IBM VERSION

THE MICRO GOES TO SCHOOL

Instructional Applications of Microcomputer Technology

The Brooks/Cole Series in Instructional Computing

RUN: Computer Education, Second Edition
Dennis O. Harper and James H. Stewart

An Apple® for the Teacher: Fundamentals of Instructional Computing, Second Edition
George H. Culp and Herbert L. Nickles

Instructional Computing Fundamentals for IBM Microcomputers
George H. Culp and Herbert L. Nickles

Instructional Computing with the TRS-80
Herbert L. Nickles and George H. Culp

Instructional Computing Fundamentals for the Commodore 64®
Herbert L. Nickles and George H. Culp

The Practical Apple®: A Guide for Educators
Herbert L. Nickles and George H. Culp

Computers in Focus
Richard Austing and Lillian Cassel

Computer Education: Literacy and Beyond
William E. Schall, Lowell Leake, Jr., and Donald R. Whitaker

Logo: Principles, Programming, and Projects
George Lukas and Joan Lukas

To Logo: Activities Guide
George Lukas and Joan Lukas

Essential WordStar®
Carl Brown

Essential dBASE II®
Carl Brown

Essential dBASE III®
Carl Brown

IBM VERSION

THE MICRO GOES TO SCHOOL

Instructional Applications of Microcomputer Technology

Andria P. Troutman
University of South Florida

James A. White
University of South Florida

Programming by Douglas E. Woolley
University of South Florida

Brooks/Cole Publishing Company
Pacific Grove, California

Brooks/Cole Publishing Company
A Division of Wadsworth, Inc.

Printed in the United States of America
10 9 8 7 6 5 4 3 2 1

Library of Congress Cataloging-in-Publication Data
Troutman, Andria, [date]
The micro goes to school. IBM version.

(The Brooks/Cole series in instructional computing)
Includes bibliographies and index.
1. IBM Personal Computer. 2. Computer-assisted instruction. I. White, James A., [date].
II. Woolley, Douglas. III. Title. IV. Series.
QA76.8.I2594T77 1988 371.3′9445 87-30922
ISBN 0-534-08880-5

Sponsoring Editor: *Cynthia C. Stormer*
Marketing Representative: *Leo Simcock*
Editorial Assistant: *Mary Ann Zuzow*
Production Editor: *Sue Ewing*
Production Assistants: *Dorothy Bell and Linda Loba*
Manuscript Editor: *Janet M. Hunter*
Permissions Editor: *Carline Haga*
Interior Design: *Sharon L. Kinghan*
Cover Design: *Victoria Van Deventer*
Art Coordinator: *Lisa Torri*
Interior Illustration: *Robyn Kline, Deborah Bond*
Typesetting: *Omegatype Typography, Inc., Champaign, IL*
Cover Printing: *The Lehigh Press Co., Pennsauken, NJ*
Printing and Binding: *Diversified Printing and Publishing Services, Inc., Brea, CA*

It's funny how things happen and how one sequence of events can lead to another. It's funny how the actions of one group of people can catalyze events they never foresaw. This book is an academic endeavor; a college text written by educators for educators. Yet, it would never have happened, and the authors might never have even known each other if not for the actions of a profit-making group of people called the International Business Machines Corporation.

Around the summer of 1983, the introduction of computers in education was still very much a grass roots movement with little central leadership or organization. During this time many educators all over the country, the authors included, were searching for the meaning of the relationship between education and computers. Groups in many locations were beginning to make inroads, each of them started and supported by different factors. An event that drew us together and gave us impetus was a decision IBM made to put some computers into some schools. The intellectual exchange, professional development, and personal growth that came out of that meeting of minds was like nothing we had ever before experienced. The seeds that led to the growth of this book were planted at that time. This book is dedicated to an individual member of IBM, the man who made this event take place.

TO: Dr. Michael de V. Roberts.

PREFACE

The history of instructional computing is a short one of only a couple decades or so. Yet, in this short period, dramatic advances in technology have developed and many instructional directions have emerged. The first generation of instructional computing was typified by large mainframes delivering tutorials—mostly drill and practice sessions—to small, select populations. These efforts were expensive and limited to minute instructional goals.

The second generation showcased microcomputers with very little primary memory and inefficient devices for external storage. The emphasis during this period centered around BASIC programming, historical topics, and microcomputer architecture. Again, only small, select groups of students were exposed to the technology.

It wasn't until the development of low-cost microcomputers having 48k or more of internal memory and disk drive systems that the instructional computing movement began in earnest. During this third generation, the emphasis extended beyond BASIC programming, computer history, and architecture to Logo and the use of small programs to deliver instruction. Talk was generated about the marvel of computer assisted instruction and the cognitive rewards of using Logo, yet the promise of this dialogue was never realized. Even so, it was clear that computers were going to have a permanent impact on society and education.

As inexpensive generic programs, such as word processors and data-base managers, and as a variety of computer peripherals became common in the marketplace, schools scrambled to define the objectives of a new computer literacy that was going to be required of all individuals. Thus a fourth generation was underway and the focus once again was teaching about computers, computer peripherals, and software tools. In the process, the fact was obscured that computers, despite their power, are no more than *tools* for human achievement, just as hammers, saws, and brushes are. More than being objects for instruction, they should be vehicles for teaching and learning, whatever the subject area.

We feel that the four generations are important ones representing a substantial and necessary period of growth. Yet we also feel that, to date, the new technology has had almost no effect on the mainstream of instruction, the role of teachers, and intellectual products for most students. We feel, along with many colleagues around the nation, that a new generation is in order and that we must find ways to use the new technology to achieve the following:

- assume time-consuming management tasks that overburden a majority of teachers: tasks that diminish the time and personal resources needed to deliver sensitive instruction.
- prepare tools of instruction and learning that can be used away from as well as at the computer.
- enable students to direct their own inquiry regardless of the subject area or its relationship to formal schooling.
- provide programmed learning experiences that are "smart" enough to conform to the needs of the learner.
- provide open-ended learning environments that allow the development of a new set of cognitive abilities: abilities that are needed for successful living in the information age.

This book represents a refined perspective for the authors as we implement our teaching responsibilities at our university. We emphasize the term *refined perspective.* We wish to share this perspective with colleagues everywhere who are enjoying the same adventure. We humbly admit that not only are the answers we give tentative, but perhaps the questions are as well. After all, today's microcomputers are Model-Ts. We have come from the Altair to the Macintosh II and the IBM PS/2 Model 80 in one decade. Who can tell what will happen in the next one and the one after that?

No preface is complete without thanking the people who made the book possible. First, to family members, Bill and Elaine, thanks for putting up with us. Next, to the faculty and staff of the Florida Center for Instructional Computing, the University of South Florida and the many other educators who shared in the endeavor, thanks for helping to shape these ideas. Also, many thanks go to the dedicated staff of Brooks/Cole—especially Cindy Stormer and Sue Ewing—who epitomize the word *professionalism* and who must have set a world record in bringing this book to life. Finally, our thanks go to the reviewers who provided vital input: Gary G. Bitter, Arizona State University; John E. Castek, University of Wisconsin; Alfred L. McKinney, Louisiana State University; Margaret Niess, Oregon State University; and Harriet Taylor, Louisiana State University. Their comments and thoughts were very beneficial during the revision process.

Andria P. Troutman
James A. White

Contents

IBM VERSION

THE MICRO GOES TO SCHOOL

Instructional Applications of Microcomputer Technology

CHAPTER

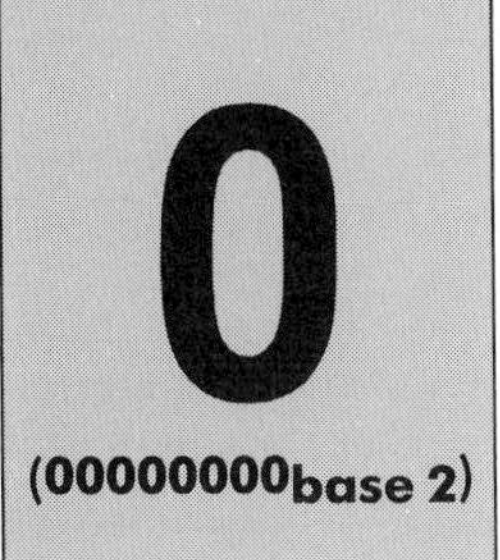

A POINT OF DEPARTURE
Where Do We Begin?

Getting Started

The purpose of this chapter is twofold. Number one, it is designed to introduce you to the format used throughout the book. For example, a section entitled "Getting Started" *begins every chapter. In each chapter, as in this one, it provides an overview of what is to come. By providing you with this advanced organizer, we are giving you a framework into which you can plug the material presented in the body of the chapter.*

Just as "Getting Started" *helps you get a handle on each chapter, the body of this chapter is intended to give you some advanced organizers for the rest of the book. In the next few pages, we'll tell you what we think about instructional computing's importance in the future of both society and education, and we'll lay some groundwork for the following chapters.*

Objectives for Teachers

After completing this chapter, you should be able to

1. Describe the format of each chapter.
2. Tell why you, as a prospective or veteran teacher, should learn about computers.
3. Hypothesize about how computers are going to continue to change our society and the teacher's role in it.

4. Briefly describe how computers are presently being used for instruction, and tell what's wrong with the current status.

5. Tell that this section, *"Objectives for Teachers,"* is designed to provide you with some formally stated objectives to keep before you as you progress through the material in each chapter.

This is the body of the chapter. In it, we hope to present you with materials appropriate to our stated objectives. We also hope to present the materials in such a way that your task of achieving the objectives is facilitated to the greatest degree.

Why Learn about Computers?

If you are a computer novice you probably have a great number of questions and probably some reservations about the use of computers in the classroom. Why should a classroom teacher learn about computers? Isn't it possible that they are just the latest fad in a profession subject to faddism? Why learn about computers if a few years from now they will have gone the way of teaching machines and new math? What guarantees do you have that computers are here to stay and that they will have significant impact on education?

Obviously, it is only after coming to terms with such questions that it is possible to move on to the topics of how to use computers and how to teach with them—the subjects of this book. In the process of achieving those goals, we think that you—the reader—will become convinced, as we—the authors—are, that computers are not just a fad. We believe that computers are going to play an increasingly larger part in American life and that education is going to have to adapt accordingly. Furthermore, that adaptation need not be a burden, for computers represent an exciting potential to revolutionize instruction. The task with which educators are faced is to see that we influence the way things are changed. That can happen only if we are knowledgeable about computers and how they can be used to teach.

American education is today faced with historically unusual and trying circumstances. The socioeconomic factors underlying the erosion of what is popularly considered to be traditional family structure and contributing to the problems of American society (and, hence, American education) are reaching extreme proportions. Many Americans, particularly those who live in large cities, are unemployed, without prospects for work, and poverty stricken. There is little question among sociologists that our society is entering a postindustrial stage. As more and more physical labor is being accomplished through automation, fewer people are involved in the actual production of goods. In 1950, 41 percent of the work force held goods-producing jobs and 59 percent worked in service occupations. In 1981, only 28 percent of the work force produced goods and 72 percent worked in service occupations. As our society becomes more information-laden and technologically oriented, the chances are that this trend will continue, and the proportions will become even more marked.

Was This Book Written for You?

This book is written for anyone who has an interest in integrating microcomputer technology and instruction. Whether you are a prospective teacher with few computer skills, a veteran teacher with computer expertise, or a curriculum coordinator with responsibility for designing curricula, we feel this book will be of value to you.

The book provides instruction on a variety of computer tools and concepts, illustrating a number of activities for use in elementary and secondary classrooms. Often the text instructs the reader to direct activities with students. Obviously, it might not be possible for you to get a class of students together with the appropriate computer equipment. The next-best option is to draft the most convenient human beings possible—spouse, friend, mother, father, next-door neighbor, classmate—to represent your class of students. Just because you can't arrange to try activities in a formal class doesn't mean you can't try your hand at planning, directing, and evaluating an activity with another audience instead. In any case, you should complete all the suggested activities yourself. Doing so will increase your computer skills, contribute to your instructional perspective, and provide you with a repertoire of instructional demonstrations.

Feel confident that the materials offered in this book were not dreamed up in an ivory tower. This material represents years of work on the front lines where the goal is to try an idea, evaluate, revise, and try again, carefully collecting that which works. The book is a labor of devotion dedicated to all those who enjoy learning and teaching. You will derive greatest benefits from it if you have the accompanying disk titled *Program Disk for The Micro Goes to School, IBM Version* and *Program Documentation for The Micro Goes to School.*

The Changing Role of the Teacher

It has been said that present-day teaching techniques are anchored in a paper culture that began with the invention of the printing press and has existed concurrently with the Industrial Revolution. It is hard for us to see today the tremendous impact the advent of inexpensive books and writing materials has had on education. The conventions of present-day American education spring directly from this phenomenon. Until printed material could be cheaply reproduced, education was steeped in an oral tradition. Since that time, the tradition has been a written one. It has been eloquently argued that the written tradition has colored not only teaching techniques but the way in which children learn to think as well. What ineffectiveness exists in the public school's ability to develop students' critical thinking skills is in large part due to an emphasis on the direct mode of instruction that is a by-product of the paper culture. Computers represent the opportunity to provide educators with the means to address those higher cognitive levels of learning that have been difficult to attain through traditional techniques.

As our society becomes more and more information-laden and as livelihoods become more and more dependent on the ability to process information, the role of the teacher is undergoing a metamorphosis. It is becoming the role of the teacher to function not as the provider of specific knowledge, but as the facilitator of learning. In other words, teachers will experience an ever-increasing need to shift the focus of teaching away from the content areas and begin teaching their students how to learn and how and where to find the information they need. Computers are the catalysts and the vehicles of this change.

Where Do We Stand Now?

Before you begin your study of computers and how to teach with them, divest yourself of any notion that you are behind the times. Resist the feeling that everyone else knows a lot about computers and you know very little, so you have to hurry to catch up. Having had the opportunity to observe schools all over the nation, we, the authors, can emphatically state that while everyone talks a great deal about how computers are currently used and how they should be used (witness this text), precious little meaningful instruction is being carried out with them.

Where computers are being used in schools right now is, with the exception of vocational education, almost exclusively in the teaching of programming and **computer literacy,** and as the tool for rote tutorial and drill and practice. While this is a passing phenomenon and probably a necessary stage in the evolution of computer instruction, it nevertheless seems that teaching students about the history and operation of the computers themselves is a little bit like teaching them about the history and theory of operation of the typewriter. Unless one plans to become a designer of typewriters, the point of the instruction is misplaced. Also, while tutorial and drill and practice computer activities have their place in the classroom, using a computer for only that application is like hiring a Ph.D. in child psychology to baby-sit your children. While the tool is certainly versatile enough to be used that way, and will probably perform admirably, it is not necessarily the most efficient use of resources.

Even though you may know absolutely nothing about computers, you are a part of the group of pioneers. The body of instructional computing curriculum does not yet exist. It is just beginning to be formed and you are in the position of being able to help shape it. The protocols are not yet in place. There are no experts.

It is our fervent wish that after finishing this text, you will be excited about using computers and eager to integrate them into your insruction. We caution you not to try to do everything at once. You cannot, single-handedly, computerize you curriculum. A task that large has to be a group effort. Even if you possess the ability, you cannot—nor should you—be your own programmer. Your energies should be focused toward teaching. What you can do is make some good instructional materials, or write one good lesson, or put your test item files on a data base, and share what you do with others. If you make just one student's learning experience come alive through the use of computers, or if you contribute just one meaningful thing to the body of instructional computing, then you will have succeeded and so will have we.

Chapter Summary

The purpose of this section is to give a brief summary of what has been presented in the chapter and, with the advantage of hindsight, make further appropriate comments. In this chapter, we have introduced you to the format of the book. We have also discussed some of the critical issues currently facing teachers, schools, teacher-training institutions, and society in general.

Chapter Review

Knowledge Exercises

1. What is the authors' purpose in providing you with fairly straightforward Knowledge Exercises that are tied pretty closely to the "Objectives for Teachers" sections?
2. Why do you think you should learn about computers?
3. How are computers changing society? How is that change affecting the role of the teacher?
4. How are most schools currently using computers? What is good about this usage? What is bad about it?

Thought Exercises

1. What is the authors' purpose in providing you with Thought Exercises that, as the name implies, require a bit more cogitation than the Knowledge Exercises?
2. If you agree with the positions taken in this chapter, come up with some further evidence that they are accurate. If you disagree, play the devil's advocate. Take other positions and try to justify them. How well do they stand up?

Activities

1. Discuss with your fellow students what you think might be the authors' purpose in providing you with a section of suggested activities for further enrichment.

2. Write up your results from Thought Exercise 2. Discuss the matter with your instructor and the other students in your class

Projects

1. The tasks included under Projects are longer-term activities. Your first project might be to convince your instructor to allow you to use a suitable project as a significant part of your grade.

2. Some of the projects may require you to explore references we have included in the bibliography for a chapter. For example, write a paper about how computers are used in schools and how they should be. For resources, you might start with publications by Henry Becker, Johns Hopkins University.

Bibliography

Anderson, Ronald E. "Inequities in Opportunities for Computer Literacy." *The Computing Teacher* (April 1984): 10–12. Wealth, community size, geographic region, race, and gender are factors involved in computer equity.

Becker, Henry Jay. "How Schools Use MicroComputers." *Classroom Computer Learning* (September 1983): 41–44. A report on the Johns Hopkins University Study on Microcomputer Usage conducted between December 1982 and February 1983.

Brady, Holly, and Melinda Levine. "Is Computer Education Off Track?" *Classroom Computer Learning* (February 1985): 20–24. An interview with Judah Schwartz (Instructional Computing, Harvard University) emphasizing use of computers as tools for learning.

Davis, Nancy C. "Yes, They Can! Computer Literacy for Special Education Students." *The Computing Teacher* (February 1983): 64–67. Discussion includes daily lesson plans for special students.

Elion, Orah. "Teaching with Computer Simulations." *Science and Children* (May 1983): 13–17. Includes a table of simulations developed by the Minnesota Education Computing Consortium.

Fisher, Glen. "Where CAI Is Effective, A Summary of the Research." *Electronic Learning* (Nov.–Dec. 1983): Vol. 3, no. 3, 82–84. CAI appears to be most effective with certain students in certain situations.

Hannaford, Alonzo E. "Microcomputers in Special Education: Some New Opportunites, Some Old Problems." *The Computing Teacher* (February 1983): 11–17. A comprehensive discussion of the use of computers in special education.

Harper, Dennis O., and James H. Stewart. *Run: Computer Education.* Monterey, Calif.: Brooks/Cole 1983. A book of readings covering the main topics in instructional computing.

Luehrmann, Arthur. "The Best Way to Teach Computer Literacy." *Electronic Learning* (April 1984): 37–44. The author suggests that all students in grades 7–9 have a computer class.

O'Brien, Thomas. "Wasting New Technology on the Same Old Curriculum." *Classroom Computer Learning* (November 1983): 25–27. Rethinking the goals of education in terms of relational knowledge.

Schall, William E., Lowell Leake, and Donald R. Whitaker. *Computer Education: Literacy and Beyond.* Monterey, Calif.: Brooks/Cole, 1986. A text for pre-service and in-service teachers to develop competencies in the usage of computers following the competencies identified by the Association of Computing Machinery.

Taylor, Robert, ed. *The Computer in the School: Tutor, Tool, Tutee.* New York: Teachers College Press, 1980. A collection of articles by Luehrmann, Papert, Suppes, and others on various issues in computer education.

Thomas, James L., ed. *Microcomputers in the Schools.* Phoenix, Ariz.: Oryx Press, 1981. A collection of articles by recognized professionals on issues ranging from teaching computer literacy in the classroom to statewide plans for integration of microcomputers into the curriculum.

1

Up and Running

The purpose of this part is to teach you to be an independent PC user. You should come away with the skills and confidence required to make you self-supporting and not dependent upon constant help from other people to run the computer. You won't be a whiz-kid (unless you already are one), but you will have a functional familiarity with the device. Teachers don't need to become computer experts; they just need to be proficient with the particular hardware and software with which they teach. Of course, the more you know, the better prepared you are to handle problems as they arise.

What is presented in the next three chapters is what we consider the bare minimum you should know about keyboarding, how computers work, and some software you may not have yet heard of: the Disk Operating System, or DOS. There are many different kinds of DOS. Some are nearly invisible to the user and require almost no attention. Others are highly visible and require a comparatively great deal of attention from the user. As a rule of thumb, the more powerful and flexible a DOS is, the more attention it requires. The DOS that we are going to study—PC DOS—is both highly visible and very powerful.

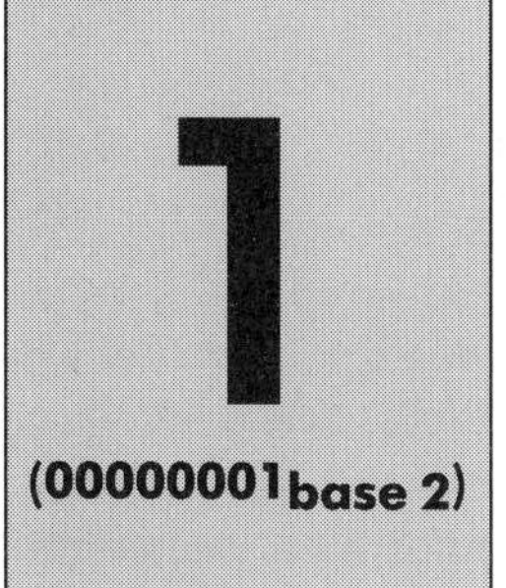

WHAT IS A COMPUTER, ANYWAY!

Relays to Microprocessors

Getting Started

Before diving into a book on computers in instruction, we had better decide just what a computer is. What is there about them that makes them valuable to educators? How do they work and how do their limitations color the decisions we must make about where they fit into schools? Before you can begin to answer these questions, you need to know something about how they work.

Objectives for Teachers

After completing this chapter, you should be able to

1. Define a computer in terms of its four essential functions.
2. Describe the difference between a calculator and a computer.
3. Name at least three input and three output devices.
4. Define primary memory, distinguishing between Random Access Memory (RAM) and Read Only Memory (ROM).
5. Define secondary memory and give examples.
6. Tell what a microprocessor is.
7. Describe the differences between first, second, and third generation computers.
8. Define the terms *bit, byte,* and *kilobyte.*
9. Describe the binary number system and explain why computers use it.
10. Describe the function of the American Standard Code for Information Interchange (ASCII) and other character codes.

The best place to start is with a definition. If we attempt to define computers in terms of physical devices, we're in big trouble because they change so much. A description of ENIAC, an early electronic computer, would probably fail to encompass the typical microcomputer in its scope. Yet both machines are certainly computers. It is better to define computers in terms of function. In other words, computers are best defined by what they do, rather than what they are.

The Definition

The following definition is a good model because it provides insight into and parallels the physical design of computers. A computer is an electronic device that

1. Accepts input. It allows the user to pass textual and numerical information into it.
2. Stores information. It is capable of storing and retrieving the information given it.
3. Processes information. It performs arithmetic and logical operations upon the information given it.
4. Produces output. It is capable of providing, in usable form, the results of the processing performed.

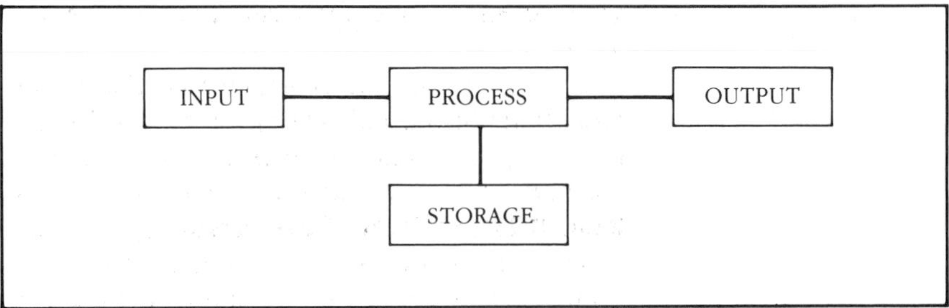

Now, one might argue that this definition falls short of being accurate because it fails to differentiate a calculator from a computer. For example, the definition makes no mention of programming. Well, some calculators are programmable. Calculators use the same kinds of components as computers and are capable of many of the same operations. This is not to say that computers and calculators are the same thing. Calculators are specific kinds of devices belonging to a larger set of devices known as computers.

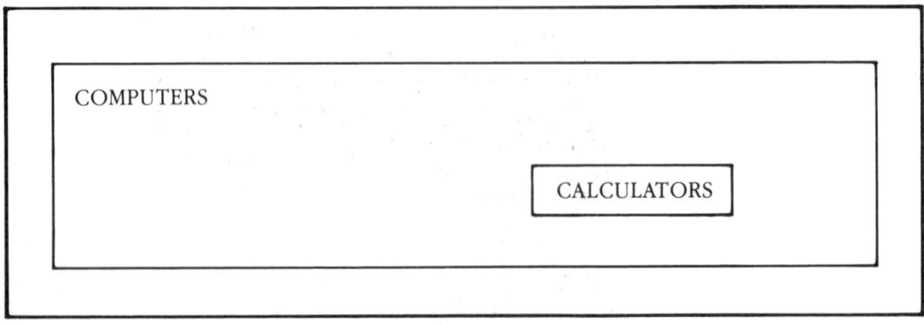

Calculators are computers that are optimized for processing numerical data and performing mathematical operations. In fact, it is easier to use a calculator for routine computation than a computer. Where calculators really fall short is in the processing of text or in repetitive calculations, two of the major uses for computers.

Computer Components

It is easy to understand the nature of the physical components that make up a computer if you understand the definition. A **computer** must be able to accept input, store information, process information, and produce output. You can view a computer's components in terms of their functions.

In order for a computer to accept input, there must be at least one component with that function. These components are called, strangely enough, **input devices.** A good example of a microcomputer input device is its **keyboard.** Some other devices are **cassette recorders, disk drives, light pens, graphics tablets,** and **joysticks.** You will find a definition of each of these devices as well as others in the Glossary. (As you've probably noticed by now, we print some words in *italic* and some in **boldface.** *Italics* are used for phrases we want to emphasize or for terms used in unusual ways. **Bold** is used for terms that are defined and that appear in the glossary.)

To store information, a computer must have a *memory.* Computer memories are usually designated as *primary* or *secondary* memory. **Primary memory** is a computer's main internal storage. This kind of memory is normally contained within the microcomputer and takes two forms, called ROM and RAM. **ROM,** or **Read Only Memory,** is where a microcomputer stores programming code that is very important to its operation. Among other things, ROM contains programming that executes automatically when you turn on the computer. This programming prepares the computer to accept input from you, the user. Most microcomputers also have a programming language called BASIC stored in ROM. Since ROM is crucial to the computer's operation, you don't normally want to change it. Therefore, ROM can only be read (looked at), not written to (changed). This means you do not use ROM to store information that you put into the computer. You can look at the information ROM contains, but you can't change it. The contents of ROM are permanently written, or hardwired. Whenever you turn on the computer, the contents of ROM are always there, waiting to talk to you.

RAM, or **Random Access Memory,** is also known as user memory. Think of it as a blank slate. RAM is the kind of memory that stores information that you input to the computer. Like ROM, you can look at the contents of RAM. The difference is that you can also change the contents of RAM. A more understandable name for RAM would be Read Write Memory. But since engineers are very fond of acronyms and RWM makes for an unpronounceable one, they call it RAM. The main disadvantage of RAM is that its contents get erased every time you turn off the computer. Power must be constantly applied to RAM chips for them to retain their memory. When the computer is turned off, RAM reverts to a blank slate.

The inability of RAM to keep its memory when a computer is turned off brings about the need for secondary memory. **Secondary memory** is a means by which the contents of RAM can be stored before the computer is turned off and restored after it is turned on again. A commonly used microcomputer secondary memory storage device is the floppy disk drive. Information in a computer's memory can be stored by the disk drive on to a **floppy diskette** in much the same way music is stored on tape.

The part of the computer that performs the processing of information, what might be called the brain, is the **central processing unit,** or **CPU.** The CPU carries out arithmetic and logic operations and controls instruction processing. It provides timing signals and does other housekeeping operations. Since the term *CPU* is defined by function and is not tied to specific devices, it is often employed to refer to everything from a single chip to an entire array of components. As far as we are concerned, the PC's CPU is the system unit (the big box with the diskette drives.)

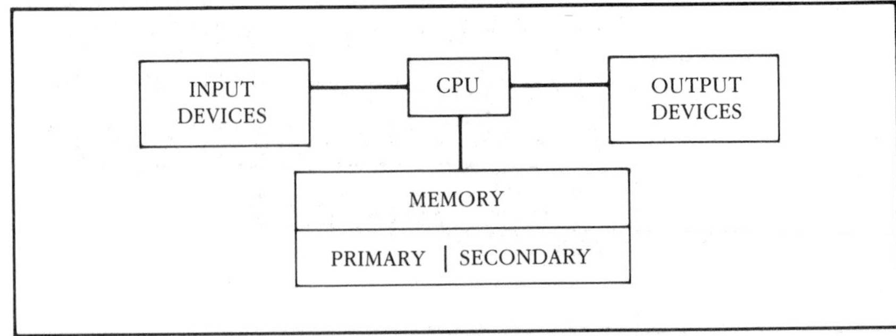

The parts of the computer that give it the ability to produce the results of processing in usable form are called **output devices.** The most commonly used microcomputer output devices are monitors, printers, and disk drives. Other types of output devices include modems that allow telephone communications and audio synthesizers that produce output in the form of speech.

You may have noticed that we have included some devices in more than one category. Most notable among these is the diskette drive. For most purposes, diskette drives are thought of as secondary storage devices. To perform that function, they must also be the objects of input and output. A computer's monitor is almost always considered an output device. Yet, when used with a light pen, it becomes part of an input system. We'll repeat our premise. It's better to classify computing devices by function, not by attribute.

CLASSROOM ACTIVITY 1.1

1. If you have access to a computer, have your students identify the various parts and classify them according to function. 2. Having volunteers research the invention and theory of operation of the various components would make good projects.

How Do They Work?

Our definition of the word *computer* and the physical components we've just discussed are common to all computers, be they mainframe, mini, or micro. **Mainframes** are very large, expensive computers usually owned by institutions and large businesses. **Minicomputers** are usually special-function computers of moderate cost typically owned by smaller institutions and businesses. **Microcomputers** are small, versatile, relatively inexpensive computers that can be purchased by individuals and small businesses. Formal definitions of these terms usually include references to cost and/or storage capacity. We're not going to use such definitions because the technology is changing so fast that the lines are blurred. Today's microcomputers have the power and capacity of yesterday's mainframes. Definitions that are tied to specific physical attributes are doomed to obsolescence.

Microcomputers began to enter classrooms rapidly in the early eighties. Right now, microcomputers are the most important type of computer to educators. Therefore, we will use the terms *computer* and *microcomputer* almost interchangeably in this book.

The three standard classifications for computers are to a large degree vestiges of the evolution of computers. Before we can trace that evolution, it is necessary to understand something about the way computers work.

Quickly, complete the following statement: Computers are

1. rapid and intelligent.
2. slow and intelligent.
3. rapid and ignorant.
4. slow and ignorant.

If you answered anything but "3," go to the back of the class. Computers are fairly ignorant. They possess little ability to reason. In fact, the most sophisticated discrimination any computer is capable of making is the difference between 0 and 1. Actually, even that statement isn't quite true because computers don't really use 0 and 1. They only know the level of voltage in a circuit. We human beings have arbitrarily assigned the value 1 to a condition of high voltage and 0 to a condition of low voltage. (Don't be afraid of the "high voltage" referred to here. It's only about five volts, the voltage of an ordinary pen light.) So, why do computers appear so smart? It's because they are very fast. Since the current in a circuit travels at the speed of light, computers can make thousands of decisions in a second. By making thousands of small 0/1 discriminations very quickly, a computer can appear to have made a very large, intelligent decision. If it's hard for you to understand how lots of small, simple decisions can add up to one big, apparently sophisticated one, you're not alone. Maybe the following analogy will help.

Suppose I tell you I am thinking of a number between 1 and 100. I want you to guess the number by asking me questions to which I can only answer yes or no (a binary state like logic based on 0 and 1). One way to obtain the answer is to ask questions in such a way that the field of possible choices is constantly narrowed. For example, asking if the number is between 1 and 50 will eliminate half the possibilities no matter what the answer is. Say, for example, that I respond yes. Now you can half the range again by asking if the number is between 1 and 25. If I answer no then you know the number must be between 25 and 50. Now you might ask if the number is between 25 and 37. If I answer yes, then you might ask if the number is between 25 and 31. I answer no again and you ask if the number is between 31 and 34. If I answer yes, then you know that the number must be either 32 or 33. If you ask if the number is 32 and I answer no, then you know it must be 33. Now, that's not too impressive, is it? The questions you ask are very simple. After enough time and repetition of variations on one basic question, you can discover the number.

When the number is between 1 and 100, the process can require no more than six steps and is infallible if performed properly. But, suppose you could ask those questions and I could answer them so fast that an objective observer couldn't detect what was going on. If the observer could only detect the first and last steps of the process, you would appear to correctly guess that number each time on the first try. Your many small discriminations would have the appearance of one large, powerful one. That is not too different from what happens in a computer.

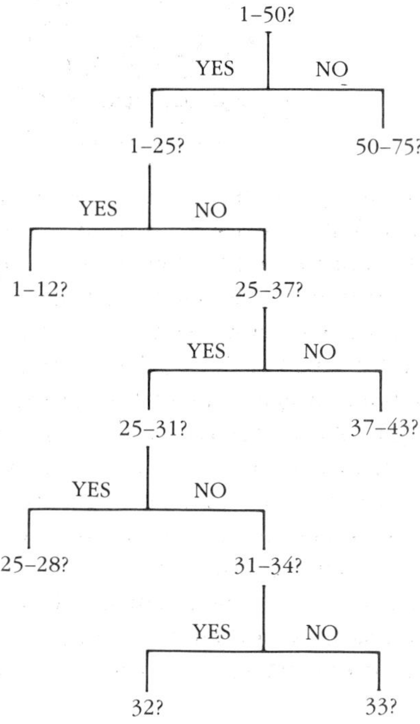

CLASSROOM ACTIVITY 1.2

1. Demonstrate the process of guessing a number between 1 and 100, as just described, to your class.
2. Have your students pair off and try it themselves.

The Computer's Roots

One way to trace the evolution of the modern electronic computer is to follow the changes in the devices used to store the zeros and ones. Some of the very first computers used switches called *electromechanical relays* that actually toggled one way or the other to indicate 0 or 1. Then it was discovered that **vacuum tubes** could be used to replace the switches. The generation of computers using vacuum tubes is considered the first generation of modern computers. **ENIAC,** the Electronic Numerical Integrator And Calculator, was one of the first true digital electronic computers. It was built in 1946 and financed by the U.S. Army to the tune of $400,000. It weighed 30 tons, covered about 1,500 square feet, and contained over 18,000 vacuum tubes. It rarely ran for more than a few minutes before a tube blew.

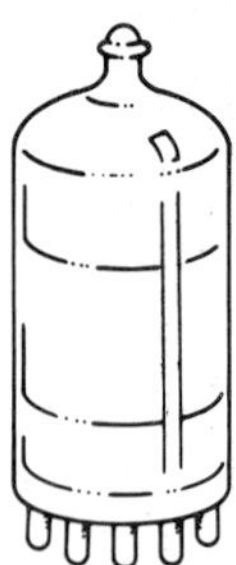

One could argue that the second generation of modern computers started at Bell Laboratories in the late forties, with the development of that revolutionary device we take for granted today, the **transistor.** Actually, the first computers using transistors didn't begin to appear until the late fifties. The use of transistors solved many of the problems associated with vacuum tubes. Transistors were extremely reliable and long-lived, compared to tubes. Tubes also generated a lot of heat and computers using them had to be cooled. Transistors had the effect of making the computer a much more practical alternative for business and science applications. Transistor technology, however, was still two steps removed from the microcomputer. Transistor circuitry was like switch and vacuum tube circuitry in that discrete electronic components (the individual transistors and other parts such as resistors and capacitors) were still assembled and connected on circuit boards.

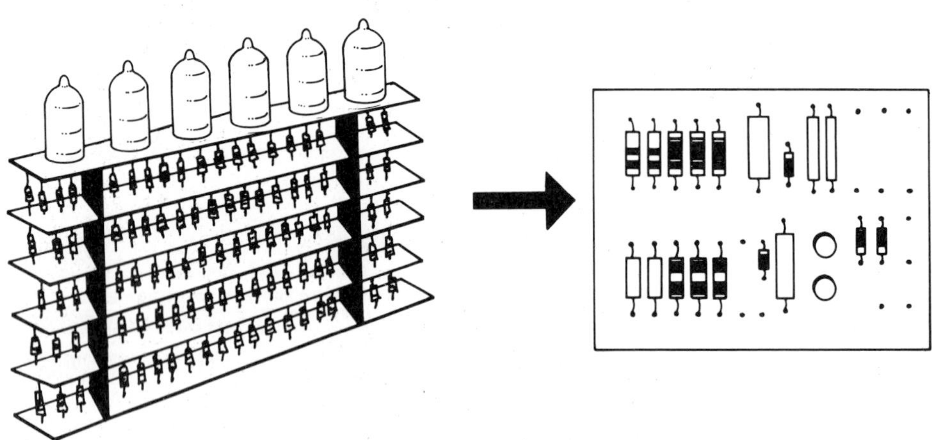

The third generation of computers appeared after the first **integrated circuit** was patented in 1959. Integrated circuits have miniature versions of all the components and all the connections making up an entire circuit crammed onto a 1/4-inch square chip of silicon. The chip is so small that it has to be enclosed in a larger outer housing so that it can be handled. Also, without the legs on the housing, it would be difficult to make electrical connections to it.

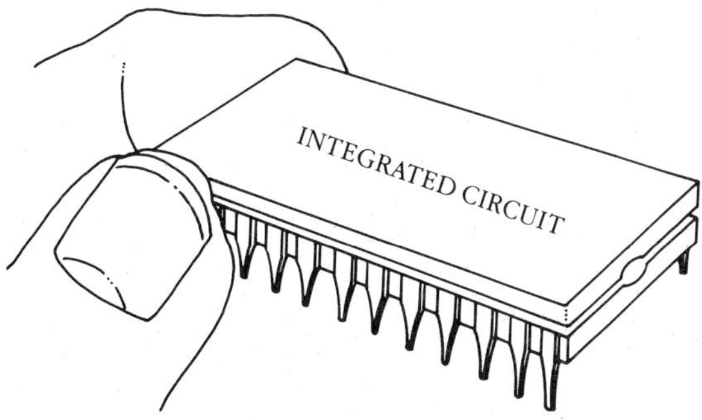

Integrated circuitry allowed computers to be much smaller than ever before, and a new breed called minicomputers appeared. Minicomputers using integrated circuitry were faster, more efficient, and rivaled the performance of much larger mainframe computers.

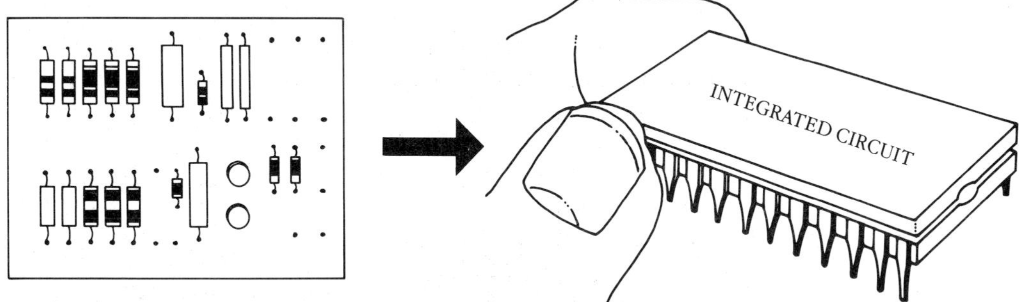

As integrated circuit technology became more refined, a fourth generation evolved. With the development of large-scale integrated circuits (LSI) and very-large-scale integrated circuits (VLSI) in the early seventies, it became possible to place an ever-increasing number of components and circuits on one chip. This led to the development of the class of integrated circuit chip that is the brain of modern microcomputers, the **microprocessor.** A microprocessor is an entire computer on a chip. Today, this innovation makes it possible to construct small, inexpensive, powerful, versatile computers. These are computers that the average person can afford to own and that schools can afford to place in classrooms. Of course, computer technology will continue to evolve. One day, computers will probably be able to approximate the abilities of the human brain.

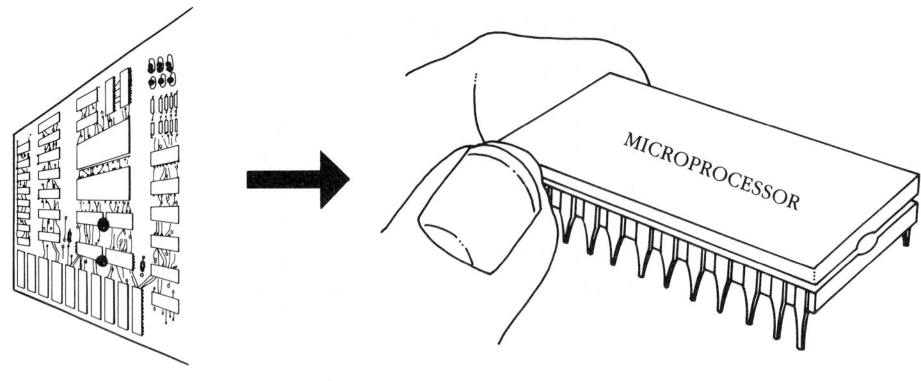

CLASSROOM ACTIVITY 1.3

Have your students research the different computers that have been developed over time. Information gathered should include cost, size, memory capacity, speed of operation, and so on. When the students are finished, you can use their findings to make comparisons with today's machines.

Numbers, Numbers, Numbers

We have already learned that computers store information in the form of 0s and 1s. This is because the switches that store the information have only two states: high and low voltage. These switches are called **bits,** short for Binary digITs. If a bit can only store the numbers 0 and 1, how does a computer operate with larger numbers? There is an established convention for grouping eight bits together to form a unit of memory called a **byte.** A byte is the amount of memory it takes for a computer to store one character, like the letter *A*. Microcomputer memory capacity is usually measured in **kilobytes.** A kilobyte equals 1,024 bytes. Why 1,024 and not 1,000? That will be explained as you read on. The maximum number that can be stored in a byte is 255. How is that so? It all has to do with a number system called **binary.**

We call our normal number system base-10, or **decimal.** Our decimal number system has ten fundamental digits, 0 through 9, with which all numbers are represented. We also have to use a convention called place value. The choice of ten digits is a completely arbitrary one based on historical factors. Since computers have only two digits to work with, they must operate in base-2, binary.

Look at the pattern in decimal counting.

```
0 10 20  . . .  90 100 110 120  . . .  900 1000
1 11 21         91 101 111 121         901 1001
2 12 22         92 102 112 122         902 1002
3 13 23         93 103 113 123         903 1003
4 14 24         94 104 114 124          .  1004
5 15 25         95 105 115 125          .  1005
6 16 26         96 106 116 126          .  1006
7 17 27         97 107 117 127         987   .
8 18 28         98 108 118 128         988   .
9 19 29         99 109 119 129         999   .
```

You can count up to 9 before you run out of digits. Then you start combining numbers. After 9, you start placing a 1 in front of all the digits. When you run out again at 19, then you start placing a 2 in front, and so on. When you get to 99, you've run out of all the combinations for two-digit numbers, so you start to use three-digit numbers. When the three-digit numbers run out at 999, you go to four-digit numbers.

Binary works the same way as decimal except that you run out of digits more quickly. The only digits in binary are 0 and 1, so you must use multiple digit numbers much sooner.

Study the following equivalence table:

Binary	Decimal
0	0
1	1
10	2
11	3
100	4
101	5
110	6
111	7
1000	8
1001	9
1010	10
1011	11
1100	12
1101	13
1110	14
1111	15

CLASSROOM ACTIVITY 1.4

Lead your students through the exercise of extending the binary-decimal equivalence table to 255.

To understand how binary is used to represent larger numbers, let's compare it to the decimal system. Consider the number 5,234. The 5 really represents 5,000, the 2 means 200, the 3 indicates 30, and the 4 is just a 4. Another way of writing 5,234 is

$$5 \times 1000 + 2 \times 100 + 3 \times 10 + 4 \times 1$$

We don't normally write anything but the digits because we understand the value each has because of its place in the number. Look closely at all the numbers that are never written: 1,000; 100; 10; and 1. They are all powers of ten. 1,000 equals ten to the third power. 100 equals ten to the second power. Ten equals ten to the first power. One equals ten to the zero power. You can find the value of a decimal number by multiplying the digits by different powers of ten. By starting with zero and counting from right to left, the appropriate power of ten is always equal to the place of the digit in the number.

Study the following table:

7	6	5	4	3	2	1	0
0	0	0	0	5	2	3	4

The numbers on the top indicate the position each digit occupies and how many powers of ten by which to multiply each digit.

$$5 \times \underbrace{10 \times 10 \times 10} + 2 \times \underbrace{10 \times 10} + 3 \times 10 + 4 \times 1$$
$$\underbrace{5 \times 1000} + \underbrace{2 \times 100} + \underbrace{3 \times 10} + 4 \times 1$$
$$5000 + 200 + 30 + 4$$
$$5234$$

Binary numbers work the same way as decimal numbers, with two exceptions. The base for all the exponents is 2 instead of 10, and there are only two digits. For example, 10110 in binary equals 22 decimal. See the following table. The numbers across the top represent how many powers of two by which to multiply each digit.

7	6	5	4	3	2	1	0
0	0	0	1	0	1	1	0

$$1 \times \underbrace{2 \times 2 \times 2 \times 2} + 0 \times \underbrace{2 \times 2 \times 2} + 1 \times \underbrace{2 \times 2} + 1 \times 2 + 0 \times 1$$
$$1 \times 16 + 0 \times 8 + 1 \times 4 + 1 \times 2 + 0 \times 1$$
$$16 + 0 + 4 + 2 + 0$$
$$22$$

Since a byte has only eight bits, the largest number it can hold is 11111111 binary. That equals

$$128 + 64 + 32 + 16 + 8 + 4 + 2 + 1$$

or 255. Now we're ready to answer the question we deferred. Why is a kilobyte 1,024 bytes? Since computers operate in binary, it's much easier for them to deal with numbers like 1,024, which is

$$2 \times 2 \times 2 \times 2 \times 2 \times 2 \times 2 \times 2 \times 2 \times 2$$

than numbers like 1,000, which is

$$10 \times 10 \times 10$$

The ASCII Set

Well, it's now apparent that a computer can represent numbers up to 255. How, then, does a computer store text? Different characters of the alphabet have been arbitrarily associated with different numbers. This convention is called **ASCII code** (American Standard Code for Information Interchange). In ASCII, the capital letter A equals 65 decimal, the lowercase a is 97; and so on through capital Z, which is 90, and lowercase z, which is 122. There is an order to the number assignation, as shown in the complete ASCII table at the end of this chapter. When a computer needs to print a character, it looks up the character's number in a table that is stored in ROM. This table tells the computer how to "draw" the character. It is important to note that the decimal digits a computer prints on the display or on a printer are characters also. The digit for zero, 0, equals the value 48 decimal; the digit for one, 1, is 49; the digit for two, 2, is 50; and so on. There are character codes other than ASCII, but ASCII is by far the most widely used of characters codes for micros.

That a byte can represent numbers from 0 to 255 might lead us to believe there are 256 different characters available. This is not true. The numbers from 0 to 31 are used for **control codes** that do such things as cause line feeds, tab stops, and carriage returns. Also, ASCII code only extends up to 128. For numbers higher than that, just about every different microcomputer has its own unique character set. From one microcomputer to another, the only characters you can be relatively sure are the same are the ones corresponding to numbers less than 123. They make up all the upper- and lowercase characters and most punctuation. For microcomputers that don't have lowercase, only values up to 96 are likely to be consistent.

The Instruction Set

Now that we understand how a computer is able to store characters and numbers, let's see how it performs operations on them. A microprocessor has a finite number of basic operations hardwired into it. They are designed right into its circuitry and are immutable. They are usually called *instructions.* A microprocessor's entire repertoire of instructions is called its **instruction set.** The microprocessor in an IBM PC has only a few hundred basic instructions in its set. Older microcomputers like the Apple II have even fewer. These instructions are the building blocks of all the different things that the microcomputer can do. By using them in combinations, the computer can do an almost infinite number of different things. The process of putting microprocessor instructions together in creative and effective ways is called **programming.**

To be versatile, the operations a microprocessor performs must be very small ones. Here are some examples of typical microprocessor operations.

- Compare two numbers.
- Increment a number by one.
- Add two numbers.

The PC's microprocessor can also multiply numbers, but many older microprocessors cannot even do that. They have to be programmed to add repeatedly.

Microprocessors are able to identify individual instructions because each has a unique number assigned to it, just like the ASCII character set. How does the microcomputer know whether a number is to be interpreted as an operation or as data? It depends upon the context. A more detailed answer would only be valuable to you if you intend to study advanced programming.

If you've ever used a microcomputer before, you're probably pretty confused right now. We've been telling you that computers only understand numbers, but you have probably seen them programmed with words like PRINT, GOTO, LET, and STOP. Programming computers with just numbers is called **machine-language** programming. It's not very easy to do. Special programs have been written that translate English-like words into machine language. These special programs are called **high-level languages.** We'll study two of them—BASIC and Logo—in Part Two.

Chapter Summary

In closing, you may be wondering why you need to know all this information to use a microcomputer. Ideally, you shouldn't need to know any more about the computer you use than you know about the car you drive. Unfortunately, the hardware and software of today has not yet reached that level of sophistication. It's just a fact of life that to be a competent computer user today requires a great deal of knowledge and understanding of both the device itself and the programming that drives it. The day when computer systems are as easy to operate as automobiles are to drive lies in the future. Even when that day arrives, however, knowledge of how computers function will still be a valuable tool. To continue the automobile analogy, knowing something about the operation of your car makes you a more intelligent driver, better prepared to deal with problems as they arise. So knowledge of the operation of your computer makes you a more intelligent, productive user.

In this chapter, we have studied how computers work. We did it so we could start to answer the questions we posed at the beginning of the book: How are computers valuable to educators and where do they fit into education? It should be pretty clear by now that computers have some limitations. Even with good programming, they are not very effective for making complex judgments. That's still a job for people. Computers are very good at handling lots of information quickly. They are useful for providing people with the tools to make decisions. We'll spend the rest of this book showing you where we think computers fit into education.

Chapter Review

Knowledge Exercises

1. Define a computer, listing its four essential functions.

   Answer: A computer is an electronic device that accepts input, stores information, processes information, and produces output.

2. What is the difference between a computer and a calculator?

   Answer: A calculator is a specific kind of device belonging to the larger set of devices known as computers. Calculators are specialized for processing numerical data and performing numerical operations, but cannot process text, one of the major uses for computers.

3. Name at least three input devices.

   Answer: Keyboard, cassette recorder, disk drive, light pen, graphics tablet, joystick.

4. What is primary memory? Differentiate between the two types of primary memory.

   Answer: Primary memory is a computer's main internal storage.

   ROM, or Read Only Memory, is where the microcomputer stores certain necessary system programming that is automatically executed when the machine is turned on. You can read the information stored in ROM, but you cannot use it to store information you put into the computer. In many computers, ROM contains BASIC, a programming language.

   RAM, or Random Access Memory, is also known as user memory, or Read Write Memory. You can look at the contents of RAM and also use it to store your information. It is very flexible, because you can change its contents, but those contents are lost every time you turn off the machine.

5. What is secondary memory? Name two secondary memory devices.

   Answer: Secondary memory makes it possible to store the contents of RAM before the computer is turned off and to load those contents into RAM at a later time. Tape recorders and floppy disk drives are some common secondary memory devices.

6. Define the central processing unit, or CPU.

   Answer: The CPU is the brain of the computer. It carries out arithmetic and logic operations, controls instruction processing, provides timing signals and performs other housekeeping operations.

7. Name at least three output devices.

   Answer: Monitor, printer, disk drive, modem, audio synthesizer.

8. What was ENIAC and why was it important?

   Answer: ENIAC, the Electronic Numerical Integrator And Calculator, was one of the first true digital electronic computers.

9. What is meant by first, second, and third generation computers?

   Answer: First generation computers used vacuum tubes as storage and logic devices, second generation used transistors, and third generation computers use integrated circuits.

10. What is a byte? What is the largest number that can be represented by a byte?

    Answer: A byte is a unit of memory that is made up of eight bits, or binary digits (represented by a 0 or 1, or by low or high voltage, respectively). The maximum number that can be represented by a byte is 255.

11. What is ASCII? Why is it used?

    Answer: ASCII is the American Standard Code for Information Interchange. Different alphabetic and numeric characters have been arbitrarily associated with numbers to form a character code. This system is used to standardize information exchange among many different computers.

Thought Exercises

1. Think of some analogies you can use with students to help them understand the difference between RAM and ROM.

2. How much detail should students have to know concerning the material presented in this chapter? How can it best be presented? Choose a grade level, describe the ability level of the class, and write a plan for how you would introduce this material to a specific student group. Describe activities you would use and how much material you would present for each lesson.

Activities

1. Divide your class into two teams. Have them try to guess a number chosen from a limited range (for example, 1 to 100, 1 to 50). Each team can use up to 20 questions, and all questions can only be answered yes

or no. After playing once or twice, discuss strategy as explained in this chapter and have the teams play again.

2. Create an activity to help students understand different number systems like binary. For example, you might have students illustrate counting in the decimal system by having three students stand in the front of the room. The student farthest to the right counts the units place on his or her fingers. When that student reaches ten, the student in the middle raises one finger to represent each group of tens. The third student keeps track of hundreds. Try to anticipate difficulties you might encounter and how to avoid them.

3. Present the activity you developed in Thought Exercise 2 to a group of students. Keep a log detailing how well things go, what modifications you have to make to the original plan, and what changes you would make if you were to present the activity again.

Projects

1. Discuss machine intelligence with a group of students. Bring in science fiction stories that show computers acting like humans and really "thinking." Compare this with what microcomputers such as the IBM PC or Apple II can presently do. Discuss what is realistic to expect out of computers in the next few years. Have the students do some type of creative activity, such as art work or creative writing. Write a short summary of the activity and collect some representative samples of student work.

Table of ASCII character code

ASCII value	Character	ASCII value	Character	ASCII value	Character
000	(null)	043	+	086	V
001	☺	044	,	087	W
002	☻	045	-	088	X
003	♥	046	.	089	Y
004	♦	047	/	090	Z
005	♣	048	0	091	[
006	♠	049	1	092	\
007	(beep)	050	2	093	]
008	◘	051	3	094	∧
009	(tab)	052	4	095	—
010	(line feed)	053	5	096	`
011	(home)	054	6	097	a
012	(form feed)	055	7	098	b
013	(carriage return)	056	8	099	c
014	♫	057	9	100	d
015	☼	058	:	101	e
016	►	059	;	102	f
017	◄	060	<	103	g
018	↕	061	=	104	h
019	!!	062	>	105	i
020	¶	063	?	106	j
021	§	064	@	107	k
022	▬	065	A	108	l
023	↨	066	B	109	m
024	↑	067	C	110	n
025	↓	068	D	111	o
026	→	069	E	112	p
027	←	070	F	113	q
028	(cursor right)	071	G	114	r
029	(cursor left)	072	H	115	s
030	(cursor up)	073	I	116	t
031	(cursor down)	074	J	117	u
032	(space)	075	K	118	v
033	!	076	L	119	w
034	"	077	M	120	x
035	#	078	N	121	y
036	$	079	O	122	z
037	%	080	P	123	{
038	&	081	Q	124	¦
039	'	082	R	125	}
040	(	083	S	126	~
041	)	084	T	127	⌂
042	*	085	U	128	Ç

ASCII value	Character	ASCII value	Character	ASCII value	Character
129	ü	172	¼	215	╫
130	é	173	¡	216	╪
131	â	174	«	217	┘
132	ä	175	»	218	┌
133	à	176	░	219	█
134	å	177	▒	220	▄
135	ç	178	▓	221	▌
136	ê	179	│	222	▐
137	ë	180	┤	223	▀
138	è	181	╡	224	α
139	ï	182	╢	225	β
140	î	183	╖	226	Γ
141	ì	184	╕	227	π
142	Ä	185	╣	228	Σ
143	Å	186	║	229	σ
144	É	187	╗	230	µ
145	æ	188	╝	231	τ
146	Æ	189	╜	232	Φ
147	ô	190	╛	233	Θ
148	ö	191	┐	234	Ω
149	ò	192	└	235	δ
150	û	193	┴	236	∞
151	ù	194	┬	237	Ø
152	ÿ	195	├	238	ε
153	Ö	196	─	239	∩
154	Ü	197	┼	240	≡
155	¢	198	╞	241	±
156	£	199	╟	242	≥
157	¥	200	╚	243	≤
158	Pt	201	╔	244	⌠
159	ƒ	202	╩	245	⌡
160	á	203	╦	246	÷
161	í	204	╠	247	≈
162	ó	205	═	248	°
163	ú	206	╬	249	•
164	ñ	207	╧	250	·
165	Ñ	208	╨	251	√
166	ª	209	╤	252	^{n}
167	º	210	╥	253	^{2}
168	¿	211	╙	254	■
169	⌐	212	╘	255	(blank 'FF')
170	¬	213	╒		
171	½	214	╓		

Bibliography

Behmer, David Edward. "Explaining Microcomputer Information Storage to Children." *The Computing Teacher* (December 1979). Using a story-analogy, teachers can help children understand these concepts.

D'Ignazio, D. Frederick. "The World Inside the Computer." *Creative Computing Magazine* (September 1980). The article presents a picture-book adventure to introduce computers to young children.

Gore, Marvin, and John. W. Stubble. *Computers and Information Systems.* New York: McGraw-Hill, 1984. A comprehensive text which includes an illustrated discussion of computer systems.

Graham, Neill. *The Mind Tool.* St. Paul: West Publishing, 1983. Chapters 3 and 4 give a thorough summary of computer hardward and how it works.

Heller, Rachelle S., and C. Dianne Martin. *Bits 'n Bytes about Computing: A Computer Literacy Primer.* Rockville, Md.: Computer Science Press, 1982. A comprehensive explanation of computer functions is illustrated.

Hopper, Grace Murray, and Steven L. Mandell. *Understanding Computers.* St. Paul: West Publishing, 1984. Chapter 3 in this comprehensive high-school-level text gives a good description of the workings of a computer.

Pfleeger, Charles P. *Machine Organization.* New York: Wiley, 1982. A small book containing in-depth discussion of computer systems.

Richman, Ellen. *Spotlight on Computer Literacy.* New York: Random House, 1985. A book with very basic explanations and illustrations.

Texas Instruments Learning Center. *Understanding Digital Electronics.* Ft. Worth, Texas: Radio Shack, 1982. A small comprehensive book explaining the underlying principles of microcomputer electronics.

CHAPTER

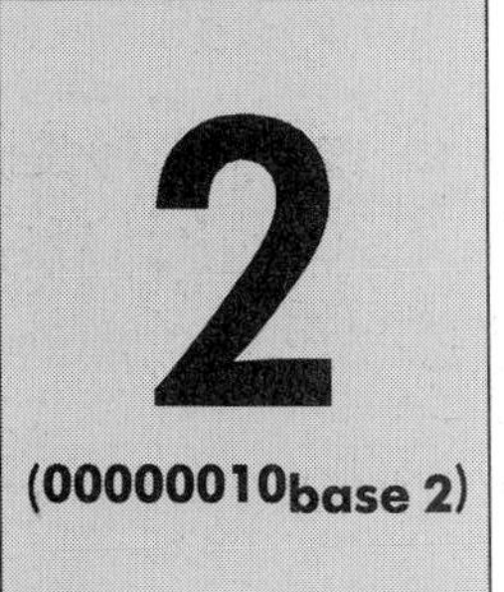

THE MOST LOGICAL PLACE TO START

Hanging Ten on the Keyboard!

Getting Started

This chapter consists of two parts. The first part is designed to familiarize you with the physical function and usage of the keyboard. The second section addresses major issues involving the teaching of keyboarding in schools and raises questions of general concern. We don't claim to have the answers to these questions, but we hope to provide information that will provoke further thought and discussion among readers.

Objectives for Teachers

After completing this chapter, you should be able to

1. Describe the difference between a computer keyboard and a typewriter.
2. Describe the three main sections of the IBM PC keyboard.
3. Describe the functions of the spacebar, cursor control, [Shift], [Enter], [Caps Lock], [PrtSc], [Num Lock], [Home], [PgUp], [PgDn], [End], [Del], [Ins], and function keys.
4. Type the extended character set.
5. Perform a warm boot of the IBM PC.
6. Define the term *keyboarding*.
7. Make recommendations concerning the appropriate grade level to begin instruction in keyboarding.
8. Develop a group activity or competitive game to use with students for keyboarding instruction.
9. Describe how to design the computer facility so that it is ergonomically sound for students.
10. Develop and implement a plan for a unit of instruction on keyboarding appropriate to your students.

The PC Keyboard

The IBM PC keyboard has been ergonomically designed for use in a variety of positions and to provide maximum typing comfort. **Ergonomics** comes from the Greek words *ergon,* meaning "work," and *economics.* It is possible to adjust the keyboard to any of three positions: level position, tilt position 1, and tilt position 2. To change positions, hold the keyboard, then push in and turn the adjustable leg handles on the upper left and right sides.

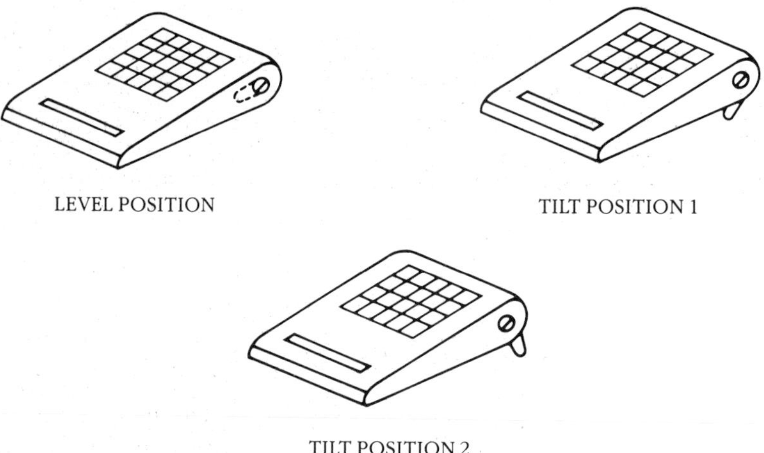

The keys themselves are concave in shape with rounded edges. These two features provide a comfortable sense of tactile feedback and make it easy to move quickly between keys. When you strike the keys, you will hear a very definite click. You will find yourself becoming quickly adjusted to hearing this sound as auditory reinforcement, especially if you are a touch-typist.

The PC keyboard, at first glance, looks very much like an ordinary typewriter keyboard. In some ways it operates similarly to a typewriter; however, it is much more powerful. As one small example, if your typewriter is relatively new, it has a few keys that are **typematic;** that is, they repeat if you hold them down. With the exception of the control keys, all of the keys on the IBM PC keyboard are typematic.

Aside from this convenience and the obvious visual similarity, the keyboard is not a typewriter; it is an input device. In fact, it is the input device that you will probably use most frequently to communicate with your computer. To this end, the keyboard itself is equipped with a small microprocessor so that when you strike the keys, information is communicated directly to the system unit. Therefore, every key generates a unique code to be transmitted to the computer. Many of the keys have more than one function, and some keys can be used in combination with others to give still other commands. So when you need the numeral *0* (zero), you must use the numeral *0*; unlike the typewriter, the computer won't be satisfied with a capital letter *O*. Similarly, when you need the numeral *1*, you must use it and not—as you may have done for years—a lowercase letter *l*. True, in typing text, this distinction will not always matter, but if you have the habit of interchanging keys, you should break it. And, as you are teaching, you should also encourage students to use the proper keys and never develop the habit.

The keys on the IBM PC keyboard are grouped into three sections: the **function keypad,** the typewriter keyboard, and the **numeric keypad.** Since you'll use the typewriter keyboard most often we'll discuss it first.

FUNCTION KEYPAD

TYPEWRITER KEYBOARD

NUMERIC KEYPAD

The Typewriter Keyboard

On the typewriter keyboard, you will notice some familiar keys and some unusual new ones. The *spacebar* will move the cursor across the screen, as you might expect. However, as it does so, each space is interpreted by the computer as a character and will be inserted as such in text. If the spacebar is used to move across existing text, it will remove the text and replace it with blank characters (spaces). The term *blank character* may sound contradictory, but to your computer, a blank space is just like any other character and is definitely not empty. It is best to use the spacebar only for the purpose of deliberately entering blank characters. To move around the screen or within text, use the cursor control keys located on the numeric keypad, which we will discuss in the next section. Remember, if you use the spacebar, you will add blank characters or replace text.

The two Shift keys are used to type uppercase letters or symbols appearing on the upper portion of a key. They are the keys with the upward pointing arrows, next to the slash and backslash keys. They will not work with the numeric keypad. Use them only with the letters and numbers on the typewriter keyboard. Note that the Caps Lock key is not the same as the shift lock key on a typewriter. Caps Lock is one of the keyboard's **toggle keys.** A toggle key is like a switch; it can be turned on and off. When depressed it will stay on until pressed again, which will turn it off. In most programs, your screen will indicate if a toggle key is on. When the Caps Lock key is on, the typewriter keyboard will produce only capital letters, much as a shift lock mechanism on a typewriter. If the Shift key is used on a letter when the CAPS mode is on, a lowercase letter will be produced. Note, however, that Caps Lock affects only letters. For example, pressing the [=] key with [Caps Lock] engaged still gets you an equal sign, not a plus sign. You must use the [Shift] key for that.

Although it may be tempting to relate the [Enter] key (the one that looks like this: ↵) to a typewriter return key, it must be stressed that the [Enter] key is quite different in function. Upon completion of a command, the [Enter] key is used to submit the information to the computer and to signal that the command is complete. When used in a text mode, such as in a word processor, it may be used to signal the end of a section of text, such as a paragraph. Remember: You don't need a carriage return mechanism on your computer; the computer will automatically wrap your text around to the next line. This is a great feature. Thanks to **wordwrap,** you will find that your typing speed will increase significantly, no matter how fast you already are. On some programs, this feature can even be set to wrap a given number of lines at a time for double, triple, or any kind of spacing you would like.

The [Tab] key customarily moves the cursor a preset number of spaces to the right. In some programs, using the [Tab] key in conjunction with the [Shift] keys will move the cursor to the left. Tab stops can be changed in most programs. Some programs take advantage of the [Tab] key to move the cursor to predetermined headings or categories where the user fills in information. An example of this is moving from column to column on a spreadsheet. The [Tab] key is a time saver. In fact, it is rumored that TAB actually stands for Take A Break, and was originally designed to save a typist from having to type in spaces or the infamous blank characters between points.

The [Backspace] key usually removes one character to the left each time it is pressed. It is a typematic key, and will continue to delete characters while depressed. In some programs, the [Backspace] key operates differently, and may simply move the cursor to the left without deleting characters.

The [Esc] (Escape) key will frequently cancel an incorrect line while editing. The [Esc] key is also used in conjunction with other keys for functions that will be discussed later. In some programs, the [Esc] key will actually let the user escape or go back to another level or menu in a program. In other programs, it may stop the execution of a command or stop the printer.

The [Ctrl] (Control) key is one of the keys that you use with other keys to produce different results. When used with the [Num Lock] key, it will stop information from scrolling on the screen. When used with the [Scroll Lock] key, it can halt some commands during execution. The [Ctrl] key is also used in conjunction with other keys for functions that will be discussed later.

The [PrtSc] (Print Screen) key, when pressed with one of the [Shift] keys, will copy the contents of the computer's screen to the printer. It copies only what is on the screen at the time it is pressed. When used with the [Ctrl] key, it copies to the printer everything that appears on the screen from the time it is pressed until it is pressed again.

The Numeric Keypad

In the numeric keypad, the **cursor keys** are important enough to get top billing. They are the keys that have arrows on them, are located on the keys labeled 2, 4, 6, and 8, and are pointing South, West, East, and North. These keys do just what their name says—they control the cursor. When you want to move around the screen or within your text without disturbing any text in place, these keys will take you where you want to go. You will use them frequently because in many situations you will need to move your cursor to a particular screen location.

With the exception of the [+] and [−] keys, all of the keys on the numeric keypad have dual functions. The [Num Lock] (Numbers Lock) key is a toggle key that turns the numeric keypad on and off. The preset value is off. When the NUM mode is on, the numeric keypad will operate numerically, and a given key will produce the corresponding number. When the NUM mode is off, the keys operate as cursor controls. With NUM mode on, your numeric keypad can operate just like a calculator keypad, depending on the program. With the NUM mode off, in many programs, the keys of the numeric keypad can be used for special functions, as shown in the following table:

Key	Function
[End] (1)	Moves the cursor to the end of the current line.
[Home] (7)	Moves the cursor to the beginning of the current line.
[PgUp] (9)	Moves the cursor to the previous screen.
[PgDn] (3)	Moves the cursor to the next screen.
[Del] (.)	Deletes, or removes, a character. Depending on the software in use, this key may delete a character to the right of the cursor, to the left of the cursor, or the character the cursor is on at the time.
[Ins] (0)	[Ins] (Insert) is a toggle key. When depressed, it changes the shape of the cursor from a thin line to a larger square, and allows for the insertion of text without removing existing text.

These functions may vary slightly from program to program.

The Function Keys

The function keys are among the most valuable attributes of the IBM PC keyboard. The function keys are located in two columns to the left of the typewriter keyboard. They are preset to differing functions depending upon the program with which they are to be used. Basically, they accomplish—with a single keystroke—commands or functions not otherwise inherent on other keys. In some programs, they can be set by the user to perform desired functions (they are redefinable); in other programs, they are preset to perform functions necessary to that program. For example, striking F5 might delete an entire line of text, bring up a set of help instructions, underline a portion of text, move the user to another menu, recall a mathematical formula, or any number of other possibilities. Although the uses of the function keys vary greatly from program to program, some standards have emerged. F1 is commonly used to invoke a *Help* function. F10 is commonly used to *back up* through a series of menus or to *quit* a program.

The IBM Extended Character Set

There are characters available from the keyboard that you can't see. They form the **extended character set.** You may recall from the previous chapter that all characters on the keyboard correspond to numbers less than 128, but that there are 256 numbers possible. Well, the numbers from 129 to 255 are the ones that we are talking about. They are not visible on the keyboard, and very few printers will print them, but you can type them by holding down the Alt key and typing a code number on the numeric keypad. For example, holding down Alt and typing 227 will print **π,** the Greek letter *pi,* on the screen. Also in the extended character set are some graphic characters for drawing lines and other simple figures. This can make for creative and innovative documents once you get the hang of combining these characters. A full chart of codes can be found in the IBM BASIC manual; an abbreviated version follows:

32		33	!	34	"	35	#	36	$	37	%	38	&	39	'	40	(	41	)
42	*	43	+	44	,	45	-	46	.	47	/	48	0	49	1	50	2	51	3
52	4	53	5	54	6	55	7	56	8	57	9	58	:	59	;	60	<	61	=
62	>	63	?	64	@	65	A	66	B	67	C	68	D	69	E	70	F	71	G
72	H	73	I	74	J	75	K	76	L	77	M	78	N	79	O	80	P	81	Q
82	R	83	S	84	T	85	U	86	V	87	W	88	X	89	Y	90	Z	91	[
92	\	93	]	94	^	95	_	96	`	97	a	98	b	99	c	100	d	101	e
102	f	103	g	104	h	105	i	106	j	107	k	108	l	109	m	110	n	111	o
112	p	113	q	114	r	115	s	116	t	117	u	118	v	119	w	120	x	121	y
122	z	123	{	124	¦	125	}	126	~	127	⌂	128	Ç	129	ü	130	é	131	â
132	ä	133	à	134	å	135	ç	136	ê	137	ë	138	è	139	ï	140	î	141	ì
142	Ä	143	Å	144	É	145	æ	146	Æ	147	ô	148	ö	149	ò	150	û	151	ù
152	ÿ	153	Ö	154	Ü	155	¢	156	£	157	¥	158	₧	159	ƒ	160	á	161	í
162	ó	163	ú	164	ñ	165	Ñ	166	ª	167	º	168	¿	169	⌐	170	¬	171	½
172	¼	173	¡	174	«	175	»	176	░	177	▒	178	▓	179	│	180	┤	181	╡
182	╢	183	╖	184	╕	185	╣	186	║	187	╗	188	╝	189	╜	190	╛	191	┐
192	└	193	┴	194	┬	195	├	196	─	197	┼	198	╞	199	╟	200	╚	201	╔
202	╩	203	╦	204	╠	205	═	206	╬	207	╧	208	╨	209	╤	210	╥	211	╙
212	╘	213	╒	214	╓	215	╫	216	╪	217	┘	218	┌	219	█	220	▄	221	▌
222	▐	223	▀	224	α	225	ß	226	Γ	227	π	228	Σ	229	σ	230	µ	231	τ
232	Φ	233	Θ	234	Ω	235	δ	236	∞	237	φ	238	ε	239	∩	240	≡	241	±
242	≥	243	≤	244	⌠	245	⌡	246	÷	247	≈	248	°	249	∙	250	·	251	√
252	ⁿ	253	²	254	■	255													

If you let your students loose with a code chart you might get some interesting results!

Key Combinations

As mentioned earlier, many keys on the IBM PC keyboard can be used in combination to produce different results than when used individually. Some of these key combinations are predefined and rarely changed, but most of them are readily programmable. Many programs take advantage of this capability by using combinations of keys for different functions. Although some standards have emerged, still far too many combinations vary from program to program. The specifics of a particular program are outlined in its documentation. It is impossible for us to detail these key combinations in this book—they are far too numerous. Let's look at the few of these combinations that were designed as or have become standards.

The Ctrl-Alt-Del key combination is not controlled by software and its function rarely varies, though a few programs disable it totally. Certainly, any IBM computer user becomes familiar with this group early on. Ctrl-Alt-Del causes a **system reset,** or what is often referred to as a **warm boot.** (In Chapter 3, we'll discuss the warm boot in more detail, and explain other methods of starting the system.) This is used when you want to reset the computer after it is already turned on and running. This is not only a time saver, but also saves wear and tear on the computer's power switch. The three keys must be held down simultaneously to perform correctly. One of the easiest methods of accomplishing this is to press the Ctrl key first, hold it down, press the Alt key next, hold it down, and finally, press the Del key. Then let all three keys go, and the system will reset.

The Ctrl-Scroll Lock key combination, sometimes referred to as *Break,* also rarely changes. It usually halts the execution of a program. The combinations with Alt and the numeric keypad numbers also rarely change. With the help of a character code table, these combinations allow you to type characters that are not represented on the keyboard. The Shift-PrtSc combination, as we discussed before, copies the exact contents of the screen to the printer. Ctrl-PrtSc toggles the print on so that everything that appears on the screen is also copied to the printer. Pressing the combination again turns it off.

Issues in Keyboarding

In recent years, particularly since the introduction of the microcomputer to the elementary classroom, a number of questions have been raised about the instruction of keyboarding at the elementary level. There are both physiological and psychological considerations, as well as concerns about the methodology of keyboarding instruction. Some educators are taking the position that we have no business allowing students to use computers until they have learned to touch-type. This strikes us as a bit like telling someone they cannot go near the water until they have learned to swim. At the other extreme are those who maintain that typing skills have no relation to computer skills. In this section, we will present some of these questions, with the aim of providing you with some insight into the issues.

What Is Keyboarding?

By definition, keyboarding is the use of, or instruction in the use of, a keyboard to input information involving either a typewriter or a microcomputer. Keyboard instruction usually involves teaching correct fingering, providing familiarity with the placement of keys on the keyboard, and instructing in the use of individual keys. By teaching the correct fingering, it is hoped that the student will develop touch-typing skills to some degree and not have to rely solely on the hunt-and-peck method.

However, in the elementary grades, while guidance should be given to provide the students with a general method of keyboarding, there should also be a great deal of room left for individual preferences and experimentation. Keyboarding instruction should focus more on results rather than techniques.

Reasons for Keyboarding at the Elementary Level

Research suggests that children are physiologically ready to learn keyboarding at about the third grade. Children at this age have mastered printing and are familiar with handwriting. As the microcomputer becomes a common tool in the elementary schools, some instruction in keyboarding may be necessary to use the computers most effectively. At this level, keyboarding is a natural extension of the existing skills of printing and handwriting and will provide a good base for the use of microcomputers in the future, especially where children will be using computers for word processing, data-base management, and programming. Also, it seems that children show an interest in developing skills on the keyboard at this age, and are receptive to instruction, knowing that it will give them greater mastery of the computer.

In What Order Should Keyboard Skills Be Taught?

Some research indicates that the order in which material is presented does not matter significantly. We disagree and believe that since the computer keyboard is so very different from a typewriter some attention should be given to the order in which keyboarding is presented. Some things to consider might be the frequency of use of particular keys, and the use of function and control keys. It is probably important to first introduce groups of keys in the major sections of the keyboard, followed by special key characteristics. For instance, a microcomputer keyboard is different from a typewriter in that most of the keys are typematic and will repeat if held down, some keys will remove information, and some keys will insert blank characters. Children should be introduced to these concepts, since errors in using these keys will produce quite different results than when using a typewriter. The general concept of computer keyboarding is entirely different from that of a typewriter. Perhaps a good way to start is to explain the differences and give children an overall understanding of what a computer keyboard does. Remember, it doesn't just type characters; it performs commands, deletes data, inserts data, and so on.

How Do Children Best Acquire Keyboarding Skills?

In learning to use the keyboard, we use tactile feedback from the keyboard to tell us if our responses are correct. This is called *kinesthesis* and is developed by repetition of a pattern until a stimulus is learned. Typing skills cannot be learned cognitively, they require repetition, and the actual use of a keyboard to provide the tactile response. Some progress may be made by teaching key locations and by using visual instruction, but it cannot replace students actually getting their hands on the keyboard. Many typing patterns are developed by using common letter combinations such as *sh, tr,* and *th,* starting with simple groupings, and moving to short sentences such as

ad as al at da la sa ta
sad fad lad gad tad had
Tad was as glad as Dad was mad

Don't Look Now . . .

Many of us learned to touch-type under the watchful eye of a strict teacher who made sure our gaze did not wander to join our fingers on the keyboard. This may have proved successful, but was undoubtedly frustrating at the beginning. Try to imagine an eight-year old in the same predicament. In the very early stages of learning keyboarding, it may actually be helpful, especially in developing confidence and providing positive feedback, to go ahead and look at whatever provides the best assistance—fingers, keys, or monitor. As confidence builds, this visual help can gradually be reduced.

What about Accuracy?

In general, keyboarding instruction has tended to stress accuracy at a fairly early stage in learning. This may not be appropriate in instructing small children. Remember, we are after an end rather than a means to it, and as confidence develops, it is likely that accuracy will improve naturally. However, students should be kept informed of their progress in speed and accuracy. Both tend to develop quickly, and constant positive feedback is important to engender high motivation.

Instructional Approaches

As in most activities with children, diversity is the key here. A teacher should not rely on one approach only, but should be flexible to meet the needs of individual learning styles. Some group activities, such as competitive games, can be motivating, as well as oral drills with the entire class. But these should be mixed with individual activities that are self-paced. Let's also not forget that the computer itself, with the right software, can provide excellent typing instruction and practice. Since the development of keyboarding skills depends so heavily upon appropriate and repeated practice, it works very well as the subject of instructional software. There are many well written, motivating programs on the market today that can be used to supplement classroom instruction in keyboarding. (See Chapter 15 for more information.)

Ergonomics—What Position Should YOU Take?

Your position is very different from that of a child. Typewriter and computer keyboards are designed for use by adult hands. The keys have been placed and spaced with average grown-up fingers in mind. Posture should be a key consideration. A 30-minute keyboarding lesson is a long one for a small child, especially in an uncomfortable position, or with a keyboard at the improper height. Some important points to consider follow:

- The child's feet should be flat on the floor.
- Chairs should be adjustable and have good back support.
- Keyboards should be at the proper height so that the upper arm is nearly vertical and the lower arm is nearly horizontal; the elbow should be at about 90 degrees.

- Hands should be able to be tilted upward slightly for better mobility.
- The top of the monitor screen should be at or below eye level to reduce neck strain.
- Copyholders may need to be considered, as well, to eliminate constant shifting of the neck and eyes from the flat surface of a desk or table.

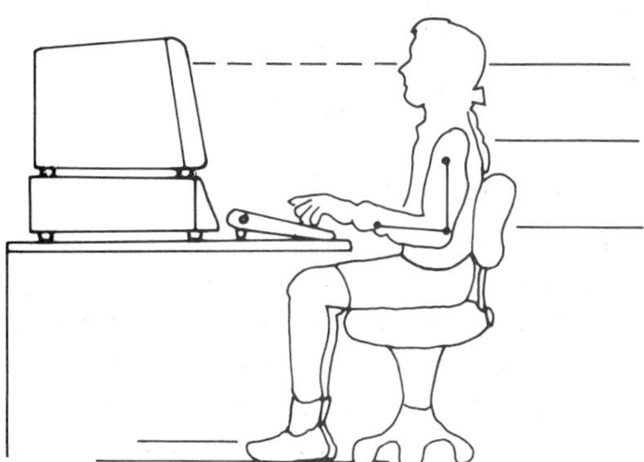

Of course, there are a lot of points to consider, and some may be economically impossible to implement immediately. It is possible, however, to make modifications that will serve the same purpose. For example, if chairs cannot be adjusted, perhaps desks or tables can be. If feet do not touch the floor, inexpensive footrests can be purchased or constructed. If neither desks nor chairs can be adjusted, then how about pillows on the chairs to raise the child's height? Monitors can be placed beside the system unit, rather than on top of it, and if necessary, can be raised slightly, or angled, with inexpensive materials.

Two more aspects to consider should be adequate lighting and glare reduction, where it presents a problem. Glare can be reduced or blocked entirely, by placing the monitors at a 90-degree angle to windows, or by installing blinds or curtains on windows. Glare reduction screens can also be purchased to cover the monitor. The manufacturers of these screens claim that they reduce glare significantly; however, you should try one in your particular environment before purchasing any large quantities. Adequate lighting will help reduce the chances of eye fatigue, as will structured periods of time on the computer with appropriately scheduled breaks.

Class Length

The length of time to spend in one keyboarding class really depends on your students. Some students could spend hours at a keyboard and not lose interest, others have much shorter attention spans. Also, susceptibility to eye fatigue varies a great deal from one individual to another. As a rule, an elementary class can probably go for 30 minutes before the students begin to tire. This length of time also varies with the activity being performed.

Organization of Keyboarding Classes

The organization of keyboarding classes will depend largely on what materials are available. If an entire classroom of computers is available, then large group instruction can be designed. This structure offers several advantages.

- The class can work as a whole and students will all get equal time.
- Students will not miss another classroom activity while working on keyboarding.
- A teacher will be available during the entire keyboarding lesson.
- Teachers with special interests and skills in keyboarding can trade duties with those who don't have those interests and skills.

If an entire lab of computers is not available, then it will be necessary to have individual or group time for keyboarding. Perhaps part of the class could work on the keyboards available, with the balance of the students working on keyboarding activities or games without the actual use of keyboards. Student time could be apportioned to assure that everyone gets equal time on the computers.

Who Should Teach Keyboarding at the Elementary Level?

This is a difficult question. It depends largely on the organization of the class. Possibilities include the following:

- A regular classroom teacher.
- A secondary business-education teacher.
- A traveling districtwide teacher for elementary schools.
- A designated teacher within the building.
- A team of teachers with a coordinator, possibly a secondary business-education teacher.

Each of the possibilities just mentioned has difficulties associated with it. An elementary-level teacher may have little formal background in keyboarding principles or techniques, and possibly little interest in teaching keyboarding. A secondary business-education teacher who does possess appropriate skills may lack the background or skills for elementary-level teaching. The ideal situation would be either an elementary teacher with formal keyboarding training, or an elementary teacher with an interest in this area acting under the guidance of a secondary business teacher.

Chapter Summary

We have provided a general introduction to the keyboard of the IBM PC and pointed out differences between it and a typewriter. While no specific material was presented on the keyboards of other members of the PC family, most of the concepts presented here generalize to them and to the keyboards of many other computers as well.

We also discussed issues concerning the teaching of keyboarding skills at the elementary level. The questions we raised cover only the basic topics for discussion when considering implementation of a keyboarding module. It should be remembered that operating the keyboard is only the tip of the iceberg in a total microcomputer curriculum, and can be an excellent introduction to advanced computer skills. It can be introduced as an entirely separate area of skill development, or can be integrated into programs involving diskette management, microcomputer hardware operation, and software applications. It can be incorporated into classes in word processing, or in English classes that use the computer to develop writing skills—to name only two examples.

Chapter Review

Knowledge Exercises

1. What are the three parts of the IBM PC keyboard?

   Answer: The function keypad, typewriter keyboard, and numeric keypad are the three parts of the IBM PC keyboard.

2. What is the most significant difference between the computer keyboard and a typewriter?

   Answer: On a typewriter, a key is represented graphically on paper just as it is on the key itself, thus making it possible to interchange some letters and numbers such as O and 0 (the capital letter *O* and zero) or l and 1 (the lowercase letter *l* and one). However, on the computer keyboard, each key represents a code to be transmitted to the computer, so letters and numbers cannot be interchanged. In fact, many of the keys have more than one function and some keys can be used in combination with each other to produce varying commands.

3. What is the function of the spacebar?

   Answer: The spacebar removes existing text as it moves across it, and inserts blank spaces or blank characters for the computer to read.

4. Where are the cursor control keys located? What is their function?

   Answer: The cursor control keys are located on the numeric keypad. They are used to move the cursor around the screen or within a text without disturbing any text already in place.

5. What is the function of the [Shift] keys?

   Answer: The [Shift] keys are used to type uppercase letters or symbols that appear on the upper portion of the keys on the typewriter keyboard.

6. What is a toggle key?

   Answer: A toggle key is like a switch; it can be turned on and off. When depressed it stays on until pressed again, at which point it turns off.

7. What is the function of the Caps Lock key?

   Answer: The Caps Lock key is a toggle key. When it is on, it functions much as the shift-lock mechanism on a typewriter, except it produces only capital letters. It affects only the letters on the keyboard. If the Shift key is used on a letter when the CAPS mode is on, a lowercase letter will be produced. The Caps Lock will not produce symbols that appear on the upper portion of other keys. The Shift keys must be used for that.

8. What is the function of the Enter key? How does it differ from a typewriter return key?

   Answer: The Enter key is used to send information to the computer and to signal that a command is complete. It is not a carriage return mechanism as on a typewriter. In many applications, the computer automatically wraps text around to the next line.

9. What is the function of the PrtSc key?

   Answer: The PrtSc key, when used in conjunction with one of the Shift keys, copies the contents of the screen to the printer. Using the Shift and PrtSc keys prints everything that appears on the screen at that time on that one particular screen only. Ctrl-PrtSc toggles on the printer so that everything that appears on the screen is copied to the printer. Since it is a toggle, pressing Ctrl-PrtSc a second time turns the function off.

10. What function does the Num Lock key serve?

    Answer: The Num Lock key is a toggle that turns the numeric keypad on and off. When Num Lock is on, the numeric keypad produces numerals. When Num Lock is off, the keys operate as cursor controls.

11. Name and briefly describe common functions of the six keys located on the numeric keypad, other than the Num Lock and Scroll Lock keys.

    Answer: Home Moves the cursor to the beginning of the current line.

    PgUp Scrolls text up one page on the screen.

    PgDn Scrolls text down one page on the screen.

    End Moves cursor to the end of the current line.

    Del Deletes or removes a character.

    Ins A toggle key that changes the shape of the cursor and allows for insertion of text without removing existing text.

12. Of what value are the function keys?

    Answer: The function keys allow you to accomplish with a single keystroke commands or functions not otherwise inherent on other keys. In many programs they are preset to perform functions necessary to that program, and in other programs they can be set by the user to perform desired functions.

13. What is a system reset, or warm boot? How do you perform it on the IBM PC?

    Answer: A system reset, or warm boot, enables you to restart the computer after it is already turned on and running. It is performed by pressing the Ctrl, Alt, and Del keys simultaneously.

14. What is keyboarding?

    Answer: Keyboarding is the use of, or instruction in the use of, a keyboard to input information. This involves a method of instruction that will teach the correct fingering, provide familiarity with the placement of keys on the keyboard, and teach the use of individual keys.

Thought Exercises

1. At what grade level should keyboarding be taught? Go to the library and find at least three references (with at least one research study) to support your recommendation. Be prepared to present your recommendations in class, along with the supporting documentation.
2. When learning keyboarding, should students be allowed to look at the keyboard? Write a one-page paper supporting your position.
3. Should accuracy be stressed in keyboarding instruction? Why or why not? Write a one-page paper supporting your position.
4. Describe a group activity or competitive game that you could use with your students to teach keyboarding.
5. Write a brief report describing how you can make adjustments in your classroom so that computer equipment will follow the ergonomic recommendations in this chapter for the smallest student in the class as well as the largest.

Activities

1. Use the extended character set to insert graphics into a short story (of at least one page) suitable for use with students. Use the IBM BASIC manual for the full chart of character codes.
2. Let students work with the extended character set to construct graphics. Encourage them to be as creative as possible. (Have them refer to the

IBM BASIC manual for the full chart of character codes.) Bring in some representative samples of their work.

3. Have students do some creative writing, using graphics they created with the extended character set to illustrate their stories. Bring representative samples to class.

Projects

1. Write a plan for teaching keyboarding to students at a particular grade level. Describe the student population you will be working with and present a rationale addressing the questions presented in the Thought Exercises. Write detailed lesson plans for at least a two-week period.

2. Implement the instructional plan for keyboarding that you developed in Project 1. Keep a daily log, recording student reactions to each lesson, any modifications that had to be made, and suggestions for improvement in case you teach it again. Keep representative samples of student work for each lesson.

Bibliography

Benamy, R. "Microcomputer Keyboarding for the Casual User." *Balance Sheet* (September–October 1984): 27–28. Describes a course at Rockland Community College for casual users of the keyboard.

Davis, B. J., and M. Little. "Keyboarding for Computer Efficiency in a Gifted/Talented Program." *Journal of Business Education* (December 1984): 104–107. Describes a keyboarding program at Nicholls State University in Louisiana for gifted/talented junior and senior high school students.

Erthal, M. J. "The Status of Keyboarding." *Journal of Business Education* (February 1985): 192–193. Describes results of a questionnaire and gives suggestions for improving the curriculum for keyboarding in elementary schools.

Kemppainen, R. "How We Use Computers for (Much) Better Education." Paper presented at the National School Boards' Association Convention, Houston, Tex., April 2, 1984.

Kisner, E. "Keyboarding—A Must in Tomorrow's World." *Computing Teacher* (February 1984): 21–22. Describes keyboarding and briefly discusses when it should be taught, who should teach it, and what level of efficiency is needed.

LaBarre, J. E., and D. K. Zahn. "Keyboarding." Madison: Wisconsin State Department of Public Instruction, July 1983. A position paper on keyboarding requested by the Superintendent's Advisory Committee for Business Education and Future Business Leaders of America.

Long, Karen J., and Roger Larkin. "Electronic Keyboarding. IBM Model Instructional Computing Program." Minneapolis: Annoka-Hennepin School District, May 1984. An introduction to keyboarding topics prepared for the 1984–85 IBM Model Schools Program.

Northwest Regional Educational Laboratory. "Technological Literacy Skills Everybody Should Learn. Ideas for Action in Education and Work." Portland, Oreg.: Northwest Regional Educational Laboratory, Education and Work Program, August 1984.

Ownby, A. C., and H. Perrault. "Keyboarding: A No-Fail Model." *Business Education Forum* (May 1983): 9–12. Although keyboarding is not complex, it is a skill that every graduate needs. Considers minimum skill levels and alternatives for teaching and learning.

Prinz, P. M., and K. E. Nelson. "Reading is Fun—With a Keyboard, a Hat, and an Alligator." *Perspectives for Teachers of the Hearing Impaired* (September–October 1984): 2–4. A program at the Pennsylvania School for the Deaf uses microcomputers to help students initiate communication and play active roles in deciding the topic of communication and the way the lesson proceeds.

Regional School District No. 10, Burlington, Conn. "Microcomputer Keyboarding Curriculum for Middle and Junior High School Students. Final Report." Hartford: Connecticut State Department of Education, August 27, 1984.

Rigby, S. "Keyboarding Is for Everyone." *Business Education Forum* (October 1983): 13–14. Computer keyboards are being used by everyone from elementary students to business executives. All need basic touch keyboarding skills to make efficient use of these computers.

Schmidt, J. B. "Keyboarding: The State of the Art." Blacksburg: Virginia Polytechnic Institute and State University, October 1983. A paper prepared as part of the University's project on "Using the Microcomputer to Teach Keyboarding Skills."

Sormunen, C. "In-Service Workshops: One Answer to the Issue of Elementary School Keyboarding." *Journal of Business Education* (October 1984): 14–17. Considers the change in attitude about teaching keyboarding in the elementary school and outlines objectives for an in-service workshop to train teachers to teach keyboarding for computer literacy.

Stewart, J., and B. W. Jones. "Keyboarding Instruction: Elementary School Options." *Business Education Forum* (April 1983): 11–12. Business education teachers have the background and knowledge to teach keyboarding basics to elementary school students, who need these skills for using microcomputers.

CHAPTER

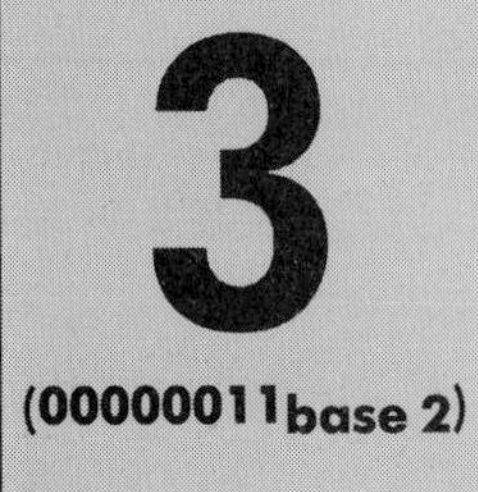

YOUR WISH IS MY COMMAND!

Introduction to the Disk Operating System

Getting Started

The process of becoming proficient with a computer like the IBM PC starts with learning to use DOS, the Disk Operating System. This chapter will introduce you to PC DOS, the Disk Operating System for PCs. You will learn what DOS is and what it will do for you. You'll also learn about floppy diskettes and how to care for them. We'll tell you how to bring your computer up to operating status and you'll learn the importance of backing up diskettes and how to do it. We'll also examine the function and format of a critical subset of the DOS commands, the minimum necessary to use software competently.

Objectives for Teachers

After completing this chapter, you should be able to:

1. Describe the Disk Operating System (DOS) and its importance.
2. Describe the various attributes of floppy diskettes and their respective functions.
3. Describe proper and improper ways to handle diskettes.

To perform the activities in this chapter, you'll need a copy of IBM PC DOS, some blank diskettes, and a felt-tip pen.

4. Define booting the machine, describe and perform both cold and warm boots.
5. Describe the importance of backing up software.
6. Describe the permitted character restrictions for DOS filenames.
7. Differentiate between internal and external DOS commands.
8. Define and demonstrate the use of the external DOS commands FORMAT, DISKCOPY, BASICA, and the BASICA command, SYSTEM.
9. Define and demonstrate the use of the internal DOS commands DATE, TIME, DIR, COPY, DEL or ERASE, and RENAME.
10. Develop and present an appropriate instructional plan for teaching the use of DOS to a specific group of students.

DOS (pronounced "doss") stands for Disk Operating System. It is a collection of utility programs designed to integrate one or more disk drives with the rest of your computer system. These programs are called utilities because they are tools that perform a variety of housekeeping functions related to the storing of information on diskettes. They are not available from the BASIC interpreter that comes with your computer, and even if they were, such a system would be difficult to operate.

The term *DOS* is generic and refers to any type of Disk Operating System. More than one is available for the IBM PC (CPM-86 and the UCSD p-System, for example). PC DOS was written for IBM by the Microsoft Corporation, which markets a similar product under the name MS DOS. There is more than one version of PC DOS. It has been modified extensively since its initial release. Different versions of computer software are indicated with decimal numbers—such as 3.10—in which a change in the digit to the left of the decimal point indicates a major revision and one to the right, a minor revision. As of this writing, PC DOS exists in versions 1.00, 1.10, 2.00, 2.10, 3.00, 3.10, and 3.20. By the time you read this, at least one more revision will probably have been released. Fortunately for users, the different versions of DOS are upwardly compatible, meaning that a later version is usually capable of operating with any diskettes or software formatted for an earlier version. All the information in this book, except where noted, is compatible with all current versions of PC DOS.

Diskettes

First of all, let's talk about diskettes and the type the IBM PC uses. Disks, diskettes, floppy diskettes, or whatever you call them, are all magnetic media. That means they store information magnetically, in much the same way as an audio cassette does. Inside the square outer cover of a diskette, there is a round plastic disk that has a coating of metallic material called flux. This flux is the part of the diskette upon which the read/write head of the disk drive encodes information.

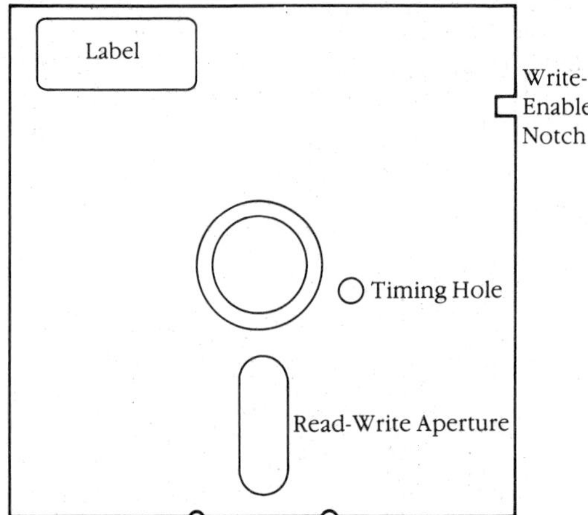

Remove a diskette from its sleeve and look at it. In the upper-left corner there is usually a manufacturer's label. Over this, or to the right of it, there may be a stick-on paper label indicating the contents of the diskette. On the right-hand side, near the top is a square notch that may or may not be covered with a small stick-on tab. This notch is called the **write-enable notch.** When it is not present or when it is covered by a tab, the disk drive cannot write to or place information on the diskette. In the center of the diskette is a large hole through which the drive grasps the diskette to turn it. Next to this hole, to the lower right, is another, smaller, timing hole that some drives make use of and some don't. The drives on your IBM PC do. Below the center hole there is an oblong opening called the read-write aperture. It is through this window that the head of the disk drive makes contact with the diskette.

The diskettes you need for your IBM PC are called (pay attention, now) *5-1/4 inch, double-density, soft-sectored, mini-floppy diskettes, single- or dual-sided.* These are the most commonly employed diskettes for microcomputers. They are called floppy diskettes because they are relatively flexible. Don't, however, bend them too much. The diskette can be destroyed that way. The 5-1/4 inch measure refers to the physical size of the diskette and double-density means that these diskettes are capable of storing information at twice the density of earlier kinds of diskettes called (what else?) single density.

Single-sided does not mean that the diskettes only have flux on one side. Just like dual-sided diskettes, single-sided diskettes have flux on both sides. The difference is that dual-sided diskettes are tested and certified for use on both sides and are therefore more expensive. Dual-sided diskettes are only necessary for dual-sided disk drives. If your PC is of pre-1984 vintage it may have single-sided drives. Newer PCs usually have dual-sided drives.

Do you have to buy dual-sided diskettes for dual-sided drives? Probably not. Many single-sided diskettes are equally good on the back. DOS also provides a safeguard by locking out bad tracks when a diskette is formatted. Buy dual-sided diskettes if you think that the additional quality and security is worth the price difference.

Before any information can be placed on a diskette, that diskette must be **formatted.** Think of a diskette as a filing cabinet. Before you start to cram information into a filing cabinet, don't you first create a filing system to organize the files that will be stored within? Isn't it important that you and other people both be able to reliably retrieve information from that cabinet? Well, the same thing goes for a diskette. All information that is placed on a diskette is placed in files. The formatting on a diskette is the filing system that DOS uses to organize the storage of files. You could create your own format, but it would be a lot of work and the end result would be that no one else would be able to retrieve your files. One major function of PC DOS, and any other DOS, is to standardize the diskette-formatting process.

Soft-sectored refers to the fact that when DOS organizes (formats) a diskette for storage, it superimposes a kind of road map that it uses to locate the files placed on it. Under an older system, diskettes were hard-sectored, meaning that the sectoring was physically accomplished on the diskette and not under the control of the Disk Operating System. Very few microcomputers continue to use hard-sectored diskettes.

You may notice that single-sided drives on the PC are called *160/180KB* drives. This is because 160KB is the amount of information the drive can place on the diskette under DOS versions 1.10 and older, and 180KB under DOS 2.00 and later. The KB stands for the word *kilobyte* (when used in reference to a computer's internal memory, the abbreviation is usually just K.) As discussed in Chapter 1, a byte is the fundamental unit of memory used in measuring the capacity of computer systems. It takes one byte to store one character of information, for example, the letter *A*. A kilobyte is equal to 1,024 bytes. If we take the number of characters on the average double-spaced typewritten page to be around 1,625 (65 characters per line × 25 lines), then that means there is room for about 100 pages of text on a 160KB diskette. Because of the space taken by the diskette's formatting and the nature of the way in which information is stored, some space is lost and you won't really be able to store that many pages.

When PC DOS versions 1.10 and older format a diskette, information is placed in 40 concentric rings called *tracks*. Each track is then subdivided into eight distinct sectors. Each of the sectors holds 512 bytes of information. A little quick arithmetic reveals that 40 × 8 × 512 equals 163,840 bytes, which is 160 kilobytes. A dual-sided drive is capable of holding 320 kilobytes. One of the major advantages of DOS 2.00 and later versions is that they format each track for nine sectors, resulting in an increase in storage capacity. Under these versions of DOS, single- and dual-sided diskettes store, respectively, 180 and 360 kilobytes of information.

Diskettes are known as volatile media because they can easily be erased, either intentionally or unintentionally. To assure the integrity of your data, handle your diskettes cautiously. Keep them away from strong magnetic fields. Television sets and airport X-ray machines, for example, have been known to cause loss of data on diskettes. Heat, like magnetic fields, can also compromise the integrity of your data. Don't leave diskettes in the window of your car on a sunny day. Dust and cigarette smoke are the enemies of your diskettes. Even the smallest particles of dust and smoke are large in comparison to the amount of area required on a diskette to store a bit.

These particles can interfere with the reading and writing of information by the head or can physically damage the flux on the diskette, causing a loss of data.

When handling a diskette, touch it only by the outer cover. Do not place your fingers on the actual disk through the read-write window. Also, don't place paper clips on a diskette. They can damage the disk through the outer cover. For the same reasons, never write on the label of a diskette with a hard-point pen. Always use a felt-tip pen. When not in use, keep your diskettes in the paper sleeves that come with them. They are made of a material called *tyvek,* which has antistatic properties. Finally, consider the purchase of containers for your diskettes. The cardboard boxes in which they come do not provide enough protection. Some diskettes come with a plastic library case as part of the purchase. The cases can also be bought relatively inexpensively.

When it comes to purchasing diskettes, don't feel that you have to buy them from the same source that your computer(s) came from. Although there are many different brands of diskettes, there are relatively few manufacturers. As long as you buy the right kind of diskette and stay away from the really cheap ones, you shouldn't have any trouble. One measure of the quality of a diskette is the length of time the retailer is willing to guarantee it. The added expense of 5- or 10-year guaranteed diskettes may be justified in the long run if they do, indeed, have a longer lifetime. The biggest problem with low-quality diskettes is that they clog the heads of your drives, causing degraded performance and requiring frequent cleaning.

Unless you know someone or have a connection, you will probably find small computer stores the most expensive place to buy diskettes. There are many reliable mail-order dealers who sell high-quality diskettes in quantity at reduced prices. Just get a copy of any computer magazine and search the ads for the best deal.

Booting the System

Now that we've discussed diskettes, let's see about booting the system. In computerese, to **boot** means to bring the system up to operational status from the off condition. The term comes from the expression "pulling yourself up by your own bootstraps." This is essentially what a computer does. When booting with a Disk Operating System, a program built into the computer's ROM tells it to look in the default disk drive for a program or series of programs to load. There is more detail to the process than we have described, but the net result is that DOS is installed, executed, and awaiting your command.

Remove the DOS diskette from its manual. If you are using DOS 1.10 or earlier, there is only one diskette in the manual. Newer versions of DOS have two, one labeled *DOS* and the other labeled *DOS Supplemental Programs.* The one you want right now, the one with most commonly used programs on it, is DOS. To boot the PC, remove the DOS diskette from its sleeve and place it in drive A:, the left-hand drive, with the label up, write-protect notch to the left, and read-write window away from you. Push the diskette in until you feel it contact the back of the drive, then close the drive door. It should close easily.

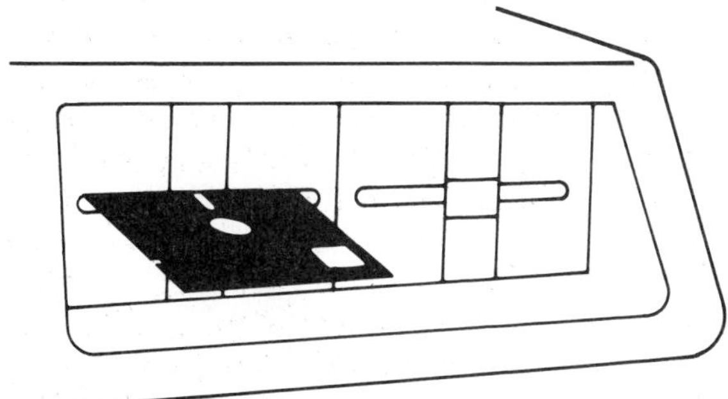

Take care opening and closing the drive doors. If you casually flip them open too many times, you may break them. Now turn on the computer's power switch and switch on your monitor. You have just performed a **cold boot.**

As you learned in Chapter 2, there is another type of boot called a warm boot or system reset. The system reset performs exactly the same function as a cold boot except that it is performed when the computer is already on. To perform a system reset, press the Ctrl, Alt, and Del keys in that order, holding each down until the last one is pressed.

Whether you've performed a cold boot or a system reset, the computer next performs a system checkout on itself, then it executes the DATE and TIME commands, prompting you to enter the current date and time. DOS uses these to date and time stamp a file when you save it and they are used by some programs as well. Enter the date in MM-DD-YY format, then press the Enter key. The time may be entered in HH:MM:SS.XX format, where XX stands for hundredths of a second. Notice that in the following illustration, only the hour and minutes have been entered.

```
Current date is Tues 1-01-1980
Enter new date: 12-20-84
Current time is 0:01:25.02
Enter new time: 8:45

The IBM Personal Computer DOS
Version 2.10 (C)Copyright IBM Corp. 1981, 1982,
1983
```

You may enter the time with just about any degree of accuracy from hours to hundredths of seconds. After you press Enter, A> will appear on the screen. This A> is called the DOS *prompt.* It means that you are now in DOS and the system is waiting for you to enter a command. Some people bypass the date and time prompts and get directly to the DOS prompt by merely pressing Enter. This is a bad habit to get into because you never know when a file was created.

Backing up a Diskette

Now that you are in DOS, the first thing you should do—indeed, the first thing you should do with any piece of software—is make a copy or back-up version of the diskette. As a general rule, you should always back up software, put a write-protect tab on the original, store it for safekeeping, and use the back-up copy. If you always have a copy on hand, then you'll never have to resort to contacting the manufacturer, who may not be very cooperative about replacing damaged software.

Unfortunately, not all software can be copied. For obvious reasons, manufacturers frequently go to great lengths to protect their merchandise from being copied. Some of these schemes allow for limited copying; others provide for no backup at all. The latter manufacturers either require you to contact them for another copy (when you return the damaged original), sell you a second copy at a reduced price, or simply provide you with two copies in the first place. We'll talk more about copy protection in Chapter 16.

Right now, we'll just go through the DOS back-up procedure step-by-step with little explanation. Later in this chapter, the full meaning of all the commands will be explained. Be sure to type all the spaces shown in the commands; for example, in DISKCOPY A: B: the spaces between the command name and the drive designations are important. It is also important to include the colons (:). They are part of the drive specification. It doesn't matter whether you type the commands in upper- or lowercase. DOS understands them both ways. Note the differing instructions depending upon whether you have two diskette drives or one.

Two Drives.

1. With the system booted and DOS in drive A:, place a blank diskette in drive B:.
2. Type DISKCOPY A: B: and press [Enter]. You should hear the drive spinning as the DISKCOPY command is started and see a small red light indicating that the drive is turning. Never insert or remove a diskette while the red light is on.
3. After a few seconds, the screen should look like this:

```
Current date is Tues 1-01-1980
Enter new date: 12-20-84
Current time is 0:01:25.02
Enter new time: 8:45

The IBM Personal Computer DOS
Version 2.10 (C)Copyright IBM Corp. 1981,
  1982, 1983

A>diskcopy a: b:

Insert source diskette in drive A:

Insert target diskette in drive B:

Strike any key when ready
```

4. At this point, you may insert a diskette to be copied (the source) in drive A: and a blank diskette (the target) in drive B:. Since we already have the diskettes we need in the drives, ignore this and press any key.
5. The screen should now indicate that DOS is copying one side. This is because DOS is capable of copying both sides of a dual-sided diskette, but in this case the copy is singled sided.
6. If everything goes well, the message following appears:

```
copy complete
another? (y/n)
```

If something went wrong, error messages will appear and you should start the entire process all over again.

One Drive.

1. With DOS in the drive, type DISKCOPY, and press Enter.
2. The program will prompt you to swap the source (DOS) diskette with the target (blank) diskette a number of times, depending upon how much memory your computer has.
3. Otherwise, the copy procedure is the same as with two drives.

An alternative to the one-drive instructions is to type DISKCOPY A: B:, just as if you have two drives. The command DISKCOPY A: B: instructs DOS to make a diskette in drive B: the mirror image of a diskette in drive A:. If you only have one drive, DOS prompts you to exchange diskettes at the proper times, treating the one drive as if it were both A: and B:. The command DISKCOPY, with no A: and B:, is the same thing as saying DISKCOPY A: A:. In both cases, A: and B: are called **parameters.** The DISKCOPY command requires two parameters to tell it which drive to copy from and which drive to copy to. When no parameters are specified, DISKCOPY assumes, by default, that you meant to use drive A:. The concept of operating by default is an important one with PC DOS because it generalizes to all DOS commands. What makes it tricky is the fact that A: is not always the default drive. We'll talk more about that later in this section.

If you are using DOS 2.00 or a later version, you may have noticed that there is a second diskette labeled *DOS Supplemental Programs* packaged with the DOS manual. This is because the later versions of DOS are too large to fit on one diskette. You may want to make a backup of this diskette also. Place your new copy of DOS in drive A:, type DISKCOPY A: B: once again, and press Enter. When the drive stops spinning and the prompts appear to place the source and target diskettes in drives A: and B:, respectively, remove the DOS diskette from drive A: and replace it with the DOS Supplemental Programs diskette. Place yet another blank diskette in drive B: and press Enter. Complete the back-up procedure as before.

Now that you have successfully backed up your DOS diskette(s), you should put the original(s) away in a safe place and never use them unless absolutely necessary. Label your copies appropriately, remembering that it is best to write on the label before applying it to the diskette. If you must write on the label after it is applied to the diskette, avoid damage by using a felt-tip pen.

Parameters and Defaults

Take the DOS back-up diskette you made earlier in this chapter and boot your computer. (You should know how to do that by now!) After entering the time and date, your screen should look something like this, depending upon your DOS version:

```
Current date is Tues 1-01-1980
Enter new date: 12-20-84
Current time is 0:01:25.02
Enter new time: 8:45
```

```
The IBM Personal Computer DOS
Version 2.10 (C)Copyright IBM Corp. 1981, 1982,
1983

A>
```

Remember that the A> is called the DOS prompt. The letter *A* means that the A drive is the **default** drive. The term *default* is one which you will encounter frequently. In general, it means *unless you tell the computer otherwise, here's what it will assume.* Most DOS commands—DISKCOPY, for example—require parameters. Previously in this chapter we used DISKCOPY A: B: to back up the DOS diskette on a two-drive system. The A: and B: were the parameters that told DOS to copy the contents of the diskette in the A: drive to the diskette in the B: drive. With one drive, it is possible to issue the DISKCOPY command without parameters. When that is done, DOS assumes you mean DISKCOPY A: A: and copies the contents of the diskette in drive A: to another diskette in drive A:, prompting you at the proper times to exchange diskettes. Whenever you issue a DOS command and leave out an expected parameter, the default will be assumed. For the command DISKCOPY, the parameters happen to be the drives themselves. Now, the default drive doesn't always have to be the A: drive. To change it, simply type in the letter of the desired drive, followed by a colon, and press [Enter]. To illustrate, typing B: at the DOS prompt and then pressing the [Enter] key makes the B: drive the default drive. If you still feel a little shaky about default, don't worry, you'll be seeing a lot more of it. You'll need to, since the term *default* includes more than just drive references. For almost any DOS command that requires a parameter of any kind, there is some kind of default condition.

Filenames

For now, let's put the concept of default aside and begin to learn about the DOS commands. Type DIR and press [Enter]. It should be pretty obvious by now that the [Enter] key plays a pretty large role in using the PC. Therefore, we're going to stop explicitly directing you to press it. On those occasions when pressing [Enter] is not necessary, it usually doesn't matter whether you push it or not because action occurs instantaneously, before you get a chance to.

When you typed in DIR, a great deal of text appeared on the screen. That was a list of all the information stored on your DOS diskette. In computer lingo, that's a DIRectory. The information on a diskette is stored in groups called FILES and every file has a filename. Those filenames are what appear when you ask DOS to display a **directory.** Also displayed were length of file (in bytes), and the date and time of creation. Notice that when the list of files appeared, there were too many names to fit on the screen at one time, so the ones at the top were pushed, or *scrolled,* off. You can prevent that by pressing the [Ctrl] and [S] keys at the same time, temporarily freezing the display. Pressing Ctrl-S again causes the scrolling to resume. Just what are the files on your DOS diskette? Most of them are part of the collection of utility programs that comprise DOS itself. They can be other things like BASIC programs or just data intended for use with another program. Whatever the contents, all information stored on a diskette of which you can avail yourself has to be stored in a file with a filename. Filenames are generally chosen to indicate the contents of the file and can be just about anything you want them to be, with the following restrictions:

1. A filename may be no longer than eight alphabetic or numeric characters (that's **alphanumeric** in computer lingo), followed by a period and a three-character extension. You can type in more characters, but the computer will only accept that many. Many of the other characters on the keyboard may be used in filenames, but the following ones are invalid:
. " / \ [ ] : | < > + = ; ,
2. The following names are reserved for special purposes and may not be used: CON, AUX, COM1, COM2, LPT1, LPT2, LPT3, PRN, and NUL.
3. Of course, you must never give a file the same name as one already present on a diskette unless it is your intention to write on top of it, or overwrite it, because that is what will happen. The original file will be lost and your new one will replace it.

As mentioned, filenames are usually chosen to indicate the contents or function of the file. Extensions are generally chosen to convey some special information about the file such as version number (PROGRAM.001), what language it's written in (MYFILE.BAS), or if it's data (LETTER.DAT). Many extensions have acquired standard meanings. Some common ones are BAS, COM, EXE, BAT, and BAK. BAS identifies BASIC program files; COM usually identifies DOS command files; EXE is reserved for other machine code files; BAT is for batch files (sequences of DOS commands); and BAK is the extension for back-up files generated by some text-editing programs.

External Commands

The files on DOS with which we will be concerned are FORMAT.COM, DISKCOPY.COM, BASICA.COM, and COMMAND.COM. These four files are all

DOS commands, hence, the COM extension. We only know two commands so far: DISKCOPY and DIR. You'll notice that there's a file for DISKCOPY, but not for DIR. DISKCOPY is an external command; DIR is an internal command. COMMAND.COM is called the command processor because when a DOS command is entered, COMMAND.COM either executes it, as in the case of internal commands (which will be discussed in the next section), or executes another program file, as in the case of external commands. This means that to use any of the external commands, the DOS diskette must be in the default drive or else the files containing the commands won't be there to be found by the command processor. You never have to run COMMAND.COM, however, because it is executed automatically when DOS is booted, and stays in memory. This means that the internal commands are available even when the DOS diskette is not in the drive. Right now, let's take a look at the external commands. Make sure you have a blank diskette handy so you can try them, even if you aren't specifically instructed to do so.

FORMAT

In order for DOS to be able to locate files by name, it must maintain a kind of road map by which it knows the layout of any given diskette. As mentioned previously, before any information at all may be stored on a diskette, the

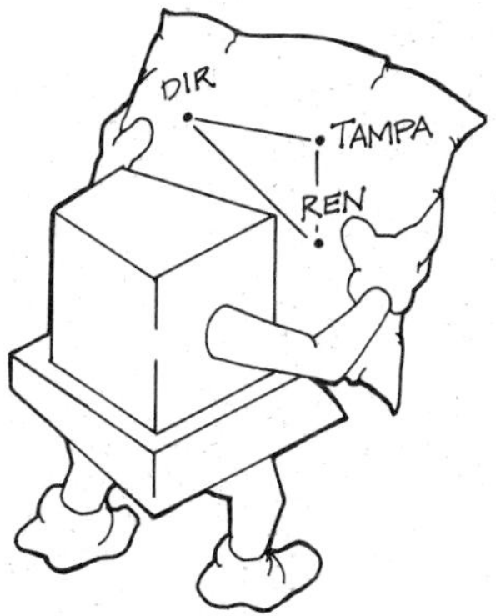

diskette must be formatted. So, why didn't we FORMAT the DOS backup we made with DISKCOPY? DISKCOPY automatically formats diskettes before it copies. Why then do we need FORMAT? The files that make up DOS occupy a considerable amount of space on a diskette, even a dual-sided one. It doesn't make sense, even on a one-drive system, to have all of DOS on every diskette. FORMAT puts a very minimal amount of system information on a diskette, leaving most of the space for data. This kind of diskette, however, cannot be used to boot the computer. Another form of the command,

FORMAT/S, places enough of the system, along with COMMAND.COM, to format a diskette that will boot. It contains none of the external command files, so there is still room for data. If you have DOS 2.00, 2.10, or later and at least one dual-sided drive, you can use the FORMAT/S command to place the contents of both the DOS and the DOS Supplemental Programs diskettes on one dual-sided diskette. You'll also need to use the COPY command, which is discussed in the next section. The command FORMAT B: formats a diskette in the B: drive on a two-drive system, and FORMAT/1 forces only one side to be formatted on dual-sided drives that normally format both sides of a diskette. *Only use FORMAT on new diskettes or old ones containing files you no longer need!!* FORMAT destroys any information already on a diskette. Just for practice, FORMAT a blank diskette so you'll be familiar with the process.

DISKCOPY

You've already seen a good example of how to use DISKCOPY, but just for the record, DISKCOPY is used to copy entire diskettes. Before copying, it automatically formats diskettes that need formatting. DISKCOPY has two normal parameters: the source drive (the one from which you're copying), and the target drive (the one to which you're copying). If you omit parameters, DISKCOPY uses the default, of course. So, on a one-drive system, DISKCOPY is all you need to type since it performs the same action as DISKCOPY A: A:. On a two-drive system, DISKCOPY A: B: copies the contents of drive A: to drive B:. With dual-sided drives, DISKCOPY copies both sides unless you specify DISKCOPY/1.

BASICA

The IBM PC, like almost all other personal computers, has a built-in BASIC interpreter for writing and executing programs written in a computer language called **BASIC.** To give this BASIC interpreter the ability to interact with DOS, it must be augmented by executing BASICA.COM. The BASICA file also adds the advanced graphic capabilities of IBM BASIC as well as some powerful commands for making music. To execute BASICA.COM, just enter BASICA and your PC will load the file, leave DOS, and pass control over to the BASIC interpreter. To get back into DOS from BASIC, type SYSTEM. Since the BASIC programs on your diskettes cannot be run directly from DOS, the normal procedure is to first go to BASIC and then load and run your BASIC programs. We'll discuss another, faster method in Chapter 5, where we also explain the other BASIC commands that communicate with DOS. For now, you'll have to content yourself with going from DOS to BASIC and back again. Do that several times. Got the hang of it?

It is interesting to note that the PCjr does not use BASIC.COM or BASICA.COM, even though they are on the DOS 2.10 diskette. The jr's advanced BASIC is contained on a software cartridge, much like the

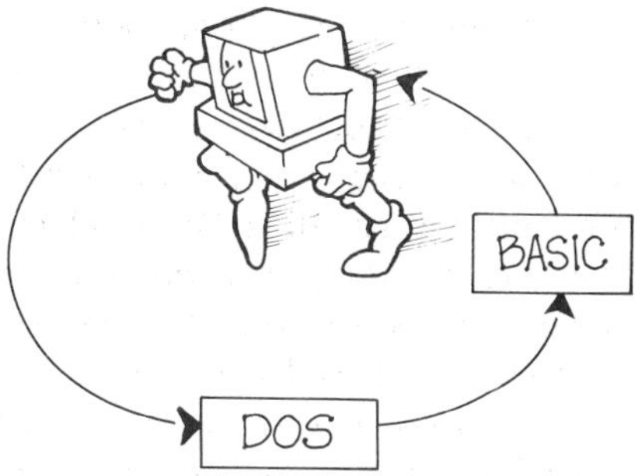

cartridges sold for video-game devices. Programming is contained on a cartridge, much like it is in the computer's ROM. Just as with the ROM contained in the computer, you can't change the programming in a cartridge. The procedure for getting into BASIC on the PCjr is the same, however. Just enter BASIC from the DOS prompt.

Well, these are all the external commands we'll be concerned with for now. There are other external command files on your DOS diskette, but they are not within the scope of this discussion.

Internal Commands

Now it's time for us to take a look at the internal commands with which we are concerned. You won't see them listed on your directory because the programming for them is contained in COMMAND.COM. They are DATE, TIME, DIR, COPY, DEL or ERASE, and RENAME.

DATE and TIME

Every time DOS is booted, the DATE and TIME commands are executed. DOS then prompts you to enter the date in MM/DD/YY or MM-DD-YYYY format and the time in HH:MM:SS format. Of course, you can execute DATE or TIME whenever you wish to reset them. DATE and TIME can be bypassed by simply pressing Enter, but resist the temptation to do this on a regular basis. DOS dates and time stamps a file when it is created or updated and there will be times when knowing which of two similar files is the later edition will be crucial. If you really despise typing in the time and date, there are multifunction cards available for the PC that have battery-run clocks and software that automatically enter the correct date and time when the computer is started.

DIR

You already know that DIR displays a diskette directory, but there are some other ways to use DIR. DIR B: displays the directory of a diskette in drive

B:. DIR also provides ways to keep a long directory from scrolling off the screen. DIR/W causes the files to be displayed horizontally, but it leaves off most of the other information normally shown. DIR/P works just like DIR except that it pauses when the screen is full and waits for you to press a key before it continues. The following entry causes a hypothetical file named TEST.BAS on the B: drive to be displayed:

```
DIR B:TEST.BAS
```

Now it may seem fairly peculiar to you to execute a command that tells us nothing more than what we already knew; here, for instance, it simply reassures us that yes, the file TEST.BAS is on drive B:. But with the addition of the concept of **wildcards,** or **global filename characters,** this form of DIR becomes the most powerful of all. Any character in a filename may be replaced with ? or *. The ? character is used to replace any single character and means that any character may occupy that position. For example, the command

```
DIR VERSION?
```

causes the VERSION1, VERSION2, and VERSION3 files to be displayed. It would not, however, display these files VERSION1.BAS and VERSION2.REV, because the ? is only good for one character. To replace more than one character, use the * wildcard. Used as a wildcard, * means any character may occupy a particular position as well as all following positions. For example, DIR *.* lists all files on a diskette. DIR ST*.BAS would list all the BASIC files whose names begin with ST. DIR PROGRAM.* would list all the files named PROGRAM, no matter what extension they have. The possibilities are almost endless.

COPY

The COPY command is used for copying single files. It can also be used to copy more than one file by using the wildcard characters. The command

```
COPY PROGRAM.BAS B:
```

will copy a file named PROGRAM.BAS on the default drive to the B: drive and will give it the same name. On one-drive systems, you may not issue a copy command like

```
COPY PROGRAM PROGRAM
```

since that tells DOS to copy a file over itself. You can't have two files with exactly the same name on the same diskette. For example,

```
COPY PROGRAM1 PROGRAM2
```

is valid because—although it causes two copies of the same file to exist on the same diskette—it gives them different names, so as far as DOS is concerned, they are different files. As mentioned, wildcards may be used with the COPY command. The command

```
COPY *.BAS B:
```

for example, copies all the BASIC files on the default drive to the B: drive.

DEL or ERASE

DEL and ERASE are different names for the same command. They are used to remove a file or a number of files from a diskette. Well, they don't actually remove the files, they just make DOS forget the filenames. Just the same, files on which you use DEL or ERASE are "dead" and you can't get them back under normal circumstances. There are some commercially available programs that can, under some circumstances, resurrect dead files by causing DOS to remember their names. DEL and ERASE have single filename parameters such as

```
DEL B:PROGRAM.BAS
```

but you can use wildcards to make them delete more than one file at a time. For example, DEL *.BAS deletes all files with the extension .BAS. Be careful with this form of the command.

RENAME

RENAME (the abbreviation, REN, also works) is used to change a file's name. Note: This is different than using COPY to create a second copy of a file with a different name. RENAME creates no additional copies. It actually changes the name of the file. It works like this:

```
RENAME BOY SUE
```

This command changes a file named BOY to a file named SUE. Of course, you can't change a file's name to that of a file already on the diskette. Although it might not seem that wildcards would be appropriate here, you could use something like

```
RENAME THISFILE.* THATFILE.*
```

to change all the files named THISFILE, no matter what extension, to files named THATFILE with the same extensions.

Chapter Summary

In this chapter, we have discussed DOS, the Disk Operating System of the IBM PC. You have studied what DOS is and what its functions are. We have also described the floppy diskettes you must use with your disk drives. We have looked at how diskettes store information, how much information can be stored, what kind of diskettes you need for the PC, how to handle diskettes, and purchasing diskettes. We have seen how to boot the computer to bring it up to operational status, discussed the importance of backing up software, and gone step-by-step through the process of backing up the DOS diskette. We have also clarified the definition of the term *default,* and seen how it functions when command parameters are omitted. We have seen that all DOS commands are either internal or external in nature. You should understand the difference between the two types, how the ways you use them are affected, and be able to tell which commands belong in each

It's de fault of
de computer!

category. You have seen examples of correct DOS command syntax and should be able to use them correctly yourself as well as be able to issue proper filenames and extensions. Finally, we discussed the use of global filename characters, or wildcards, to cause action on more than one file.

Chapter Review

Knowledge Exercises

1. What is DOS?

   Answer: DOS, or the Disk Operating System, is a collection of utility programs designed to integrate one or more disk drives with the rest of your computer system. These programs perform a variety of housekeeping functions related to the storing of information on diskettes.

2. What is the write-enable notch on a floppy diskette? What difference does it make if it is covered or not?

   Answer: The write-enable notch is a square notch near the top on the right-hand side of the floppy diskette. When this notch is not present or is covered, the disk drive cannot place information on the disk.

3. What is the difference between single-sided and dual-sided floppy diskettes?

   Answer: Both single-sided and dual-sided diskettes have flux (the metallic material upon which the read-write head of the disk drive encodes information) on both sides. The difference is that dual-sided diskettes are tested and certified for use on both sides, and are more expensive.

4. What does it mean to format a diskette?

   Answer: When DOS formats a diskette, it organizes the diskette for storage, or superimposes a kind of road map that it uses to locate the files placed on the diskette.

5. Why are diskettes known as volatile media? What precautions should be taken in their handling?

   Answer: Diskettes can easily be erased, and should be handled with care. Keep them away from strong magnetic fields (for example, television sets and airport X-ray machines), heat, dust, and cigarette smoke. Never touch the flux with your fingers. Don't use paper clips or write on them with a hard-point pen; keep them in their sleeves.

6. What does the term *booting the system* mean?

   Answer: To boot means to bring the system up to operational status. The term comes from the expression "pulling yourself up by your own bootstraps," which is essentially what a computer does.

7. What is the difference between a cold boot and a warm boot?

   Answer: A cold boot is performed by turning on the power switch to the machine and switching on the monitor. A warm boot, or system reset, is performed when the computer is already on, by pressing the Ctrl, Alt, and Del keys simultaneously.

8. Why should you always make a back-up copy of your software?

   Answer: You should always make a back up for regular use and store the original in a safe place. Thus, you will never be caught without a copy of the software you have purchased. It can be difficult to get a replacement from the manufacturer.

9. What does the DOS command DIR stand for? What does it do?

   Answer: DIR stands for DIRectory. It lists the names of all the files contained on a particular diskette.

10. What are the restrictions on filenames for PC DOS?

    Answer: A filename may be comprised of up to eight alphabetic or numeric characters, followed by a period and an extension of up to three characters. (Refer to this chapter for a listing of other acceptable characters.)

11. What happens when you give a file the same name as one already present on the disk?

    Answer: The old file is replaced or overwritten by the new file.

12. What are the five common filename extensions discussed in this chapter? What does each indicate?

    Answer: The five extensions are BAS, COM, EXE, BAT, and BAK. BAS identifies BASIC program files; COM identifies DOS command files; EXE is used for other machine code files; BAT indicates batch files consisting of sequences of DOS commands; and BAK indicates a back-up copy of a file, often generated by some text editing programs.

13. What is the difference between internal and external DOS commands?

    Answer: Internal commands are contained in the COMMAND.COM file, which is executed automatically when DOS is booted and stays in memory. Thus, internal commands are available even when the DOS diskette is not in the drive. External commands have files separate from COMMAND.COM, and the DOS diskette must be in the default drive in order for the commands to be executed.

14. What are the differences between the commands FORMAT and FORMAT/S?

    Answer: The FORMAT command puts a very minimal amount of system information on a diskette, leaving most of the space for data. The FORMAT/S command places enough of the system, along with COM-

MAND.COM, to format a diskette that will boot. It doesn't contain any of the external command files, leaving room for data.

15. What happens if you format a diskette that already contains data on it?

    Answer: Any previously existing information on the diskette will be erased.

16. How do you go from DOS into BASIC, and back to DOS?

    Answer: Enter BASICA (or BASIC) and your PC will leave DOS and pass control over to the BASIC interpreter. Type SYSTEM to get back into DOS from BASIC.

17. What is a wildcard? Explain the difference between using the ? and the *.

    Answer: Wildcards are global filename characters. The ? character is used to replace any single character and means that any character may occupy that position. The * character is used to replace more than one character, and means that any character may occupy that position as well as all following positions.

Thought Exercises

1. How much instruction in DOS is needed for students in a third grade class? For a sixth grade class? For a tenth grade class? For the teacher who is going to have to use computers in the classroom?
2. How should the question of illegally copying material be presented to students? Support your position.
3. Compare PC DOS with some other microcomputer Disk Operating Systems. What suggestions would you make for improving the usability of any or all of them?

Activities

1. Make a DISKCOPY of your DOS diskette (or any other easily copied diskette) using a one-drive system.
2. Make a DISKCOPY of your DOS diskette (or any other easily copied diskette) using a two-drive system, if it is available.
3. FORMAT two new diskettes or old ones containing files you no longer need. Use FORMAT on one and FORMAT/S on the other. Can you tell any difference?
4. Use the DISKCOPY command to make an exact duplicate of any diskette that is not copy protected. Try it twice, once using a one-drive system and again using a two-drive system.
5. Use the COPY command to copy a file from one drive to another.

6. Practice going from DOS to BASIC and back again.

7. Practice entering the date and time in the proper format when you boot DOS. Get into the habit of always entering both.

8. Practice using DIR to display the directory for drive A: and for drive B:. What happens when you use DIR/W and DIR/P? Try it.

9. Use wildcards to list all the files with a BAS extension on the DOS diskette. How else can you use wildcards to pull up particular classes of files?

10. Use the COPY command with wildcards to copy all the files with the BAS extension onto a diskette in the B: drive. How else can you use the COPY command in conjunction with wildcards?

11. Use the DEL or ERASE command to remove a file or a number of files from a diskette. Try using wildcards with this command.

12. Use the RENAME (or REN) command to change a filename. Try it in conjunction with wildcards.

Projects

1. Use posterboard to prepare charts showing the DOS commands appropriate for a specific student group.

2. Write an instructional unit on teaching DOS. Describe the grade level and student population, and write detailed lesson plans. In addition, include a rationale for including or not including certain topics discussed in this chapter.

3. If possible, present the instructional plan developed in Project 2 to a group of students. Keep a log detailing student reactions, possible motivating factors, and listing any modifications necessary to the lessons.

Bibliography

Cain, Thomas, and Nancy Woodard Cain. *Hard Disk Management.* New York: Prentice-Hall, 1986. A good resource for setting up directories and using more sophisticated facilities. Many examples are given.

Chertok, Barbara Lee, Dov Rosenfeld, and James H. Stone. *IBM PC and XT Owner's Manual.* Bowie, Md: Robert J. Brady, 1984. A complete tutorial on the computer with many hands-on exercises.

Cortesi, David E. *Your IBM Personal Computer: Use, Applications, and BASIC.* New York: Holt, Rinehart & Winston, 1983. Chapter 7 provides a good introduction to IBM DOS system.

DeVoney, Chris. *PC DOS User's Guide.* Indianapolis: Que Corporation, 1984. An instruction handbook on the popular Disk Operating System.

Goldstein, Larry Joel, and Martin Goldstein. *IBM PC: An Introduction to the Operating System.* Bowie, Md.: Robert J. Brady, 1984. An elementary guide to DOS.

Graham, Lyle J., and Tim Field. *Your IBM PC: A Guide to the IBM PC.* Berkeley, Calif.: Osborne/McGraw-Hill, 1984. The usage of DOS is described with explanation of program development tools.

King, Richard Allen. *The IBM PC DOS Handbook.* Berkeley, Calif.: Sybex, 1983. A complete guide to PC DOS, including its filing system, graphics, and command structure.

Norton, Peter. *Inside the IBM PC.* Bowie, Md.: Robert J. Brady, 1983. A reference book explaining the advanced features of DOS.

Poole, Lon. *Using Your IBM Personal Computer.* Indianapolis: Howard W. Sams, 1983. Part One gives a introductory description of the uses of the operating system.

Sachs, Jonathan. *Your IBM PC Made Easy.* Berkeley, Calif.: Osborne/McGraw-Hill, 1984. Beginner's introduction to the IBM PC, PC/XT, and PC DOS 2.0.

Shillingburg, Patricia M. *IBM PC: A Beginner's Guide.* Denver, Colo.: Love Publishing, 1984. A simple guide to MS/PC DOS operating system.

PART

2

SINE QUA NON

Without programming, computers are just worthless piles of silicon and metal. Although we are not suggesting that you should become a programmer, you do need to understand something about the art. Therefore, this section is all about programming. First we are going to examine the concept of programming from the approach of problem solving. That way, you don't even need a computer. Then it will be hands-on time as you become familiar with BASIC, the most widely used microcomputer language. After that, we'll step back and take a look at the overall process of constructing a meaningful instructional program. Finally, we'll take a less comprehensive look at another programming language that has become important in education: Logo. You'll learn, however, that Logo represents much more than just a language for programming computers.

CHAPTER

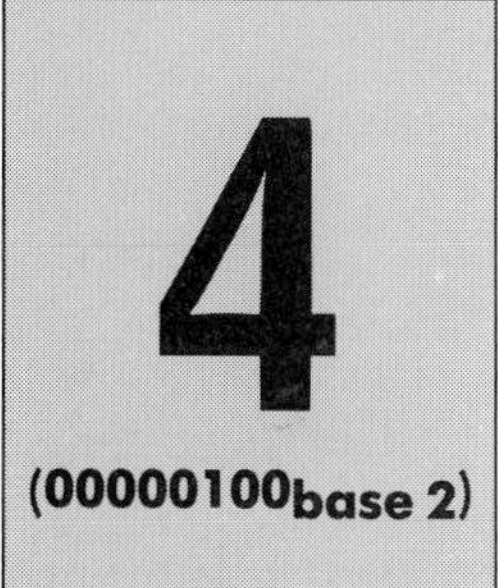

WHAT IS IT ALL ABOUT?

Programming without Computers

Getting Started

To perform a given task, you must know what steps to take or you must determine what the steps are. If you don't know how to handle the task, then you need resources to help you. Even with help, you may have to analyze the task. If you analyze carefully, you may come up with a method for completing the task. If you're smart, you'll record or somehow memorize the method for future use.

To make a computer do what you want, you must tell it precisely what you want done. This means communicating in a language it can interpret. In doing so you must be very specific. The computer task must be analyzed in advance and conveyed in literal terms. You are the mastermind. You perform the analysis and draw up the plan, then you tell the computer to do all the work required to implement the plan.

This chapter, then, is devoted to a very fundamental process: analyzing problems so we can tell computers how to solve them. We won't use computers, though, since we don't want the medium to obscure the message. There will be plenty of time for microcomputer hands-on in the next two chapters.

Objectives for Teachers

To successfully complete this chapter, you should be able to

1. Distinguish between hardware and software.
2. Give the definition of a computer program.
3. Distinguish between machine code and high-level programming.
4. Name two high-level programming languages.
5. Define the term *algorithm,* describing its important features.
6. Design a simple algorithm.

7. Design a sketch, plan, or flowchart for a simple algorithm.
8. Describe algorithms that all programming languages should support.

What Is a Computer Program?

In Chapter 1, we indicated that a microcomputer is a device manufactured to recognize and carry out a limited set of instructions. A program is a logically organized sequence of these instructions, designed to perform a specific task. As a computer user, when you have a task that you want the computer to accomplish, you can either write a program designed to accomplish the task or you can obtain a program written by someone else. Computer programs are called **software.** Computer elements are called **hardware.** These are frequently used terms, so they bear repeating. The term *software* refers to computer programs; that is, sequences of instructions for directing computers to perform specific tasks. The term *hardware* refers to all the physical components of computers that enable general operation. Sometimes computer programs are built into or *hardwired* into a computer. Even so, the program is still referred to as software. We also discussed in Chapter 1 how the instructions that make up a program have to be given to the computer in the form of lots of 0s and 1s. A program in this form is said to be written in *machine code.* Machine code is the only thing that a computer is capable of understanding without translation.

Writing programs in machine code is difficult to do. People are much better at expressing themselves with words than with digits. Working with all the digits required in machine-code programming can be very tedious.

In order to cope with this difficulty, *programming languages* have been developed. Think about it. What would be the ideal programming language? How about a conventional language like English? Wouldn't computers be very easy to program if one could just describe the task to be accomplished in English?

Using English would certainly solve the problem we have identified, but it would create a host of new ones. One major problem with English is that it is not accurate enough. Though people have superior reasoning powers, they frequently fail to communicate accurately with English. That's not good enough for work on computers. Computers must have exact directions. So, the development of programming languages has involved compromise; highly accurate, English-like languages have been developed that are used to instruct computers with exactness. BASIC and Logo are such languages. (BASIC stands for Beginner's All-purpose Symbolic Instructor Code.)

It is important to remember that, while you may be programming a computer in BASIC, the computer doesn't really understand what you are writing. Somewhere between your giving of instructions and the computer's execution of those instructions, the BASIC language you are using has to be translated to the machine code that the computer can understand. Because languages like BASIC and Logo have to be translated to machine code before they can be executed, they are often called *high-level languages;* meaning that they are further removed from the actual operation of the computer than *low-level languages* like machine code. There are many high-level languages other than BASIC and Logo; in fact, there are hundreds. We choose to present BASIC and Logo because they are important to education. They are comparatively easy to learn and are versatile, having broad appeal to people with varied interests. BASIC is by far the most widely used programming language. Next to BASIC, Logo has had the greatest impact on education. This is because Logo is designed specifically for instruction.

Some Common Features of Programming Languages and Computer Programs

Different programming languages such as Logo and BASIC vary greatly. A programming language like BASIC will vary from microcomputer to microcomputer. Nevertheless, there are fundamental elements every programming language must have. Every programming language has **statements.** These statements involve special words that the computer translates into machine code. Every programming language has rules of **syntax** that specify how statements in a program are to be organized. No matter what language is used, a program will consist of a *finite number of precise statements.* There can be no guesswork. A computer program should achieve goals.

An example will illustrate these ideas. Suppose a person, say Madam X, secretly chooses a geometric figure and gives you clues as to its identity. You are to draw the figure illuminated by the clues. The clues can't name any figures except line segment and point. You must do what each clue tells you to do, but you must avoid drawing the secret figure as long as possible. In other words, you don't read between the lines or guess. You accept no ambiguity. You do only as directed.

Madam X might say, "Draw three segments." You may guess what Madam X wants but you may not. In any event, you do exactly as asked and draw the following:

Madam X is disappointed, so she tries again. Madam X says, "Draw three segments that are the same size." You draw the following:

Again, Madam X is disappointed and says, "Draw three line segments that are the same size and that are connected." You draw the following:

By now, Madam X is really frustrated, but it's her own fault. She reconsiders and says, "Draw three line segments of equal length, that are connected, and that enclose a region." Now she feels secure. You draw the following:

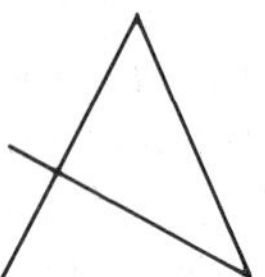

At last, Madam X sees the errors of her ways. Finally, she says, "Draw three line segments that have equal length, are connected at their endpoints, and enclose a region." Phewww! Now you're disappointed; you can't hold off any longer. You draw the following:

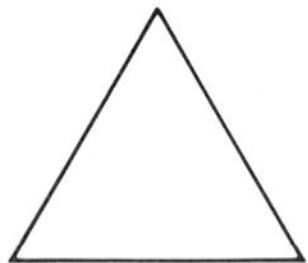

Madam X is relieved. Her goal was to make you draw a triangle having sides of equal length, but you did only what you were told to do. So, she had to give you a finite set of precise instructions that required you to draw the triangle. This example should lead you to an intuitive definition for the term *computer program.* Now let's make it more formal.

> *Computer Program.* A computer program is a finite set of precise, logically organized statements. The program will achieve goals when executed.

This definition leads to a discussion of **algorithm.** Every program involves at least one algorithm, and some programs involve many. The definition for algorithm is about the same as the definition for computer program.

> *Algorithm.* An algorithm is a finite set of steps that, when executed, will consistently achieve specific goals.

There is, however, a difference between an algorithm and a computer program. Algorithms are processes, used with or without computers, that produce consistent results. When adding two numbers, you use an addition algorithm even though you may not be conscious of it. If you and a friend add the same numbers using the same algorithm, you expect to get the same results. It doesn't matter if you compute at different places, for different reasons, and at different times. An algorithm represents a method or strategy, rather than just an end result. You can perform the process repeatedly without rethinking it. Thus, you may be able to use the same algorithm with different sets of data to obtain different results. Once an algorithm is developed, it can be passed on to other people.

An example will serve to illustrate how to design an algorithm. Suppose you want to find all the numbers between 10 and 100 whose digits total 5. One such number is 23, since $2 + 3 = 5$. You start guessing, "Hmmm, 41 is one of them." But guessing is not systematic. How will you know when you've found them all? So, you start at 10 and begin working your way toward 100, "14, 23, ..." That's systematic. You're sure you'll find all numbers meeting the criteria, but it's too time-consuming. There's got to be a better way. Ah yes! You must build an algorithm by selecting the smallest

Algorithms were here
long before I was.

number that can be a digit in a number (that's 0) and stop after using the largest number (that's 5). This process is shown in the following table:

Algorithm Design	Algorithm Results
1. Start on the left with 0.	
2. While left addend < 6, make sums for 5 using two addends; increase left addend by 1.	0 + 5 = 5 1 + 4 = 5 2 + 3 = 5 3 + 2 = 5 4 + 1 = 5 5 + 0 = 5
3. Stop making sums.	
4. Use addends in sums to make numbers with two digits. Use left addend for 10s. Use right addend for 1s.	14 23 32 41 50
5. If number > 10 then list it.	
6. Stop when you get to last number.	

Now you have an algorithm. You don't have to think about it anymore. Whenever you want the numbers, you just follow the algorithm. That's not all: you can share the algorithm with others. You also have the basis for developing a more general algorithm. Even so, implementing the algorithm could become tedious and time-consuming. Suppose you had to find all the numbers between 10 and 10,000 whose digits totaled 18. It would be nice to have an algorithm to generate the correct numbers, but it would be better yet to have a computer program to implement the algorithm.

In summary, all programming languages consist of special words and rules of syntax. Computer programs consist of algorithms that are expressed using the special words and rules. Problems that can be solved with algorithms can be solved with computers and problems involving repetition or lengthy calculations are particularly suited for computers.

Special Types of Algorithms

With any programming language, you can design any number of algorithms, but there are certain ones that any language is expected to support. These are worth mentioning because they enable computers to solve substantial problems common in everyday life.

Count. Many times it is necessary to get a count related to some event. Suppose a city official must decide whether or not to install a traffic light at a particular intersection. The official may want to know the number of times any vehicle passes through the intersection. One way to get a total would be to station a human being at the intersection to count. This isn't realistic, since a human gets tired, loses concentration, and may not be able to keep up with traffic flow. Another way would be to design a computer program with a counting algorithm. The program could accept signals generated by a cable in the intersection that senses a crossing vehicle. All programming languages must have statements that can be used to design efficient *counting algorithms.*

Repeat. Many mundane, time-consuming jobs require numerous repetitions of the same task. Take, for example, balancing a checkbook. The task is routine and can be boiled down to a specific set of steps that are performed often. A programming language must support algorithms that endlessly repeat the same boring task, such as balancing your checkbook. Algorithms that repeat or iterate are called *loops.*

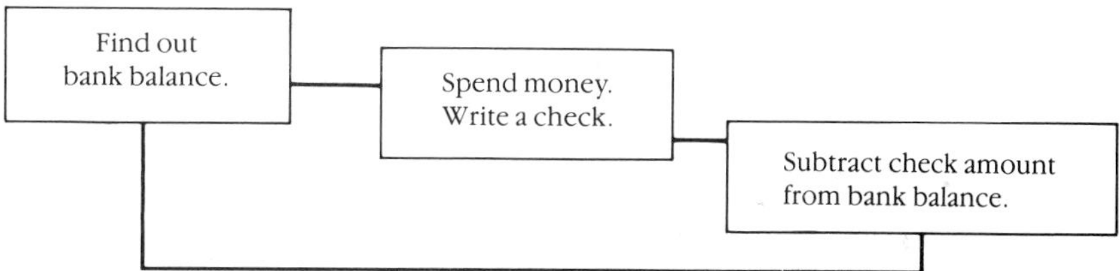

Compute. Programming languages must have statements supporting the design of algorithms that perform complex computations. Most languages can handle the four arithmetic operations (addition, subtraction, multiplication, and division), roots and powers, a variety of functions, and special logical operations from a branch of mathematics called *Boolean algebra.*

Sort. Programming languages must have statements supporting the design of algorithms that sort data; that is, that arrange data in alphabetic or numeric order.

Compare. Programming languages must have statements that support the design of algorithms that compare data. For example, suppose you want to find all students at Chamberlain High who had been absent more than five days during a given year. A program with an algorithm for comparing could be written that would quickly locate and list students with more than five absences.

Decide. Programming languages must have statements that support the design of algorithms that not only make comparisons, but also make decisions based on the outcomes of those comparisons. For example, a program could be written to compare dates for locating customers whose payments are overdue. After checking an account, the program would decide whether or not a customer was delinquent, either writing a payment reminder to the delinquent customer or continuing to examine data for another customer. To execute different sets of steps based on a decision, the program must be able to *branch*.

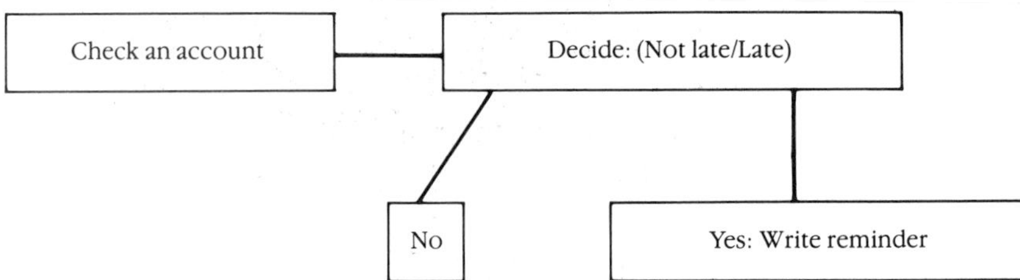

Format and report. Once a program has done a lot of computing, comparing, and deciding, then it must report the results of this activity some way. This means that the language must have statements that support the design of algorithms that format and report data.

Save and retrieve. Ultimately, programs are useful only if they can be saved and retrieved and only if the data they create or manipulate can be saved and retrieved. A useful programming language must have statements that support the design of algorithms that save and retrieve.

Interact. Microcomputer languages should make provisions for user-computer interaction. The computer language must support a variety of statements that allows users to directly pass data into the computer's memory.

This just about covers the types of tasks a programming language should be able to do. The ideas are simple and few, but the results can be astounding. Enabling the computer to count, compare, repeat, compute, sort, compare, decide, format, report, save, retrieve, and interact will produce amazing results.

Writing a Microcomputer Program

To write a program with efficient algorithms, you must devise a plan. Usually, spending time to devise a good plan pays off in a number of ways. Writing the program is usually easier and the resulting program is often more efficient and easier for others to understand. What are the ingredients of a good plan? You can't nail down all the specifics, but you can establish a general framework.

Planning a Program

There are at least seven steps to devising a good plan. These include the following:

1. Defining the task.
2. Breaking the task into small steps.
3. Ordering the steps, designing algorithms.
4. Translating to program statements.
5. Evaluating the program.

6. Modifying the program.
7. Documenting the program.

The rest of this chapter will be devoted to a discussion of the first three steps. The other steps are covered in later chapters.

Step one: Define the major task to be accomplished. When writing a program, it is very important to clearly describe the desired goals. Take the problem in the last section about a city official who wants to decide whether or not to install a traffic light. The official needs a program that will count vehicles as they move through the intersection. Will certain times of the day be more important than other times? Will certain days be more important than other days? These questions need to be addressed. Otherwise, the resulting program may not yield information needed for sound decision making.

Step two: Break the task into small discrete steps. This step is very important, since most of the time you can't tackle an entire problem all at once. Usually, a good program is made up of a lot of small programs that each perform a small task. The small programs work together logically to accomplish the major task. So, each programming project should be broken down into smaller projects. Then each of the smaller projects must be analyzed.

Step three: Put the steps in logical order, design algorithms. Here, you are required to arrange steps in logical order so that the program will be accurate and efficient. Check the steps to make sure they are not ambiguous. Each time the steps are performed on the same set of data, the results must be the same.

The three steps just outlined are reasonable for analyzing any kind of problem, regardless of whether or not you are going to write a computer program. This kind of reasoning is not new; it has been around a long time. Nevertheless, with computers and the right kind of logical thinking, we can solve highly complex problems that would otherwise require much human time. Let's look at some routine problems and use these steps to analyze them.

Define the task. We have a jigsaw puzzle that has 1,000 pieces. The puzzle container shows a scene almost entirely occupied by a multicolored hot-air balloon. The colors are red, blue, and yellow. Our task is to put the puzzle together.

In this case, the problem statement is easy to develop since almost everyone has, at some time, put together a jigsaw puzzle. So the statement would go something like this: Fit all the pieces of the puzzle together so that the resulting picture is a replica of the one shown on the puzzle container.

Break the problem into parts, order the parts. We can tackle this problem as follows:

1. Separate the border pieces from the inside pieces.

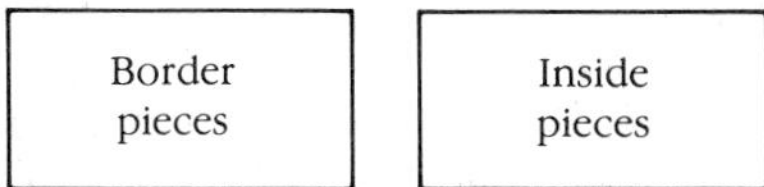

2. Separate the pieces according to color.

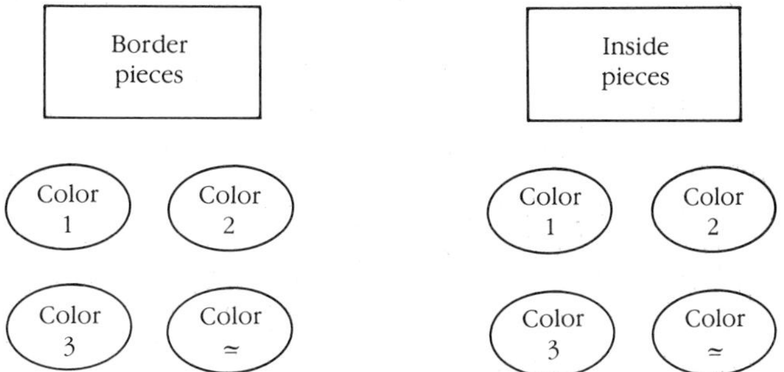

3. Separate pieces according to shape; that is, according to the type of connection that is made.

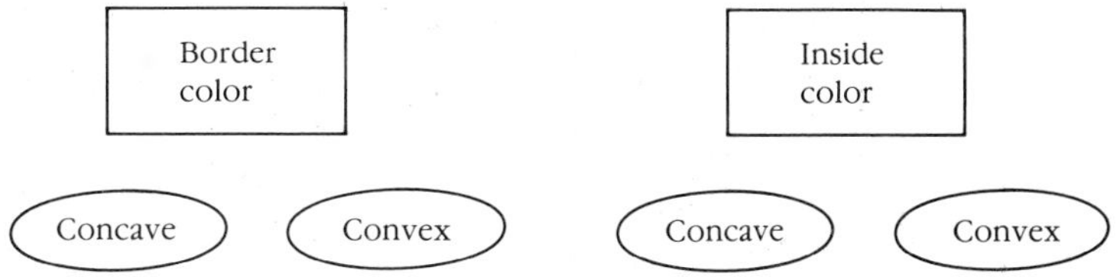

4. Use trial and error to test pieces in each pile. When pieces fit, put them together, otherwise try other pieces.
5. Pick out the corner pieces.

6. Put the border together.

7. Put the interior together.

8. When you discover that a piece has been placed in the wrong pile, put it in an I-don't-know-where-it-goes pile.
9. Continue trying to fit the pieces in the piles together until you are out of pieces.
10. Fill up holes with pieces from the I-don't-know-where-it-goes pile. Continue until you run out of pieces.

It would be nice if the steps could be executed sequentially to reach the desired goal of completing the puzzle. Unfortunately, this and most problems are too complex for so simple a solution. Some steps will have to be repeated a number of times. For example, you could pick out all the border pieces and separate them first according to color, then shape. Then you could use trial and error to fit together pieces in each pile until you produce chunks, and finally fit those chunks together in order to produce the border. You would then have to go through the same set of steps with the pieces on the inside. What about the trial-and-error step that must be performed with each little pile? This step could be phrased as follows:

> Try a couple of pieces. If they fit, connect them and go on to two more pieces. If they don't fit, discard one of the pieces and try another piece. Repeat the process until all the possibilities have been exhausted.

Obviously, you will be performing this procedure a number of times.

We realize that you can put a jigsaw puzzle together without all this folderol. In fact, it is probably easier to put one together than to tell how it's done. But suppose the puzzle had 20-million pieces? Wouldn't it be nice if you, the human, could separate the task into a finite number of logically ordered steps and leave the work to the computer, especially the trial-and-

error steps? Otherwise, you might spend a lifetime buried neck deep in puzzle pieces. Isn't this a powerful concept? We humans can mastermind human-like tasks for machines to implement. The machine has the advantage of working on electricity, and electrical current travels at the speed of light. So the machine, running the right program, can complete highly technical tasks involving large amounts of data in a small amount of time.

Drawing Pictures

Not enough good things can be said about graphs, charts, diagrams, and pictures. These tools allow us to capture intricate concepts and hold them still for examination. The eye is allowed to perceive and transfer relationships to the brain that might otherwise escape our awareness. Given that, it's time to introduce **flowcharts.** The term *flowchart* is the fancy name that is given to a diagram that illustrates the steps in a computer program or in an algorithm. Using flowcharts is more useful to some people than to others. Its purpose is to help you conceptualize the steps in a process. There are standard rules for drawing flowcharts and the degree to which you stick by these standards depends a lot on your purposes. If you are not going to share your flowchart with anyone and you are not teaching anyone to use flowcharts, then you are on your own: anything goes. The following illustration shows the most widely accepted symbols that are used to draw flowcharts for programming in BASIC.

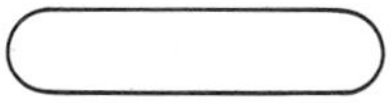

START/END — Indicates the START or END of a program.

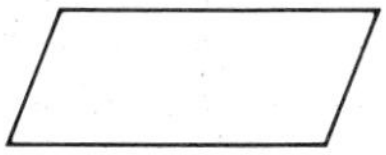

INPUT/OUTPUT — Information is entered into the computer's memory and outputted from the computer's memory.

DECISION — The computer is to decide whether a statement is true or false.

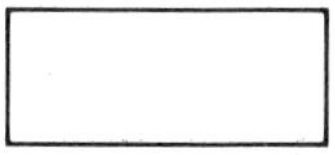

ASSIGNMENT/OPERATION — The program assigns a value to a variable. The variable is found on the left and the value on the right. This symbol is also used to indicate that a process is being implemented.

CONNECTOR — Indicates the connection between two parts of the program.

Now, let's use these symbols to draw some flowcharts. The height a person can jump is dependent on the pull of gravity on that person. This is true on earth or on any planetary body in the solar system. On earth, the pull is said to be one gravity (1 g.). On the moon, the pull is 1/6 g. The following flowchart illustrates an algorithm that will convert the height one jumps on earth to the height one can jump on the moon.

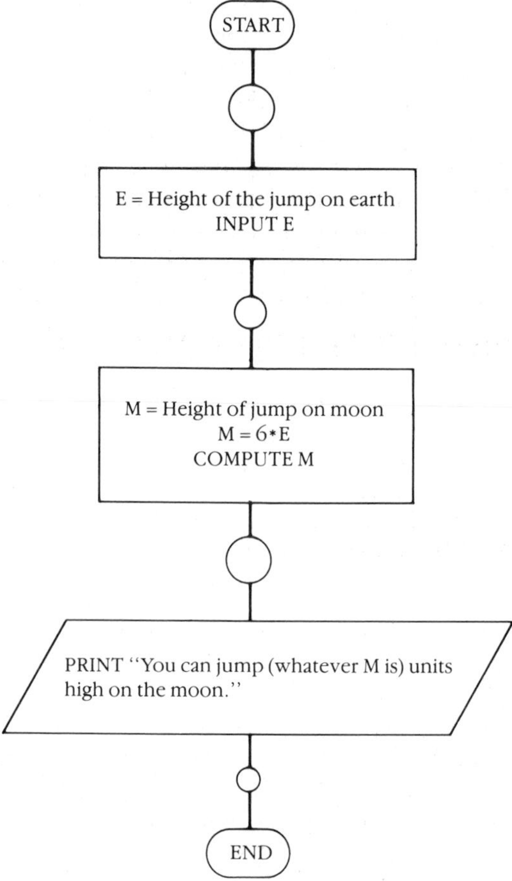

Here is a tougher problem. There are three boxes. Each box is labeled incorrectly. The labels are *Cupcakes Only, Doughnuts Only,* and *Both Doughnuts and Cupcakes.* We know that one box contains cupcakes, one contains doughnuts, and the other contains both. We can take a sweet from only one box, after which we must identify and relabel the contents of each box correctly.

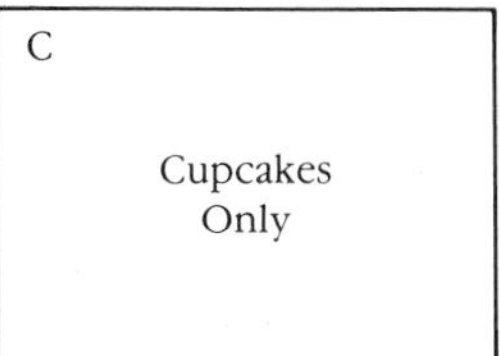

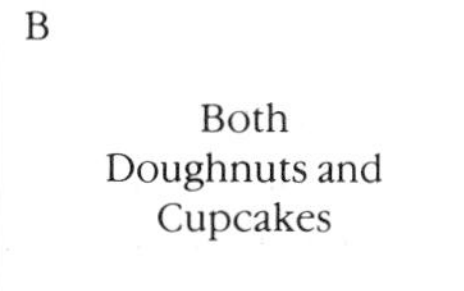

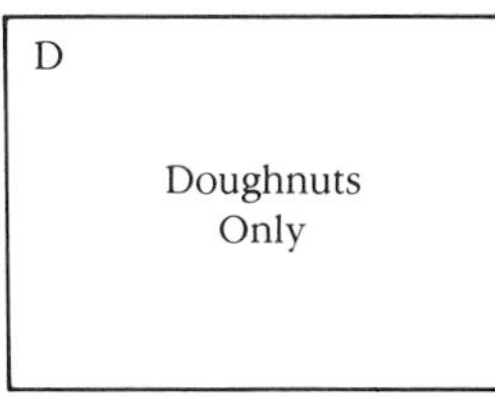

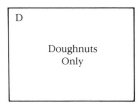

Solution. Let C represent the *Cupcakes Only* label, D the *Doughnuts Only* label, and B the *Both Doughnuts and Cupcakes* label. Suppose we reach in the C box and pull out a doughnut. The evidence indicates that the box contains doughnuts only or doughnuts and cupcakes, but we can't tell which. A similar situation may occur if we reach in the D box and pull out a cupcake. If we reach in the B box and pull out a doughnut, we know that's it: doughnuts! We also know that cupcakes can't be in the C box. Why? Evidently then, cupcakes are in the D box and both cupcakes and doughnuts are in the C box. Now we relabel boxes. At this point we can prepare a flowchart or plan for consistently solving this dilemma should we encounter it again. We certainly don't want to go through the reasoning again. (See Thought Exercise 1 in the Chapter Review section.)

Implications for the Classroom

Reasoning did not begin with the advent of microcomputers. That happened a long time ago. Since the beginning of time, people have been rearranging the elements of their environments to produce tools that could perform work efficiently and that would do tasks humans disliked, were bored with, or couldn't do; the wheel, the fulcrum and lever, and the printing press were all results of these efforts. The microcomputer is just another dramatic example of human ingenuity. So, in the classroom, we should not focus primarily on who invented what in what year, upon what name is given to this or that piece of equipment, or upon producing perfect flowcharts. We should focus on the phenomenon that has always led to the development of technology: the need to solve problems and the process for satisfying this need. So far this chapter has introduced a plan for solving problems, algorithms, flowcharts, and elements of computer programs. With this backdrop, the chapter now introduces activities representing appropriate learning experiences for elementary and secondary education that should be implemented apart from computers. Precollege teaching experience and observations in precollege classrooms have convinced us, the authors, that the essence of problem solving and how computers can help is often lost in the milieu of the little-bitty steps that make the computer go.

Activities for the Classroom

We set forth a number of activities in this section. Read each activity carefully, making sure that you could implement each one. Whether you are preparing to teach, are a veteran teacher, or are developing personal skill, the activities can be instructive.

Activities such as our first one—Activity 4.1—help students develop skills for giving precise directions and for accurately describing procedures. If the activity is very simple, it can be delivered at grade levels lower than the third. This kind of activity should be repeated often, regardless of the level.

ACTIVITY 4.1

Make Me Draw It!

Learning Objective. Giving precise directions.

Materials. Cards with simple line drawings. Some examples follow:

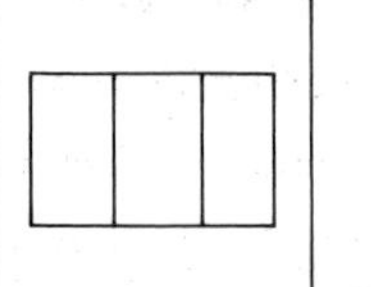
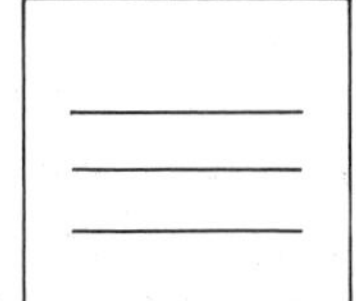
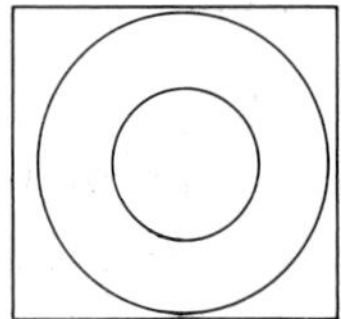
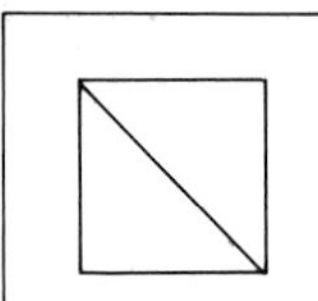

Directions. Have students play this game in groups of four. Shuffle the pictures and place them face down in a pile. A team of two students should pick a picture from the pile. Their task is to give small sets of directions so that the other two students are forced to draw a picture like the one on the card. The students giving the directions cannot use names of figures such as triangle, square, and so on. They can, however use terms such as line, point, and inside. The students who are drawing are *playing computer.* They will do only as they are told, no more, no less.

LEVEL: Third grade and up, depending on the complexity of the pictures.

Giving directions and following directions are two separate tasks. No doubt, learning to do either one aids in learning to do the other. Nevertheless, students should have experiences in pretending to be a microcomputer and in carrying out sets of directions. If properly prepared, this type of activity could be presented at almost any level. As written, Activity 4.2 is suitable for students in fourth grade and higher.

ACTIVITY 4.2

Act It Out

Learning Objective. Interpreting written objectives.

Materials. Cards with directions for completing tasks. An example card follows:

1
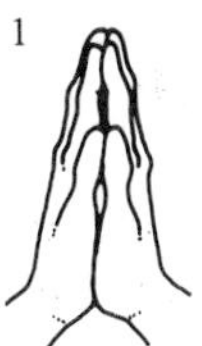
2
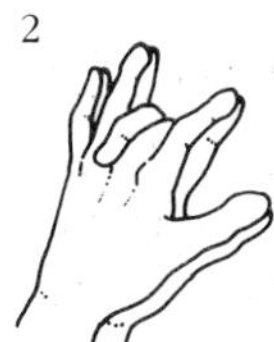
3
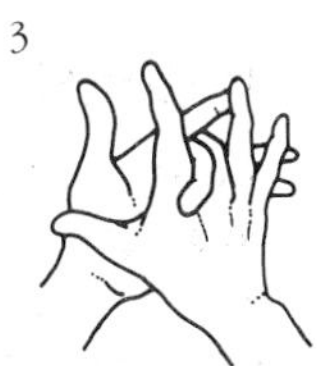
4
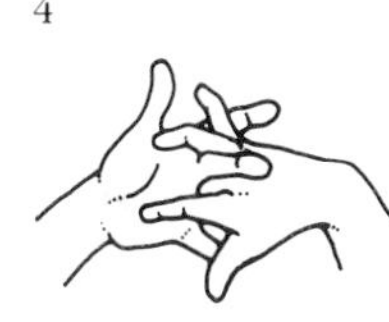

DIRECTIONS: Students enjoy doing this activity in a large group. Have individual students pick a card at random and play computer by attempting to act out the directions that are on the card. Put directions on the chalkboard or use the overhead projector. Let the entire class try to perform the task.

LEVEL: Fourth grade or higher.

You guessed it. In the next activity, students learn to write precise directions.

ACTIVITY 4.3

Preparing Algorithms

Learning Objective. Writing precise directions.

Materials. Cards indicating small tasks. Cards might include tasks such as looking up a phone number or crossing a busy street.

Directions. Let students choose cards and try to write algorithms for their tasks. Have students exchange cards and critique each other's algorithms.

Level: Third grade and up, depending on the complexity of the tasks.

This next activity is very important. (Not that the others aren't!) When implementing this activity, it is important that the teacher help students explain why given tasks require given strategies. It is not enough for the students to simply match tasks and strategies.

ACTIVITY 4.4

Compare, Repeat, and Decide

Learning Objective. Generating tasks that require certain strategies.

Directions. Have students work in pairs. Have small competitions where students identify tasks that require repetition for completion, comparisons of data for completion, and decision making for completion. Have them make lists such as the following:

Tasks that repeat steps

1. Knitting a sweater.
2. Walking up a set of steps.
3. Shuffling cards.
4. Chewing gum.

LEVEL. Third grade and up.

In Activity 4.5 and Activity 4.6, students use manipulatives to find strategies for solving problems. This technique is very useful no matter how old or sophisticated you become. The object is to

1. Examine a complicated problem under simple circumstances.
2. Get a hunch or pattern.
3. Plan a strategy.
4. Tackle the more complicated problem.

In these activities we expect students to achieve the first three steps of this objective.

ACTIVITY 4.5

Swapping Plans or Flowcharts

Learning Objective. Developing plans or flowcharts for algorithms.

Materials. Prepare square grids like the following:

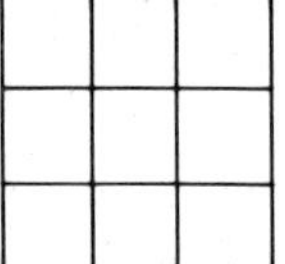

Directions. Have students use these aids to find an algorithm for the following problem:

> You have an $N \times N$ square grid. You are to place an X in every row. However, no two Xs can be in the same row, column, or diagonal.

The following shows how a 3 × 3 board will look:

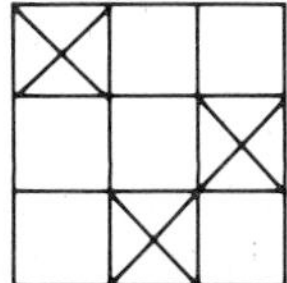

After students discover a pattern, have them write an algorithm and draw a sketch or flowchart. Let students exchange, compare, and critique each other's products.

Level. Third grade and up, depending on the size of the grid.

ACTIVITY 4.6

Let's Have Order

Learning Objective. Designing algorithms, outlining instructions, drawing sketches or flowcharts.

Materials. Resource Sheet 4 located after the Chapter Review. (Cut that page out to complete this activity.)

CARDS	HOLD
A	1
B	2
C	
D	3
E	4
F	5

Directions. Resource Sheet 4 has six *letter cards* labeled with the letters *A–F.* The right half of the sheet is a slot board with six slots. One of the slots is called a *holding slot.* The others, numbered 1–5, are *card slots.*

Cut out the cards and the slot board. Then try to do the following:

> Shuffle the cards and randomly place them face up on the board in the card slots. Then put the cards in ascending or descending order. There is a trick, though. You can never move more than one card at a time. That is, you must put a card down on the board before you pick up another card. You can, however, put a card temporarily into the holding slot. Find a strategy or a plan for solving this problem. Draw a sketch or a flowchart if you can.

Level. Fourth grade and up.

Chapter Summary

In this chapter, you have learned to distinguish between software and hardware. We hope that you have come to appreciate the importance of good software and the planning required for its development. You should also realize that without software, microcomputers would sit and do nothing. In this chapter, we explained that software programs are developed with programming languages or in machine code. Programs written in high-level languages, such as Logo and BASIC, are written with precise statements that employ English-like terms. Writing programs requires abilities to interpret problems and their solutions in terms of algorithms that yield predictable and consistent results.

Talking about these concepts and learning to use them are two different things. Learning to use these concepts requires understanding and special practice. The understanding is this: Computers can't do anything that humans can't do; and what computers do well, humans have been doing for some time. The difference is that humans problem solve and computers implement solutions at high speed. Thus, it is important that humans learn to design procedures for solving problems. The best way to learn this is to practice doing it!

Chapter Review

Knowledge Exercises

1. Give the definition for the term *computer program.*

   Answer: A computer program is a finite set of precise, logically organized statements. The program will achieve goals when executed.

2. What is the difference between hardware and software?

   Answer: Hardware refers to all the physical components of computers that enable general operation. Computer programs are referred to as software.

3. Why is it easier to program in a programming language such as BASIC than it is to program in machine code?

   Answer: High-level languages use English-like statements for programming, whereas machine code employs thousands of the digits 0 and 1, making program statements unintelligible to humans.

4. Name the two high-level programming languages referred to in this chapter. Find the name of two other high-level programming languages.

   Answer: BASIC and Logo. Answers will vary. (COBOL, FORTRAN, Pascal, PL/I, and so forth.)

5. List and describe some features all programming languages should support.

   Answer: All programming languages should support the following features:

   Statements written in words or terms the computer can interpret.
   Rules of syntax for organizing statements.
   Programs can be written in a finite number of steps.
   Programs can be written that will achieve goals.

6. Define the term *algorithm*.

   Answer: An algorithm is a finite set of steps that, when executed, will consistently achieve specific goals.

7. What is the difference between a computer program and an algorithm?

   Answer: Algorithms are processes, used with or without computers, that produce consistent results.

8. List and describe seven special algorithms that every programming language should support.

   Answer: The algorithms you've listed should be seven of the following: count, repeat, compute, sort, compare, decide, format, report, save, retrieve, and interact. For descriptions of these algorithms, see the section entitled "Special Types of Algorithms."

Thought Exercises

1. Reread the problem concerning labeling boxes of cupcakes and doughnuts. Design a plan that will enable a person to consistently select correct labels for the goodie boxes. Describe your plan using statements or by using a sketch or flowchart.

2. Complete Activity 4.2. Then find a similar physical feat that can be described in a sequence of steps. Write a plan—set of steps—for accomplishing this feat. Have at least one other individual evaluate your plan. Refine your plan on the basis of the evaluation.

3. Develop 10 cards that are suitable for use with Activity 4.3.

4. Many tasks require the repetition of certain steps in order to be completed.

Make a list of five tasks that have this characteristic. For each task, indicate the steps that require repetition.

5. Develop an algorithm for finding all numbers up to 1,000 in which the sum of the digits is either 9 or a multiple or 9.

Activities

1. Complete each of the activities provided in this chapter. Prepare a log for each activity describing difficulties you experience and listing responses. Consider ways in which you might improve the activities.
2. Prepare two activities similar to the activities provided in this chapter. For each, list the learning objective, materials needed, directions, and level. You may use other resource materials to find ideas for your activities.
3. Make up a programming language that includes the statements described in the following table:

Statement	Abbreviation	Example
START	S	S means that you assume a position facing North.
MOVE FORWARD	MF	MF5 means move forward five units.
MOVE BACKWARD	MB	MB5 means move backward five units.
TURN LEFT	L	2L means turn left two times.

Write programs that allow one to make precise movements on a flat surface. Have other individuals verify your programs.

Projects

1. Locate students of the appropriate age or level and instruct them in two of the activities provided in this chapter. Keep a log of student responses. Compare your results with your classmates.
2. Write a student activity using the programming language developed in Activity 3 of the Chapter Review.

Resource Sheet 4

This Resource Sheet is for use with Activity 4.6

CARDS	HOLD
A	1
B	2
C	3
D	4
E	5
F	

Bibliography

Bradbeer, Robin, and Peter DeBono. *The Beginner's Guide to Computers.* Reading, Mass: Addison-Wesley, 1982. A firm beginning discussion of programming concepts is given.

Burns, Marilyn. "Getting Kids Ready for Computer Thinking—Thoughts for Teachers, Grades 4–8." *The Computing Teacher* (September 1980). Games and activities to prepare children for programming computers.

Dunlap, Michael. "Strategies in Searching and Sorting." *The Computing Teacher* (October, November, December 1984): 23–24, 31–35, 42–45. A comprehensive series on the development of algorithms.

Ershov, A. P. "Programming: The Second Literacy." *Monitor* (November 1981): 7–11. Programming is discussed as a tool to greatly enhance the intellectual power of humanity.

Horn, Carin E., and James L. Poirot. *Computer Literacy.* Austin, Tex: Sterling Swift, 1981. Chapter 11 and 12 offer good examples of programming principles and development of algorithms.

McCarley, Barbara. "A Disk of My Own." *Classroom Computer Learning* (November–December 1984): 60–61. Strategies for motivating beginning programming students are reviewed.

Marchionini, Gary. "Teaching Programming: A Developmental Approach." *The Computing Teacher* (May 1985): 12–15. A sequence of programming activities is outlined and discussed.

CHAPTER

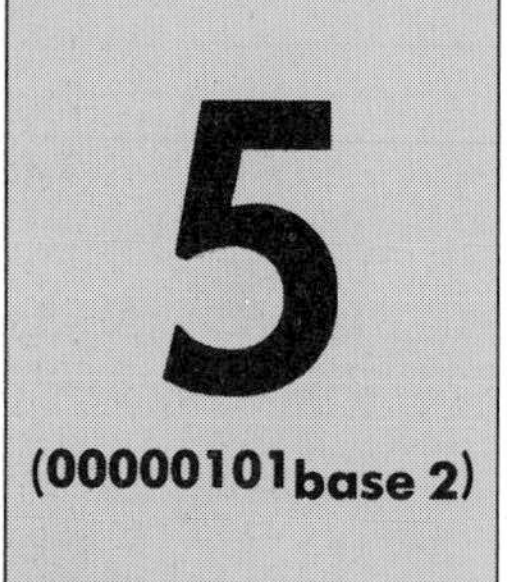

JUMP STARTING BASIC

The Hands-On, Sit Down at the Computer, and Do It Chapter

Getting Started

This chapter is a bit unlike all the other chapters of this book. The format and style are different. Its purpose is to introduce you to the environment of a programming language called BASIC. This job is best done by giving you brief descriptions and then letting you experiment. Therefore, this chapter is hands-on. You should go through it with your computer close at hand.

Of course, we can't cover all of BASIC in one chapter. Even if we could, it wouldn't be appropriate to do so. It is not our goal to teach you to program. If you come away from this chapter with an awareness of what BASIC is and how to load, run, edit, and save programs, then you will have achieved everything we intended. We'll also cover a few of the features that are unique to IBM BASIC. If you want to learn more about BASIC than what we cover here, read the BASIC Minibook included as Appendix A. Also, everything you could possibly want to know about BASIC is covered in detail in the manual that comes with the computer. You might also want to take a course that is devoted to studying nothing but BASIC.

Well, it's time to begin. Dive in and don't be afraid to experiment. You can't hurt the computer. We'll meet you in the next chapter.

Objectives for Teachers

To successfully complete this chapter, you should be able to

1. Access the BASIC interpreter.
2. Describe the differences between command mode and program mode.
3. Load and execute a BASIC program.
4. Edit a BASIC program.
5. Save a BASIC program.

Lesson 5.1

Preliminaries

Let's refresh your memory about how to get into BASIC. If your computer doesn't have any disk drives, you won't have much choice. When you turn on the computer, it automatically places you in cassette BASIC. This is the BASIC interpreter that is contained in the PC's ROM. The only provision it gives you for saving programs is on audio cassettes, hence the name.

If your PC has at least one disk drive, it is capable of booting up into DOS when you turn it on, as we discovered in Chapter 3. To get to BASIC from DOS, you must execute it like a program. There are two BASIC files on the DOS diskette: BASIC.COM and BASICA.COM. If you execute BASIC.COM, your PC will place you in the BASIC interpreter and will also augment cassette BASIC to give it the ability to interact with diskette drives. BASICA.COM also provides some advanced sound and graphics capabilities that are not included in BASIC.COM. If you have a PCjr, you must have purchased the BASIC cartridge in order to program in BASIC. The BASIC interpreter contained in the PCjr's cartridge is much like BASICA.COM except that it is even more powerful.

Turn on your PC with DOS in the A: drive. When the DOS prompt appears, type BASICA, and press Enter. Whenever you are asked to enter a program in this chapter, we will assume that you are in BASICA.

Discovery 5.1: Command Mode

Objectives. In this lesson you will learn the difference between *command mode* and *program mode*. You will also learn the commands CLS, LIST, LLIST, and RUN, and the statement PRINT.

Materials. For this lesson you will need DOS.

Just to make sure that you are in BASICA, check to see if your screen looks something like this:

```
The IBM Personal Computer Basic
Version A3.00 Copyright IBM Corp. 1981, 1982, 1983, 1984
60887 Bytes free

Ok





1LIST 2RUN 3LOAD" 4SAVE" 5CONT 6,"LPT1 7TRON 8TROFF 9KEY 0SCREEN
```

What you see might be slightly different, depending upon what version of DOS you are using and how much memory your computer has. Don't pay any attention right now to the legend at the bottom of the screen; we'll get to that later in this chapter.

The little flashing line underneath Ok is called the *cursor.* Like the DOS prompt (A>), it shows where you are right now on the screen. Unlike the DOS prompt, you can move the cursor around on the screen with the cursor keys on the numeric keypad (2, 4, 6, and 8). Do that now.

Well, here we are, sitting at the controls of a powerful engine of knowledge. Hear it throb? Let's see what this machine can do! Type the following text:

```
What is the volume of Lake Okeechobee?
```

What happened? Probably nothing, unless you also pressed the Enter key. Just as in DOS, pressing the Enter key tells the computer to operate on what you have typed. From now on, when we want you to do something, we will use the term *enter* to mean: "Type in the indicated text and then press the Enter key."

Now what? The computer replied with the message: "syntax error." Does that mean that the computer doesn't know the volume of Lake Okeechobee? Let's try another question. Surely this powerful computing device knows how to add two to two. Enter this:

```
What is 2+2?
```

Another syntax error, right?

The computer doesn't know the volume of Lake Okeechobee unless someone programs it to. It does, however, know how to add 2 + 2. Syntax error means that the computer doesn't even understand your question! The BASIC language is a very strictly defined subset of the English language, with some extensions. The computer must be addressed in its own tongue. Enter the following:

```
PRINT 2+2
```

Aha! Now we're getting somewhere. Try this.

```
PRINT Emma
```

0? Why 0? Is this computer evaluating Emma's worth? Try putting quotation marks around Emma, like this:

```
PRINT "Emma"
```

Now, that's better. Why did the computer print 0 before? We'll answer that question later in this chapter. Right now, use the cursor keys to move up the screen to

```
PRINT "Emma"
```

Then move the cursor right to the first letter of Emma. Now type your name, close the quotes, and press Enter.

```
PRINT "your name"
```

Place the cursor on the first letter of your name again. This time press the Del key until your name is deleted. Then press the Ins key one time. Now type a capital letter *I* followed by a comma and a space. (From here on, we'll use single quotation marks to enclose text for you to type, as here, type 'I, '.) Then press the End key, followed by the backspace key (←), to the right of the + key on the top row. Now type ', don't know the volume of Lake Okeechobee." ' and press Enter.

```
PRINT "I, Emma, don't know the volume of Lake
Okeechobee."
```

The screen must be getting pretty cluttered by now, so let's clear it off. Enter the following:

```
CLS
```

So far, while we have been exploring BASIC, you have been in command mode. All the things you have typed have been BASIC commands that the computer executes immediately. This is why command mode is also sometimes called *immediate mode.* None of the things you have typed so far have been kept in the computer's memory. Although you have been commanding the computer, you have not yet written a program. You can verify that by giving the command LIST. LIST commands the computer to display whatever program is in memory. Try it.

```
LIST
```

Nothing happened, right? To be in program mode, you must put program line numbers in front of the commands. Once that is done, they are no longer considered commands. Instead, they are called *statements.* Enter the following:

```
10 PRINT "I am I. B. Emma"
```

Did the computer print anything when you pressed Enter? Now LIST your program. This is what you should see.

```
LIST
10 PRINT "I am I. B. Emma"
Ok
```

If there is a printer attached to your computer, you can get a program listing there by using the LLIST command. Computer printouts are sometimes called hard copy.

Typing a line number in front of the PRINT statement causes its execution to be deferred until you issue another command to run it. For this reason, program mode is also called *deferred mode.* The command to run a program is (you guessed it) RUN. Try that now.

```
RUN
I am I. B. Emma
Ok
```

Congratulations! Unless you have programmed before, you just entered and ran your first BASIC program.

Programming Particulars

The difference between a command and a statement is often confusing because many commands are also often used as statements. CLS, for example, is used in both command or program mode. LIST and RUN, however, are rarely used in a program. Generally, commands tell the computer what to do with a program that is in memory. For instance, the command RUN tells the computer to execute the program in memory. When you type a command and press the Enter key, the computer carries out the command immediately. If you give commands line numbers, they become part of a program and are no longer considered commands. By the same token, if you take the line number off of what is normally considered a statement, then it becomes a command. A good rule to use is this: If it is issued without a line number, it's a command; otherwise, it's a statement.

The Ins, Del, and ← (backspace) keys are all active in BASIC. Backspace and delete have immediate effect. The Ins key is a *toggle*. If you press it once, the cursor becomes a flashing rectangle and text that you enter is pushed to the right. A second press on the Ins key (or pressing some other keys, such as End or Enter) returns the cursor to its normal status.

Line numbers cause program statements to be kept in the computer's memory. You can only enter as many lines as your computer has room for in its memory. When you are ready to execute a program, use the RUN command.

Lesson 5.2

Preliminaries

Now you are ready to write some programs. First, there are some details that you should know about BASIC. When entering a program, you must press the Enter key at the end of each program line. This signals the computer that the line is complete. When a program is run, lines are executed in order of line number.

Sometimes the display becomes untidy and you want to get a fresh start. As we saw in the last lesson, the command CLS will clear the display. Fortunately though, the program remains in memory and you can display it by issuing the command LIST. Some frequently used commands, which we will be using in this chapter, are LIST, LOAD, and SAVE.

Program statements don't have to be entered in order of their line numbers even though a program is executed in order of line numbers. If you discover that you have forgotten an important statement, you can insert it between two other statements providing there is an available number that can be assigned to the new statement. This is why programmers seldom, if ever, use consecutive numbers for program statements. We'll say more about this later.

When you want to modify a line, just reenter it. The computer remembers only the last line entered for a given number. If you want to get rid of a line, simply enter the line number and press the Enter key.

In the previous chapter we discussed procedures for developing algorithms. You won't see any more about that here. It's not that we don't believe in what we say, it's just that at this point, we don't yet have the necessary programming tools. This chapter focuses on presenting BASIC statements and simple programming techniques. The sample programs here are intended to demonstrate how statements work. In Appendix A, you can put what you have learned to work by defining a programming task and then achieving it with the intellectual tools discussed in Chapter 4. Now—finally—it is time to start programming.

Discovery 5.2: Printing

Objectives. In this lesson you will learn to use these statements: REM, KEY, LOCATE, WIDTH, and END. You will also learn to use the RUN, NEW, and RENUM commands. Analyze each program carefully. Try to discover how each statement works. Check your observations by reading the Programming Particulars section for this lesson.

Materials. For this lesson you will need DOS.

1. We are going to experiment with the PRINT statement. To do so we will give you a set of small programs to enter. The PRINT statement is used in each program, but the results are not always the same. Enter the programs one at a time and then use the command RUN to execute each program before entering the next one. You will not have to enter every line each time. With each new program, simply enter the new lines and retype the old ones that have changes. Actually, you will not be entering a new program. You will be editing the one in memory.

Notice that the first line of each program begins with REM. REM is short for REMark. REM lines are used to put comments in a program.

IBM BASIC does not require an END statement in a program, but it is a good practice to use one. Not only does the END statement give your programs a neater appearance, it makes the logic easier to follow in large programs. Also, for reasons that may seem unclear right now, properly placed END statements make it easier to discover and correct program errors. Thus, every program in this book will terminate with an END statement. Remember, after you enter a program line, you must press the Enter key. Record your observations.

```
90 REM PROGRAM #1 - HELLO
100 CLS
```

```
110 PRINT "Hello Y'all!"
120 END
```

Retype 110, then run again.

```
110 PRINT "   Hello Y'all!"
```

Retype 110, then run again.

```
110 PRINT "20 + 40"
```

Retype 110, then run again.

```
110 PRINT 20 + 40
```

Now type in Program 2.

```
90 REM PROGRAM #2 - PIG
100 CLS
110 LOCATE 5,20
120 PRINT "Never try to teach a pig to program."
130 END
```

Retype 130, add 140, and run again.

```
130 PRINT "It will bore the pig and tire you."
140 END
```

Add 125 and run again.

```
125 LOCATE 6,21
```

Retype 125 and run again.

```
125 LOCATE 15,21
```

Retype 110 and 125 and run again.

```
110 LOCATE 20,5
125 LOCATE 21,15
```

2. Enter Program 3 just as it is. Run it and then decide whether the message prints appropriately.

```
90 REM PROGRAM #3 - M, M & M
100 CLS
110 PRINT "Maynard";
120 PRINT "Millie";
130 PRINT "and Mackelroy"
140 END
```

3. Reenter lines 110 and 120, but use commas instead of semicolons. Run the program. Observe the difference between the first and the second program.

4. Reenter lines 110 and 120. Leave out all commas and semicolons. Run the program again. Notice differences between the third program and the other two.

5. Add the following two lines to Program 3:

```
115 PRINT
125 PRINT
```

Run the program and observe the results. Now add lines 95 and 105 and observe the results.

```
95 KEY OFF
105 WIDTH 40
```

6. Okay, let's play with Program 3 a bit. First enter CLS and then enter LIST. Observe what happens. Do this a few times. Notice the sequence of program line numbers. Notice how we kept inserting lines. This illustrates an important point. *You should never use consecutive numbers for program lines.* You should provide for flexibility. Depending upon how thoroughly you think your programs through before you enter them, the need will arise to enter statements between two existing statements.

7. Inserting lines results in a sequence of line numbers that is not logical. Fortunately, IBM BASIC allows us to renumber them. Try this: Clear the display, then enter RENUM. List the program. Observe what has happened. Do this again, but this time enter RENUM 100. Observe what has happened. Try each of the following renumber statements in sequence. Observe what happens in each case.

```
RENUM 200,130   RENUM 300,230 RENUM
RENUM 100,10,5 RENUM ,,1      RENUM 1,,1
RENUM
```

Finally, enter the command NEW. Then enter LIST. What happens?

Programming Particulars

The PRINT statement tells the computer to print text and numbers on the display. Text must be enclosed in quotation marks. Numerical expressions that are enclosed in quotation marks are printed literally. Without the quotation marks, expressions are first evaluated, and then the answer is printed. For example, PRINT "1 + 2" displays 1 + 2 literally. PRINT 1 + 2 displays 3, the sum. The LOCATE statement locates the position where printing is to begin on the display. To use LOCATE correctly, you must know the dimensions of the display. You can select a width of 40 or 80 characters using either the WIDTH 40 or WIDTH 80. When you turn on the computer, the display generally has a width of 80 characters. (The width depends upon some switch settings inside the computer.) Regardless of the width, the text display is always 25 lines long. You cannot LOCATE line 25, however, until you turn off the function key display.

When using LOCATE, you should provide two numbers, one for the line and one for the column, like this: LOCATE *l,c*. This program statement will position the cursor at line *l* and column *c*. For example, LOCATE 3,5 will place the cursor on line 3 and column 5. Commas and semicolons also control the placement of the cursor. If you end a PRINT statement with a semicolon, then the next message to be printed will begin immediately following the first one. A comma at the end of a PRINT statement tabs the next PRINT statement over to a predetermined print zone. An 80-column line has six print zones that are 14 characters wide except for the sixth zone, which is 10 characters wide.

REM statements allow you to put comments in a program. When BASIC sees REM at the beginning of a line, it disregards the rest of the line and does not attempt to execute it. BASIC will also accept the apostrophe (') as an abbreviation for REM. Placing remarks inside a program is called *internal documentation* and it is very important. Programmers use REM statements to explain details about a program so that they, or someone else, will be able to interpret the program more easily at a later date. The importance of REM will become more clear to you as you proceed through this chapter.

The statement CLS clears the display, except for the function key display on row 25. When you begin BASIC, the function keys on the leftmost end of the keyboard are programmed with commonly used commands. These commands are displayed on row 25. KEY OFF turns this display off. KEY ON turns it back on. Note, however, that the function keys continue to operate even after KEY OFF has been executed. All three of these statements can be conveniently used in command mode as well as program mode.

When you want to rid the computer's memory of a program, you use the command NEW. Don't get CLS and NEW confused. CLS does not affect program memory and NEW does not affect the display. Just because the display is cluttered does not mean that there is a program in memory. Likewise, a clean display does not mean that a program is not in memory. Always execute the NEW command to clear the program in memory before loading another program.

IBM BASIC conveniently provides the RENUM command for renumbering program lines. RENUM has three **arguments:** the new number of the first line, the first line to begin renumbering with, and the line numbering increment. For example, RENUM 100,55,5 means to start renumbering by 5s at line 55 of the current program. Line 55 becomes line 100. The next line after 55 becomes 105, the next becomes 110, and so on. Any or all of the arguments may be omitted. RENUM without any arguments is equal to RENUM 10, first line of program 10.

Lesson 5.3

Preliminaries

It is time-consuming to enter a program, so once you have entered one, you may want to store it for later use. To save a program, give the command SAVE in command mode. Before you can save though, you must also supply a name for the program. Programs are saved as diskette files, so they follow the same conventions as the DOS filenames discussed in Chapter 3, with two important exceptions. First, when programs are saved from BASIC, the name must be enclosed in quotation marks. For example, you must enter

```
SAVE "MYFILE.001"
```

to save a program with the name MYFILE.001. The second difference is that if you issue a program name with no extension, like MYFILE, BASIC automatically appends the extension .BAS. DOS doesn't do that.

This command

```
SAVE "ART#1"
```

will save a program in memory to a file named ART#1.BAS. Once the program has been stored, you can retrieve it by issuing the command LOAD like this:

```
LOAD "ART#1"
```

Notice that you do not need to enter the extension, .BAS. However, if you have given a program name any extension other than .BAS, you must include the extension when you load the program. For example, you must enter

```
LOAD "MYFILE.001"
```

to load a program named MYFILE.001. *Before saving a program in BASIC, the diskette you are saving on must have been previously formatted in DOS.*

To see what programs are on a diskette, BASIC has its own equivalent of the DOS command DIR. It is called FILES. To view the directory from BASIC, just type "FILES *.BAS". This command will display all the files with the BAS extension. You can use FILES to verify that a program has been saved.

There will be times when you will make errors and times when you will want to change program lines for some other reason. A convenient command in IBM BASIC is EDIT. To use this command you enter the command name followed by the line number of the statement you want to edit. If you enter

```
EDIT 100
```

line 100, if it exists, will print on the screen. The cursor will rest at the beginning of the line, waiting for you to begin entering changes. You can use the cursor keys, the [Del] key, and the [Ins] key to make as many changes as you wish. Whenever you are finished editing, press [Enter]. You can do this at any time; that is, you don't have to be at the beginning of the line. *Editing a program in memory does not also change it on the diskette.* You must resave the program with the same name.

Discovery 5.3: Saving, Loading, and Editing

Objectives. In this lesson, we will work more with the PRINT statement to produce what are called *character graphics*. You will also learn to SAVE, LOAD, and KILL programs and to use the FILES command. Whenever necessary, you should use the EDIT command to make changes.

Materials. For this lesson you will need DOS and a formatted diskette.

1. Enter this program. Be sure to insert all the spaces that are indicated. Run the program to check it, then correct any errors. Save the program using the name PGM04.

```
90 REM PROGRAM 4 AUTO
100 CLS
110 PRINT "         ____    "
120 PRINT "    --__/_¦_o\__ "
130 PRINT "  -- /__________]"
140 PRINT "   --   O     O  "
150 END
```

2. Enter the next program to get a picture of a tree. Don't forget to NEW the previous program!

```
90 REM PROGRAM 5 TREE
100 CLS
110 PRINT "    /\     "
120 PRINT "   //\\    "
130 PRINT "  ///\\\   "
140 PRINT " ////\\\\  "
150 PRINT "////¦¦\\\\ "
160 PRINT "   _¦¦_    "
170 END
```

3. Run Program 5. Change some of the keyboard characters if you wish. When you are sure that the program is correct, save it using the name PGM05. Then enter NEW. (What will this do?) Now load and run the program to make sure that it saved successfully.

4. Now let's really cut loose with the PRINT statement. Enter Program 6 and run it. When you are satisfied that it is correct, SAVE it. Use the name PGM06.

```
90 REM PROGRAM 6 HOUSE1
100 CLS
110 PRINT "    ________________            "
120 PRINT "   /////////////////\           "
130 PRINT "  //\\\\\\\\\\\\\\\\\\\         "
140 PRINT " //////////////////////\        "
150 PRINT "//\\\\\\\\\\\\\\\\\\\\\\\       "
160 PRINT "[                       ]       "
170 PRINT "[  []  []  []  []  []   ]       "
180 PRINT "[  []  [] ____ []  []   ]   *  *"
190 PRINT "[         |UU|          ] *  *\/"
200 PRINT "[_________|__|__________]  \/   "
210 END
```

5. Do you like the placement of things on the screen? Modify the program by inserting spaces so that the picture moves closer to the center of the screen. Save the program again using the same name. This time when you save the program, the modifications will be saved.

6. As you learned in Chapter 2, the IBM PC has characters that are not displayed on the keyboard. To use them, you must depress the Alt key, type in a code for the character, and release the Alt key. The codes are given in the BASIC manual. For example, the code for pi (π) is 227. Use this symbol and others of your choice to change PGM06 so that the house looks more like a house. *Character codes must be entered on the numeric keypad, not on the numbers at the top of the keyboard.* Also, you don't need to press the Num Lock key, although it won't matter if you do.

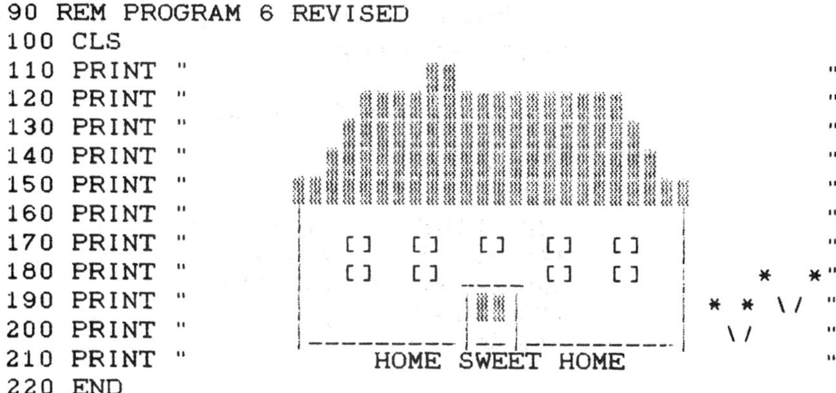

```
90 REM PROGRAM 6 REVISED
100 CLS
110 PRINT "                                                  "
120 PRINT "                                                  "
130 PRINT "                                                  "
140 PRINT "                                                  "
150 PRINT "                                                  "
160 PRINT " |                                      |          "
170 PRINT " |   [ ]  [ ]  [ ]  [ ]  [ ]            |          "
180 PRINT " |   [ ]  [ ]  ____  [ ]  [ ]           |   *    * "
190 PRINT " |              |  |                    | * *  \/  "
200 PRINT " |----------|--|----------|                 \/     "
210 PRINT "        HOME SWEET HOME                            "
220 END
```

Programming Particulars

In this lesson, you learned to SAVE and LOAD programs. Some other commands that you may find useful are FILES and KILL. FILES will display a directory of all the files on a diskette. KILL is used to remove files from a diskette. To use it, you must type the entire file name, including extension. For example, KILL"MYFILE.001" will remove the file MYFILE.001 from the diskette.

You have also learned to use PRINT statements to create character graphics. You have learned of the special characters that can be used to create text graphics. These characters are referred to as the *extended character set*. You obtain them by holding down the Alt key and entering three-digit codes on the numeric keypad.

We hope that as you worked, you became familiar with using the EDIT command. You should have noticed, also, that spaces serve as a useful formatting tool in PRINT statements.

Chapter Summary

We hope that our discovery approach to BASIC has given you a worthwhile introduction to the BASIC environment. You should know how to load, run, edit, and save BASIC programs. We hope that you have a feeling for what the language is like. Some of you have probably decided that programming is pretty boring. Others of you are probably eager to learn more. Now, if you really want to learn the language, move on to Appendix A.

This chapter has been but a small sampler; we've only scratched the surface. Programming is just one small aspect of how computers can be applied to education. If you don't care for it, that's fine. Teachers shouldn't have to write their own software. That's a job for people who can devote all of their time to the task. However, teachers need to understand how programming works, and you should have gotten some of the flavor from this chapter. The remainder of this book will be devoted to other aspects of computers in education.

Chapter Review

Knowledge Exercises

1. Describe the difference between command and program mode.

   Answer: In command mode, instructions to the computer are executed immediately by the interpreter and are not stored in memory.

   In program mode, line numbers in front of instructions cause them to be stored in memory and not executed until the RUN command is entered.

2. Describe the function of the following commands: LOAD, RUN, SAVE, EDIT, LIST, LLIST, CLS, NEW, KEY, RENUM, KILL, and FILES.

   Answer: See Chapter.

3. Describe the function of the following statements: PRINT, REM, END, LOCATE, WIDTH.

   Answer: See Chapter.

4. Why aren't BASIC program lines numbered consecutively?

   Answer: To allow new lines to be inserted.

Thought Exercises

1. What are the reasons for teaching students and teachers to program in BASIC?

2. What are the reasons for not teaching students and teachers to program in BASIC?

Activities

Locate and run the following programs on the *Program Disk for the Micro Goes to School, IBM Version.*

a. PGM54.BAS
b. PGM55.BAS
c. ESTIMATE.BAS

Projects

1. Attempt to modify the ESTIMATE.BAS program so that when the student responds with the exact answer, instead of flashing

   ```
   PERFECT!!!
   ```

   the program flashes

   ```
   TOO GOOD!
   ```

Bibliography

Cassell, Don, and Richard Swanson. *BASIC Made Easy.* Reston, Va.: Reston Publishing, 1980. An introductory text with emphasis on problem solving and flowcharting.

Clark, James F., and William O. Drum. *Structured BASIC.* Cincinnati: South-Western Publishing, 1983. A secondary-level text on BASIC programming.

Culp, George, and Herbert Nickles. *Instructional Computing Fundamentals for the IBM Microcomputers.* Monterey, Calif.: Brooks/Cole, 1985. A text in BASIC programming for the design and development of instructional computing programs.

Cummins, Jerry, and Gene Kuechmann. *Programming in BASIC.* Columbus, Ohio: Charles E. Merrill, 1983. A high-school-level text in BASIC programming.

IBM Corporation. *BASIC by Microsoft.* U.S.A.: IBM Corporation, Boca Raton, Fla., 1984. Official BASIC programming reference manual for IBM PC BASIC.

Kitchen, Andrew. *BASIC by Design.* Englewood Cliffs, N.J.: Prentice-Hall, 1983. A comprehensive text in BASIC, emphasizing the structured design.

Luehrmann, Arthur. "Structured Programming in Basic." *Creative Computing* (May, 1984): 152–163. An important article on top-down BASIC.

Luehrmann, Arthur, and Herbert Peckman. *Computer Literacy: A Hands-On Approach.* New York: McGraw-Hill, 1983. The examples of programming concepts are paired closely with internal memory of the computer.

Presley, Bruce. *A Guide to Programming the IBM Personal Computer.* Lawrenceville, N.Y.: Lawrenceville Press, 1982. A secondary-level text in programming.

Quasney, James S., and John Maniotes. *BASIC Fundamentals and Style.* Boston: Boyd & Fraser, 1984. This text emphasizes problem solving and good program design in BASIC.

Shelly, Gary, and Thomas J. Cashman. *Introduction to BASIC Programming.* Brea, Calif.: Anaheim Publishing, 1982. A solid BASIC text with many illustrations.

Simon, David E. *IBM BASIC from the Ground Up.* Rochelle Park, N.J.: Hayden Book Company, 1983. An introductory text with particular emphasis on IBM functions.

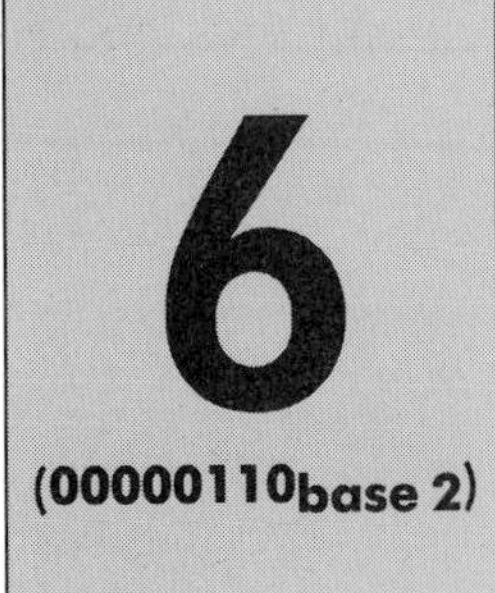

The Lowdown on Logo
Taming the Turtle

Getting Started

Logo, like BASIC, is a high-level programming language, which means that computers don't really understand programs written in Logo. High-level languages have to be translated into a computer's real language, machine code. That translation can be accomplished with two different kinds of translator programs: interpreters or compilers. Interpreted programs usually execute much more slowly than compiled programs; however, interpreters are usually much easier for beginning programmers to learn to use. Logo, like BASIC, is an interpreted language. If you don't already know how to program in Logo, you aren't going to learn it from one chapter in this book. There are a number of excellent texts listed in the Bibliography at the end of this chapter. Get one of them if you really want to learn the language. What we hope to do in this chapter is to introduce you to Logo. You should come away with an understanding of where Logo came from, what it is all about, and how you can teach with it.

Objectives for Teachers

After completing this chapter, you should be able to

1. Briefly detail the history of Logo, specifying its creator and the mainframe language from which it was derived.
2. Briefly explain the philosophy behind Logo.
3. Boot Logo on the IBM PC.
4. Define and use simple Logo primitives.
5. Create Logo procedures to perform simple tasks.
6. Describe some well-known Logo prototype activities.
7. Identify instructional activities for which Logo can be used.
8. Describe the role of the classroom teacher in the Logo environment and give supporting arguments for this role.

9. Identify other programs designed to supplement and/or substitute for Logo by simplifying its syntax and/or making it easier to use.
10. Describe how to first introduce Logo to students.
11. Present a Logo lesson to students.

What Is Logo All about?

If you already know the name *Logo,* you may know that it has gained a reputation as the "elementary" language. While that reputation doesn't really characterize Logo very well, it is easy to see how it came about. **Logo** was created as a tool for learning. It was designed to make the computer into a learning environment. The name *Logo* is derived from the Greek word for thought. Most of the research associated with Logo has been done with children and most of the teaching that has been done with Logo has been at the elementary level, hence the reputation. Another reason for Logo's reputation as elementary is that, up to now, microcomputers haven't had enough memory to run true Logo. You see, Logo was derived from a mainframe language called **LISP,** short for LISt Processing. LISP is the language used most frequently for research in **Artificial Intelligence (AI).** Artificial Intelligence research centers around efforts to give computers the ability to reason. Logo, like LISP, has the ability to deal in powerful ways with large lists of words. However, on 8-bit microcomputers, there just isn't enough room in memory for very large lists, so the emphasis in teaching with Logo has been placed on the language's other features, mainly graphics. As more powerful microcomputers capable of having more memory (enter the IBM PC family) become more prevalent in schools, we should see more of Logo's powerful features being exploited. Logo's reputation as elementary can then become a thing of the past.

Most of what has been done with Logo grew out of the work of the Massachusetts Institute of Technology (MIT) Logo Group. The father of Logo is a professor at MIT, a man named Seymour Papert. To get the full philosophy behind Logo, you must read Papert's book, *Mindstorms: Children, Computers, and Powerful Ideas.* It is not appropriate for us to relate that information here. We just want to give you the gist of it.

To date, Logo stands as the sole major application of computers to education that breaks with the programming-literacy-tutorial-drill and practice model that has dominated the field. We talk in this book about how computers are extensions of the mind and should be used in education as learning tools; the student, not the computer, should be in control of the process. There is a strong element of this in Logo. At one time in his career, Papert worked in France with Jean Piaget and was greatly impressed with what he observed. He feels strongly that children should be what he calls "architects of their own intellectual development" and that computers should not be used just as teaching machines. Logo was created to answer this need. The best way to grasp the concepts embodied in Logo is to use it and to observe how teaching is done with it. We must begin by learning to load Logo.

Loading Logo on the IBM PC

Many different versions of Logo are available for the IBM PC family of computers and they all have minor differences between them. Where it is necessary in this text to refer to a specific Logo, we will use IBM Personal Computer Logo Version 1.00, which runs on all the members of the PC family. If you don't have IBM Logo, you won't be able to use the sample files provided on the diskette that comes with this book. Listings of all those files are, however, provided after the Chapter Review; with some modification they can probably be made to run with virtually any version of Logo. If you have no Logo at all, you should be able to get along with the pictures and descriptions in this chapter.

Unlike BASIC, Logo does not reside in the ROM of a microcomputer. The language must be loaded from a diskette. With most versions of Logo, that is as easy as inserting the diskette and turning on the computer. If your PC is already on, just reset the system. Enter the date and time when prompted, and after a few seconds, the screen should look like this:

```
IBM Personal Computer Logo Version 1.00
(C) Copyright IBM Corp. 1983
(C) Copyright LCSI 1983
Serial Number 0123456789

WELCOME TO LOGO
?█
```

Dynatrak*

Once Logo is booted, the program diskette need not remain in the drive. Take it out and replace it with the data diskette provided with this book. Type LOAD "DYNATRAK" and press the Return key. After a few seconds, your screen should look like this:

```
THE OBJECT OF THIS GAME IS TO SEE
HOW LONG YOU CAN KEEP THE DYNATURTLE
MOVING ON A CIRCULAR TRACK WITHOUT
CRASHING!

* * * * * * * CONTROLS * * * * * * *
6 ROTATE CLOCKWISE
4 ROTATE COUNTERCLOCKWISE
8 GIVE THE TURTLE A "KICK" IN THE
DIRECTION IT IS POINTING
* * * * * * * * * * * * * * * * * *
```

*© 1982 by MIT/Terrapin. Reprinted by permission.

```
( PRESS 'NUMLOCK' TO USE NUMBER PAD )
HOW WIDE DO YOU WANT THE TRACK TO BE?
( 50 IS A GOOD SIZE. )
```

Answer DYNATRAK's prompts until you get this screen.

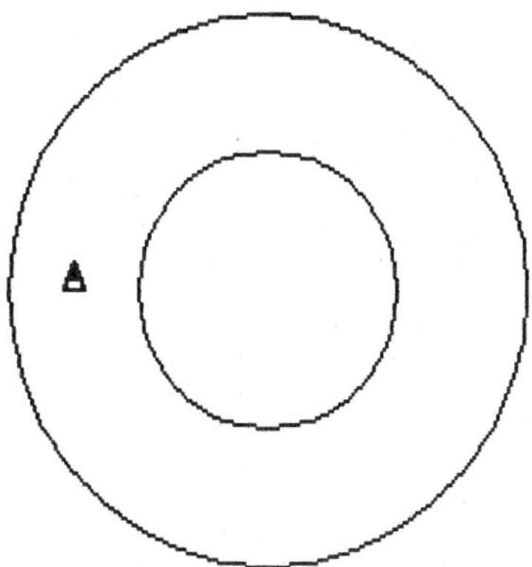

The triangle on the screen is the Logo turtle. The object in DYNATRAK is to drive the turtle around the track without crashing through the walls. Use the [R] and [L] keys to steer the dynaturtle right and left; use the [K] key to give the dynaturtle a kick. Not too much! Go to the computer now and try to drive around the track. Come back when you've had enough.

It wasn't easy, was it? The dynaturtle doesn't drive like a car. If you operate it under that assumption, you'll crash every time. Children and adults alike possess intuitive knowledge that things go the direction in which you push them. Does the dynaturtle behave that way? Let's try it. From a stop, give the dynaturtle a kick. Then press the [R] key three times and give it another kick. If things always go the way we push them, the dynaturtle should move like this:

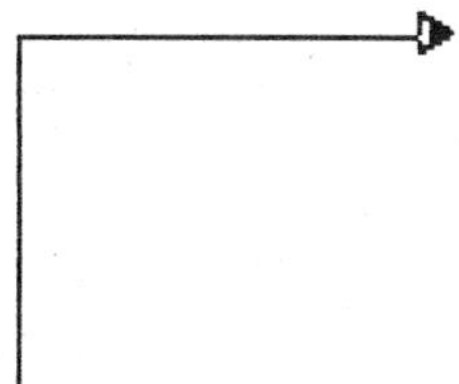

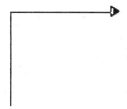

But, doesn't the dynaturtle really move like this?

Objects usually move the way we push them because there are other invisible forces acting upon them such as friction and gravity. The dynaturtle moves only according to the obvious forces applied to it, as if it were an object on a plane with no friction and no gravity. After you have used DYNATRAK long enough to master navigating the dynaturtle around the track, wouldn't you think you'd have a pretty good intuitive sense of how

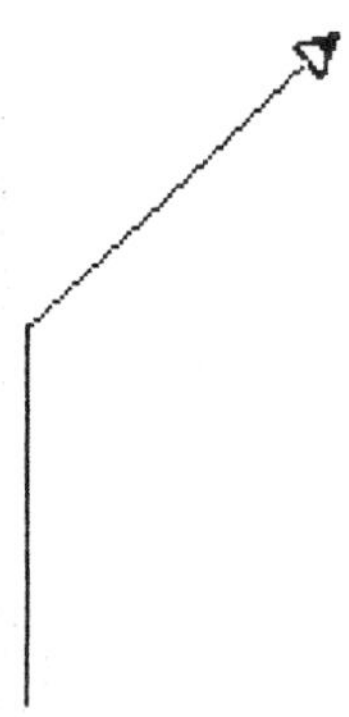

forces really affect object movement? Studies show that conventional physics instruction doesn't change intuitive beliefs concerning the laws of physics. College-level physics students hold many of the same intuitive notions as elementary-school students. DYNATRAK, however, provides an environment in which the learner can explore and experiment with an object that, unlike most things on earth, is unaffected by forces that are not obvious. In Logo, learning environments such as DYNATRAK are called microworlds. When using a Logo program such as DYNATRAK, it is the teacher's job to provide guidance, not instruction. It is the student who drives the learning process.

Polygons

We saw with DYNATRAK how Logo can be used to develop a concept from physics. The DYNATRAK program could be written, however, in just about any programming language. Let's take a look at what it is about Logo itself that is unique, and how the programming process can be used to teach something other than programming. We are going to develop some geometry concepts and at the same time learn a little about programming with Logo.

If you haven't already done so, boot your computer with Logo. Type CLEARSCREEN to get the Logo turtle and experiment with these commands. (Note abbreviations in parentheses.)

FORWARD (FD) *n*	BACK (BK) *n*
RIGHT (RT) *n*	LEFT (LT) *n*
PENUP (PU)	PENDOWN (PD)
CLEARSCREEN (CS)	

These simple Logo commands are called *primitives.* FD 100 moves the turtle forward 100 units. RT 120 turns the turtle right 120 degrees. If you type PU before FD 100, the turtle moves without leaving a trail. This is because PU, or PENUP, makes the turtle lift up his pen so it won't draw as he moves. The command PD makes him put the pen back down.

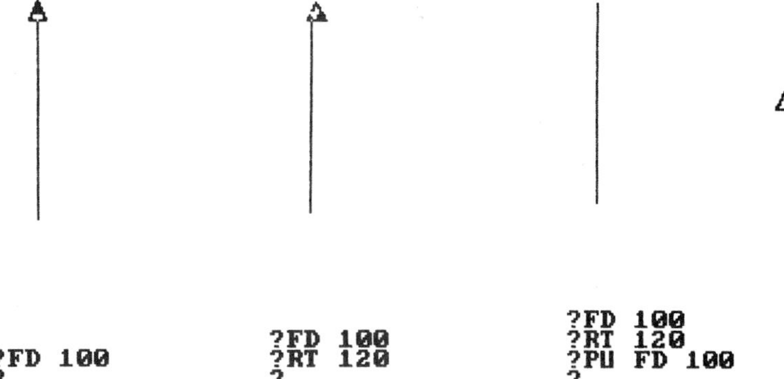

Note that forward movement is in the direction that the turtle points. Type CLEARSCREEN followed by PENDOWN and try the following:

```
?FD 40  RT 90
```

What did the turtle do?

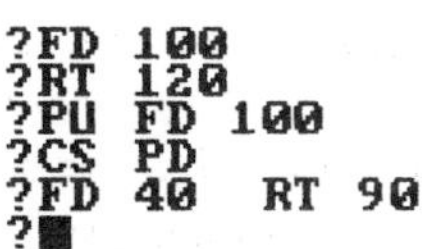

?FD 100
?RT 120
?PU FD 100
?CS PD
?FD 40 RT 90
?

Now let's add something to it. CLEARSCREEN and try

```
?REPEAT 4 [ FD 40  RT 90 ]
```

What did the turtle draw this time?

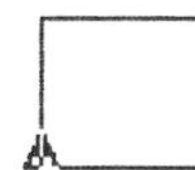

```
?PU FD 100
?CS PD
?FD 40  RT 90
?CS
?REPEAT 4 [ FD 40  RT 90 ]
?
```

The concept that an action can be composed of many smaller equal actions is an important one for students.

A critical feature of Logo is that the language can be extended by making new words, called *procedures.* Type the following:

```
?TO SQUARE
>REPEAT 4 [ FD 40  RT 90 ]
>END
```

When you have finished, CLEARSCREEN and type

```
?SQUARE
```

What does the turtle draw?

```
>REPEAT 4 [ FD 40  RT 90 ]
>END
SQUARE DEFINED
?CS
?SQUARE
?■
```

The TO statement in Logo allows new words to be defined from the Logo words that already exist. These new words can be used just like all the old ones. CLEARSCREEN and try

```
?REPEAT 12 [ SQUARE  RT 30 ]
```

What happens?

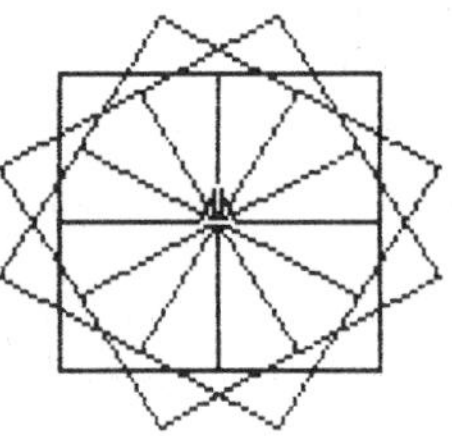

```
SQUARE DEFINED
?CS
?SQUARE
?CS
?REPEAT 12 [ SQUARE  RT 30 ]
?■
```

The new words that you create with Logo are called procedures. Variable values can also be given to procedures. Let's create a new procedure called SQUARE2 that allows us to tell the computer how large a square to draw.

Type

```
?TO SQUARE2 :SIZE
>REPEAT 4 [ FD :SIZE  RT 90 ]
>END
```

Now CLEARSCREEN and enter SQUARE2 10. What happens? Try SQUARE2 20. What happens? Use values of 30, 40, 50, 60, and so on and observe what happens.

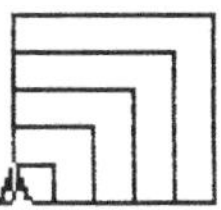

```
?SQUARE2 10
?SQUARE2 20
?SQUARE2 30
?SQUARE2 40
?SQUARE2 50
?
```

A Logo variable written as :SIZE allows us to tell the procedure SQUARE2 how big we want our square to be. We type the command SQUARE2 *n* where *n* is the length of one side. The ability to pass a variable value to a Logo procedure is a very powerful one. We can easily modify the SQUARE2 procedure to allow us to draw equilateral (all sides having same length) triangles instead of squares. Rather than just telling you how to write this new procedure, we want you to figure it out for yourself. Now, we know that's a lot to ask of you at this point. We have covered a lot of ground in just a few short pages, certainly much more than you would ever attempt to cover with students in that time. However, discovery is a key ingredient to the philosophy of Logo and the best way to get a feel for it is to experience it yourself. If you think you can write the procedure now, go ahead and try it. Don't be afraid. Experiment! The whole idea is that you can solve the problem by experimentation and successive approximation. In Logo, there is no such thing as a mistake. Call your procedure TRI. If you don't feel ready or if you try it and get stuck, then read on.

The first step in creating TRI is to examine SQUARE2 to see how it works.

```
REPEAT 4 [ FD :SIZE  RT 90 ]
```

REPEAT 4 causes the statements inside the brackets to be executed four times. What are the statements inside the brackets? Forward the number of units specified (FD :SIZE) and then a right turn (RT 90). Do you see how drawing a line and then making a right turn makes a square if you do it four times? Okay, what has to be changed to make the procedure draw a triangle?

Whether you feel ready or not, try to write the procedure now. The first step is

```
TO TRI :SIZE
```

Read on when you have finished.

The first attempt a student might make could be

```
TO TRI :SIZE
REPEAT 3 [ FD :SIZE  RT 60 ]
```

Everybody knows triangles have three sides and that the sum of the three angles is 180 degrees. Does this procedure work?

```
?CS
?TRI 60
?
```

The correct angle is not 60 degrees, is it? See if you can find out the correct angle. Come back when you are finished.

Did you get this?

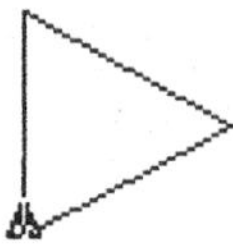

```
?TRI 60
?
```

Look at the following picture and you'll see that we're not concerned with the interior angle, which is 60 degrees. What is important is the supplement of that angle, or the number of degrees through which the turtle must turn.

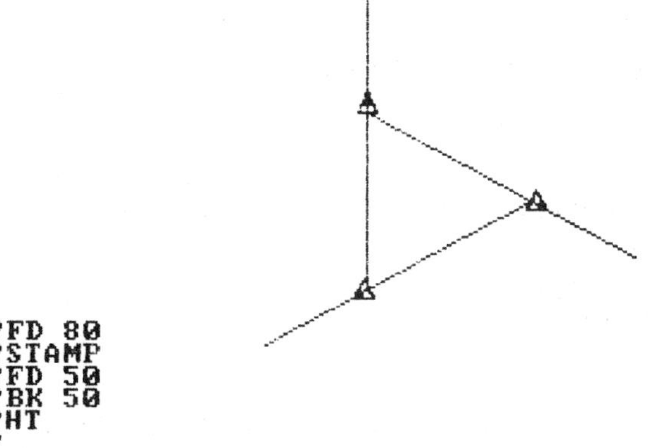

How did you find it out? By trial and error? It surprises many people to find out that the solution is 120 degrees, but just about anybody can determine it through trial and error. Now that you have the triangle and the square under your belt, you should be able to draw any other regular (all sides having same length) polygon; for example, a pentagon (five sides), hexagon (six sides), octagon (eight sides), and so on. Use Logo to complete the following table. Come back when you have finished.

Number of sides	Procedure
3	REPEAT 3 [FD :SIZE RT 120]
4	REPEAT 4 [FD :SIZE RT 90]
5	REPEAT ___ [FD :SIZE RT ____]
6	REPEAT ___ [FD :SIZE RT ____]
8	REPEAT ___ [FD :SIZE RT ____]
10	REPEAT ___ [FD :SIZE RT ____]
12	REPEAT ___ [FD :SIZE RT ____]

The following table summarizes the results you should have gotten in your experimentation:

Number of sides	Procedure
3	REPEAT 3 [FD :SIZE RT 120]
4	REPEAT 4 [FD :SIZE RT 90]
5	REPEAT 5 [FD :SIZE RT 72]
6	REPEAT 6 [FD :SIZE RT 60]
8	REPEAT 8 [FD :SIZE RT 45]
10	REPEAT 10 [FD :SIZE RT 36]
12	REPEAT 12 [FD :SIZE RT 30]

Can you find a relationship between the number of sides and the angle required to complete the polygon? If so, we can write a new procedure for drawing polygons with any number of sides and of any size. Think about how you would modify TRI to do this. Try it now. Call the procedure POLY :SIDES :SIZE. Come back when you are finished.

The first step in writing POLY :SIDES :SIZE is to determine the relationship between the number of sides of a polygon and the angle the turtle must turn after drawing each side. No matter what polygon is drawn, no matter how many sides, doesn't the turtle turn a total of 360 degrees each time? Wouldn't the proper turn after each side be 360 divided by the number of sides to be drawn? Do our experimental results bear this out?

Number of sides	Times	Angle	Equal	Result
3	*	120	=	360
4	*	90	=	360
5	*	72	=	360
6	*	60	=	360
8	*	45	=	360
9	*	40	=	360
10	*	36	=	360
12	*	30	=	360

That the turtle must turn a multiple of 360 degrees to get back to its original heading is often called *The Total Turtle Trip Theorem*.

The procedure TRI had a fixed number of sides and a fixed angle written into it.

```
TO TRI :SIZE
REPEAT 3 [ FD :SIZE  RT 120 ]
```

POLY must have expressions that use the variable :SIDES.

```
TO POLY :SIDES :SIZE
REPEAT   ??   [ FD :SIZE  RT        ??        ]
```

If you couldn't write POLY before, try it again now.

Here is the solution we had in mind.

```
TO POLY :SIDES :SIZE
REPEAT :SIDES [ FD :SIZE  RT 360/:SIDES ]
```

As you can see, the variable :SIDES is used two times in the procedure. It tells how many times to repeat and it is also used in the expression 360/:SIDES to tell how many degrees to turn. To execute POLY, you must type 'POLY *n*1 *n*2', where *n*1 is the number of sides and *n*2 is the length of each side. See the following illustrations for examples.

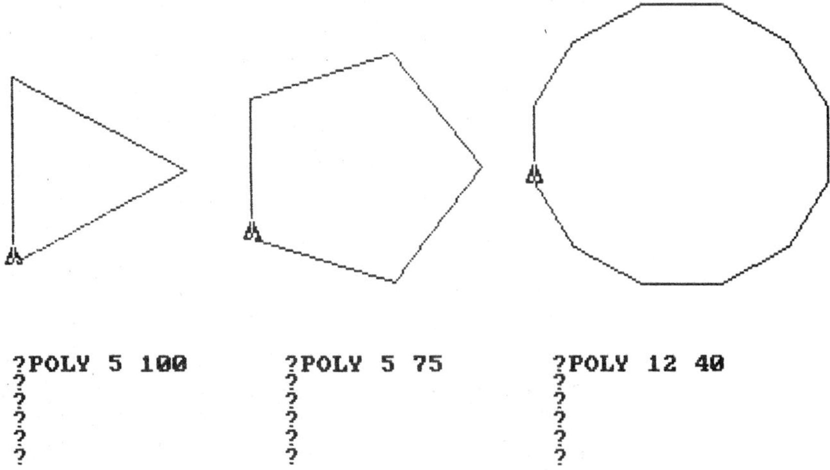

```
?POLY 5 100        ?POLY 5 75        ?POLY 12 40
?                  ?                 ?
?                  ?                 ?
?                  ?                 ?
?                  ?                 ?
?                  ?                 ?
```

Synonyms

All the Logo applications shown so far in this chapter have been very widely used and are well known in Logo circles. While the graphics and drawing capabilities of Logo have been explored broadly, one area of Logo that has received less attention is its list handling capabilities. Logo has very powerful features for manipulating words and large lists of words. These features haven't received as much attention up to now because 8-bit microcomputers just haven't had enough memory to store very many words. This isn't a problem with the IBM PC family and other 16-bit microcomputers.

SYNONYMS, the application to be shown in this section, accomplishes two goals. First, it demonstrates the power of Logo's list handling. Second, it models a different kind of educational application than those shown so far: the computer's role as a tool for augmenting a student's abilities.

If your computer is off, turn it on and boot with the Logo language diskette. If you already have Logo loaded and have been writing procedures, let's get rid of all of them. Type ERALL (ERase ALL) to clear every procedure. Now, with the diskette provided with this book in drive A:, type LOAD "SYNONYMS" and press Return. After the program has been loaded, execute it by typing SYNONYMS and pressing Return. Your screen should look something like this:

```
?LOAD "SYNONYMS
?SYNONYMS
WORD?
█
```

Type in 'HAPPY', press Return, and see what happens. Now try 'SLIM'. Try 'LOGO'. By now your screen should look something like this:

```
?LOAD "SYNONYMS
?SYNONYMS
WORD?
HAPPY

HAPPY
CONTENT
JOYOUS

WORD?
SLIM

SKINNY
SLENDER
SLIM

WORD?
LOGO
NOT IN THIS DICTIONARY

WORD?█
```

SYNONYMS is a computerized thesaurus. It gives two synonyms for any word that you input, as long as the word is in its dictionary. Of what use is a program like this? Just like a paper thesaurus, it is a writer's tool. Can't think of just exactly the right word? Let the computer look it up. Now, SYNONYMS is just a sample of what is possible with this kind of program, so there aren't many words in its dictionary. It's easy to add more if you want to. Press the Ctrl-Scroll Lock key combination to break the execution of SYNONYMS and type 'POTS.' This Logo command prints the names of all the procedures in its memory.

```
WORD?
SLIM
```

```
SKINNY
SLENDER
SLIM

WORD?
LOGO
NOT IN THIS DICTIONARY

WORD?
STOPPED! IN SYNONYMS:
MAKE "WORD READWORD
?POTS
TO FIND :WORD :POS :WHICH :LEN
TO WORDLISTS
TO RESTARTS
TO DISPLAY :POS
TO SYNONYMS
?■
```

The procedure WORDLISTS contains the dictionary. To see it, type PO "WORDLISTS."

```
WORD?
LOGO
NOT IN THIS DICTIONARY

WORD?
STOPPED! IN SYNONYMS:
MAKE "WORD READWORD
?POTS
TO FIND :WORD :POS :WHICH :LEN
TO WORDLISTS
TO RESTART
TO DISPLAY :POS
TO SYNONYMS
?PO "WORDLISTS
TO WORDLISTS
MAKE "SYN1 [HAPPY SAD SOFT HARD FAT SKI→
NNY ZZZ]
MAKE "SYN2 [CONTENT UNHAPPY PLIANT TOUG→
H ROTUND SLENDER ZZZ]
MAKE "SYN3 [JOYOUS DOWN MALEABLE DIFFIC→
ULT CORPULENT SLIM ZZZ]
END

?■
```

The word lists are contained within the brackets. The first list of words contains the first word in each set of three synonyms, the second list contains the second word in each set of three synonyms, and so on. Notice that order is important in the lists. The words occupying the first position in each list make up one set of three synonyms, the words occupying the second position in each list make up another set of synonyms, and so on. The last entry in each list, ZZZ, is a **flag** that the program uses to know where the end of the list occurs. To add words to the dictionary, first decide on three synonyms. Then, you must enter the Logo Editor. To do this, type ED "WORDLISTS". Your screen should now look like this:

```
TO WORDLISTS█
MAKE "SYN1 [HAPPY SAD HARD SOFT FAT SKI→
NNY ZZZ]
MAKE "SYN2 [CONTENT UNHAPPY PLIANT TOUG→
H ROTUND SLENDER ZZZ]
MAKE "SYN3 [JOYOUS DOWN MALEABLE DIFFIC→
ULT CORPULENT SLIM ZZZ]
END








███████████LOGO EDITOR███████████
```

Use the cursor keys to move down and right to place the cursor on the first Z in ZZZ in the first word list. Now type in the new word followed by a space. This is important. A space must separate each word. Now cursor down to place new synonyms in the second word list and the last word list. When you are finished, press the Esc key. Your screen should now say

```
WORDLISTS DEFINED
```

To save your new version of the program, type SAVE "SYN2" and press Return.

CLASSROOM ACTIVITY 6.1

Instruct students to collect synonyms. Then have them enter the words into the Logo SYNONYMS word list. Encourage them to consult the program when they write.

Instant*

In an effort to make Logo more accessible to children just beginning school, a number of products have been released that simplify Logo's already simple syntax and make it easier to use. Some of these products may have been inspired by yet another classic Logo program called INSTANT. Yes, you guessed it: a version of INSTANT is also on the diskette provided with this text. LOAD "INSTANT" and experiment with it. Once loaded, you can run the program by typing INSTANT. For those of you without Logo or the diskette, the opening screen looks like this:

```
F: MOVES TURTLE FORWARD
R: TURNS IT RIGHT
L: TURNS IT LEFT
D: DRAW ( CLEARS THE SCREEN )
Q: EXIT TO DOS
N: NAMES THE PICTURE
P: SHOWS A PICTURE  ASKS FOR ITS NAME
?: GIVES HELP

PRESS ANY KEY TO CONTINUE
█
```

You'll find that INSTANT allows you to draw pictures using just the F, R, and L keys. You can also use the N key to name any pictures you draw. Once named, any picture can be redrawn by pressing P and typing the name of the picture. By repeatedly pressing P and redrawing many pictures, you can then use N to name the combined pictures as one big picture. What you may not figure out is that INSTANT is keeping track of and recording your every move. As you move the turtle around, INSTANT translates those moves into FORWARDs, RIGHTs, and so on. When you name a drawing, INSTANT creates a procedure with that name. These procedures are exactly like procedures you might write yourself. You can even view their contents with the PO command. Here is a drawing made with INSTANT and the procedure that draws it.

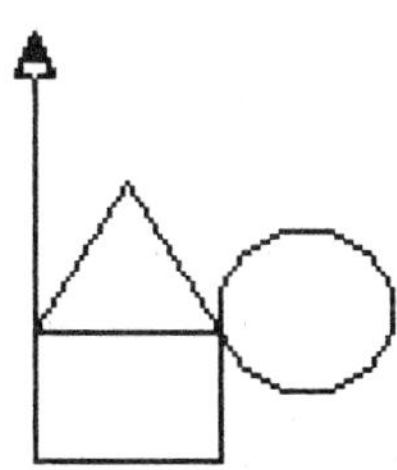

```
TO SAMPLE
FORWARD 10
RIGHT 30
FORWARD 10
RIGHT 30
FORWARD 10
RIGHT 30
FORWARD 10
RIGHT 30
FORWARD 10
RIGHT 30
FORWARD 10
RIGHT 30
FORWARD 10
RIGHT 30
FORWARD 10
RIGHT 30
FORWARD 10
RIGHT 30
FORWARD 10
FORWARD 10
FORWARD 10
FORWARD 10
FORWARD 10
LEFT 30
LEFT 30
LEFT 30
FORWARD 10
LEFT 30
LEFT 30
LEFT 30
LEFT 30
FORWARD 10
FORWARD 10
FORWARD 10
FORWARD 10
RIGHT 30
RIGHT 30
RIGHT 30
FORWARD 10
RIGHT 30
FORWARD 10
FORWARD 10
FORWARD 10
FORWARD 10
RIGHT 30
RIGHT 30
RIGHT 30
FORWARD 10
FORWARD 10
FORWARD 10
FORWARD 10
FORWARD 10
```

```
RIGHT 30       LEFT 30        FORWARD 10   FORWARD 10
FORWARD 10     FORWARD 10     FORWARD 10   FORWARD 10
RIGHT 30       FORWARD 10     RIGHT 30     FORWARD 10
FORWARD 10     FORWARD 10     RIGHT 30     END
```

If you like INSTANT, there is a product on the market that could be described as INSTANT to the *n*th degree, and you don't need Logo to use it. This product is called DELTA DRAWING and it was developed by the Computer Access Corporation and is published by the Spinnaker Software Corporation. The authors of DELTA DRAWING frankly admit to having been inspired by INSTANT. Like INSTANT, DELTA DRAWING allows you to draw with a turtle using single keystroke instructions, all the while recording your moves. It goes beyond INSTANT, however, including many more features that give you control over color, scale, and moving increments. It also makes use of the PC's programmable function keys. Here is a sample of a picture created with Delta Drawing.

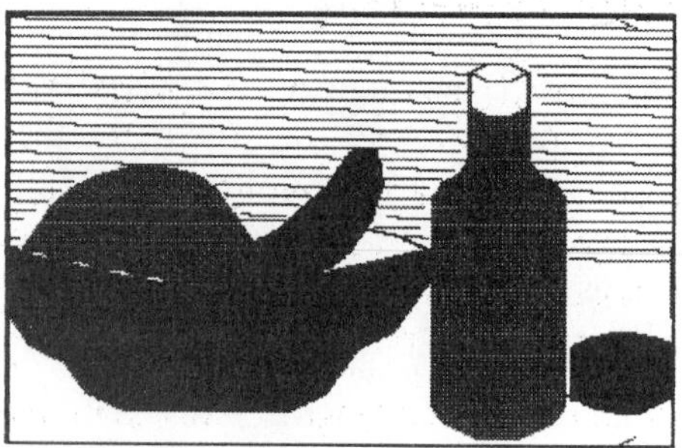

Chapter Summary

In this chapter, we have shown you a number of Logo applications in an attempt to portray the nature of Logo without explaining all the philosophical principles behind it. But now it's time to get more specific. What are the educational benefits to be gained from using Logo (according to the Logo believers)? What evidence is there that Logo delivers the goods?

Papert claims that what he calls *mathophobia,* and defines as fear of learning, is one reason so many people are poor learners, particularly in the area of mathematics. Mathophobia results from being forced into unnatural learning environments. In Papert's opinion, many modern schools are just such environments. He believes that there exists a natural mode of learning, what he calls *Piagetian learning,* or *learning without being taught,* that is far superior to conventional instructional techniques. As evidence of this, he points to the fact that preschool children acquire a great deal of knowledge in the absence of formal instruction. For example, at age two, the average child's vocabulary can be measured in hundreds of word. By the time the child reaches first grade, that vocabulary must be measured in thousands of words. That's somewhere between two and six new words learned per day over those four years.

Logo, then, is an attempt to tap this natural mode of learning. The implication is that, if Papert and others are right, effective teaching with Logo will result in greater student gains. Those students should possess both superior reasoning ability and a healthier attitude about learning. What's the bottom line? Nobody knows for sure. Very few objective studies have been done on the effects of learning with Logo. The few that have been done are inconclusive. There is as yet no clear-cut answer. There may never be. If you become involved with Logo, be prepared for controversy. The observation has been made in many different quarters that educators who come to know about Logo become either stout devotees or severe critics; few are fence sitters.

Chapter Review

Knowledge Exercises

1. Who is known as the father of Logo? What publication gives his philosophy of Logo?

   Answer: The father of Logo is Seymour Papert, who is a professor at MIT, working on the development of Artificial Intelligence. Papert's publication, *Mindstorms: Children, Computers, and Powerful Ideas,* gives the full philosophy behind Logo.

2. From what mainframe language was Logo derived?

   Answer: Logo was derived from a mainframe language called LISP, which stands for LISt Processing. LISP, as well as Logo, has the ability to deal in powerful ways with large lists of words.

3. What famous cognitive theorist greatly influenced Papert's ideas on learning?

   Answer: Jean Piaget.

4. Does Logo reside in the ROM of the IBM PC?

   Answer: No, it must be loaded from a diskette.

5. Of what educational use is a microworld like DYNATRAK? What concepts does it teach?

   Answer: DYNATRAK provides an environment where the learner can explore and experiment with an object that is unaffected by forces that are not obvious (such as friction and gravity). It can be used to provide students with an intuitive understanding of the physics involved.

6. What is a Logo primitive?

   Answer: Primitives are the commands that are built into Logo. It is from these basic commands that procedures are constructed.

7. Define in your own words the following Logo terms: FORWARD, BACK, RIGHT, LEFT, CLEARSCREEN, REPEAT, LOAD, ERALL, POTS.

   Answer: Definitions for these terms can be found in the sections discussing POLYGONS and INSTANT.

8. What is a procedure in Logo?

   Answer: A procedure is the process of making a new word in Logo. The programmer usually starts by using Logo primitives to create procedures that perform very small tasks. Then more powerful procedures can be created using the procedures already defined. The concept of procedures is similar to the BASIC concept of subroutines.

9. What is The Total Turtle Trip Theorem?

   Answer: The Total Turtle Trip Theorem describes the principle that the turtle returns to its original heading when turned in multiples of 360 degrees.

10. How would you first introduce Logo and its turtle graphics to elementary students? Be as specific as possible.

    Answer: You might either have a student act as the turtle, or you, as the teacher, could be the turtle. Then have students in the class tell the turtle what to do. Commands must be limited to those available in Logo. The turtle must carry out the commands and move exactly as told.

Thought Exercises

1. Read *Mindstorms,* by Seymour Papert, and write a reaction paper at least two pages in length, particularly addressing Papert's assertions that effective teaching with Logo will result in greater student understanding. Discuss the importance that you feel Logo should be given in education. How would you plan to use Logo in your classroom?

2. In using the language Logo, what is the role of the teacher? Does it differ from the traditional role? In what way(s)?

3. Do you agree with Papert's premise that teaching with Logo will result in superior reasoning ability and a healthier attitude about learning? Why or why not?

4. Try to think of some potential microworlds that would have instructional value. A good place to start is to examine your own field of endeavor and try to identify activities you would like to have students do, but can't because of time, cost, or other considerations.

Activities

1. After loading Logo into the computer, write procedures to draw three squares, each a different size. Use the REPEAT command in at least one of them.

2. Define a procedure that will draw an equilateral triangle. Use the REPEAT command in the finished product.

3. Define a procedure that accepts variable input to draw squares of different sizes. (Try to define the procedure without looking back in the chapter.)

4. Define a procedure that accepts variable input to draw equilateral triangles of different sizes.

5. Write procedures for drawing at least three other polygons you haven't yet drawn with Logo.

6. If possible, present a Logo lesson to a specific student group. Write a short report describing successes, problems, and student reactions. Bring in a sample of the group's work, if possible.

Projects

1. Read Papert's *Mindstorms,* and books by at least two other writers influential in the field of educational learning and psychology (such as Piaget, Bruner, Skinner, and others). Compare and contrast their ideas, and state your analysis of which principles will be best for a given group of students, and why. Describe how you would plan to implement these ideas in your classroom.

2. If possible, develop at least three activities using the ideas of Papert or any other important writer in the field of learning theory or psychology, and present these to a specific student group. Keep a log detailing student reactions and suggestions for improvement that you would make the next time around.

Program Code for Logo Programs

Dynatrak

Andrea diSessa, a member of the MIT Logo group, developed DYNATRAK. It is a Logo program.

```
TO NODRAW
CLEARTEXT
CLEARSCREEN
TEXTSCREEN
END

TO REPLAY
NODRAW
INSTRUCTIONS2
DTRACK :W
END
```

```
TO REQUEST
OUTPUT READLIST
END

TO REPLAY?
PRINT [DO YOU WANT TO PLAY AGAIN?]
IF (FIRST FIRST REQUEST) = "Y [REPLAY STOP]
TOPLEVEL
END

TO ENDGAME
CLEARTEXT
SETTEXT 6
PRINT []
PRINT []
PRINT [YOU CRASHED]
PRINT SE [YOUR TIME WAS] :T
REPLAY?
END

TO KICK
MAKE "VX :VX + :FORCE * SIN HEADING
MAKE "VY :VY + :FORCE * COS HEADING
END

TO DISTANCE.SQUARED :X :Y
OUTPUT (XCOR - :X) * (XCOR - :X) + (YCOR - :Y) *
(YCOR + :Y)
END

TO CHECK.STOPPED
IF AND :VX = 0 :VY = 0 [MAKE "T :T - 1]
END

TO SETXY :X :Y
SETPOS SENTENCE :X :Y
END

TO RCIRCLE :R
REPEAT 36 [RCP :R]
END

TO INSTRUCTIONS2
PRINT [HOW WIDE DO YOU WANT THE TRACK TO BE?]
PRINT [( 50 IS A GOOD SIZE. )]
MAKE "W FIRST REQUEST
PRINT []
PRINT [HOW STRONG DO YOU WANT THE KICK TO BE?]
PRINT [( 3 IS A GOOD STRENGTH.)]
MAKE "FORCE FIRST REQUEST
END

TO INSTRUCTIONS1
PRINT [THE OBJECT OF THIS GAME IS TO SEE]
PRINT [HOW LONG YOU CAN KEEP THE DYNATURTLE]
```

```
PRINT [MOVING ON A CIRCULAR TRACK WITHOUT]
PRINT [CRASHING!]
PRINT []
PRINT []
PRINT [* * * * * * * CONTROLS * * * * * * *]
PRINT []
PRINT [6 ROTATE CLOCKWISE]
PRINT []
PRINT [4 ROTATE COUNTERCLOCKWISE]
PRINT []
PRINT [2 GIVE THE TURTLE A "KICK" IN THE]
PRINT [ DIRECTION IT IS POINTING]
PRINT []
PRINT [* * * * * * * * * * * * * * * * * * *]
PRINT []
PRINT []
PRINT [( PRESS 'NUMLOCK' TO USE NUMBER PAD )]
PRINT []
END

TO INSTRUCTIONS
INSTRUCTIONS1
INSTRUCTIONS2
END

TO CIRCLE :R
LEFT 90
PENUP FORWARD :R PENDOWN
RIGHT 90
RCIRCLE :R
RIGHT 90
PENUP FORWARD :R PENDOWN
LEFT 90
END

TO START
PENUP
MAKE "VX 0
MAKE "VY 0
END

TO CHECK.DTRACK
CHECK.STOPPED
IF DISTANCE.SQUARED 0 0 < 2500 [ENDGAME STOP]
IF DISTANCE.SQUARED 0 0 > (50 + :W) * (50 + :W)
[ENDGAME]
END

TO DYNAMOVE
SETXY XCOR + :VX YCOR + :VY
END

TO DT.DTRACK :T
DYNAMOVE
CHECK.DTRACK
```

```
COMMAND
DT.DTRACK :T + 1
END

TO DRAW
CLEARSCREEN
END

TO DTRACK :W
DRAWTRACK 50 :W + 50
START
DT.DTRACK 0
TO SETUP
NODRAW
INSTRUCTIONS
END

TO SETUP
TEXTSCREEN
CLEARTEXT
INSTRUCTIONS
END

TO DYNATURTLE
SETUP
DTRACK :W :A
END

TO NOWRAP
FENCE
END


TO DRAWTRACK :R1 :R2
DRAW FULLSCREEN
HIDETURTLE
CIRCLE :R1
CIRCLE :R2
LEFT 90
PENUP FORWARD (:R2 + :R1) / 2
RIGHT 90
SHOWTURTLE
END


TO RCP :R
RIGHT 5
FORWARD 3.14159 * :R / 18
RIGHT 5
END


TO READKEY
IF RC? [OUTPUT READCHARACTER]
OUTPUT "
END
```

```
TO COMMAND
MAKE "COM READKEY
IF :COM = "  [STOP]
IF :COM = "6 [RIGHT 30 STOP]
IF :COM = "4 [LEFT 30 STOP]
IF :COM = "8 [KICK STOP]
END

TO RC?
OUTPUT KEYP .
END

TO READCHARACTER
OUTPUT READCHAR
END

TO TOPLEVEL
THROW "TOPLEVEL
END

MAKE "FORCE 10
MAKE "VY 0
MAKE "VX 10
MAKE "W 50
MAKE "COM "6
MAKE "STARTUP [DYNATURTLE]
```

Synonyms

```
TO DISPLAY :POS
PRINT []
PRINT ITEM :POS :SYN1
PRINT ITEM :POS :SYN2
PRINT ITEM :POS :SYN3
END

TO RESTART
PRINT []
PRINT []
SYNONYMS
END

TO SYNONYMS
WORDLISTS
MAKE "LEN COUNT :SYN1
PRINT [WORD?]
MAKE "WORD READWORD
MAKE "POS FIND :WORD 1 :SYN1 :LEN
IF :POS = 0 [MAKE "POS FIND :WORD 1 :SYN2 :LEN]
IF :POS = 0 [MAKE "POS FIND :WORD 1 :SYN3 :LEN]
IF :POS = 0 [PRINT [NOT IN THIS DICTIONARY]
RESTART]
DISPLAY :POS
RESTART
END
```

```
TO WORDLISTS
MAKE "SYN1 [HAPPY SAD SOFT HARD FAT SKINNY ZZZ]
MAKE "SYN2 [CONTENT UNHAPPY PLIANT TOUGH ROTUND
SLENDER ZZZ]
MAKE "SYN3 [JOYOUS DOWN MALEABLE DIFFICULT
CORPULENT SLIM ZZZ]
END

TO FIND :WORD :POS :WHICH :LEN
IF :WORD = FIRST :WHICH [OUTPUT :POS]
IF :POS < :LEN [MAKE "POS FIND :WORD :POS + 1
BUTFIRST :WHICH :LEN]
IF :POS = :LEN [OUTPUT "0] [OUTPUT :POS]
END

MAKE ":POS 1
MAKE "SYN3 [JOYOUS DOWN MALEABLE DIFFICULT
CORPULENT SLIM ZZZ]
MAKE "SYN2 [CONTENT UNHAPPY PLIANT TOUGH ROTUND
SLENDER ZZZ]
MAKE "SYN1 [HAPPY SAD SOFT HARD FAT SKINNY ZZZ]
MAKE "LEN 7
MAKE "POS 1
MAKE "WORD "JOYOUS
```

Instant *by Harold Abelson*

```
TO UNDO
IF :HISTORY = [] STOP
MAKE "HISTORY BUTLAST :HISTORY
DRAW
RUN.ALL :HISTORY
END

TO UNDOALL
DRAW
MAKE "HISTORY[]
END

TO LEARN
PRINT [WHAT DO YOU WANT TO CALL THIS PICTURE ?]
MAKE "NAME (FIRST REQUEST)
DEFINE :NAME (FPUT [] :HISTORY)
UNDOALL
END

TO RUN.AND.RECORD :ACTION
RUN :ACTION
MAKE "HISTORY (LPUT :ACTION :HISTORY)
END

TO ASK
PRINT [WHAT PICTURE DO YOU WANT TO SHOW ?]
RUN.AND.RECORD REQUEST
END
```

```
TO RUN.ALL :COMMANDS
IF :COMMANDS = [] STOP
RUN FIRST :COMMANDS
RUN.ALL (BUTFIRST :COMMANDS)
END

TO REQUEST
OUTPUT READLIST
END

TO HELP
TEXTSCREEN
CLEARTEXT
SETCURSOR [0 0]
PRINT [F: MOVES TURTLE FORWARD]
PRINT [R: TURNS IT RIGHT]
PRINT [L: TURNS IT LEFT]
PRINT [D: DRAW ( CLEARS THE SCREEN )]
PRINT [Q: EXIT TO DOS]
PRINT [N: NAMES THE PICTURE]
PRINT [P: SHOWS A PICTURE. ASKS FOR ITS NAME.]
PRINT [?: GIVES HELP]
PRINT [] PRINT []
PRINT [PRESS ANY KEY TO CONTINUE.]
PRINT READKEY
SETCURSOR [0 20]
FD 1 BK 1
PD
END

TO INSTANT.COMMAND
COMMAND READKEY
INSTANT.COMMAND
END

TO DRAW
CLEARSCREEN
END

TO SETUP
MAKE "HISTORY []
DRAW
INSTANT.COMMAND
END

TO INSTANT
HELP
SETUP
END

TO READKEY
IF RC? OUTPUT READCHARACTER
OUTPUT "
END
```

```
TO COMMAND :COM
IF :COM = "F [RUN.AND.RECORD [FORWARD 10] STOP]
IF :COM = "R [RUN.AND.RECORD [RIGHT 30] STOP]
IF :COM = "L [RUN.AND.RECORD [LEFT 30] STOP]
IF :COM = "D [UNDOALL STOP]
IF :COM = "Q [.DOS]
IF :COM = "N [LEARN STOP]
IF :COM = "P [ASK STOP]
IF :COM = "? [HELP STOP]
END

TO RC?
OUTPUT KEYP
END

TO READCHARACTER
OUTPUT READCHAR
END

MAKE "HISTORY [[SQ]]
MAKE "NAME "SQ
```

Bibliography

Abelson, Harold. *Apple Logo.* New York: Byte Books, 1982. A comprehensive text including graphics and list processing.

Abelson, Harold. "A Beginner's Guide to Logo." *BYTE* (August 1982): 88–112. This early classic article contains a comprehensive coverage of the language.

Abelson, Harold, and Andrea diSessa. *Turtle Geometry.* Cambridge, Mass.: MIT Press, 1981. An advanced-level book which utilizes Logo to teach advanced math concepts.

Babbie, Earl. *Apple Logo for Teachers.* Belmont, Calif.: Wadsworth Publishing, 1984. A thorough text for teachers, includes teaching objectives, techniques, and materials.

Bamberger, Jeanne. "Logo Music." *BYTE* (August 1982). An early article on the music capabilities of Logo.

Barnes, B. J., and Shirley Hill. "Should Young Children Work with Microcomputers—Logo before Logo?" *The Computing Teacher* (May 1983). Discusses appropriate times to begin computer activities with reference to Piagetian stages.

Bearden, Donna. *1, 2, 3 My Computer and Me: A Logo Fun Book for Kids.* Reston, Va.: Reston Publishing, 1983. An elementary-level workbook.

Bearden, Donna, and J. Muller. *The Turtle Sourcebook.* Reston, Va.: Reston Publishing, 1983. This guide for teachers includes many Logo activities.

Carter, Ricky. "The Complete Guide to Logo." *Classroom Computer News* (April 1983). The article outlines the various Logo packages.

Harvey, Brian. *Computer Science, Logo Style.* Cambridge, Mass: MIT Press, 1985. This college-level text teaches programming concepts using Logo including extensive coverage of list processing.

Lough, Tom, and Steve Tipps. "Is There Logo after Turtle Graphics?" *Classroom Computer News* (April 1983). Examples of word activities are given including creating words and writing stories.

Maddux, Cleborne D. *Logo in the Schools.* New York: Haworth Press, 1985. A series of articles from the journal *Computers in the Schools* contains current research findings on incorporation of Logo in the curriculum.

Minnesota Education Computing Consortium. *Apple Logo in the Classroom.* St. Paul, Minn.: Minnesota Education Computing Consortium, 1983. A comprehensive resource with student activities and teacher notes for each Logo concept.

Moore, Margaret. *Logo Discoveries.* Palo Alto, Calif.: Creative Publications, 1984. A handy book which can be used as a teacher's guide or individual worksheet for students; however, it is limited to Turtle Graphics.

Papert, Seymour. "Computer as Mudpie." *Classroom Computer Learning* (January 1984): 37–40. Logo is discussed as an important problem-solving language to foster learning.

Papert, Seymour. *Mindstorms: Children, Computers, and Powerful Ideas.* New York: Basic Books, 1980. The classic book by the author of Logo contains his discovery philosophy and practical examples.

Sharp, Pamela. *Turtlesteps,* Bowie, Md.: Brady Communications, 1984. A tutorial text with particular emphasis on Turtle Graphics.

Tobias, Joyce. *Beyond Mindstorms: Teaching with IBM Logo.* New York: Holt, Rinehart & Winston, 1985. Logo programming is presented with an emphasis on problem solving.

Upitis, Rena. "Logo and the Primary-Junior Pupil: One Student's First Encounter." *The Computing Teacher* (November 1982): 28–31. The article describes fifth grade students' interaction with Logo.

Watt, Daniel. *Learning with Logo.* New York: McGraw-Hill, 1983. This comprehensive beginning text places emphasis on Turtle Graphics and includes interesting illustrations of powerful ideas.

PART

3

REAL SHOP TALK

Now it's time to take a look at what has been the bread-and-butter of instructional computing to date. Once upon a time, this was all called *CAI*, or *Computer Assisted Instruction*. Of late, the term *CAL*, for *Computer Assisted Learning*, has come into vogue. We think that the territory has become too big to be encompassed by those terms. We propose that it needs more accurate definition.

In the next few chapters we'll take a look at some pretty traditional CAI, what we call *Computer Directed Instruction*. Then we'll look at programs that place the emphasis on the teacher, not the student: *Computer Enhanced Instruction*. Finally, we'll examine what is meant by *Computer Managed Instruction* and what potential it holds for education.

CHAPTER

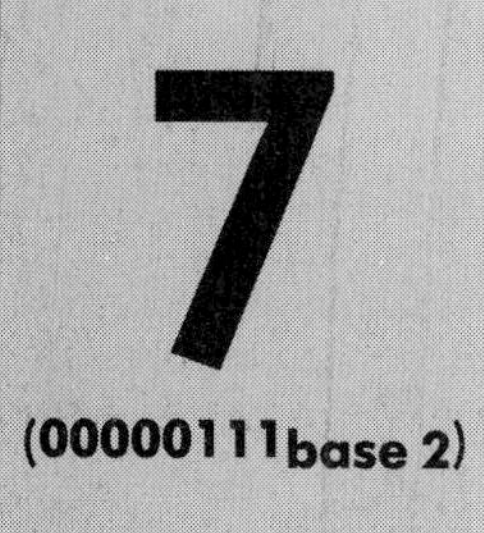

COMPUTER DIRECTED INSTRUCTION
Coming of Age

Getting Started

In this chapter we are concerned with the role computers can play in the delivery of instruction. For that role to be significant, there must be computer programs that effectively deliver instruction in a cost-efficient and a time-efficient manner. These programs must have qualities that go beyond the qualities of traditional instructional materials. Effective use of such programs will require a change in the traditional teaching role. The new role for the computer-savvy teacher includes selecting and using programs that deliver instruction so that the amount and quality of time that the teacher can spend with individual students increase. To implement this responsibility, teachers must be familiar with the different types of programs for Computer Directed Instruction (CDI). They must be capable of identifying advantages or disadvantages of CDI programs and must be able to identify the levels of learning they offer.

Objectives for Teachers

To successfully complete this chapter, you should be able to

1. Define Computer Directed Instruction (CDI).
2. Describe educational goals that can be accomplished using CDI programs.
3. Describe desirable features of CDI programs.
4. Describe undesirable features of CDI programs.
5. Classify CDI programs according to the levels of learning offered.
6. Prepare computerized lessons using a simple authoring tool.

What Is Computer Directed Instruction?

Let's begin the discussion in this chapter with a definition.

Computer Directed Instruction (CDI). The definition is implied by its name—the computer directs instruction. It may involve a whole lesson, a set of lessons, or part of a lesson. The assumption is that learners, by pressing the right keys, are able to move through lessons without other human intervention. This definition does not assume anything about the learner or the quality of the program. The definition simply states that once a CDI program has been installed in the memory of a computer, sufficient conditions for completing the lesson involve only the computer and the learner.

CDI programs can be used to address many different learning modes, including the following:

Developing concepts and skills.
Practicing concepts and skills.
Applying concepts and skills.
Solving problems.
Simulating experiences.

A CDI program may deliver a short practice lesson requiring answers in the form of fill-in-the-blank, multiple choice, and so on. On the other hand, the program may deliver a lesson that is of longer duration and requires the learner to apply both concepts and skills to solve problems. When choosing a CDI program for use in the classroom, we must perform two kinds of evaluation. First, we must evaluate the program in terms of the types of educational goals it successfully addresses and decide if these goals accommodate our instructional plan. Second, we must decide whether the program is technically sound. For example, is the program well formatted? Is the reading level appropriate? Is the program user-friendly? Will the program adequately handle mistakes the user might make?

In this chapter we are concerned with the first kind of evaluation—determining what and how instructional goals are achieved through the use of CDI programs. To evaluate systematically we need a simple instructional framework. The framework should allow us to qualitatively classify CDI programs; for example, the program develops concepts and provides for the practice of skills. After we determine the instructional goals, we examine attributes of the program to determine how computer capability is being used. The bottom line rests in the answer to this question: What advantages related to instruction does the computer program provide that could not be more inexpensively achieved with traditional instructional materials?

Building an Instructional Framework

Schools have the responsibility to transmit knowledge and build abilities so that as students grow into adults they become competent to purposefully manage the events of their lives. This important responsibility implies that schools must help students develop concepts that can be readily integrated and applied to solving problems. Educators must do much more than teach rote skills. As computers take over more and more of the drudgery of data manipulation, it will become more important for students to learn to apply concepts. Of course, this doesn't happen without a plan. We teachers need to be able to analyze learning experiences to determine what is taught and how it is taught. As we review computer programs aimed at instruction, we should relate programs to desirable learning objectives, then classify programs in terms of student behaviors that are stressed: concept development, skill development, or concept application.

Here we present a framework for classifying programs in terms of which student behaviors are emphasized. Make sure you understand the framework before moving on. We will use it throughout the chapter; later we refer to it as the Framework table.

The Framework

To become educated we must learn concepts and skills. The young child who learns to recognize any dog whatsoever and discriminate it from a cow or any other animal has learned the concept dog. When the child learns to say, write, and read the word *dog,* the child is learning related skills.

When concept classes are mentally related and organized (for instance, barnyard animals), the child has integrated concepts. A cow is a barnyard animal, a pig is a barnyard animal, a chicken is a barnyard animal . . . . The child must think two things: What kind of animal is it and does it have anything to do with farming or barnyards? As we acquire and integrate concepts and skills, we build the foundations for solving problems encountered either in or out of school. For example:

> I don't usually live on a farm; more often I'm found in the jungle or zoo. I like to eat bananas. I can climb very high and swing from tree to tree. What kind of animal might I be?

This framework, shown graphically in the following table, categorizes the types of learning experiences children should have in school. It can be used to review and classify classroom activities. Doing so can help maintain balance in the quality of activities that are presented to students.

When we classify an activity as a CD activity, then we are saying that the activity is one that will help children develop new concepts; that is, understanding is involved. Such a classification would be indicated by shading the CD cell in the table. If we say that an activity is of the SD type, then we mean that a skill is being developed; that is, memorized behavior is the focus. From here you can surmise the rest. Of course, an activity may be classified in terms of more than one type. Indeed, when a learning activity requires students to develop, reinforce, and apply concepts/skills to solve unfamiliar problems, the activity could possibly be classified in terms of all eight types. The resulting activity is probably a problem-solving activity.

FRAMEWORK	Develop	Reinforce	Apply to Solve Problem
Skill	SD	SR	SA
Concept	CD	CR	CA

It is not important to be picky about the application of the table. What is important is that you develop a broad view of instruction. Only then will you be able to review and select appropriate computer experiences for learning.

Tutorials

Students sometimes need special help in learning particular skills or concepts. The tutorials provided here should give you an idea of the kinds of instruction possible with CDI.

Rounding Numbers One
A Program for Learning Skills

The first program that we will discuss requires users to round numbers to the nearest ten. This program can be found on the Program Learning Diskette for *The Micro Goes to School IBM Version* (the Program Disk for short) under the filename ROUND1. First the program asks for the learner's name and the date. Then the program gives the learner 10 exercises to complete, one at a time. The numbers in the exercises are randomly generated by the computer. After each exercise the learner is told whether or not the response is correct. If correct, positive reinforcement is provided. If incorrect, the learner is given another opportunity to complete the exercise. When 10 exercises are completed, the learner is given a progress report and is asked whether or not a printed copy of the report is desired. At this point the learner can exit the program or get another set of exercises to complete.

You should run this program a couple of times to see how it accomplishes each of these steps. Remember, the filename of the program is ROUND1. Now let's list the characteristics of this program.

1. The program certainly meets the conditions of being a CDI program. After the program is installed in memory, it is possible for a learner to go through the program without outside help.
2. Although some instruction is provided, the program is primarily a drill program.
3. The program tells the user whether responses are correct and allows incorrect answers to be corrected. If the learner gets the exercise wrong a second time, the program explains the exercise, provides the correct answer, and gives the learner a new exercise.
4. The program gives positive reinforcement for correct responses and gives an explanation of how the exercise should be done.
5. The program gives a progress report and allows the learner to make a printed copy of the report.

Now let's list characteristics that the program does not have.

1. The program does not give instruction on the concept or on how to use the program. To use this program effectively, prior learning is necessary.
2. The program does not require the learner to apply concepts or solve problems in any significant sense.
3. Feedback that is provided for incorrect responses does not address the specific errors the learner makes; the learner is simply given information on how to do the problem correctly.
4. The program does not provide the teacher with a way to change the types of exercises that are presented without actually rewriting part of the program.
5. Even though the program provides a progress report, the information provided on the report is limited. All that is given is the student's name, the date, and the percentage correct. There is no record of the exercises that the student missed, so there is no way that a teacher might analyze the errors that the student is making.
6. The program uses neither graphics nor sound to instruct or motivate.

FRAMEWORK	Develop	Reinforce	Apply to Solve Problem
Skill	SD	SR	SA
Concept	CD	CR	CA

Now let's assume that this program meets all technical requirements: among other things, it is formatted properly and the reading level is okay. Could we say the program was good? This question is not appropriate. What we really should ask is this: Does the program have instructional value and if so, under what circumstances?

The program can be classified as both a skill development (SD) and skill reinforcement (SR) activity. The conclusion is that it will be effective only in learning situations in which drill is the primary focus.

Points to Consider

Once the teacher has provided instruction on rounding numbers to the nearest ten, then this program could efficiently give learners practice experiences. It would provide the teachers with a printed progress report indicating the percentage correct out of 10. The program is limited because the teacher is unable to adjust exercises to individual learners and the progress report that is furnished does not indicate the types of exercises that the student is missing. Before purchasing a program such as this, an important question must be answered: How is using this program more effective than using pencil and paper activities? Unless the program is improved, there is little justification for using it.

Rounding Numbers Two
A Program for Concept Development

How about another program for rounding numbers? This program is also on the Program Disk under the filename ROUND2. It represents a substantial improvement over ROUNDING NUMBERS ONE. First of all, the program offers instruction that embodies concept development as opposed to listing mechanical steps. The program has another important feature that aids learning: it does not let the learner enter errors. No matter how hard the learner may try to make errors, the program just sits and patiently waits for correct responses. The program provides five random exercises, each requiring two preliminary responses that help the learner find the final answer. This program does not provide a progress report since there is nothing to report. This is a hand-holding program. The purpose is to stay right with the learner and guide him or her successfully through given exercises.

A Point to Consider

This type of program can be very valuable if not used too often. When programs such as this are used over and over, students become bored and build negative attitudes toward computer learning.

Classifying the lesson presented by ROUND2 is left as an exercise. (See Thought Exercise 2 in the "Chapter Review" section.)

Rounding Numbers Three
A Program with Teacher Information

Just one more time and then we'll look at programs for other topics! Run this program (found under filename ROUND3). This program has features that neither ROUND1 nor ROUND2 has. First, the program offers instruction in two different ways.

1. From the main menu, the learner can choose to get brief but substantial instructions on how to round numbers to ten. The learner doesn't have to suffer through these instructions each time the program is run, but can elect to go straight to the lesson. Furthermore, the sample exercise given in the instructional routine changes each time the program is run. After all, who wants to see the same exercise demonstrated each time instructions are needed?

2. Instructions are also given as the learner completes each exercise in the practice routine. Each exercise requires two preliminary responses that aid the learner in finding the final answer. Unlike ROUND2, this program will allow the user to enter a final response that is incorrect. The program keeps track of right and wrong answers for a progress report. After 5 exercises are completed, the learner can press [Ctrl]-[P] to get a progress report related to the completed exercises. As many as 25 exercises can be completed before the program automatically evaluates user progress. The user can exit anytime to the program menu by pressing the [Esc] key. The program keeps track of the exercises done incorrectly and, upon request, will furnish a printed list of wrong answers and corresponding exercises. This kind of information can be very helpful to a teacher who must provide efficient reteaching.

Did you notice that this program makes no use of the computer's graphics and sound capabilities?

Points to Consider

Although ROUNDING NUMBERS TWO and THREE are both better programs than ROUNDING NUMBERS ONE, there are still other desirable features that could be added. A good feature to have would be one in which the computer checks for commonly occurring errors and tailors exercises on the basis of what errors a learner is making. Also, it would be convenient for the teacher to be able to change or tailor the types of exercises that learners are given—without having to rewrite part of the program. In all three programs, the exercises are randomly generated according to the program specifications. Take a moment to consider the advantages and disadvantages of this technique before moving on to the next section.

Authoring Systems

Many times it is helpful if an instructional program provides a method for entering lessons designed by the instructor. The method should be easy to learn and easy to use. Specifically, it should not require programming skills. The next program that we discuss has this feature. The program can be classified as indicated in the following table:

FRAMEWORK	Develop	Reinforce	Apply to Solve Problem
Skill	SD	SR	SA
Concept	CD	CR	CA

Mentor
An Authoring System

Here is a program that presents the learner with a stimulus for which the learner is to enter correct responses.

The learner's response is checked character by character as it is entered. The program will not accept incorrect characters, so the learner can experiment to arrive at the correct answer.

The teacher using the program can develop custom lessons and tailor the program to present them. In developing a custom lesson, the teacher must prepare the following:

1. Prepare a set of directions that will appear on the screen for the student. Use up to ten lines with no more than 38 characters in each line. These directions should be planned in advance and then entered using the program ENTER. (See Activity 1 at the end of the chapter for an exercise that will help you learn to use this program.)

Here is an example of how to plan directions:

INVENTION QUIZ
I am thinking of some famous
scientists or inventors.
I will give you some clues.
Then you are to guess the person
I am thinking of if you can!

2. For each exercise, you must design a stimulus. The stimulus can be one word or can occupy up to two lines with 38 characters in each line.

3. For each exercise, you must give a hint or some statement that clarifies the stimulus. You can use up to two lines with 38 characters in each.

4. For each exercise, you can specify up to four responses that you will accept.

Here is a possible exercise set:

```
Stimulus: Who invented the phonograph?
Hint/Information: He was hard of hearing and had
                  a winter home in Florida.
Acceptable Responses: Thomas Edison, Edison,
                      edison, ThomasEdison.
```

The most likely response should be entered first, exactly as you would want it to look on the screen. The rest of the responses should be entered without spaces. When the program accepts student answers, it removes spaces in case the student has accidentally entered undesirable spaces. The only reason you provide the first acceptable response with appropriate spaces is because this response will appear on the screen when reinforcement is provided.

You must design a minimum of 10 exercise sets. There is no maximum number; however, after the last exercise is entered you must enter the word QUIT. This last statement signals the computer that all exercises have been entered.

Run the program on the diskette, using the filename MENTOR. Choose the lesson INVENT from the MENTOR menu. This lesson will quiz you on famous inventors.

With a little imagination, a teacher can do a great deal with this program. Here are some specific ideas.

1. Scramble the letters of each word in a spelling lesson, then give a brief definition. Have students enter the unscrambled word.
2. Provide sets of pictures made from keyboard characters, then give the number name for the set. Have students enter the corresponding numeral.
3. Provide a word in Spanish, tell what the word means. Have students provide the English equivalent.
4. Give an important historical event, provide related facts. Have students give a name for a related historical figure.

For more information on the MENTOR program, you should read the documentation that comes with the Program Disk. (See Activity 1 in the Chapter Review for more details.)

Points to Consider

MENTOR's ability to accept more than one correct answer provides flexibility. Obviously, if a history lesson involves names that are unfamiliar and hard to spell, you might not want to penalize a student who gave the correct answer but failed to spell it correctly. Allowing four acceptable responses provides teacher alternatives. When you want a specific answer and are not willing to accept variation, simply enter the same response four times.

You can enter any number of exercises, depending upon the available memory in the equipment you are using. However, the program will only present 10 during a lesson. We don't want students becoming restless while doing a computer activity. Notice, however, that the student can elect to do another 10 if desired. With this scheme it is helpful if the teacher enters a large number of exercise sets, so that the program can be run a number of times without becoming stale.

This program must be classified according to the activity that is designed by the teacher. A creative teacher could even design an activity that required some problem solving. Generally, the program would be used to stress concept and skill development.

Problem Solving

The programs we have discussed so far have not been specifically designed to foster thinking abilities or problem-solving strategies. We have mainly been concerned with concept or skill development. Both concept and skill development are extremely important, but neither is ultimately important if one does not learn to use these abilities in problem-solving modes to manage life events. In education it is important to require learners to find similarities and differences, see relationships, and draw conclusions. In this section we will present two programs that have more or less the same content goal. However, each achieves the goal in different ways. The first program lacks imagination and routinely goes about achieving a content objective; the second requires learners to do some thinking.

Guess the Secret Number One
A Program for Thinking

In GUESS THE SECRET NUMBER ONE (found under filename GUESS1), the computer gives the learner a random number and requests that a series of operations be performed in a certain order, starting with the random number. The learner is to find and enter the result.

Here is a sample run.

```
If you take . . . 9
```
(9 is chosen randomly.)
```
Multiply by . . . 2
```
(2 is chosen randomly.)
```
Add the results to 4 and then
```
(4 is chosen randomly.)

```
Subtract . . . 3
```
(3 is chosen randomly.)
```
What number do you end with?
```

Run GUESS1 a few times. Get a feel for how the program carries out its mission. As you can see, this program involves only direct computation. If the learner uses the indicated operations in the indicated order and computes accurately, then the correct answer is inevitable. Very little thinking is involved, just the orderly performance of rote skills. Now let's add a little imagination to the program and get a new program that is instructionally more powerful and more fun to boot. (Pardon the pun.)

Guess the Secret Number Two
A Program for Deeper Thinking

In GUESS THE SECRET NUMBER TWO, learners are given a riddle. The computer chooses a secret number and gives the learner clues that must be used to find the number.

Here is a sample run:

```
I have a secret number and if you
```
(The computer has chosen a random number.)
```
Multiply by . . . 3
```
(The 3 is chosen randomly.)
```
Divide the results by . . . 4 and then
```
(The 4 is chosen randomly from all possible divisors.)
```
Add . . . 9
```
(The 9 is a random number.)
```
You will get 17.

What is the secret number?
```

Run GUESS2 a few times. To solve this riddle, learners must be able to identify opposite operations (addition and subtraction are opposites). They need to recognize that computational steps must be performed in the reverse order. For example, if multiplication is the first operation performed, then its opposite, division, will be the last operation performed. Though not fancy, the program requires learners to make decisions. Thus, this program could be classified as one that fosters problem-solving strategies, especially for children who have not learned algebra concepts. In fact, this program is a useful tool for getting students ready to learn rules for solving number sentences. Can you explain why? It is easy to see that this program requires more decision making than GUESS1 and involves a higher level of thinking.

Points to Consider

If you drew flowcharts for each of these programs, they would be very similar. The difference in the programs is simply the question asked of the user: What number do you end up with? or What number did I start with? This subtle difference significantly changes the quality of thinking that students must achieve. GUESS2 is classified as indicated in the following table:

FRAMEWORK	Develop	Reinforce	Apply to Solve Problem
Skill	SD	SR	SA
Concept	CD	CR	CA

It is left as an exercise for the reader to classify GUESS1.

Simulation

As we have seen, Computer Directed Instruction Programs (CDI) can help achieve a number of instructional goals. With the appropriate characteristics, CDI programs can aid in the development of concepts and related skills and can foster the growth of problem-solving abilities. Another very powerful teaching tool that CDI programs can provide is simulation. A computer simulation is a program that allows the user to have an artificial experience that resembles a real experience. Computer simulations are used whenever it is not feasible to have the real experience. The real experience may be impossible to create, too dangerous, too expensive, technically difficult to arrange, or too hard to manage. For example—at least at the time of writing this book—it would be hard to let students experience walking on the moon. However, it would be possible to use a computer program to provide some type of simulation in the classroom. It would not be possible for students to return in time and travel across the Atlantic with the Pilgrims in order to appreciate the experiences of that voyage. However, it is possible to create a computer program that, to some degree, would allow learners to simulate that experience.

Shopping Mall
A Program for Simulation

In this section we will present a simulation involving a skill that all citizens should acquire: the ability to make change for a dollar. It would be possible to provide this experience in the classroom without a computer, but it wouldn't be as effective or as efficient. It is effective because of the variety of experiences that the computer can deliver and monitor. It is efficient because of the limitless repetitions the computer can provide. Run the program (filename SHOPMALL) several times.

Let's review some of the characteristics of the program. It randomly chooses an item that might be found at a convenience store and establishes the price. The learner is told that a customer is going to pay for the item with a certain number of dollars. The learner is to make change, starting with the smallest realistic coin. The program puts restrictions on the number of coins of a given type the user can use to make change. When pennies, nickels, dimes, and quarters are all available, the program will permit the learner to use up to 4 pennies, 2 nickels, 2 dimes, and 3 quarters. The program does not allow for the possibility of half-dollars. The learner is prompted by a how-many question for each coin starting with pennies. For example: How many pennies will you use? Often the most efficient way to make change involves *not* using a particular coin. For example, take the problem of making change from a dollar when an item costs $0.62. The most efficient way would be to give 3 pennies, 0 nickels, 1 dime, and 1 quarter. In this case, the learner would have to enter a 0 for the number of nickels. At the start of the program, users are given an example exercise and are warned that 0s may have to be entered. The user is also told what coins are available for making change. For example, if the cash register contains no dimes, the user will be informed that change must be made using pennies, nickels, and quarters.

If the learner has difficulty with two consecutive exercises, the computer will make a printed copy of the incorrect exercises and exit the user from the program, advising him or her to seek help. We leave it as an exercise for the reader to list other important features of this program.

Points to Consider

A CDI program is most useful when it is used in conjunction with other classroom activities, especially a program like SHOPPING MALL. This program could be followed by a classroom activity where the teacher restricts the type of coins that can be used to give change for a particular item. Students could use play money to actually make the required change with the indicated coins (for example, using only pennies and dimes to make change from $4.00 for a book that costs $3.37).

This program is classified as indicated in the following table:

FRAMEWORK	Develop	Reinforce	Apply to Solve Problem
Skill	SD	SR	SA
Concept	CD	CR	CA

Chapter Summary

In this chapter we have described computer programs for Computer Directed Instruction (CDI). We have illustrated characteristics these programs may have and explained why it is important that teachers examine these characteristics to see how well a program meets particular instructional needs. At the risk of being redundant, we list important attributes to look for when choosing instructional software.

1. A CDI program can provide instruction. The instruction may involve developing a concept in which understanding is stressed, or it may involve developing a skill and emphasize rote procedures. In general, a program that develops understanding is more valuable than one that stresses memorization.
2. A CDI program can provide reinforcement. This reinforcement may involve exercises that require the learner to apply important concepts, or the practice may involve performing memorized routines. Generally a program is more valuable when it requires the learner to apply concepts.
3. A CDI program can deliver exercises that are randomly chosen within specified limits. This is convenient because of the large number of different exercises that can be generated. Often these programs are limited because they repetitiously drum away at the same type of boring exercise.
4. A CDI program can be designed so that teachers can input their own lesson, including questions and answers. This is a valuable feature of a program since it allows the teacher to use the program in a wide variety of circumstances with learners having different needs. These programs are sometimes limited because only a small number of exercises can be conveniently entered. To avoid staleness, a teacher must enter different lessons often.

5. A CDI program can provide remediation. A program can provide exercises for learners, analyzing wrong answers that are entered. Common errors can be identified and, based on the error, appropriate instruction can be provided. These programs must be designed by educators who have expert knowledge in diagnosis and remediation with respect to a particular subject. Programs having this feature usually require substantial computer memory, since a great deal of program branching is required if errors are to be carefully remediated.

6. A CDI program can provide problem-solving opportunities. Problem solving is a very complex topic involving every field of study. Whether the subject under study is mathematics, history, English, or science, it is important that learners acquire abilities for finding similarities and differences, seeing relationships, drawing conclusions, and synthesizing information, events, or experiences. Since time in the ordinary classroom is limited and since the average teacher's time is divided among many students, programs offering problem-solving experiences would be of high value.

7. A CDI program can provide simulations. Using computer simulations allows teachers to provide educational experiences that might otherwise be impractical or impossible. A computer program can simulate anything from navigating a simple maze to exploring the moon. The range is broad enough to provide meaningful simulations to virtually any student population, from learning disabled to gifted. Through the use of computer simulations, the secrets of the universe could dramatically unfold in the classroom. The big question is this: Will the teacher look for and insist upon this kind of program, not settling for programs that present repackaged pencil-and-paper drill?

8. A CDI program can keep track of each student's performance in a computerized lesson. Scores, missed exercises, and wrong answers can be stored or printed. Teachers can plan further instructional experiences for learners by using these records.

Well, we could go on, but we think you have the gist of it. Besides, there is other important territory to cover! The main point is this: A good CDI program should have many of these characteristics. Furthermore, educational objectives should be determined, and then CDI programs should be purchased that best fit the objectives; not the other way around. Last, but most important, educators should insist upon programs that are substantial and that lead to the acquisition of important goals. If a goal can be achieved efficiently and inexpensively without a computer, then why use one?

To date, most of the software that has been developed expressly for education has been CDI programs. In many instances, the quality has been poor. Not only has quality suffered, but the learning objectives that have been chosen, more often than not, have emphasized drill at the exclusion of concept development, problem solving, and simulation. Many of the programs that are currently on the market lack many of the features we have discussed. Moreover, to date, educators have not realized the potential of using computer programs to produce instructional tools other than CDI programs. In the next chapter, we will discuss that potential.

Chapter Review

Knowledge Exercises

1. What three categories will be substituted for the term *Computer Assisted Instruction (CAI)?*

   Answer: Computer Directed Instruction (CDI), Computer Enhanced Instruction (CEI), and Computer Managed Instruction (CMI).

2. Define Computer Directed Instruction (CDI).

   Answer: The computer directs instruction. This may include the entire lesson, a part of a lesson, or a set of lessons. The CDI program installed in memory, the computer, and the learner are sufficient conditions for completing the lesson.

3. What are some goals that CDI programs may be used to accomplish?

   Answer: Some goals are developing, practicing, or applying concepts and skills; solving problems; and simulating experiences.

4. How should you classify the program ROUNDING NUMBERS ONE, whose filename is ROUND1?

   Answer: It develops and reinforces skills.

5. How does ROUND2 differ from ROUND1?

   Answer: ROUND2 offers instruction that embodies concept development and it does not allow the learner to enter errors. It does not provide a progress report, since there is essentially nothing to report.

6. What four features does ROUND3 have that neither ROUND1 nor ROUND2 have?

   Answer:
   - The learner can make a choice as to whether to receive instructions on rounding.
   - The sample exercise presented in the instructional routine changes each time the program is run.
   - After 5 exercises, the learner can hit the Esc key to exit; otherwise, as many as 25 exercises can be completed.
   - The program keeps track of the exercises done incorrectly and will furnish a printed list of the exercises and the wrong answers.

7. Name at least two other desirable features that are not demonstrated in ROUND1, ROUND2, or ROUND3.

Answer:
- The computer checks for commonly recurring errors and tailors exercises on the basis of those errors.
- The teacher can change or tailor the types of exercises without having knowledge of programming.

8. What kinds of thinking skills are used in problem solving?

   Answer: Problem solving requires learners to find similarities and differences, see relationships, and draw conclusions.

9. What are the differences between the programs run by GUESS1 and GUESS2?

   Answer: In GUESS1, the student is asked for the result of a carefully enumerated series of instructions. The thinking is very straightforward and little problem solving is required. In GUESS2, the student must work backwards to find the number that the computer started with, which involves quite a bit of problem solving.

10. What is a computer simulation? When is it used?

    Answer: A computer simulation is a program that allows the learner to have an artificial experience that resembles a real experience. It is used whenever it is not feasible to have the real experience, whether because it is too expensive, too dangerous, or too time-consuming.

Thought Exercises

1. Would you use the program run by ROUND1 with your students? Under what conditions? Write a brief paragraph to support your answer.
2. How would you classify the program run by ROUND2? Use the Framework table.
3. If you could choose only one of the rounding programs presented in this chapter for use with your students, which would you choose? Why?
4. Other than those suggested in the chapter, what are some ideas that you could use with the program MENTOR to develop programs suitable to use with your students?
5. How would you classify the program run by GUESS1? Use the Framework table.
6. Describe a CDI program—not presented in the chapter—that promotes problem solving.

Activities

1. Develop a lesson using MENTOR that would be appropriate for students at a level of your choice. (See the *Program Documentation for the Micro Goes to School* for more detailed directions on how to run this program.)

After you finish developing it, go through it as a student might, so you can check to see if the lesson does exactly what you want.

2. Run the program run by SHOPMALL several times. List some important features of the program not described in the chapter.
3. Design a concept development lesson that you think could be converted to a CDI program.

Projects

1. Take the lesson you developed from MENTOR in Activity 1 and use it with some students. Keep a log showing student response and motivation, and any modifications that are necessary before using it again. Record any outstanding successes.
2. Use the concepts presented in this chapter to develop a checklist for identifying and reporting features of CDI Software. Your Checklist should include such features as the following:
   - Does the CDI lesson provide a printed report?
   - Does the CDI Lesson provide lesson instructions?

Bibliography

Balajthy, E. "Artificial Intelligence and the Teaching of Reading and Writing by Computers." *Journal of Reading* (October 1985): 23–32. Discusses how computers can "converse" with students for teaching purposes, demonstrates how these interactions are becoming more complex, and explains how the computer's role is becoming more "human" in giving intelligent responses to students.

Dreyfus, H. L., and S. E. Dreyfus. "Putting Computers in Their Proper Places: Analysis versus Intuition in the Classroom." *Teachers College Record* (Summer 1984): 578–601. The computer in the education setting can serve as tutor, tool, and tutee. A five-stage model of skill acquisition is offered that explores the use of computers and learning styles.

England, E. "Interactional Analysis: The Missing Factor in Computer-Aided Learning Design and Evaluation." *Educational Technology* (September 1985): 24–28. Describes two experiments on computer-assisted instruction interaction in which interactional analysis is utilized to provide information on the interaction of students with microcomputers.

Frank, A. R., and others. "Teaching Selected Microcomputer Skills to Retarded Students via Picture Prompts." *Journal of Applied Behavior Analysis* (Summer 1985): 179–185. Five mildly retarded students were taught to use picture prompts to help them access and terminate a computer program. Results indicated that the program was successful in teaching the microcomputer skills to students.

Geller, D. M., and M. Shugoll. "The Impact of Computer-Assisted Instruction on Disadvantaged Young Adults in a Non-Traditional Educational Environment." *AEDS Journal* (Fall 1985): 49–65. Describes a study which assessed impact of computer-assisted instruction on reading and mathematics achievement of disadvantaged youths participating in U.S. Department of Labor's Job Corps, a federal vocational and educational program.

Hartley, J. R. "Some Psychological Aspects of Computer Assisted Learning and Teaching." *Programmed Learning and Educational Technology* (May 1985): 140–149. Considers three aspects of Computer Assisted Learning: instructional program design, software tools needed for their realization, and assimilation of CAL in the classroom.

Hunter, B. "Powerful Tools for Your Social Studies Classroom." *Classroom Computer Learning* (October 1983): 50, 55–57. Lists and describes currently available software useful in social studies classes.

Hythecker, V. I., and others. "A Computer-Based Learning Strategy Training Module: Development and Evaluation." *Journal of Educational Computing and Research* 1, no. 3 (1985): 275–283. Describes a study that involved development of evaluation of a training module that uses Computer Assisted Instruction and cooperative learning to facilitate acquisition of learning strategies by university students.

Kanevsky, L. "Computer-Based Math for Gifted Students: Comparison of Cooperative and Competitive Strategies." *Journal for the Education of the Gifted* (Summer 1985): 239–255. Computer Assisted Instruction and flashcard presentation of math drills were equally effective in increasing basic math skills of 40 gifted third and fourth graders.

Kemppainen, R. "How We Use Computers for (Much) Better Education." Paper presented at the National School Board's Association Convention, Houston, Tex., April 2, 1984.

Levin, B. B. "A Dozen Ways to Put Your Classroom Computer to Work . . . at Last." *Curriculum Review* (September–October 1985): 40–43. Discusses specific ways to maximize computer use in elementary and secondary schools.

Lewis, R. "Teachers, Pupils, and Microcomputers." *Technological Horizons in Education* (February 1983): 81–87. Discusses factors related to the design of computer software, focusing on student notes, teacher's guides, and the computer program itself. Also discusses computer training courses for teachers at different levels.

McGrath, D. "Artificial Intelligence. A Tutorial for Educators." *Electronic Learning* (September 1984): 39–43. Discusses Computer Assisted Instruction from the perspective of Artificial Intelligence researchers and describes program features of intelligent CAI, which the researchers feel will help resolve CAI's deficiencies.

Mevarech, Z. R. "Computer Assisted Instructional Methods: A Factorial Study within Mathematics-Disadvantaged Classrooms." *Journal of Experimental Education* (Fall 1985): 22–27. This study reported the contribution of Computer Assisted Instruction employed in traditional and individualized classrooms to cognitive and personal growth of third grade disadvantaged children.

Nelson, P., and W. Waack. "The Status of Computer Literacy/Computer-Assisted Instruction Awareness as a Factor in Classroom Instruction and Teacher Selection." *Educational Technology* (October 1985): 23–26. Describes a study that surveyed Iowa elementary and secondary school principals to determine Computer Assisted Instruction use in different grade levels and subject content areas and their opinions on importance of computer literacy awareness in teacher selection.

Passmore, David L., and others. "The Role of Personal Computers in Vocational Education: A Critical View." *Journal of Epsilon Pi Tau* (Spring 1984): 10–15. Personal computers are inexpensive, portable, accessible, and adaptable for vocational education instruction, administration, and communications. Successful infusion of microcomputers into vocational education requires staff orientation, improvement in software quality, and careful planning.

Roberts, Franklin C. "An Overview of Intelligent CAI Systems." *Peabody Journal of Education* (Fall 1984): 40–51. Intelligent Computer-Assisted Instruction (ICAI) allows both student and program a flexibility resembling a one-on-one interaction between student and teacher. This paper reviews the components of artificial intelligence, describes the structure of ICAI systems, and examines the relative strengths and weaknesses of such systems.

Ryba, K. A., and others. "Computer Aided Training of Cognitive Processing Strategies with Developmentally Handicapped Adults." *Australia and New Zealand Journal of Developmental Disabilities* (March 1985): 17–25. Correlational results involving 60 developmentally disabled adults indicated that a computerized cross-modal memory game had a highly significant relationship with most cognitive and motor coordination measures.

Sauve, Deborah. *Guide to Microcomputer Courseware for Bilingual Education.* rev. and exp. Rosslyn, Va.: InterAmerica Research Associates, 1985. The guide to courseware for CAI and CMI in bilingual education, English as a second language, and second language instruction contains entries from the National Clearinghouse for Bilingual Education's data base and selected courseware for the related areas of special education, vocational education, and adult basic education.

Shuman, R. Baird. "A Dozen Ways for English Teachers to Use Microcomputers." *English Journal* (October 1985): 37–39. Suggests ways that teachers and administrators can integrate computers in their schools, including record keeping, writing instruction, tutoring aids, and adapting tests to individual needs.

Stasz, C., and R. J. Shavelson. "Staff Development for Instructional Uses of Microcomputers." *AEDS Journal* (Fall 1985): 1–19. Presents recommendations for the topics and organization of pre-service and in-service teacher-training activities based on a literature review on staff development for CAI, and on opinions on successful microcomputer-using teachers in elementary and secondary science and math instruction.

Stubbs, M., and P. Piddock. "Artificial Intelligence in Teaching and Learning: An Introduction." *Programmed Learning and Educational Technology* (May 1985): 150–157. Discussion of ICAL systems considers both those that offer natural language communication to the user and those that are adaptive, generative, or self-improving.

Tennyson, Robert. "Artificial Intelligence Methods in Computer-Based Instructional Design. The Minnesota Adaptive Instructional System." *Journal of Instructional Development* 7, no. 3 (1984): 17–22. Reviews educational applications of Artificial Intelligence and presents empirically-based design variables for developing a computer-based instructional management system.

Tobin, Kenneth, and Barbara Tobin. "The One Computer Classroom: Applications in Language Arts." *Australian Journal of Reading* (August 1985): 158–167. Describes a study showing that primary grade students can benefit from using a word processor in activities that involve the creation of text. Suggests further word processing activities.

Watkins, M. W., and Webb, C. "Computer Assisted Instruction with Learning Disabled Students." *Educational Computer* (September–October 1981): 24–27. Results of an investigation of the effectiveness of Computer Assisted Instruction with learning disabled students in an elementary school indicate that CAI increased students' mathematics skills.

Wehrenberg, S. B. "Is the Computer the Ultimate Training Tool?" *Personnel Journal* (April 1985): 95–96, 98. Gives examples of how several companies are using computers in training programs and describes Computer Assisted Instruction and Computer Managed Instruction. Elements of computerized training such as standardization, flexibility, quality, security, expense, and expertise are examined.

Wyer, J. "New Bird on the Branch: Artificial Intelligence and Computer Assisted Instruction." *Programmed Learning and Educational Technology* (August 1984): 185–191. Surveys some of the Intelligent Computer-Assisted Instruction programs that have been developed and differentiates them from traditional Computer Assisted Instruction.

CHAPTER

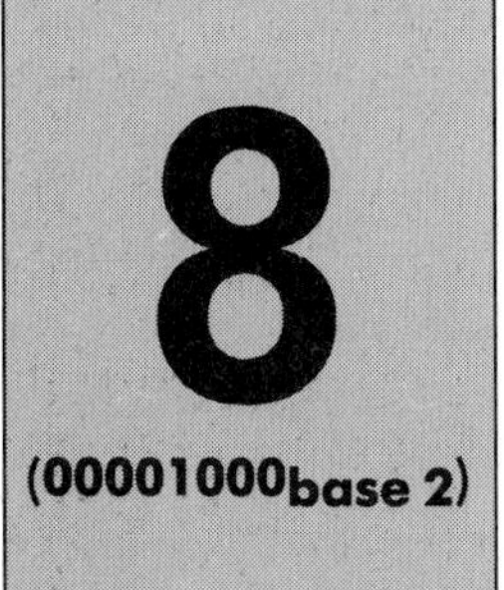

COMPUTER ENHANCED INSTRUCTION

The Best Is Yet To Come

Getting Started

Using computers to direct instruction only begins to tap the potential uses for education. There are innumerable ways in which computer applications can streamline instructional efforts. In this chapter, we will examine some of these ways by looking at a category of applications referred to as Computer Enhanced Instruction (CEI). *We will encourage you to let your imagination go and to experiment by implementing some of the ideas we present.*

Objectives for Teachers

To successfully complete this chapter, you should be able to

1. Define Computer Enhanced Instruction (CEI).
2. Identify teaching and learning aids and give examples of each.
3. Describe the CEI programs FRACTION, SLIDE SHOW, MR. CLOCK, MULTIMAN, AMAZE, MY STORY, SUPER SPELL, SCRAMBLE, FANCY NOTES, and PICPAL.
4. Prepare aids and activities using the CEI programs.
5. Present activities to students and report the results using CDI programs.
6. Design units of instruction using CEI, CDI programs, and other traditional learning materials.

Computer Enhanced Instruction—A Definition

First of all, you should know that **Computer Enhanced Instruction (CEI)** refers to using computers to bring additional dimensions to the way you teach, dimensions that may be impractical to access without the aid of the computer. What are the applications? They range from the creation of teaching aids and instructional support materials to the enhancement of student self-directed learning with appropriate software tools. The best way to get a feeling for what we mean is to study the sample applications presented in this chapter.

Using Computers to Create Teaching and Learning Aids

To start, let's look at the objects of instruction—those things that are used in the classroom to directly influence learning. Basically these objects fall into two categories: teaching aids and learning aids.

Teaching aids are objects that teachers use to clarify instructional ideas or provide demonstrations. For example, using transparencies in a lesson provides visual impact. A set of slides or a sequence of transparencies can visually demonstrate an idea that might be difficult or cumbersome to explain. However, preparing slides or transparencies is not easy and takes special skills. No matter how expert you are at doing either, the jobs are time-consuming. Another teaching aid that is often used is a set of flash cards. After concept development has taken place, it is often useful to have quick reinforcement lessons where learners respond to stimuli presented on flash cards. As we will show you later, the computer can be very helpful in quickly preparing attractive and useful flash cards. And what about templates? Teachers are noted for searching out templates or patterns to trace when preparing classroom visuals. Just look in almost any teacher's file cabinet and you are sure to find patterns for making holiday displays, constructing bulletin boards, making game boards and any high-interest material one might imagine that calls for a picture. Well, there are many computer programs that can efficiently help teachers create attractive visuals that can be used for a variety of purposes. What about certificates, badges, and awards? Wouldn't it be nice to have a computer program that could produce an endless supply of attractive rewards for positive attitude, cooperative behavior, and achievement? Such programs currently exist, just waiting for teachers to take full advantage.

Learning aids are primarily used by students as they carry out a lesson. A learning aid can have visual, auditory, or kinesthetic impact on learning. A learning aid might be a model like a clock with movable hands, a game providing educational experiences that students play, or a set of cards that students arrange or stack in certain ways. When you get right down to it, a simple black-line master from which activity sheets are reproduced is a learning aid.

There is a fine line between what constitutes a teaching aid and a learning aid. In fact the line is probably artificial. What is important is that you become aware of specific things that are used in the classroom to stimulate learning.

Teaching/learning aids are either purchased by the school or constructed by the teacher. Most school budgets are limited so teachers either make their own aids or go without. Many teachers shy away from constructing aids because they lack skill, time, or both. Often they resort to rendering last-minute sketches on an acetate or on the chalkboard. They pick up objects that are easily found in the environment and use these as manipulative aids. The results are sometimes inaccurate and unattractive. A lesson that is supported by poor visuals and manipulative aids will most probably lack motivational quality and could lead to faulty concept development.

With computers this needn't be the case. The availability of programs in journals and the availability of good commercial programs make it easy and inexpensive to create a myriad of useful instructional tools. If you have programming skills, you can write simple but useful programs that generate good materials. If you can't program or if you don't want to spend time programming, you can enter and modify programs found in a growing number of publications. There are also programs you can purchase for creating classroom tools. Some of the commercial tools are designed specifically for designing educational tools and others are generic. Generic software programs are general-purpose programs like word processors, graphics programs, spreadsheets, and data-base managers, all of which we will discuss in depth in later chapters. Meanwhile, we hope you are convinced. There are plenty of sources, but first you must take two steps to tap this potential.

1. You must become aware of the types of aids microcomputers can produce.
2. You must learn to use computer tools to produce the aids.

Some Special Programs

The rest of this chapter will be devoted to helping you take these two steps. We will demonstrate programs that have been designed for CEI. Some of these programs are designed to generate specific classroom aids. Some of them are more general and will generate a variety of aids. In order to familiarize you with the programs, we will describe a set of aids that the programs will produce. Whenever a particular program is complex we give detail on its operation. Here goes.

Fraction
A Program for Creating Learning Models

The first program we discuss is called FRACTION. This program can be used to create aids showing models for fractions. When you start the program you will get six choices:

```
1. Draw models-Alike and unpainted
2. Draw models-A Fraction Family
3. Draw models-Fraction Comparison
4. Draw one large model
5. Load a model
6. Get instructions
ESC Return to Main Menu
```

To use this program effectively first read the instructions by choosing Option 6, then proceed with other options. Option 1 lets you construct models for a denominator of your choice. After a denominator has been specified, the program draws six circular regions that are separated into the number of parts designated. For example, the picture that is drawn when a denominator of 6 is chosen follows:

SIXTHS

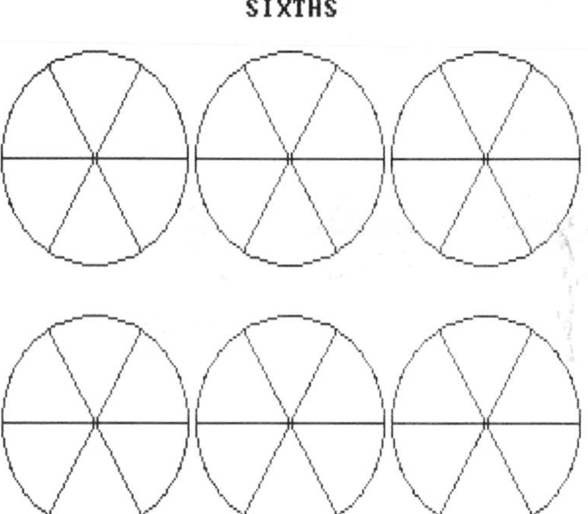

After the picture is generated, it can be saved to disk, printed, copied, and supplied to students for a number of activities. Here are suggested activities that use Option 1.

ACTIVITY 8.1

Finding Equivalent Fractions

Learning Objective. Finding sets of equivalent fractions.

Materials. Copies of the picture generated by Option 1 of the program FRACTION.

Directions. Have children color parts of each circular region to discover sets of equivalent fractions.

Example. Color 1/2 of the first circle. How many sixths is this? Color 2/6 of the second region. Can you give another fraction to tell how much is shaded? Color 2/3 of the third circular region. Tell how many sixths this is. Write number sentences to tell what you have found out.

Student Response. The coloring portion of this activity might result in a picture such as the following:

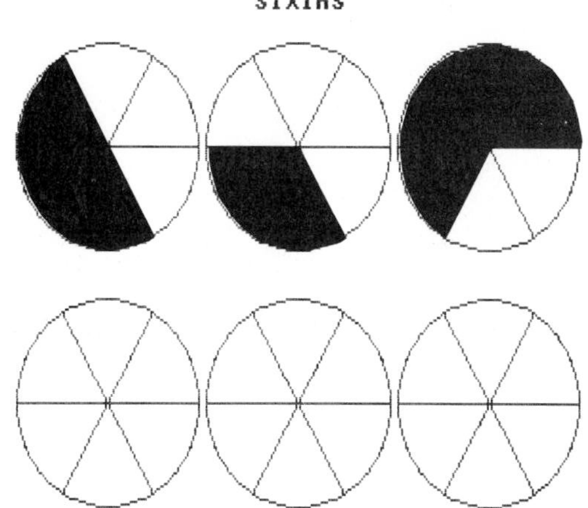

Level. Fourth, fifth, or sixth grade.

The next activity demonstrates addition concepts.

ACTIVITY 8.2

Using Models to Add Fractions

Learning Objective. Using pictorial models to demonstrate addition.

Materials. Copies of the picture generated by Option 1 of the program FRACTION.

Directions. Have students color circular regions to illustrate addition with fractions having different denominators.

Examples. Color parts of a circular region to show that

$$1/3 + 1/2 = 5/6$$

Color two regions to show that

$$5/6 + 1/2 = 1\,1/3$$

Student Response.

SIXTHS

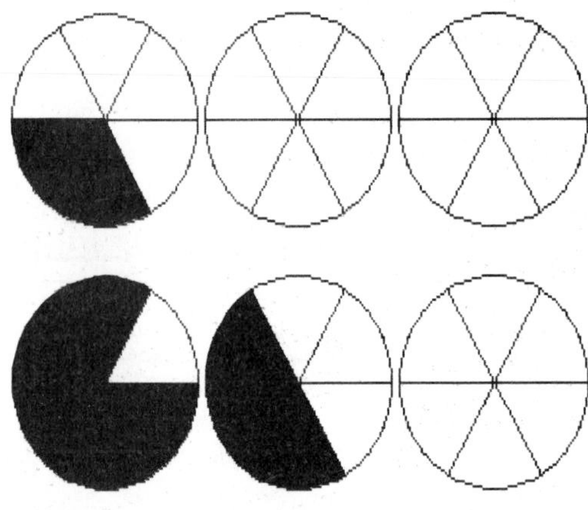

$\frac{1}{3} + \frac{1}{2} = \frac{5}{6}$

$\frac{2}{6} + \frac{3}{6} = \frac{5}{6}$

$\frac{5}{6} + \frac{1}{2} = 1\frac{2}{6} = 1\frac{1}{3}$

Level. Fourth, fifth, and sixth grades.

If you choose Option 2, the program produces the model we refer to as Fraction Family. This model demonstrates 1/2s, 1/3s, 1/4s, 1/6s, 1/8s, and 1/12s. Obviously, there are a lot of concept development activities for which this model could be used; Activity 8.3 demonstrates just one.

ACTIVITY 8.3

Using Models to Order Fractions

Learning Objective. Ordering fractions.

Materials. Copies of the picture generated by Option 2 of the program FRACTION.

Directions. Label the circular regions with the letters A, B, C, D, E, and F. Prepare a set of exercises in which students are to replace a ? in the exercise with either =, <, or > in order to make a true number sentence. Your exercises might include the following:

1. 1/2 ? 2/4
2. 1/3 ? 1/2
3. 1/8 ? 1/6
4. 3/8 ? 5/12

Students are to tell which circular regions can be used to verify each answer they give.

Example. Replace the ? in this sentence

3/4 ? 5/8

with one of these signs

=, <, or >

Student Response.

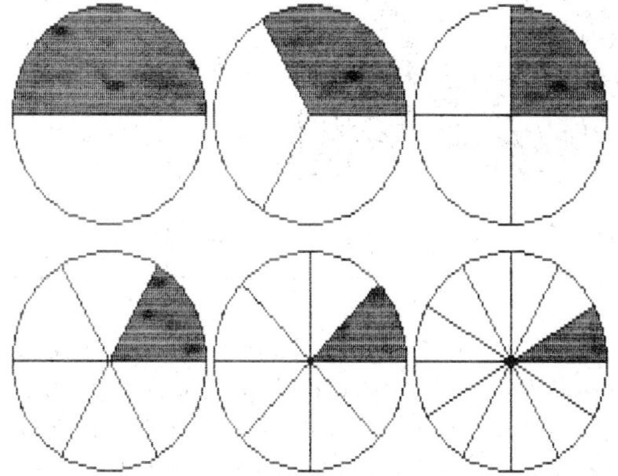

$\frac{1}{2} = \frac{2}{4}$ A,C

$\frac{1}{3} < \frac{1}{2}$ B,C

$\frac{1}{8} < \frac{1}{6}$ E,D

Level. Fourth, fifth, and sixth grades.

Option 3 allows the user to choose two denominators. The program then subdivides three circular regions for each of the denominators. If you were to select Option 3 and then specify denominators of 3 and 6, here is the model that you would obtain.

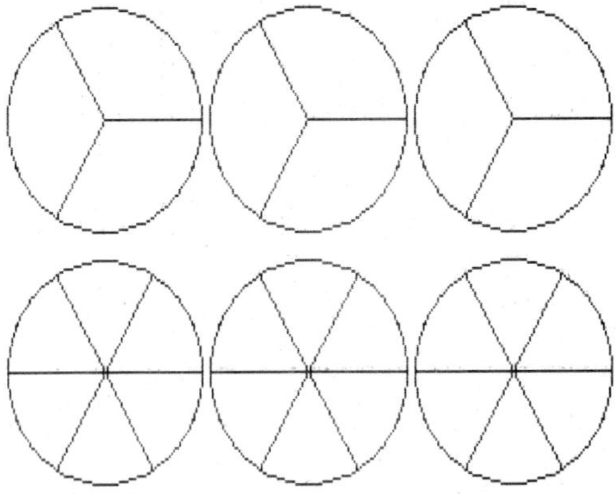

Pictures generated as a consequence of the third option could be used in a variety of instructional ways. An exercise that uses fractional models generated using this option is in the Thought Exercises at the end of this chapter.

Option 4 allows the user to obtain a large circular region that is subdivided and painted as the user specifies. This option is useful when transparencies or slides are desired. Here is a model that was generated using Option 4.

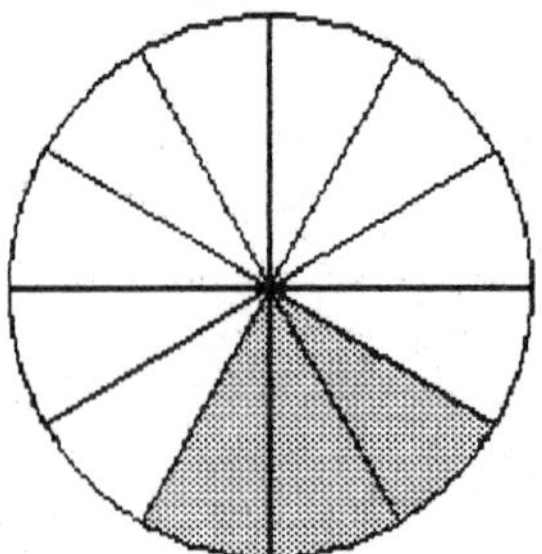

Option 5 allows the user to load a picture or model that was previously saved.

Option 6 provides instructions for using program FRACTION. The instructions go something like this:

Once the computer has drawn a fractional model you can

Save it by entering S
Load the program by pressing L
Rerun the program by entering R
Quit by entering Q

The saved image can be used for a computer slide presentation or as a master for an activity sheet or transparency. (Check PROGRAM DOCUMENTATION for details on how to print your pictures.)

Whenever you want to exit the program just press the ESC key. This will take you back to the main menu.

So what's the big deal? The big deal is that you can provide accurate models for learning fractional concepts in a few heartbeats and you don't have to be an artist to do it. Run the program several times to see how easy it is to generate a multitude of pictures with fractional models.

Slide Show
A Program for Making Presentations

The next program we discuss is called SLIDE SHOW. When you run this program you should use the filename SHOW. After the program has been booted, you will see the main menu. From this menu you can select one of these four options:

```
1. Design Slide Show
2. View a Slide Show
3. Run demo show
4. Get Instructions
ESC Return to Main Menu
```

Option 1 allows you to design a small slide show. Here's how. The program asks how many slides will be in the show and what the name of the presentation will be. You enter the number of pictures desired and the slide show's filename. When these entries are complete, the program asks for the names of the pictures that will be included in the show. When prompted, you enter the desired filename without any extension for each picture. The program saves the name and adds the extension .pic. When it comes time to view the presentation, the program will look for files on the data disk with the .pic extension. Obviously, you will have to make sure that pictures saved on the data disk are saved or renamed with the .pic extension.

The second option allows the user to view a show that has already been designed. After entering the name of the show that you would like to view, you must decide whether you want timed pauses between each slide or whether you want to move through the sequence of slides by pressing the spacebar. If a timed pause is chosen, then you will have to specify the number of seconds for each pause (0–30).

Option 3 allows you to run the demonstration show that we have supplied on the Program Disk. This demo will not win any Academy Awards and you will hardly know that it has started before it ends. Pictures require a lot of disk space so we had to limit our effort. Our goal is to show you how the program works and then have you prepare your own show using the utilities that are presented in this chapter. Run SHOW and select Option 3 (Run demo show). Sit back, relax, and watch the show. Then you should be eager to do your own thing!

Option 4 will take you to a screen giving you general instructions on how to run the program. More detailed instructions are found in *Program Documentation for the Micro Goes to School.*

Mr. Clock
A Program for Solving Time Problems

Next on the agenda is the program MR. CLOCK. With this program you can produce pictures of clock faces that show any time you specify. This program also generates related time problems for students to solve. The program can be used as a tutorial or can be used to produce student activity sheets. Each activity sheet shows a picture of a clock and provides several related problems for students to solve.

To run this program you need the file named CLOCK. After the program is loaded in memory, you are given a number of options. The first three options allow you to choose a single clock face, a tutorial, or to construct a student activity sheet. In any case, you can choose the time to be displayed or you can let the computer randomly select clock times. If you choose to construct an activity sheet, the computer will let you choose either color or black and white. At this point you can create a new work sheet or load and print one you have previously saved.

Option 4 provides brief instructions telling you how to save and how to print. The most important idea to remember is this: Make sure there is sufficient space on your data disk if you want to save a picture or you may lose important files.

There are a number of learning activities that could be constructed with the clock faces you can obtain using this program. One possibility involves the creation of a bulletin display. This display might illustrate routine activities and related times of the day. Here is an example.

Of course, a set of clock faces could be used in a slide presentation where students identify the time shown on each face and describe routine events that occur at the given time. A set of clock faces could be prepared and students could order them according to the times shown on the clock faces. There is no end! The real beauty of this program is this: The program can be used as a tutorial—a CDI program—or as a program for developing visual aids—a CEI program. This program provides continuity between what students do at computers and what they do in traditional classroom settings.

Read the suggested activity that follows and then think of some activities using clock faces.

ACTIVITY 8.4

Illustrating Time Concepts

Learning Objective. Depicting clock times.

Materials. Copies of Mr. Clock generated by Option 1 of the program MR. CLOCK.

Directions. Give students several pictures of Mr. Clock showing different times. Have students cut pictures from magazines or draw pictures to illustrate things they do at the time that is shown by Mr. Clock. Have students write short stories to go with their pictures.

Example. A student is given a clock face with eight o'clock showing.

Student Response.

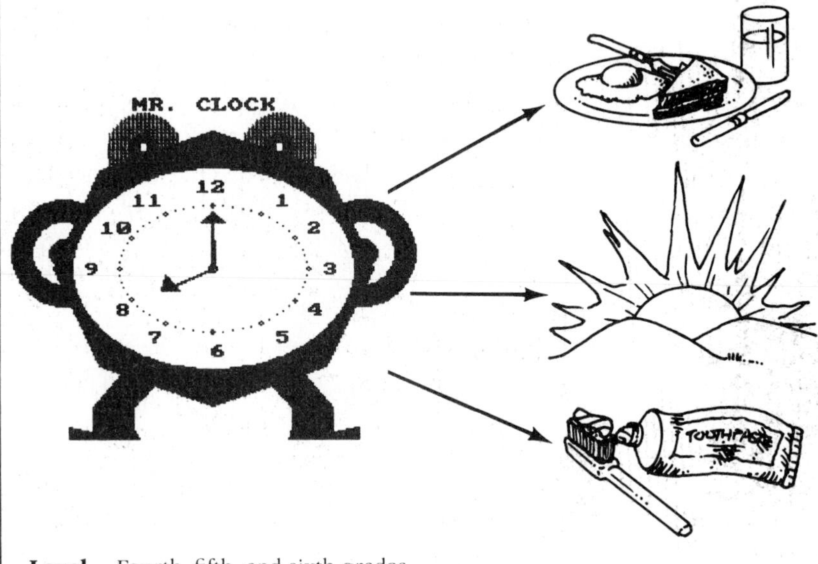

Level. Fourth, fifth, and sixth grades.

Multiman
A Program that Teaches the Multiplication Facts

MULTIMAN is another big mileage program. This program provides the teacher with three options. These options are as follows:

```
1. Student Practice
2. Printed Activity Sheet
3. Printed Flash Cards
ESC Return to the Main Menu
```

Option 1 provides a practice lesson that relates basic multiplication facts to rectangular models. As students practice the facts, they also practice related concepts. Option 2 prints out a master for a student activity sheet. The teacher may use this master for special instruction with a single student or may make multiple copies to use for large group instruction. The third option allows the teacher to print a set of 12 flash cards for practicing the facts. Each option of the program is based on the random generation of appropriate conceptual models for multiplication facts. For each model the computer generates two random numbers: one for rows and one for columns. Then the computer draws a corresponding array of rectangles. The goal is to have students associate arrays with basic multiplication facts.

Every math teacher knows how important it is to have aids for teaching the multiplication facts, and using any one of the options that the program delivers can result in a learning activity that does more than just provide drill. Students must view each model and make an interpretation relating a model to an abstraction. The computer can easily provide a tutorial that can be followed with seat work using the student activity sheet or with a game using the flash cards. Either the activity sheet or the cards will print in seconds instead of the precious time a teacher might spend making similar aids as attractive and accurate. Since the models are randomly generated, the activity sheet and the flash cards will be different each time the program is run.

The following are examples of the material that can be generated with this program. Look over these examples, and then run the program several times, using the filename MMAN.

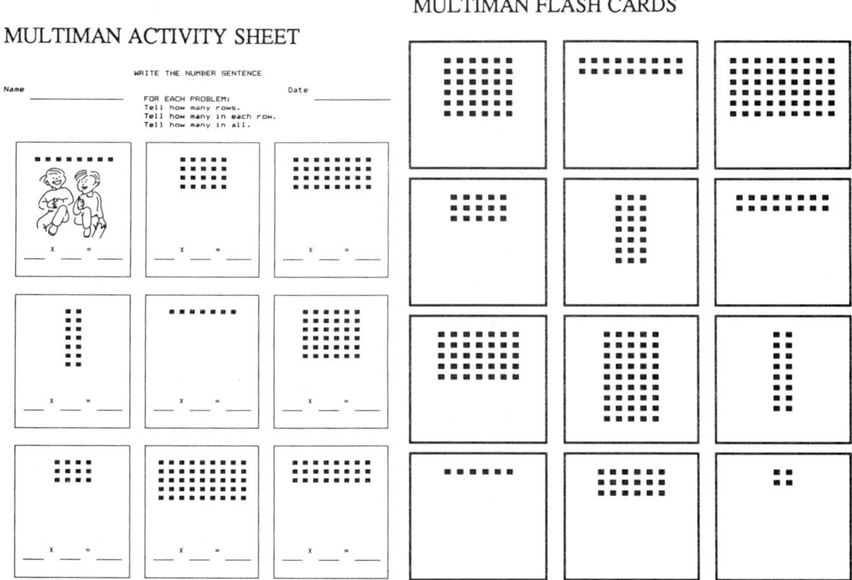

Flash Cards for Multiplication Facts

Welcome to Amaze
Program of Mazes

The next program we will discuss is called AMAZE. This program is guaranteed to produce more mazes than a teacher could ever use.

When you run the program, use the filename AMAZE. Once the program is in memory, you must specify how many vertical paths and how many horizontal paths you want in your maze. The program does the rest. It lets you save all or part of the maze to disk and you can get a printed copy.

Now, what can you do with mazes? One use could be for creating activities for children with learning disabilities. For example, you could provide a set of directions with a maze, giving a special student instructions for navigating through the maze; for example, start at the X, find the second opening from the top, go three units, turn right, and so on. You could also create high-interest activities with mazes for different subject areas.

Look at the activity and the activity sheet we have designed using program AMAZE. The activity's purpose is to provide practice following directions. The activity sheet is a lesson for identifying words that have similar meaning.

ACTIVITY 8.5

Giving Directions

Learning Objective. Learning to give simple directions.

Materials. Copies of a simple maze generated with program AMAZE.

Directions. Create a simple maze with program AMAZE. Use the filename AMAZE to run the program.

Help students draw a path through the maze. Then let students take turns giving others directions for getting through the maze. Have a group of students compile a written set of directions. Collect the sets of directions and in a large group activity refine the set of directions.

Example. Here is a maze that was generated for a small class of students who were classified as emotionally handicapped. Labels were put on the tops of students' hands so that identifying left and right would be easier. Students were also given a set of words that could be used in their directions: doorway, wall, hall, through, first, second. The starting point on the maze was identified with an X.

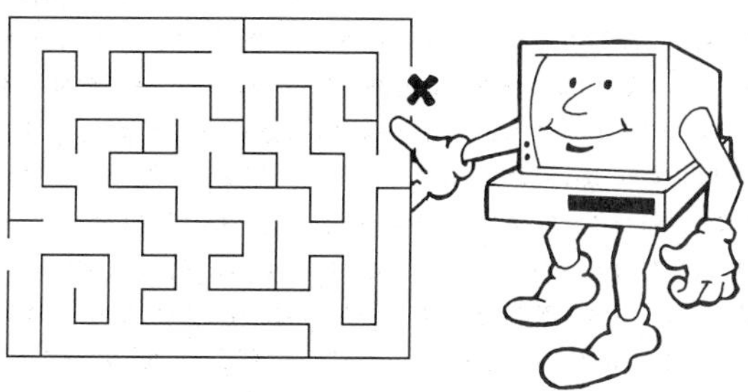

Student Response. Here is a set of directions that the students came up with. Not bad, eh?

1. Start at the X.
2. Go in the door and turn left.
3. Walk just a little until you find a doorway.
4. Turn right through the doorway.
5. Turn right again.
6. Follow the only path until you hit a wall.
7. Turn left.
8. Walk until you find a doorway on the right. Go through the doorway.
9. Turn left.
10. Walk until you run into the wall (a long way).
11. Turn left.
12. Walk a little less than before and turn left again.
13. Walk some more to the next doorway. Turn right through the doorway.
14. Turn right again.
15. Keep on until you hit a wall.
16. Turn left.
17. Keep on going until the exit appears on the right. You're OUT!

Level. Third grade or above; special education students at various levels.

It is important to note that students who are classified as emotionally handicapped typically have short attention spans, cannot stay on tasks for long periods of time, become easily frustrated, and sometimes lack social skills required for group work. Activities such as Activity 8.5 encourage development in all of these areas as well as help students learn to articulate their thoughts.

The next maze has words typed in its paths. Students are told to find all the words that relate to the word *happy* in order to find the way to the word *treasure*.

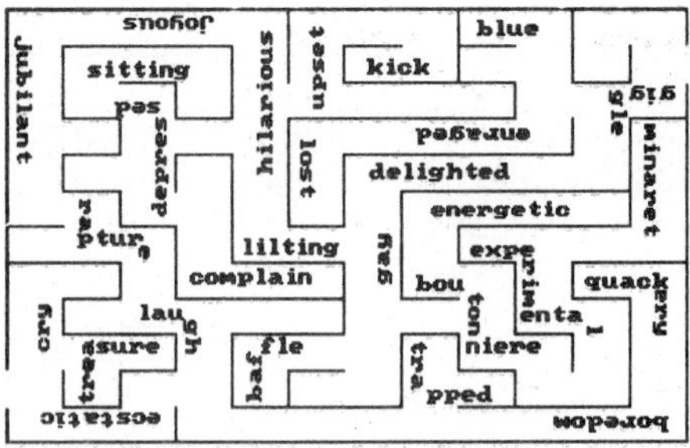

Teachers are expected to do a lot more than teach and it is not unusual for teachers to prepare programs for school productions, study guides, and other booklets. The neat thing about the maze program is that you can stop the drawing of the maze at any point. The resulting picture can be saved, printed or loaded into another graphics program to be written on, drawn on, and colored. Now you know where we obtained the color slide in our slide presentation back in program SLIDE SHOW. The following is an example of a cover for the program of a school production:

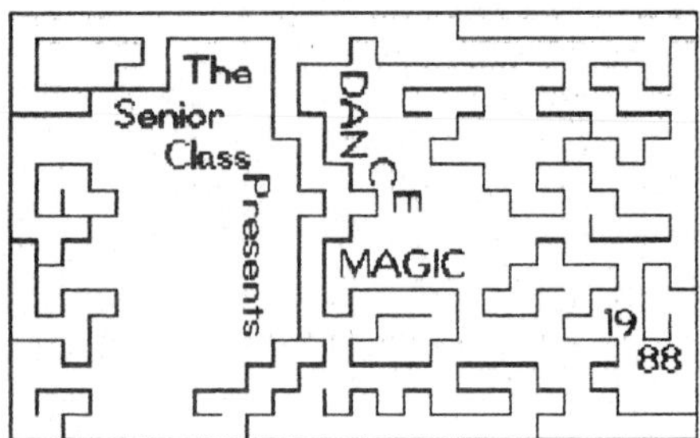

My Story
A Program for Personalizing Stories

This program is one of our favorites. It prints stories for students to illustrate and read. The nice thing about each story is that it can be personalized for the individual student. Here's how the program works. The menu has eight options that are chosen by pressing the right key, as shown in the following table:

Function key	Option	Explanation
F1	Add Record	This option allows you to enter personal data about a student, friend, or relative. When you enter personal data, you enter the first and last name and other information such as the person's

Function key	Option	Explanation
		best friend, the person's sex, nicknames, pets' names, and birthday.
F2	Edit/Delete Records	This option allows you to maintain records once they have been stored. You may want to change entries or delete records.
F3	Print Stories	Here is the good part. Once you have entered records for people, you can tell the computer to use that information to write stories using one or more of your records. What happens is that the computer takes names and other pertinent information from the records and places the information into stories that are on the disk. In other words, you obtain stories that are personalized for your friends or students. What fun!
F4	Print All Records	Choosing this option provides you with a printed copy of all your records.
F5	Print Some Records	Choosing this allows you to select a set of records to print.
F6	Input a Story	This is another goodie. This option allows you to write your own stories.
F7	Change the Data Drive	This is a sophisticated program and—as you can imagine—if you start entering names for all your students, friends, and neighbors, not to mention your cousins, you might run out of disk space. So this option allows you to create data disks that are independent of the main program. To run the program efficiently, you must tell the computer where your data are. This option allows you to do this.
F8	Exit	Choose this option when you want to quit.

As we said before, this is a sophisticated program and it takes more than this brief discussion to get thoroughly up and running. You should consult *Program Documentation* for instructions that are more detailed. You must also spend a lot of time at the computer trying one option after another. Experience at the keyboard pays off.

Once you have some experience with the program and have entered some records, you can write your own stories or you use ones we have on store on the Program Disk to print stories for people in your file. One of our stories is called RAINY; try printing it for some of the names you have entered.

If you decide to enter your own story, you must use variables in your story. When you print the story for a particular person, the computer will substitute data about the person for these variables. For example FNAME$ is the variable that represents the student's first name. If you were to print a story for a person named Ryan Smith, the variable FNAME$ would be replaced with the name Ryan. Again, see *Program Documentation* for details how to enter your own story.

The following illustration should give you some idea of how this program works. The program, MY STORY, will take this record from the names file

```
Last Name.......Smith
First Name......Ryan
Sex (M or F)....M
Birthday........07/12/83
Friend's Name...Tanner
Kind of Pet.....dog
Pet's Name......Scruffy
.
.
```

and substitute the data about Ryan in the story shown on the left. The printed story will look something like that shown on the right.

```
   This is a story on the Program Disk
   called RAINY

■    One night \FNAME$\, his \PET$\,■
■\PETN$\ and his best friend, \FRIEND$\■
■were playing a game of checkers. Of■
■course, \PETN$\ was winning. All of■
■a sudden there was a loud thumping■
■on the roof. \PETN$\ barked, 'That■
■loudnoise bothers my concentration.'■
■The other two giggled, hoping that■
■\PET$\ was truly bothered. When a■
■lightning bolt and a roar of thunder■
■hit the house, the giggling stopped.■
■All three left the checkerboard at■
■once and flashed to the window. There■
■were more than droplets plummeting■
■from the dark sky. The sounds on the■
■roof grew louder: Bow-Wow, Meow, Meow!■
■\FNAME$\,\FRIEND$\,and\PETN$\ stared■
■at each other in shock. It was raining■
■cats and dogs.■
```

```
                 RAINY

    One night Ryan, his dog, Scruffy
and his best friend, Tanner were
playing a game of checkers. Of course,
Scruffy was winning. All of a sudden
there was a loud thumping on the
roof. Scruffy barked, 'That loud
noise bothers my concentration.' The
other two giggled, hoping that Scruffy
was truly bothered. When a lightning
bolt and a roar of thunder hit the
house, the giggling stopped. All
three left the checkerboard at once
and flashed to the window. There were
more than droplets plummeting from
the dark sky. The sounds on the roof
grew louder: Bow-Wow, Meow, Meow!
Ryan, Tanner, and Scruffy stared at
each other in shock. It was raining
cats and dogs.
```

How can this program benefit the classroom? An obvious answer is that it can be a motivation for reading activities. Stories for individual students can be printed. Students can draw pictures for their stories and even prepare their own personal books. What a great way to experience education.

So far we have talked mostly about teaching and learning aids that are used to enhance instruction. These activities and materials are controlled by the teacher. What about the activities and materials that students control? Computers are tools for extending the human intellect and augmenting human abilities. How do we go about constructing activities in which students are actively involved in structuring their own learning processes? The following programs fall into this category.

Super Spell
A Program for Sharpening Spelling Skills

SUPER SPELL is another program you will find on the disk that comes with this book. This program serves several purposes. The main purpose is to provide spelling practice for a student while keeping track of words he or she finds difficult. One of the program's nicest features is that teachers can enter word lists of their own. These word lists are saved as lessons (files) on a data disk. At any time students can run SUPER SPELL and retrieve any lesson the teacher specifies. The program is saved under the name of SUPSPELL.

Here are some details on how the program works. After the program has been loaded into memory, the student is presented with the program's logo and a request for name, date, and filename for the spelling lesson to practice. We have provided one spelling lesson on the disk entitled ELSOUND, which we will describe later. A student taking a lesson is to give his or her name, the date, and the name of the lesson. At this point the program retrieves the work list for the lesson and randomizes it. A clue is given for each word and then very quickly the word to be spelled is flashed on the screen. The clue is either a synonym, a brief definition, or some word that is logically related to the one that is to be spelled. The student can take as much time as needed to enter the word that was flashed on the screen.

For each word, the student is given two tries. If, on the third try, the spelling is still incorrect, the program moves on to a new word. However, the misspelled word is stored for listing in a final report.

After the lesson is completed, the student is given a progress report that gives the student's name, the date, the percentage correct, and lists the words that were misspelled and the corresponding errors that were made. The bottom of the report has a checklist that helps the student categorize the types of errors made: Were letters left out of a word, did the student fail to double letters that should have been doubled, were endings used for plurals correct, were like sounds with different spellings handled correctly, and so on. The program does not perform this analysis since we want students to consciously analyze their mistakes. Up to now you probably thought that this was just another drill and practice program and that we weren't living up to the promise we made about involving the student in the learning process. This last part of the program addresses that concept. By saving the misspelled words, presenting them with the correct spelling, and presenting the categories of common spelling errors, the program encourages the student or teacher to diagnose mistakes. It is through this analysis (which rarely occurs under normal circumstances) that the student can become aware of the kinds of mistakes he or she makes consistently. Armed with that knowledge, improved spelling can occur more rapidly.

ELSOUND, the spelling lesson we included on the Program Disk as part of SUPER SPELL, is a lesson written on the fifth grade level stressing words ending with the el sound. Some words that fit this category are puzzle, pedal, and nickel. Words such as these are particularly bothersome since the ending sound is the same but the spelling is different. This condition requires that one memorize correct spellings. Using the computer for a word list of this type is particularly helpful since the computer fills the traditional role of the teacher by calling out the words. But more than that, the words are flashed on the screen so that the student is also exposed to visual stimuli.

The next program is an even better example of how computers can be used as tools for enhancing learning experiences.

Scramble
A Program that Produces Word Puzzles

This program produces word puzzles that can be presented on the computer display or can be printed out. Here's how the program works. The program selects a secret word and several other words from a library of words that has been stored on the disk. Each letter of the secret word can be found in at least one of the other words. Each of the words is presented to the student in scrambled form. Hints are given and the student is to unscramble each word. After all the words have been unscrambled, letters from each word are indicated. The learner is to use the indicated letters to form the secret word.

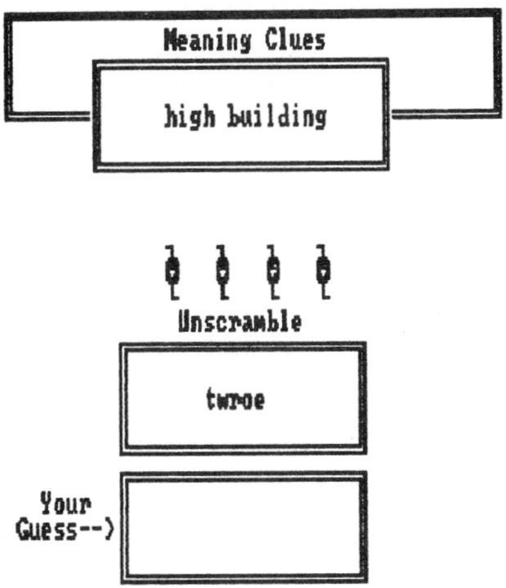

The program has a library of about 275 of the most frequently used words. Along with each of these words, there is an associated hint. Each puzzle is randomly generated by the program using the library. The program gives the user the option to add new words to the library.

Obviously this program could be used with other instructional materials to build interesting lessons for vocabulary development. If desired, Word Scramble lessons can also be printed and distributed to students for completion away from the computer.

Fancy Notes and Picpal
Programs for Preparing Graphics

The next two programs that we discuss are less limited in application than the ones we have discussed so far. We classify these programs as generic since they allow us to carry out general tasks as opposed to specific ones. Also, both programs produce files that are compatible with program SLIDE SHOW. The first program we will discuss is FANCY NOTES.

This program has the ability to print a wide variety of certificates and bordererd notes. The user can select a border from among hearts, diamonds, smiley faces, lace, musical notes, blocks, and many other patterns. Certificate mode allows the user to specify a title, four short lines of text, and up to two signers. Note mode allows a note of up to ten lines and a one line closing, either centered or not centered. Whether certificate or note, all text can be easily edited. This means that the user can experiment by putting letters in and removing letters until the text appears as desired. When you have finished designing your creation and are satisfied with it you can press CTRL - D. This signals the program that the potential slide is ready to be displayed. The computer then draws the picture the full size of the screen. If you like the picture, you can also save it to disk. Here is the menu and an example graphic that was produced by the program.

```
Fancy Notes

1. Print a Certificate
2. Print a Note
3. Load a Certificate or Note
4. Get Instructions
ESC Return to Main Menu
```

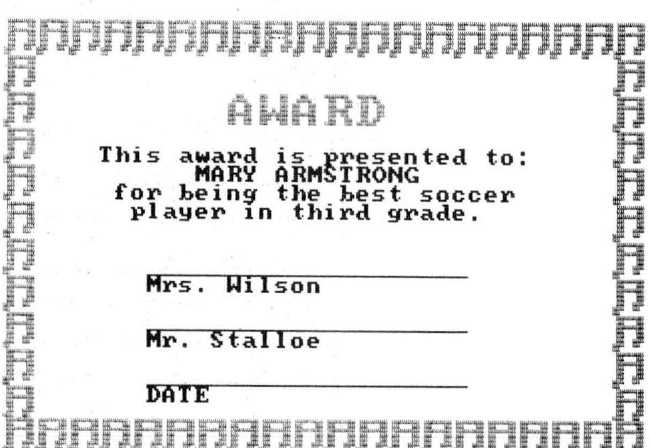

Now, FANCY NOTES will not let you draw. It will only let you put large colorful text characters on the screen. However, there is a lot you can do with these characters. Run the program several times. To do so you use the filename FNOTES. After you have the program in memory, load the text file named SMILE. After you have seen SMILE, it is your turn to try. FANCY NOTES can be used for poems, invitations, greeting cards, thank-you notes, rainy-day stories, and many other applications. Experiment; the possibilities are almost endless!

ACTIVITY 8.6

Publishing Poetry

Learning Objective. Writing short poems.

Materials. Program FANCY NOTES loaded in the computer.

Directions. Instruct each student to write a short poem using program FANCY NOTES and publish it. Poems can be centered around holiday themes or other subjects with which students are familiar. When finished, they can be displayed on bulletin boards or mailed to the school board to encourage the purchase of more computers for your class.

Example. Here is an example of what can be accomplished by even very young students using FANCY NOTES.

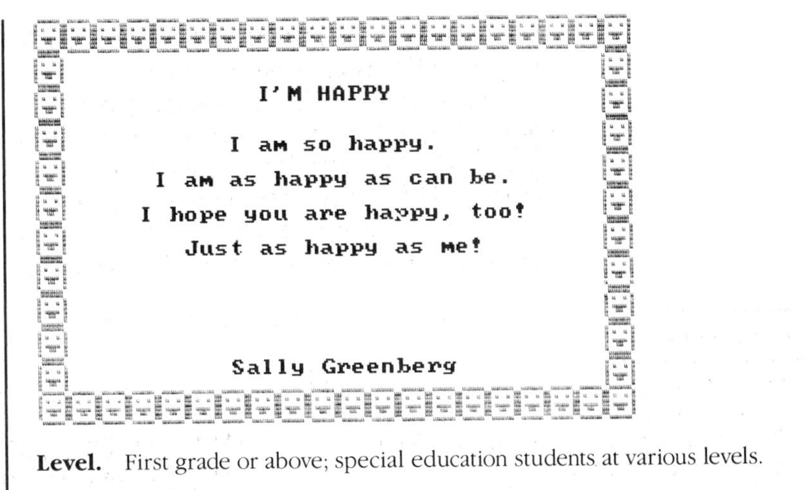

I'M HAPPY
I am so happy.
I am as happy as can be.
I hope you are happy, too!
Just as happy as me!
Sally Greenberg

Level. First grade or above; special education students at various levels.

Now let's turn our attention to another generic program called PICPAL. This program will let you do freehand drawings with the cursor keys. It will also let you draw lines, circles, and rectangles. These pictures can be used to make a variety of aids. Here are some examples:

Chapter Summary

Well, we could wax on for probably another year and not exhaust the possible ways computers could enhance instruction. However, our purpose is not to be exhaustive. Neither is our purpose to be representative. The purpose is to help you create a broad image of how computers can be used in the classroom. We want to help you avoid the stale stereotype of a room full of computers with students sitting behind each engaged either in a tutorial or in programming. The materials presented in this chapter should make it obvious that there is a host of ways in which teachers can use computers to aid in the preparation of learning materials. Right now you should be thinking, *"How can I evaluate software that enhances the curriculum?"* The answer to this question is not so easy. The programs illustrated in this book are not full-blown commercial programs. They have been designed to give you insight. Actual commercial programs have to be more sophisticated, more comprehensive. If a program is technically sound and smoothly performs what it sets out to do, then the program must be given an okay. The burden of determining quality is really on the teacher. It is the ends to which these programs are directed that will affect learning. If a teacher creates learning materials that lack depth and creativity, then learning may proceed accordingly.

Enough said. It's your turn. Try your hand at the exercises in the "Chapter Review" section that follows. That section contains exercises as well as more directions for using the programs presented here to create some learning/teaching aids. We think that you'll enjoy it!

Chapter Review

Knowledge Exercises

1. Define the term *Computer Enhanced Instruction (CEI).*

   Answer: CEI refers to the use of the computer to create teaching aids and instructional support materials, and to enhance student self-directed learning with appropriate software tools.

2. Give two examples of teaching aids. Two examples of learning aids.

   Answer:
   - Teaching aids. These include slides, transparencies, and flash cards.
   - Learning aids. These include a clock with movable hands, an educational game, cards, and activity sheets.

3. Describe the program FRACTION. Be sure to discuss each option.

   Answer: FRACTION can be used to create aids showing models (circular regions) for fractions. It includes six options, as follows:

   1. Lets you specify the denominator of a fraction for which you would like to construct a model, and then draws six circular regions separated into the number of parts indicated.
   2. Produces a fraction family.
   3. Allows you to choose two denominators and then produces three circular regions for each.
   4. Allows you to obtain a large circular region that is subdivided as you specify.
   5. Allows you to load a picture or model that was previously saved.
   6. Provides instructions for using the program.

   Finally, you can press Esc to return to the main menu.

4. Describe the program SLIDE SHOW. Be sure to discuss each option.

Answer: SLIDE SHOW is a program containing options that allow you to

1. Design a slide show.
2. View a slide show.
3. Run a demonstration slide show.
4. Get instructions.

You can press [Esc] to return to the main menu.

5. What extension does the program SLIDE SHOW look for to identify the pictures that are to be used in the slide show?

   Answer: The .pic extension.

6. Describe the program MR. CLOCK. Be sure to discuss each option.

   Answer: This program has three options.

   1. Enables you to produce pictures of clock faces that show any time you specify.
   2. Provides a tutorial.
   3. Enables you to produce randomly generated pictures of clock faces and associated problem sets for student activity sheets.
   4. Provides instructions for using the program.

   You can press [Esc] to return to the main menu.

7. Describe the program MULTIMAN. Be sure to discuss each of the three options.

   Answer: MULTIMAN relates basic multiplication facts to rectangular models. It uses the following options:

   1. Provides a practice lesson so the student is practicing facts and related concepts.
   2. Prints out a master for a student activity sheet.
   3. Prints a set of 12 flash cards for practicing the facts.

   You can press [Esc] to return to the main menu.

8. Describe the program AMAZE. What types of input must the teacher give?

   Answer: AMAZE will generate mazes with user-specified numbers for vertical and horizontal paths.

9. Describe the program MY STORY.

   Answer: MY STORY allows the user to save student data that can be transferred and inserted into stories that the program can print. This personalizes stories for individual students. The program also allows the users to input their own stories.

10. Describe the program SUPER SPELL.

    Answer: SUPER SPELL provides spelling practice for a student while keeping track of words the student finds difficult. Teachers can enter their own word lists, and students can run the program retrieving any lesson the teacher specifies.

11. Describe the final report compiled by the program SUPER SPELL.

    Answer: The report lists the student's name, the date, the percentage correct, and lists the words that were misspelled and the corresponding errors made. The bottom of the report has a checklist that helps the student categorize the types of errors made.

12. Describe the program SCRAMBLE.

    Answer: The program SCRAMBLE randomly generates word puzzles requiring the learner to unscramble a set of words. The program uses a library of words to which the teacher can add new words.

13. Describe the programs FANCY NOTES and PICPAL.

    Answer: FANCY NOTES allows you to prepare a certificate, note, or other message using any characters that can be entered from the keyboard. PICPAL allows you to draw with the cursor keys, and allows you to draw lines, circles, and rectangles.

Thought Exercises

1. Design an student activity illustrating equivalent fractions, using Option 1 of the program FRACTION. Use different fractions than those used in the chapter.

2. Develop a student activity to teach addition of fractions using pictorial models generated with Option 1 of FRACTION. Use different fractions than those used in the chapter.

3. Use Option 2 of FRACTION to write an activity using circular regions to teach the ordering of fractions. Use different fractions than those used in the chapter example.

4. Use Option 3 of program FRACTION to develop an activity to teach equivalent fractions, addition or subtraction of fractions, regrouping of fractions, or some other topic in the area of fractions.

5. Use Option 4 of program FRACTION to generate at least five models that can be used to make slides or transparencies, or to use on a bulletin board. The generated models may all use the same denominator with different regions painted, use different denominators, or some combination thereof.

6. Sketch and/or write a brief outline of a lesson that you could develop for use with students using Options 1 and 2 of the program SLIDE SHOW.

7. Write a problem-solving lesson on the topic of time appropriate for students of a level of your choosing. Use the program MR. CLOCK to prepare learning/teaching aids. Use a different idea than the one presented in the chapter.

8. Use the program MULTIMAN to print out three different activity sheets and one set of flash cards. Write a brief description of how you would use them in a classroom setting with your students.

9. Use the program AMAZE to print out at least two mazes, one small and fairly simple and one larger and more complicated. Type or write appropriate words in the paths of one maze so students can find their way through. (Use different words than those used in the chapter.) Write down directions to help students find their way through the second maze.

10. Choose a list of at least 15 words suitable for your students. Enter them using the program SUPER SPELL and save them as a lesson on a data disk. Specify the grade level, student population, and rationale for choosing these particular words.

11. Write a short paragraph explaining how you would use the programs FANCY NOTES and PICPAL to make a teaching/learning aid for use with students. Include a sketch of the proposed aid.

Activities

1. Use the activity you developed in Thought Exercise 1 with students. Write a short paragraph or two describing successes, problems, and student reactions to the lesson.

2. Use the activity you developed in Thought Exercise 2 with students. Write a short paragraph or two describing successes, problems, and student reactions to the lesson.

3. Use the activity you developed in Thought Exercise 3 with students. Write a short paragraph or two describing successes, problems, and student reactions to the lesson.

4. Use the activity you developed in Thought Exercise 4 with students. Write a short paragraph or two describing successes, problems, and student reactions to the lesson.

5. Use the activity you developed in Thought Exercise 5 to present a lesson on fractions to students. Write a short paragraph or two describing successes, problems, and student reactions to the lesson.

6. Make a slide show using the activity you developed in Thought Exercise 6 and use it to present a lesson to students. Write a short paragraph or two describing successes, problems, and student reactions to the lesson.

7. Use the activity you developed in Thought Exercise 7 to present a lesson on time to students. Write a short paragraph or two describing successes, problems, and student reactions to the lesson.

8. Use the activity you developed in Thought Exercise 8 to present a multiplication lesson to students. Write a short paragraph or two describing successes, problems, and student reactions to the lesson.

9. Use the activity you developed in Thought Exercise 9 to present a lesson using mazes to students. Write a short paragraph or two describing successes, problems, and student reactions to the lesson.

10. Use the activity you developed in Thought Exercise 10 to present a spelling lesson to students. Write a short paragraph or two describing successes, problems, and student reactions to the lesson.

11. Use the activity you developed in Thought Exercise 12 to present a lesson to students. Write a short paragraph or two describing successes, problems, and student reactions to the lesson.

Projects

1. Develop a unit of instruction on fractions. Describe the grade level and student population. Include detailed lesson plans for at least two weeks. Use the program FRACTION to generate teaching/learning aids. Present the unit to the students, keeping a log describing student reactions to each lesson as well as suggestions for improvement, and representative samples of student work.

2. Develop a unit of instruction on any topic. Describe the grade level and student population. Include detailed lesson plans for at least two weeks. Use any programs (other than FRACTIONS) presented in the chapter to generate teaching/learning aids. Present the unit to the students, keeping a log describing student reactions to each lesson as well as suggestions for improvement, and representative samples of student work.

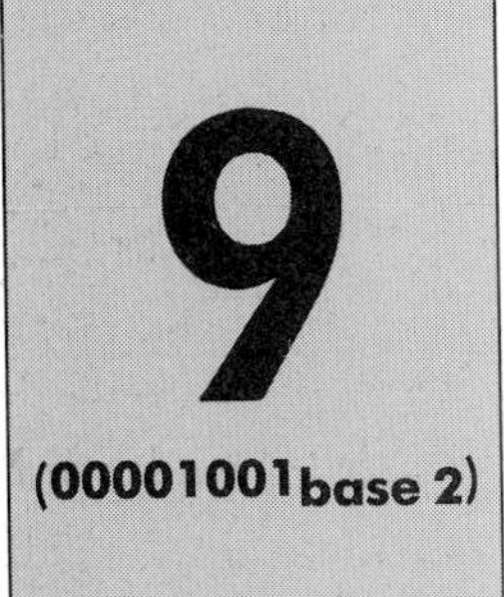

COMPUTER MANAGED INSTRUCTION

Reaching Maximum Potential

Getting Started

For the last several decades, educators have insisted on the goal of individualizing, even though this admirable goal is difficult to achieve. Programs for individualization have been planned and implemented, but few have survived on a broad scale. Tied to these programs are masses of paperwork and heaps of data manipulations and, until recently, using computers to do the job was too expensive for the average school. This burden of completing so much paperwork, piled on top of the normal chores of teaching, overtaxed teaching personnel, diminishing the quantity and quality of teacher-student contact. Most of these programs faded away, not because their philosophy or intent was in question, but because the technical resources available were not commensurate with the dream.

Today, powerful microcomputers are within reach of the poorest school, and the dream of individualizing instruction can become a reality, but educators must learn new roles. In this chapter we illustrate ways in which teachers can use the computer to organize and manage the tools of instruction as well as manage the learning environment itself.

Objectives for Teachers

To successfully complete this chapter, you should be able to

1. Define Computer Managed Instruction (CMI).
2. Describe the programs CLASSROOM ROSTER, BIBLIOGRAPHER, LABEL MAKER, and TEST ITEM BANK.
3. Describe seven important features of a gradebook program.
4. Generate labels using LABEL MAKER.
5. Use TEST ITEM BANK to store and generate at least 20 test items.
6. Use BIBLIOGRAPHER to create a file with references related to instructional computing applicable at a specific grade level, and establish search codes for retrieving and printing records.

7. Enter at least 10 student names using ROSTER and get a printed copy.
8. Outline a plan for using computers to manage some instructional environment—a subject area, a grade level, or some other environment.

The Scene

In almost every aspect of business life there are computers present, crunching numbers, manipulating text, and churning out tables, graphs, and reports. In education, at the administrative levels, there are computers responsible for student registration, for maintaining student profiles, and for compiling attendance reports. Yet, in the average classroom, the teacher still performs most of the teaching tasks, while manually maintaining mountains of records that are due next Tuesday everywhere! In fact, it is an understatement to say that **Computer Managed Instruction (CMI)** has barely impacted the average classroom, whether you are speaking of college level or kindergarten level.

As we discussed earlier, the first uses of computers in the classroom were instructional. In fact, if you were to glance over the last 10 years of microcomputer literature, you would find that the instructional computing movement started from the bottom up, with teachers who had a compelling desire to compute as well as an enthusiasm for teaching. Articles extolling instructional computing have been common but comparatively little clamor has been made with regard to how computers might transform classroom management. As with most revolutions, our enthusiasm for the goal—instructional computing—has outstripped our capacity to deliver. Without coherent plans, without a substantial research base, we have plunged headlong into instructional computing, talking a lot and learning as we go. Some reflection may indicate that early experiences may have been more productive if greater consideration had been given to instructional management. One computer with the right software placed in the teachers' lounge or a classroom corner could make a big dent in the management tasks for which the ordinary teacher is responsible, freeing the teacher to teach. In this chapter, we will focus on this "big dent," the main objective being to demonstrate how teacher potential can be released to do things that computers can't do.

There are many kinds of managerial tasks that computers can handle. In this chapter we will concentrate on two basic types. An informal definition for each type follows:

Type 1. Management tasks that involve students indirectly. These tasks generally require collecting, organizing, and reporting various types of student information. Examples include grade reporting, attendance reporting, maintaining classroom inventories and book lists, creating and updating course outlines, and establishing test item banks.

Type 2. Management tasks that involve students directly. These tasks involve the delivery of instruction where teachers assume the role of managers, expected to analyze educational objectives and plan related learning experiences. Teachers in this role break learning experiences into parts: those parts that teaching personnel deliver and monitor and those parts that computers deliver and monitor. As overseers, teachers collect the parts into meaningful wholes so that teaching, and consequently learning, become efficient and effective.

We will discuss each of these types of management in some depth, giving you a number of concrete examples as we go. These examples will include computer programs that have been designed expressly for this book. These programs will not have the characteristics that commercial programs should have but they will be sufficient to demonstrate desirable attributes. In many cases, however, the programs will be a valuable addition to the tools you use in your classroom. You should be aware that the programs designed for this chapter are revised on a continuous basis. Thus a program may run slightly differently from the description in the book. Consult the *Program Documentation for the Micro Goes to School* for further explanation.

Now it's time to discuss the tasks we've categorized as Type 1.

Collecting, Organizing, and Reporting

Okay, we are going to start with the obvious: there are some important differences between computers and people, thank goodness! No matter how sophisticated computer technology becomes, these distinctions will continue to exist. Let's analyze some of these distinctions. Humans can feel, computers cannot. Humans can initiate, computers cannot. Computers can accurately perform tedious and repetitious tasks at very high speeds, humans cannot. Humans get bored, lose concentration, become impatient, get tired and irritated; computers do not. Humans can make important value judgments, computers cannot. A human can laugh and fill the void for a lonely companion, a computer cannot.

If a task can be broken into a finite number of steps, it is probable that a computer can perform the steps and complete the task, even if that task is so large that it would consume a human lifetime to do so. Then doesn't it make good sense to explore how computers can be used in the classroom to maximize human vitality and minimize human frailties?

Classroom Roster
A Program for Making Lists

So let's leave the boring, the time-consuming, and the tedious tasks related to teaching to a computer. For openers, let's start with CLASSROOM ROSTER. The filename for this program is ROSTER. Teachers are constantly called upon by various departments or administrators to construct lists of students. The person who maintains textbook records wants a list of students with their book number assignments. The main office wants a periodic attendance report. The transportation department may require teachers to keep an updated list of students and their bus number assignments. Some school programs require teachers to keep lists of students who are eligible for federal aid. Then there are grade records to be maintained and, of course, teachers must keep up with the clubs to which their students belong, must know which student is going on what field trip, and the list of lists goes on. The fact that there are so many lists to be made is frustrating in itself, but the situation is compounded further because the lists keep changing. List making is not what teachers are educated to do; such a job should be primarily carried out by the computer. So here we will describe a program that makes a class roster for a teacher.

Here's what the program does. The program opens by providing the following options:

```
1. Create a New List
2. Add to List
3. Delete from List
4. Print a List
ESC Return to Main Menu
```

By choosing Option 1, Create a new list, the teacher may enter the first and last names of up to 200 students as well as a student number for each student, if desired. Names can be entered in any order. When finished, the teacher simply presses Enter an extra time. The program then provides the option to sort the list alphabetically, and then returns to the program menu, saving the list automatically. At the program menu, the teacher can choose

```
                    PRINT WITH NO LINES
   NAME
1. Black, Peter
2. Blue, Emory
3. Brown, Mary
4. Green, Jim
5. White, Suzy

   Print to Printer? (Y/N):
```

```
                    PRINT WITH HORIZONTAL LINES
   NAME
1. Black, Peter________________________________________
2. Blue, Emory_________________________________________
3. Brown, Mary_________________________________________
4. Green, Jim__________________________________________
5. White, Suzy_________________________________________

   Print to Printer? (Y/N):
```

PRINT WITH CELLS

NAME											
1. Black, Peter											
2. Blue, Emory											
3. Brown, Mary											
4. Green, Jim											
5. White, Suzy											

Print to Printer? (Y/N):

another option. If Option 2 is chosen, a list can be loaded into memory, after which additions, deletions, and corrections can be made. By choosing Option 4, the teacher can print a list choosing from three different print formats. Each of the formats is pictured here; as you can imagine, they can be used for a multitude of purposes.

Run the program a few times (it can be found on the Program Disk under the filename ROSTER) and print copies of the different forms. Notice how easy it would be to add new names or delete names when they are no longer valid. This sure beats the purple ditto with all the pencil marks on it.

The Electronic Grader
A Must for the Teacher

The program CLASSROOM ROSTER is handy to have, but when it comes to record keeping an *electronic gradebook* is a must. We are past the days when a teacher must sit for hours recording and averaging grades. In fact, if there are teachers still doing this, all we can say is, "What a waste!" Now, we can't provide you with a full-fledged gradebook program with this book, but we can tell you what the bare essentials of such a program should be.

First, a good gradebook should provide flexible features for entering data. You should be able to enter student names and correct any resulting errors easily. When necessary, you should be able to make additions or deletions to your list. Once a list has been completed, there should be several options for sorting it: alphabetically, by student number, by class standing on a given test or assignment. The gradebook should hold information on an adequate number of students for each class and should allow the user to enter more than one class. You should be able to enter a sufficient number of scores for each student in the list and for each score you should be able to enter a scaling factor. A special character (such as -1) should be provided, allowing you to indicate that a given student is absent on the day of a certain assignment. This is important for makeup purposes and ensures that inappropriate scores of zero are not figured in student or class averages. The program should be able to take all scores you enter, along with respective scaling factors, and find an average score for each student. For each set of scores that is entered, the program should also calculate other important statistics. These should include the range of the scores for the assignment, the class average, the class median, and the standard deviation. If you desire it, the computer program should be able to translate individual student grades to letter grades using a range you have prescribed. When computation of statistics is complete, you should be able to request a printed copy from a variety of print formats. Formats we suggest include the following:

Individual Student Progress Report. This type of print format allows the teacher to keep students, parents, and other administrators constantly informed of progress. When problems begin to develop they can be handled immediately. On Friday afternoon it is easy to print out up-to-date progress reports for those students who must meet eligibility requirements for Friday night's football game.

```
                WASHINGTON SENIOR HIGH SCHOOL
                   *** PROGRESS REPORT ***

STUDENT: Halfback, Harold     GRADE: 11         DATE: 11/07/87
CLASS: Functional English     SEMESTER: 1
LETTER GRADE: C               AVERAGE: 79
```

Class Status Reports. These reports give the teacher a clear view of the range and show gaps in the data. With the report and with statistics such as class averages, class median scores, and standard deviations, the teacher can more realistically make decisions related to assigning letter grades. The teacher can also make decisions related to the quality of the reported lesson or the learning activities that lead up to the lesson.

FUNCTIONAL ENGLISH
STATISTICAL ANALYSIS - UNIT TEST SEVEN

PERIOD	MEAN	MEDIAN	STD. DEV.
1	78.67	85.31	7.79
5	73.26	78.04	7.23
7	80.55	79.97	6.53

Student Number and Score Reporting. Often it is desirable to make a list available that does not include student names. Such a list makes it possible to determine grades when the teacher is not present.

MRS. GREEN - FUNCTIONAL ENGLISH
PERIOD 3 MIDTERM EXAMINATION RESULTS

STUDENT NO.	GRADE	STUDENT NO.	GRADE
1257843	95	5672896	87
9836476	67	9146276	78
0128754	88	5170653	82

Alphabetized List. Of course we cannot forget the old standard. This type of list is very important for reference purposes.

MRS. GREEN - FUNCTIONAL ENGLISH
PERIOD 3 CLASS ROSTER

NAME	GRADE	GENDER
Aaronson, Michael	11	M
Black, Amy	10	F
Douglass, Sarah	11	F
Everett, Kelly	11	M

Assignment Makeup List. Finally, the program should provide a printout of all students who have missed an assignment and should indicate the name or number of the assignments each student needs to complete.

```
MRS. GREEN - FUNCTIONAL ENGLISH
        PERIOD 3 MAKEUPS

NAME                      MISSING GRADE
Aaronson, Michael         Chapter 7 test
Black, Amy                Term paper
```

There are other features that a gradebook could have but the features we have described would provide an indispensable tool. Features in excess of these would just be "gravy!"

We have included a very simple gradebook program on the Program Disk so that you can get an appreciation for what one should be like. The program is called MINIGRADER and its filename is GRADE. For more information on this program, consult the *Program Documentation for the Micro Goes to School.* There are more powerful programs available commercially and in the user-supported/public domain network. (In fact, if you want information on obtaining a public domain gradebook program, just write to us care of the publisher of this book.) You should locate some of these programs and review them in the light of the comments we have made in this section.

Bibliographer
Keeping Track of Resources

What teacher has not mused, "I wish I could keep up with all the good references that I find." As educators we all find reference materials that we would like to keep track of. Storing these references in an organized fashion is one problem, but a bigger problem is finding them once they're stored. With a computer around there is an answer to this problem. You can use a program designed to prepare bibliographies to keep track of important references you want to maintain. There are several of these programs on the market for the IBM PC. Generally, these programs allow the user to enter identifying information about a given reference. The information is maintained on a disk file that can be readily accessed and printed. Usually there is a choice of print formats. The choices should include a standard bibliographic format as well as a retrieve record format. The bibliographic format should comply with some standard that is accepted by the educational community. The retrieve record format should be just that: the user should be able to retrieve records in essentially the same format as they were entered. The retrieve record format should include a provision for making annotations.

Now guess what? We just happen to have a program that does some of these tasks. Our program—found under filename BIBLIO—allows you to save desired information about references, search for references with respect to codes you have established, and retrieve and print records in the retrieve record format.

Here are the program particulars. To use our bibliography program efficiently, you must copy the program to another diskette. Doing so will provide disk space for your references. For more discussion on this program, see *Program Documentation for the Micro Goes to School.*

Once the program is on your disk you can try it. First the program will give you a main menu that lists the following options:

```
F1. Add to File
F2. Edit/Delete Items in a File
F3. Retrieve Records
F4. Print Entire File
F5. Print Selected Records
F6. Change Data Files
F7. Exit
```

If you choose Option 1, the screen will clear and the program will open the file on your disk and allow you to enter data. You should be ready with the appropriate information: subject; topic; subtopic; author; title; pages; publisher; publisher's address, including street address, city, state, and zip code; and any comments. A typical entry will look something like this:

```
SUBJECT: Math
TOPIC: Elementary
SUBTOPIC: Methods
AUTHORS: Troutman/Lichtenberg
TITLE 1: Mathematics: A Good Beginning
TITLE 2: (You would use this if your reference
         was an article.)
PAGES: (You would use this if your reference was
       an article.)
PUBLISHER: Brooks/Cole
ADDRESS: 511 Forest Lodge Road
CITY/STATE: Pacific Grove, CA
ZIP: 93950-5098
DATE OF PUBLICATION: 1987
COMMENT #1: Text for elementary school
            mathematics methods.
COMMENT #2: Many sample activities various levels
            of diff.
```

After you have entered data, you will be able to search for specific items by choosing Option 3, Retrieve records. You can search for items by subject, topic, subtopic, authors, title 1, title 2, or publisher. When you have decided how you will search, you must type in specific search characters. For example, if you wanted to find all the references in your file for math you would search by SUBJECT, typing in MATH.

To use the program productively you will have to make some decisions. First, decide what codes you will use for the subject entry. It is important that you choose a specific set of codes and use them consistently. Otherwise, when you search for references, the computer may not recognize the characters you enter. That is, if you have saved items under a subject as Eng and you search for ENGLISH, the program will not find any records. Remember: The computer cannot second guess you, it can only do what it is told. In the Review Exercises, we provide an exercise requiring you to create a file of references; there you will determine search codes, search for references, and get printed copies.

Label Maker
A Tool for Organizing

The next program, LABEL, is a simple one, but it is also very handy. This program allows you to make labels with 3–16 lines of information. Each line of information can have up to 35 characters. The labels can be address labels, labels for notebooks, shelves, boxes, closets; you name it! The program allows you to make several copies of the same label or several different labels. We won't make a big fuss about this program because it's easy to use and the results speak for themselves. Try it. It's located on the Program Disk under filename LABEL.

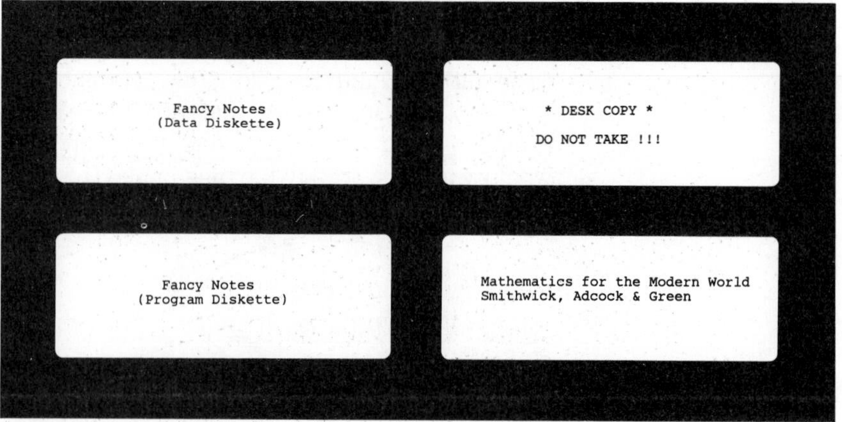

Test Item Bank
A Real Time Saver

We have saved one of the best programs for last. This is the TEST ITEM BANK. This program allows you to create, classify, and save test items. Once you have a sufficient number of items in the bank, you can search for ones meeting the criteria that you indicate and print a test of your choice. This program will allow you to save up to 500 items. To use the program, you must copy it to a formatted disk, just as you did with BIBLIOGRAPHER. The filename is ITEM.

Once the program is on your disk, you can begin to enter test items. The first menu will provide the following options:

```
F1. Add Items
F2. Edit/Delete
F3. Design Lessons or Tests
F4. Print a Lesson
F5. Print the Entire File
F6. Print Part of File
F7. Change Data Drive
F8. Exit
```

If you choose Option 1, the screen will clear and the program will provide a **template** into which you enter items. If this is the first time you have used the program, the item number will be 1. Thereafter, the number will correspond to the number of items that have been entered in the file. The test item template looks like this:

```
SUBJECT:              (10 characters)
TOPIC:                (15 characters)
SUBTOPIC:             (15 characters)
LEARNING OBJECTIVE:   (50 characters)
OBJECTIVE CODE:       (10 characters)
LINE1:                (34 characters)
```

```
LINE2:                   (34 characters)
LINE3:                   (34 characters)
LINE4:                   (34 characters)
LINE5:                   (34 characters)
LINE6:                   (34 characters)
LINE7:                   (34 characters)
LINE8:                   (34 characters)
LINE9:                   (34 characters)
ANSWER:                  (34 characters)
```

Here's how an item entry may look.

```
SUBJECT: Science
TOPIC: Biology
SUBTOPIC: Mammals
LEARNING OBJECTIVE: Classifying animals
OBJECTIVE CODE: SCI-B-25
LINE1: Circle the animals that are mammals.
LINE2: The bear was scratching furiously.
LINE3: There was a fat flea biting his hide.
LINE4: The duck and the rabbit laughed.
LINE5: The dog didn't laugh, he knew what
LINE6: it was like to have flea bites.
LINE7:
LINE8:
LINE9:
ANSWER: bear, rabbit, dog
```

After you have entered data, you will be able to search for and select specific items by choosing Option 3, Design Lessons or Tests. You can search for items on the basis of item number, subject, topic, subtopic, or objective code. When you have decided how you will search, you must type in specific search characters. As with BIBLIOGRAPHER, it is important to use search words that are consistent with the original entries made for the subject or objective. When all of your items have been chosen, you can use Option 4 to get a printed lesson containing the items. If desired, the program will print an answer key.

Now, although this item bank program is very sophisticated, it is not a commercial product. Its purpose is demonstration. By using it you will be able to imagine what might be done with commercial program. A good test item bank allows you to systematically save all those items that take so long to write. Once you have typed them into the computer, you never need to type them again. With a few keystrokes you can make changes that produce parallel items or refresh old ones. In seconds you can produce a printed copy of a test whether it is for an entire class, for a special student, or for a makeup exam. Several teachers working collectively can produce a good item bank. Just think of all the hours of teacher time such a program can save.

Well, that's it for Type 1 management programs. The programs that we have presented and the concepts we have covered should spell one thing: Teachers are too important a resource to be wasted on tedious tasks that the computer can do faster, more accurately, and more efficiently. Teacher time should be devoted to making important instructional judgments that computers can't make.

Managing Instructional Delivery

We want to start this section with this statement: "No lesson stands alone." This is an obvious statement, but oh, so important. We think this statement is so obvious that it is often overlooked. We frequently hear educators, when discussing educational software, make statements such as the following: "That's just a drill and practice program. It would be better if it were a problem-solving program." Such a statement can be misleading and downright false under some instructional circumstances. Furthermore, it is unwise to make subjective statements about a single piece of software without a frame of reference. Certainly a major function of education is to teach human beings to solve problems, but you must develop and learn to apply skills in order to solve problems. It is a wiser use of teacher time to let computers monitor skill development if the overall instructional plan is organized and managed properly. If computers handled most of the drill and practice that went on in schools today, there would be a tremendous amount of teacher time released to organize and implement problem-solving opportunities. Let's face it, a computer can provide mundane practice exercises for days and not become upset or frustrated with a learner who continues to make mistakes. The computer could politely say on the 50th try: "That's not the answer I'm looking for. Would you like to try again?" A teacher in the same circumstances might be tempted to jump out the nearest window yelling "How many times do I have to tell you———!?" So, the conclusion is this: A computer program that efficiently delivers drill and practice exercises may be an important part of an instructional plan. As the availability of computers and software in schools increases, the role of the teacher must change. Teachers must become more and more responsible for developing and managing instructional plans. The teacher will still direct instruction, but he or she will reserve energy for situations in which direct teacher-student contact pays the greatest benefits and builds the best partnerships. To make this point clear, we will build an instructional plan around a program introduced in Chapter 8, called SUPER SPELL.

An Instructional Plan

It is pretty well accepted that you must memorize the English spelling for many words. Oh, there are many rules to learn, but even if you master all the rules, there are still many exceptions. Generally speaking, it takes a lot of drill and practice for most students to learn to spell correctly. In most schools, even in high school, the student gets a set of words to learn each week. Furthermore, all students in a given classroom or grade level get the same words. Sometime during the week, the teacher calls out the same words to all the students. Now, this happens whether or not particular students already know the words. Spelling tests are graded and returned to students so that they can examine their mistakes. In most cases, specific difficulties that students are experiencing are not diagnosed. This teaching scenario can be greatly improved with the use of a computer, an efficient spelling program, and a good plan.

Let's look at the ingredients of an efficient spelling program. First, the program should contain at least 32 lessons that contain words on a given grade level. Each lesson should be built around a spelling concept. For example, at the upper elementary level students have difficulty with the el sound that occurs at the end of many words; for example, nickel, pedal, temple, and evil. There are no consistent rules that will help students decide when an ending is correct. Thus it's appropriate for lessons to be designed for practicing words such as these. Other problems students have occur when two or more vowels are used to make a single vowel sound, or when silent *es* occur at the end of words, or when letters in a word must be doubled, or when suffixes are being annexed, or . . . , or . . . , or! Consequently, each lesson should revolve around a theme that can be built upon. Second, the program should include several diagnostic lessons containing sample words provided in the weekly lessons. For example, a set of 32 lessons could be separated into four groups with 8 lessons in each group and a diagnostic lesson could be included for each of the four groups. Third, the program should provide a way for teachers to enter spelling lessons of their choice. These lessons could be for enrichment, for review, or for random practice. Fourth, the program might also include computer components involving related high-interest or application activities. Fifth, the program should come with a teacher's manual with suggestions and tips for each lesson. Sixth—last, but very important—the program should include a component for analyzing and organizing specific information on individual students and facilitating the design of activities. Here is an example of how such an analysis might look.

```
STUDENT: Sammy Jones PERIOD: 3
TEACHER: Ms. Arcman


OBJECTIVES MASTERED
Student is able to divide words of two and three
syllables.
Student is able to read basal three vocabulary.


OBJECTIVES TO BE MASTERED
Student is able to write simple sentences with
verbs in present tense.
Student is able to draw simple conclusions after
reading short passages.
```

```
DIFFICULTIES EXPERIENCED
Does not correctly apply ves endings to make
plurals.
Does not correctly double consonants in words.
Mistakenly employs o in ou words like pour.
```

Now let's talk about how all the pieces would fit together. That is, what is a possible instructional plan? First, students should take a diagnostic test. The test is then computer scored. (Remember: Neither of these statements means that students must sit at computers to take tests.) Based on results, the computer plans a personal lesson profile for each student. The teacher then groups students having similar profiles. The teacher directs small group instruction using his or her own ideas or using the suggestions provided in the teacher's manual.

There are a number of interesting ideas the teacher might pursue. The students can use spelling words for a given lesson in sentences or in original stories or in poems. Games for finding synonyms, homonyms, and antonyms can be played. Dictionary explorations can be conducted. The object is for teachers to lead exciting activities that prepare students for spelling quizzes, after which students use the computers for further concept development, practice, and final evaluation. The teacher then uses evaluation results and diagnostic information as a basis for teacher-student consultations and designing further lesson profiles.

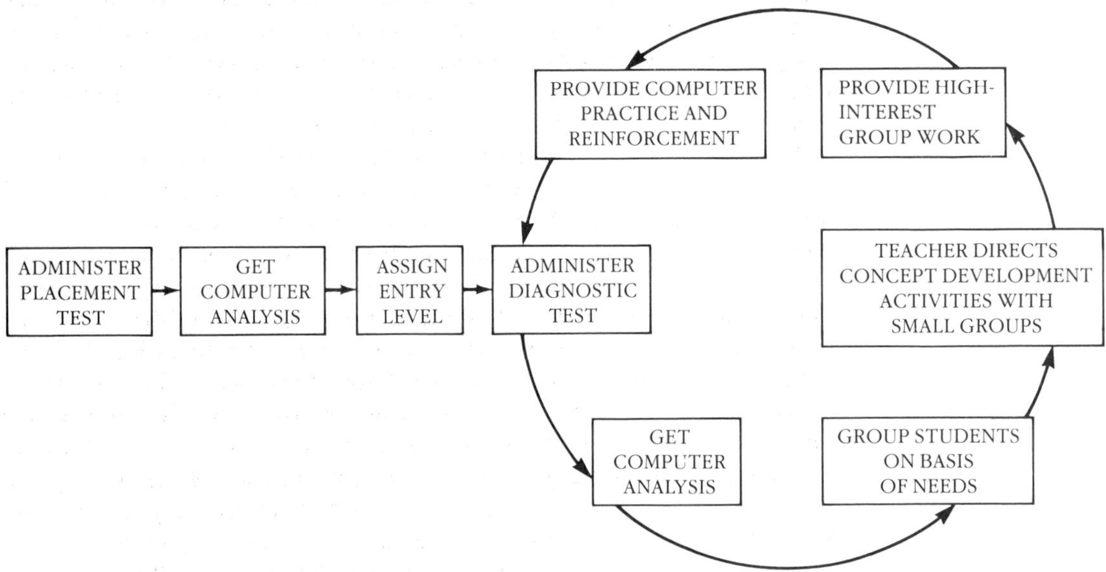

If you study this instructional plan, you will find that the teacher is a manager with the goal of efficiency as well as effectiveness. The teacher does not call out the same words to the same group of students on the same day.

The computer is used to provide practice and evaluation for students based upon their particular needs. The teacher directs instruction when it really counts, when the human element is important. Using the computer to perform routine, mundane, but time-consuming tasks, the teacher becomes available for higher levels of instructional support and more teacher-student contact.

On the Program Disk for this book, there is a sample set of spelling lessons, a sample program for diagnosis, and a sample high-interest activity that reflects ideas we have been discussing. In the Review Exercises, there are teaching tips and suggestions that should be found in the teacher's manual for a spelling program such as the one we have described. Your job will be to add more lessons to the program as well as to prepare learning activities and teaching tips for your lessons. Since the "proof of the pudding is in the tasting," you will be asked to organize an instructional plan and to try it out on a small scale.

Managing the Instructional Environment

Well, we have seen how to use a carefully designed program to manage one aspect of learning in one specific content area. But what about all the other subjects? Even if you narrow the field to just language arts, aside from spelling there are grammar, composition, literature, and a host of other topics. Granted, not all of them may lend themselves to computer aided learning, but if just a few of them do, how are you going to handle it? Do you get a different program for each subject? What if you are an elementary teacher who has to teach other subjects as well? Do you need to get management programs for math, social studies, and science?

This may seem like a pretty ludicrous scenario, but it describes just exactly what is beginning to happen in the classroom now. Many major textbook publishers are beginning to sell computer management software (little of which has the necessary attributes as just described) to go with their products. Not only do all these programs work differently, since there is no established standard for information storage, none of them can even exchange information. Should the teacher have to maintain half a dozen different class rosters? Are we to expect the classroom teacher to learn to master six or seven different management systems to organize the learning environment? The answer is a resounding NO! It doesn't have to be that way.

Computers should help the teacher manage an entire learning environment, but the horror story we've described is not the way to do it. An instructional management system must interact successfully with a number of elements in the instructional environment. To do so, an effective system must draw upon important components. To build or select a functional management system, we must know what these components are and how they can be controlled by the computer. We'll spend the remainder of this chapter examining the attributes of ideal classroom management software.

Performance Standards

If we expect the computer to help us manage learning, then we must have some idea of what is to be learned. The very first component to consider is a set of *student performance standards* or *learning objectives*. How should these standards or objectives be written? There are several answers to this question, but two things are sure. Each learning standard or objective must be distinct and small enough to be measurable.

An objective may involve a fact, a skill, a concept, or a process. The objectives, when arranged in related clusters, should represent substantial learning. To manage this component with a computer, the objectives can be stored in a data base along with numeric codes. Using the numeric codes, the computer finds and manipulates desired sets of objectives. Related information about each objective—information concerning learning difficulties associated with objectives, the levels at which objectives are normally introduced and normally mastered—should also be stored in the data base. The main topic and related topics should be part of each objective's record. Information about necessary prerequisites will also be useful.

Here is what a record for a mathematics objective might look like.

```
OBJECTIVE: Adds numbers (n<100), regrouping in
           the ones place.
OBJECTIVE #: 104
TOPIC: Addition
SUBTOPIC: Place value
TYPE: Computation
LEVEL OF INTRODUCTION: 1-9
LEVEL OF MASTERY: 3-5
PREREQUISITES: Facts greater than 10; Regrouping
DIFFICULTY #1: Does not regroup; ex. 28+37 = 515.
DIFFICULTY #2: Regroups, doesn't increment tens
               place; ex. 28+37 = 55.
DIFFICULTY #3: Hasn't mastered basic facts, sums
               greater than 10.
```

Now, what good are objectives if we don't have a way to measure them? A good management system must be capable of evaluating student performance. This requires two components: the evaluation instruments and the evaluation utility.

Evaluation Instruments

One component must include evaluation instruments. This might be a set of criterion-referenced tests measuring student performance related to learning objectives. This component might also include instruments that evaluate student learning styles, their strengths and weaknesses. Using computers for test administration with large student populations requires considerable computer access. This could result in giving up instructional time for testing purposes. Usually, this is not efficient use of computer time, so in general, evaluations should be implemented with pencil and paper.

Evaluation Utility

The second part of the evaluation component is a utility for data analysis. This utility must have an efficient method for data entry—either manually or by electronic scanning. Once data are entered, the utility interprets, organizes, and stores student test data in files that can be accessed over and over again. The goal is to track student performance and provide individual learning plans. Ideally, this component should identify and store information related to specific errors students make, indicating their learning styles. Obviously this information is critical for designing individual learning plans.

Once performance has been measured, learning plans for individual students can be designed. Two computer components are required to accomplish this task: a library of instructional activities and a planning utility.

Instructional Activities

There must be a component that contains information about instructional materials used in the learning environment; in short, a computerized library of readily available learning activities. The library of learning activities should be comprehensive. Activities should be written around software, books, kits, work sheets, teacher directed learning activities, and audiovisual materials. In other words, the library should reflect a multisensory approach to teaching and learning. Activities in the library should be coded to learning objectives found in the objectives library. Records for each activity should contain important descriptive data. What materials are needed? How long should the activity take? What objective does the activity address? Is the activity related to particular difficulties that children experience? What type of learning experience is involved: skill or concept development, problem solving? A record for an activity might look like this.

```
TITLE: How many over ten?
ACTIVITY #: 1007
TYPE: Concept development
ARRANGEMENT: Teacher directed, student pairs
OBJECTIVE #: 104
DIFFICULTY: Regrouping
MATERIALS NEEDED: Software-Grannie's Confidence
                  Builders, Option 2
EQUIPMENT: Microcomputer X
```

The Planning Utility

A related component should be a utility that builds learning plans. This utility searches the library of instructional activities and locates materials suitable for building plans for individual students. The learning plan should be comprehensive and substantial. It should provide opportunities for concept or skill development, problem solving, and review.

Here is an example of a learning plan.

LEARNING PLAN FOR TANNER SMITH

EVALUATION DATE: 1-16-86
STUDENT #: 103567
OBJECTIVE STATEMENT: **Identifying and using adjective in speech and writing.**

LESSON 1. CONCEPT DEVELOPMENT (15 MIN) **Teacher directed activity #306**

LESSON 2. CONCEPT REINFORCEMENT (15-30 MIN) **Game "Say it better"**
MATERIALS: **Software "Say it better"**
EQUIPMENT: **PC JR & Speech attachment**

LESSON 3. SKILL DEVELOPMENT (15 MIN) **Individual seatwork**
MATERIALS: **The circus workbook, level 4, page 69**
EQUIPMENT: -----

LESSON 4. CHALLENGE (15-30 MIN) **Self-directed activity**
MATERIALS: **I Can Write, lesson #4-8, I Can Write Word Processor**
EQUIPMENT: **Microcomputer**

LESSON 5. REVIEW (30 MIN) **Student pairs**
MATERIALS: **Software "Word Scramble"**
EQUIPMENT: **Microcomputer**
COMMENT1: **Tanner has difficulty completing written tasks, works well with partners.**
COMMENT2: **Tanner may have trouble distinguishing adverbs and adjectives.**

The learning plan should engage students in a variety of instructional settings: seatwork, small groups, large groups, teacher/student interaction, or student pairs. Some activities should be supervised by a teacher or aide and some should allow students to work independently. Computer activities should include ones in which students can exhibit initiating behaviors and control computer outcomes. Computer lessons should not be restricted to tutorials or drill and practice programs in which the computer controls the student.

Student Data Utility

A good management system must have a utility that maintains and updates student data, using this data to produce useful reports, charts, and graphs. These include classroom profiles, indicating acquisition of learning objectives by student groups; individual student profiles, indicating individual student performance; and achievement by objective, indicating student performance on a particular objective. This utility should be able to identify difficulties students are experiencing and automatically write letters to parents, indicating how they may help their children. In short, the utility should be capable of providing any report that is necessary for implementing effective instruction. The utility's capability should be limited only by the data that are collected.

Features You Can't Do Without

Dynamic and Open Ended

Educators should be able to modify, add to, and delete from the objectives or instructional activities files of the system. They should have the ability to design student files to meet particular program needs. The process of adding and deleting student information should be flexible and easy to accomplish. New test data should be easy to enter and unwanted test data should be easy to delete.

Choice of Materials

Many commercial management programs depend upon sets of specially prepared instructional materials. Because the materials are developed by the same company following a particular format, their cosmetic appeal does not vary. For many learners this repetition leads to lack of interest and an unwillingness to learn. Often these materials duplicate lessons found in textbooks, kits, filmstrips, videos, games, and good software already available from numerous vendors throughout the country. Usually these materials are very expensive, often more expensive than similar products from vendors who specialize in developing certain instructional products.

An open-ended management system allows users to select their own instructional materials from a variety of sources, consciously making specific selections. Users can enter and delete activities for learning objectives at will. By taking advantage of vendors nationwide and other noncommercial sources, teachers and administrators can select products that have been properly reviewed, are more attractive, more substantial, and usually lower in costs. The big payoffs are greater variety, less dependence on particular products, customized planning, and the capability to expand.

Multisensory and Flexible

The system should not rely solely on computer tutorials. Learning activities stored in the learning library should involve teacher directed activities, computer tutorials, problem-solving experiences, simulations, text materials, audiovisual experiences, large group work, small group work, individual student work, and students working in pairs. Students should have ample opportunities to direct their own computer experiences, to be initiators, not just subjects of computer teaching.

The planning utility that searches for lessons to include in a learning plan must be capable of generating variety. An abundance of lessons should be entered in the learning library so many learning plans can be generated for a single objective. When plans are generated for the same objective at different times, lessons selected from the library should also be different.

Progressive and Compatible

The system should be sophisticated enough to manage large student populations. It should be compatible with other management systems used in the same instructional setting; certainly within the school, and within the district or state if possible. This implies that the system should be capable of sharing data files. Once student information, test data, and activity data are entered in the management system, that data should be transferable to other management systems that might be in use. The system should have the capability of sharing files with statistical and graphics utilities so that long-range studies on student growth can be initiated and automatically maintained.

Small rigid management systems built for specific purposes that cannot be modified or expanded have little long-range potential. They are useful for learning concepts and skills related to computer management but will not bear up under serious instructional use. Several small management systems used in the same learning environment, but each designed for a different purpose, could become more taxing to teachers than traditional methods of managing instruction.

Ownership

A substantial management system requires a considerable expenditure of resources, both human and financial. Once a system is purchased or developed, it should be expandable to accommodate changes as they arise. Also provisions should be made so that users obtain the right to operate the management system with any instructional unit in their jurisdiction. Educators should be wary of companies that sell lock-step systems that cannot be modified and inexpensively installed for use in a number of district sites.

Reinforcement

A good management system should be supported by other important computer utilities—word processors; data-base managers; and programs that generate learning/teaching aids such as transparencies, certificates, work sheets, and tests. Such utilities allow teaching personnel to prepare attractive aids in a reasonable amount of time. A good management system supported by useful utilities can free teachers from the bonds of paperwork to do what is their most important task—teach!

Chapter Summary

Certainly the perspective offered in these pages doesn't come close to delivering the last word on Computer Managed Instruction. To say that it offers a beginning is more like it. We believe, however, that important aspects for effective implementation of computer management have been identified. Also we stress that *a management system is no panacea; using one will not cure all of the ills of education.* Educators and their decisions make the real difference! If the most sophisticated management system is developed, but learning objectives are trite, then learning will be trite. If the objectives are substantial, but the learning activities are superficial, repetitious, and boring, then learning will limp along. If students are passive participants in the learning endeavor, they will not learn responsibility for achieving their own goals. There are a lot of ifs. On the other hand, a committed team of educators, willing to expend the emotional, mental, and physical demand for getting a good management system up and running could change the whole meaning of education as it is now understood.

In this chapter, we have discussed Computer Managed Instruction and have identified two types of CMI. The first type does not involve students directly. This type is the most obvious and easiest to implement. The second involves students directly and is much harder to implement. This type requires teachers to embrace a role that is not traditional, a role that casts the teacher as one who orchestrates, one who carefully weaves the instructional pieces so that computers do what it is that they do best, and teachers gain greater freedom to do what they do best—motivate and guide learning.

Chapter Review

Knowledge Exercises

1. Define Computer Managed Instruction (CMI).

   Answer: CMI uses the computer to manage routine, boring tasks so the teacher will have more time for meaningful interaction with students. Two basic types of managerial tasks are

   - Type 1 tasks that involve students indirectly; for example, grade reporting, attendance reporting, course outlines, and test item banks.
   - Type 2 tasks that involve students directly; for example, using student records of acquired objectives accomplished to track progress, using computer graded tests to identify learning difficulties and design appropriate activities, and so on.

2. Describe the program ROSTER.

   Answer: ROSTER allows the teacher to input first and last names of up to 200 students, order the names either alphabetically or by student number, add to or make deletions from an existing list, and print out class rosters in three different formats.

3. Describe seven essential features of a good gradebook program.

   Answer: A good gradebook should

   - Allow you to enter student names and correct errors easily, as well as make additions or deletions to your list.
   - Sort the list alphabetically, by student number, or by class standing on a given assignment.
   - Allow you to enter enough scores for each student and a scaling factor for each score.
   - Allow you to indicate the absence of a given student for makeup purposes by use of a special character.
   - Find an average score for each student.
   - Furnish statistics for a set of scores, such as range, class average, class median, and standard deviation, and be able to translate student averages to letter grades using a teacher prescribed range.
   - Allow you to choose from a variety of print formats for reports.

4. Describe the program BIBLIOGRAPHER.

   Answer: The program allows you to save desired information about references, search for references with respect to codes you have established, retrieve and print a record in the retrieve record format.

5. Describe the program LABEL MAKER.

   Answer: This program allows you to make labels with 3–16 lines of information, each line containing up to 35 characters. You may make several copies of the same label or several different labels.

6. Describe the program TEST ITEM BANK.

   Answer: This program allows you to create, classify, and save up to 100 test items. You can also search for the ones meeting the criteria that you indicate and print a test of your choice.

7. Describe six crucial management features that a spelling program should have.

   Answer: The program should

   - Contain at least 32 lessons that contain words on a given grade level, and each lesson should be built around a spelling concept.
   - Include several diagnostic lessons containing sample words provided in the weekly lessons.
   - Provide a way for teachers to enter spelling lessons of their choice.
   - Include computer components involving related high-interest or application activities.
   - Come with a teacher's manual with suggestions and tips for each lesson.
   - Include a component for analyzing and organizing specific information on individual students.

Thought Exercises

1. Run the program GRADE several times and describe its features.
2. Are there other features that you think would improve GRADE? List them and provide a rationale for each suggested feature.
3. Write four spelling lessons appropriate to students at some instructional level. Structure each lesson around some theme or objective. Write a diagnostic lesson containing sample words from each lesson.

Activities

1. Direct a group of students (or any group of people) to list characteristics of humans and of computers. Discuss the list as a group, and assist in a refinement of the list. (You may want to present a list of characteristics and have individuals decide which characteristics belong to humans and which to computers.)

2. Enter grades for at least five students using the GRADE program. (Use at least three grades for each student.) Turn in hard copy showing examples of all possible print formats.

3. Copy the program BIBLIOGRAPHER onto another diskette, following the directions given in *Program Documentation for the Micro Goes to School.* Create a file by entering at least ten references related to instructional computing. Search for and print at least three references.

4. Copy the program TEST ITEM BANK onto a formatted diskette, following directions given in *Program Documentation for the Micro Goes to School.* Then enter at least 20 test items related to some subject and topic. Using specific search characters to search for and select 8 test items to prepare a lesson. Print the lesson and an answer key.

5. Use the program SUPER SPELL to enter the spelling lessons developed in Thought Exercise 3. Use the diagnostic test with some students and, based on the results, have them go through the appropriate lessons. Keep a log of their progress.

6. Use the program LABEL MAKER to generate at least 10 different labels.

Project

1. Develop an instructional plan for spelling suitable for a selected level of students. Include the components discussed in this chapter. Describe grade level, student population, objectives, spelling lists, and concept or reinforcement lessons.

Bibliography

Becker, Henry Jay. "Computers in Schools Today: Some Basic Considerations." *American Journal of Education* (November 1984): 25. Teachers may use computers as administrative tools to manage individualized instructional programs, including analyzing student performance and routing students to different instructional or practice activities.

Bergen, Steve, and Lynne Schalman. "Who's Pushing the Buttons?" *Classroom Computer Learning* (November–December 1984): 52. The teacher's familiarity with commercially available software is necessary in order to gain control of its use in the classroom.

Bernstein, Harriet T. "The Information Society: Byting the Hand That Feeds You." *Phi Delta Kappan* (October 1983): 109. School leaders and business people often merge to produce high-tech education for students only to end up with students who are narrowly trained and lacking in basic intellectual skills.

Bork, Alfred. "Computer-Based Learning in the Schools—The Two Major Problems." *Educational Computer Magazine* (January–February 1983): 18. Training teachers to recognize quality software will help persuade publishers to provide more useful materials.

Griswold, Philip. "Elementary Students' Attitudes During Two Years of Computer Assisted Instruction." *American Educational Research Journal* 21, no. 4 (Winter 1984): 751. Low achievers reflect positive attitudes towards their academic achievement after two years of participation in computer instruction.

Honig, Bill. "Computer Assisted Learning." *Computers in Education: Goals and Content* (1985): 5. Though hard to prove, it is a very appealing concept that as students gain control over the knowledge being acquired and the method of acquiring it, the benefit of the learning experience with computers is enhanced.

Judd, Wallace. "A Teacher's Place in the Computer Curriculum." *Phi Delta Kappan* (October 1983): 120. Computers can increase a teacher's power in the classroom.

Mevarech, Zemira, and Yisrael Rich. "Effects of Computer-Assisted Mathematics Instruction." *Disadvantaged Pupils' Cognitive and Affective Development* (1981): 8. Computer-assisted mathematics instruction given to disadvantaged elementary school pupils helped them to score higher on mathematics achievement than did their peers in traditional instruction classes.

Potts, Michael. "Still?" *Educational Computer Magazine* (September 1983): 22. Expensive tools are being used for limited goals.

Rosenbaum, Nina Joy. "Problems with Current Research in Writing Using the Microcomputer." *The Computing Teacher* (February 1984): 11. Because traditional textbooks used in remedial writing courses have failed to help underachievers, word processing may help to motivate students by making composing and revising easier and more enjoyable.

Ryba, Kenneth, and James Chapman. "Toward Improving Learning Strategies and Personal Adjustment with Computers." *The Computing Teacher* (August 1983): 49. Computers help to give students a feeling of internal control which appears to be vital for improving academic achievement.

Sheingold, Karen, et. al. "Microcomputer Use in Schools: Developing a Research Agenda." *Harvard Educational Review* (November 1983). New approaches in computer learning emphasize letting the child take the initiative—actually becoming the computer programmer—which is thought to facilitate powerful learning for the child.

Tolor, Alexander. "An Evaluation of a New Approach in Dealing with High School Underachievement." *The Computing Teacher* (September 1969): 16. An instructional computing program used to show underachieving students that their behavior determines their success or failure in school academics produced no significant change in grades.

Troutman, Andria. "Computer Managed Instruction, What Is It?" *Perspective* (March 1986): 1–4. Florida Center for Instructional Computing, Tampa. How can microcomputers be used to manage a test-driven, criterion-referenced, multimedia learning environment? What to look for in commercial software of this genre.

Ulloth, Dana. "The Computer Highway." *Media and Methods* (November 1984): 29. The traditional method of teaching large groups of students prevents the teacher from devoting individual attention to students.

Wager, Walter. "Microcomputers and the Management of Instruction." *Educational Computer* (October 1983): 47. An effective management system requires cooperation between a subject expert, an instructional designer, an evaluator, and a computer applications person.

Zemke, Suzanne. "Microcomputers and Education—Choices and Consequences." *Educational Computer Magazine* (March–April 1983): 43. The use of computer assisted instruction without teacher interaction locks students into passive learning roles.

PART

4

TOOLS OF THE TRADE

In the last section we discussed programs that illustrate how computers can be used in the classroom to direct, enhance, and manage instruction. In this section we're looking at the heavyweights, the tools that turn the IBM PC into a powerhouse: applications software. We are going to discuss a special category of commercial programs that have significant implications for instruction. These programs are referred to as *generic software tools*.

A generic software tool is a program that allows the user to carry out general tasks. For instance, a program that transforms a computer into the ultimate typewriter is called a word processor. A word processor is indeed generic because there is no end to the type and number of documents that could be prepared using it. There are several other types of generic software: data base, spreadsheet, and telecommunications.

None of these tools was created with teachers in mind, but they all have educational applications. That is the emphasis we place on them in the ensuing chapters. We will describe how they might be used to create materials for instruction. We will also discuss two kinds of learning objectives. The first involves skills and abilities that must be acquired in order to use a particular generic software tool. The second involves academic skills and abilities related to content in the traditional curriculum. Our hope is to show you how a generic software tool can be used to improve the effectiveness and efficiency of teaching traditional learning objectives. For each type of generic software discussed, we will demonstrate sample lessons and teaching or learning aids.

WORD PROCESSORS
Writing without Cramps

Getting Started

Is there a soul alive who doesn't feel a need to communicate in writing? It seems not, for we humans have contrived many tools for doing so. Yet until recently, using even the most sophisticated tool available locked the user into a static time-consuming writing mode. In recent years, one of the most important computer tools ever conceived made its way into the average school and home. This computer tool is called a word processor. *It has been said that a word processor with a printer is nothing more than a glorified typewriter. This hardly describes its vast potential. A word processor turns the written word into a fluid medium, parallel to the fluidness of thought. With word processing, your fingers become extensions of your mind; recording, inserting, deleting, and quickly moving ideas around the screen until the words, finally captured, do not betray the ideas that inspired them. A word processor will not make a writer out of someone who does not want to write. But for those who have the inclination, it will hasten the flow of ideas from the mind to the page. Thus we maintain that word processors should play a major role in education at all levels.*

In keeping with this fundamental premise, this chapter has three primary goals. The first is to describe important features of word processors, spell checkers, and thesauri so that users can become better buyers. The second is to provide a few word processing lessons for you so that you can accomplish personal word processing goals. The third is to illustrate how word processors can be used to enhance the traditional school curriculum. The important distinction among these three goals is this: The first two involve teaching about word processors whereas the third involves teaching with word processors. Ultimately, the latter is most important.

Objectives for Teachers

To successfully complete this chapter, you should be able to

1. Define the term *word processor.*
2. List and briefly describe the important features of a word processor's editor, file manager, and print component.

3. Describe other computer utilities that may work in conjunction with a word processor.
4. Briefly describe the important attributes of a spell checker.
5. Describe the difference between a literal or root-word dictionary.
6. Compare and contrast a typewriter and a word processor.
7. Perform fundamental word processing functions.
8. Describe or develop word processing lessons for different student populations.

What Is a Word Processor?

The first word processors were machines that had built-in programs dedicated solely to the task of creating, editing, and maintaining documents. Appropriately, they are known as **dedicated word processors.** Unlike dedicated word processors, microcomputers can perform an almost endless number of different tasks. When you talk about word processing on a microcomputer, you are talking only about the software, the program that gives it that function. All microcomputer word processors are descended from dedicated word processors, and with the arrival of powerful micros like the IBM PC, they are beginning to exceed the capabilities of the dedicated machines. From now on in this chapter, we will use the term *word processor* to refer to microcomputer programs designed to create, edit, and maintain documents.

Word processors come in two basic types. Which one you choose is almost completely a matter of preference. It has nothing to do with the sophistication of the program. Since neither type has been officially named, we'll call them WYSIWYG (pronounced "wiziwig")—popular slang for what-you-see-is-what-you-get—and LOWIP (pronounced "lo-wip")—a term we just invented meaning looks-OK-when-I-print-it. Almost all word processors are a combination of both types.

The ultimate WYSIWYG word processor would display text on the screen that looks exactly like it does when it is printed. That means on-screen italics, line spacing, underlining, boldfacing, margins, footnotes, page numbers, and any other characteristic possible. To accomplish the polished appearance, the program would have to maintain codes in the document that the user cannot see.

At the other end of the spectrum would be the most extreme LOWIP word processor possible, which wouldn't care what text looks like on the screen and would display codes and commands that tell the printer what to do with the text. To illustrate the difference between the two, when you want a

WYSIWYG word processor to center a title, it centers it right on the screen like this:

```
                    THIS IS THE TITLE
```

The screen of a LOWIP word processor performing the same function would look something like this:

```
\ctr
THIS IS THE TITLE
```

or this:

```
@C34THIS IS THE TITLE
```

The codes \ctr and @C34 are both embedded codes that tell the printer to center the text line that follows the command when printing. The exact code employed depends upon the program.

It used to be that you had to put up with LOWIP if you wanted a program that could make use of all features of the printer; the WYSIWYG word processors just didn't have the horsepower. This is no longer true. There are WYSIWYGs today that handle just about any task, and they are getting better all the time. As mentioned earlier, most word processors combine both techniques, using LOWIP techniques for functions that are difficult to accomplish otherwise. Many people prefer their screens to show all codes. They maintain that they have greater control if they can see all codes that are sent to the printer. If this is your preference, then you are definite LOWIP material.

All word processors must have three capabilities: editing, file saving and loading, and printing, but beyond this, the range of features may vary greatly. We will now explain the basic functions that every word processor should have.

The Editor

When you are using the editor, the screen resembles a blank piece of paper. With special keys or key combinations, the user is able to move to various locations on the screen and enter desired text. Commands can be issued that cause the text to be manipulated in certain ways. The following sections describe some of the important features different editors might have.

Full-Screen Editing

There are special keys, called cursor keys, that allow the user to move anywhere on the screen. This is called full-screen editing. Other special keys allow the user to quickly browse through a document or move rapidly to its beginning or end.

Margins and Tabs

Commands are available that allow the user to define margin and/or tab settings. Usually margins can be set so that printed line widths can vary from 10 to 132 or more characters. This feature accommodates **dot matrix printers** that can produce text that is standard, double-wide, or compressed. It also accommodates extra-wide printers. Tabs are usually preset at five-unit intervals and can usually be reset to any position on the current margin line.

Automatic Wordwrap

When text is typed to the end of a line, it automatically wraps to the next line, bringing any partial word with it. The user does not have to press the RETURN key, which is usually reserved to indicate that the end of a paragraph has been reached and that text is to be continued on the next line. This feature allows a writer to concentrate on what is being written and not worry about typing off the right-hand side of the page.

A feature that is becoming more and more common is *hyphenation*. Words that can be hyphenated at the margin are indicated by the program. The user can decide whether the suggested hyphenation is desired or whether the entire word should be wrapped to the next line.

Insert/Delete Features

There are special keys that allow the user to insert or delete characters, words, or lines. With this feature you are never totally locked in. You can change lines, phrases, or words at will and quickly move on. Some word processors even have what is called an undelete key; this key allows you to recover text should you change your mind about deleted text.

Justification

Right-justified text has a right margin that is a straight line rather than a ragged one. Text can usually be right-justified anywhere in a document. Furthermore, commands should be flexible enough so that justification commands can be turned on and off from paragraph to paragraph.

Special Effects Available

Passages can be isolated and identified as text to be underlined, printed in boldface, italics, printed with overstrike, or ignored when printing takes place.

Block Commands

There are block commands that allow the user to identify a block of text to be copied, moved, or deleted, or have some other operation performed upon it. The moves or copies may affect the working document (the document in memory being edited) or a document that is in a file on a data diskette. Perhaps the user would like to take excerpts from a working document and save these to a separate file. This would be easily accomplished with appropriate block commands.

Import/Export Commands

There are read commands that allow the user to take materials from other files on the disk and copy that material into the text that is being edited. When this is done with commonly used passages, it is sometimes referred to as boilerplating. There are other commands that allow the user to block off parts of the text that is being edited and save the blocked text as a new file.

Paging Features

Line, column, and page displays tell you where you are in the document. It's pretty nice to know when you are on line so-and-so and column such-and-such. Most programs also display page breaks. It's often useful to know where one page ends and another begins. No one wants the last line of a document straggling over to an extra page.

Search-and-Replace Commands

Commands are available that allow the user to search for and find any set of characters (a character string) in the text. Provisions are made that allow the user to replace the first character string with another string. The user has the option to make replacements one at a time or all at once. The word *global* is often used in reference to search-and-replace commands because they can affect the entire document.

Some programs allow wildcards to be used. Sometimes you want to find a certain passage or a certain name in a document, but you don't know the exact spelling. You have the first, last, or middle few letters. For these situations you need a word processor that has a wildcard search. This search allows you to use a character—such as *—as a wildcard in the character string for which you will be searching. For example, if you gave the command to search for app*, the program would search the document you were editing and find all the words that begin with app.

Some word processors allow you to ignore case (uppercase versus lowercase) as necessary. This is handy when you want to search for a word and you don't care whether or not it begins a sentence.

On-Line Help

Help commands are available that can be used anytime, anywhere in the program. These commands call up information on the program's operation. They provide helpful hints in areas of probable difficulty. Sometimes help takes the form of on-screen menus that can be turned off and on as you are editing. These menus provide information on how to issue editing commands.

Proofing Features

The program provides a utility that allows the user to see exactly what the text will look like when printed. Any LOWIP features that the word processor has will be turned off. Some programs do this by merely erasing the offending characters from the screen. Others clear the screen and then print the document to the screen exactly as it will appear when printed to paper.

The Filing Manager

Not all word processors have much in the way of file managers. But it's much easier to manipulate files from within a program than to have to exit the program and use DOS. Certain basic features are necessary if a word processor's file manager is to be efficient. Here we will list and discuss some of the more important of these features.

Save/Retrieve

Obviously a good word processor must have features that allow you to save and retrieve files. It is important that the save command have a safety feature. When saving the latest version of a file with a filename that has been used before, the safety feature should alert you to the possibility of losing the previously saved file. Of course, if you are revising a file, you will want to write over the old version. However, there are times when you want to keep several versions of the same file. So you want to be able to retract a hastily executed save command. Any word processor designed for the IBM PC family will record the date when a file is saved so that the last date of editing can always be determined. Of course, this means that you will have to first enter the date when you boot the computer.

Copy, Delete, and Rename

There are commands that allow the user to copy files from one disk to another disk without leaving the word processor. It is also important to be able to delete and rename files. The alternative—leaving the word processor and going back to DOS to handle these housekeeping chores—is very inconvenient.

Automatic Backup

Some word processors automatically make a backup copy of any file you save. If for some reason a file is accidentally deleted, then the backup is accessible. Some people argue that this is not really a good feature, since it wastes too much disk space and isn't actually safe because the backup is saved with the original file on the same disk. Most word processors give you the option to disable this feature. Another kind of safety feature backs up your document at regular intervals while you are working on it. This save-as-you-go feature can be invaluable if the power should happen to go out in the middle of your work on an important paper.

Subdirectories

As **hard disks** become more prevalent, it is important for word processors to use DOS **subdirectories.** Simply put, a disk may be "chopped up" into several logical pieces called subdirectories. For example, you might set aside one part of your disk to catalog reading activities and call it READING, and specify another part for student records, and call it STUDENTS. Many word processors still on the market don't accommodate subdirectories. The better ones allow the user to specify paths to different subdirectories to implement filing functions. For example, let's say that Jim is operating an IBM XT and has defined a personal work space—a subdirectory—on the hard drive. The name of the subdirectory might be something like this: C:\WORDWING\JIM. This means that WORDWING is a subdirectory of the *root directory* (the one that already exists on any disk) and that JIM is a subdirectory of WORDWING (a brand of word processor). WORDWING may have many subdirectories for there may be many persons using it. When Jim is preparing his documents, it is important that he is able to tell the word processor that he wants his documents saved or loaded from the C: drive and that he wants them saved or loaded from his subdirectory. Otherwise Jim will have to do one of three things:

1. Save and load his files to and from a data diskette on the A: drive.
2. Save his file on the same directory with the word processor. Of course, everyone else might be doing the same thing, so security is lost. Plus, if a disk contains files belonging to several different people, confusion is bound to occur.
3. After he saves his files on the WORDWING subdirectory, he must copy them to his subdirectory. This is a lot of unnecessary bother. If Jim wants to load a file from his subdirectory, he must then put up with the additional bother of reversing these steps.

So the bottom line is this: A really good word processor should allow users to specify paths to subdirectories from which filing functions are to be implemented. (This is an advanced DOS topic and we have only touched on it here. Many books are available on the subject; see your library or book store if you're interested.)

ASCII Files

Believe it or not, very few word processors are able to read each other's files, since they almost always use different formats. It is important for a program to allow you to save what are called *nondocument files.* These files are saved in standard ASCII codes, eliminating codes that are defined uniquely by a particular brand of word processing program. Such files can easily be transported from one program to another (called *porting*) and can be used in telecommunication activities. Another feature that enhances any word processor is a utility that converts any previously saved file to an ASCII file. Incredibly, many word processors don't have this feature.

Record of Disk Space

The program alerts the user when there is insufficient space on a data disk to save a document that is in computer memory. It provides a way to retract a save command and prepare a new data disk. In fact, the word processor should indicate, at either the beginning of the editing process or on the screen, how much space is left on the data disk and how large the loaded document is. No one wants to spend hours preparing a file only to lose it because the program didn't keep track of disk space and one learned—too late—that there was not enough room on the disk to save the program. Unfortunately, there are widely used, expensive programs that have this inexcusable fault.

The Print Module

Certain basic features are necessary if the print module of a word processor is to be efficient. Here we will list and discuss some of the more important of these features.

Printer Configuration

The program must contain easy-to-use routines that allow the user to configure it to a large variety of printers, especially the one the user owns. There is nothing more frustrating than to purchase a word processor and a printer only to find that you must be an expert to get the word processor to communicate with the printer. It is especially important that educators check this feature, since most schools purchase their software through the mail. Good programs come with libraries of preconfigured drivers, which enable them to be used with hundreds of different printers.

Format

There should be commands that allow the user to set margins, borders, headings, footings, spacing, paragraph indentation, page lengths, automatic page breaks, and so on. You should check these features carefully for several reasons. First, you want to be sure that the available formatting commands are sufficient to create the kinds of printed documents you need or desire. While many of these instructions are usually embedded in the text, some can or must be set in the print module. Some programs allow the commands to be issued either way. Sometimes it is helpful to have the commands embedded in the document so that the document can be printed over and over again without resetting print options each time. On the other hand, you may want to print some documents in a variety of forms. For such documents, you don't want the commands embedded in the text; rather, you want to set the commands just before printing.

Some Super Extras

There are a lot of extra features a word processor could have that would make it extra special. Having these features would not excuse the nonexistence of other standard features, though. The following sections touch on some of those extras that may be suitable for your needs.

Outlining

Some word processors provide automatic outlining routines. These routines establish outline numbering and lettering setups. When in the edit mode, the user is able to insert new items and then give a renumber or reletter command that reorganizes the outline. This feature is especially suitable to individuals who write, lecture, or give professional presentations.

Calculating

Some programs allow you to stop midstream in the editor, turn on a screen calculator, compute to your heart's content, then return to edit mode with calculations inserted as you like them. This is a very nifty feature for those who work with mathematical, financial, or statistical reports. It is a super feature for those who teach or write about mathematics.

Split-Screen, Windowing, Multiple File Editing

There are word processors that will allow you to divide the screen into parts. Different parts of the same file or different files can be shown in separate sections of the screen. In other words, you can compare different sections of text while you are editing. This is a handy feature to have if you want to review sections of text or reports before you insert them in your document, or before you make conclusive statements that are based upon certain evidence.

Typewriter Mode

Once you have used a word processor you may never want to return to pencils, pens, or typewriters except for short, simple tasks. Word processors are available now that also allow you to do small jobs. These processors have a **typewriter mode.** This mode enables you to enter text that prints immediately so that typing a small note or memo, addressing an envelope, or preparing a label are all easy tasks.

Some Strong Relatives

Having a good word processor is super, but having one whose operation is coordinated with other useful programs is the ultimate. Programs that allow the user to check spelling, correct grammar, find synonyms for overused words, prepare an index for a book, or prepare a mass mailing can help you complete routine tasks that once took hours of drudgery. We leave it as an exercise for the reader to investigate indexing programs and mail mergers. Here we focus on spell checkers, grammar checkers, and thesauri since these programs have greatest implications for instruction.

Spelling Checkers/Thesauri

A spell-checking program scans and compares words in a document with words in its dictionary. When a word in the document does not match any word in the program's dictionary, then the word is somehow marked for the user's consideration (we'll discuss this later). Many advertised spell checkers brag about their large dictionaries, so it is easy to get caught up in the argument that more is better. Actually, most writing tasks can be accomplished effectively and efficiently with far fewer words than is generally suspected. A good spell checker could have a dictionary with as few as 20,000 words; 50,000 words would usually be considered more than adequate. On the other hand, if disk space, memory space, and program speed are not considerations, then more than 50,000 words will not hurt matters. Regardless of the number of words, two characteristics should be present. The dictionary should include the 10,000 most frequently used words and should allow users to add words that fit their special interests. *Conclusion:* When reviewing a spell checker it's important to get beyond the number of words in its dictionary and look for features that are equally important. In doing so, look for answers to the questions posed in the following sections.

Can I add to or delete words from the dictionary? People in different fields or affiliated with different professional groups may have reason to use special words or acronyms associated with those fields or professions. Thus, it is especially helpful to be able to add words to a dictionary, thereby tailoring it to special needs. For example, a mathematics teacher may want to add a list of technical terms and names of prominent mathematicians related to a frequently taught course. Also, since there is certainly a chance that errors made when entering technical terms into a speller's dictionary may not be caught immediately, it is important to be able to edit words added to the dictionary.

Is the dictionary a literal or root-word dictionary? A literal dictionary is one that contains root words as well as derivations of the root words. The spell checker compares a word in a document with words in its dictionary, character by character; that is, the comparison is *literal.* For example, if the dictionary contains the word *believe* then it will probably contain the words *believing, believes,* and *believable.* On the other hand, a *root-word* dictionary saves space and search time by containing only the root word *believe* and possible prefixes or suffixes, with built-in features for checking text against the root word and possible modifications. A literal dictionary is generally more accurate and requires more search time and more disk and computer memory space. A root-word dictionary can contain more words in less disk and computer memory space but is less dependable.

How large a document can I spell check? Your documents will be of different lengths. It is important to survey the kinds of writing tasks you would like to accomplish and make sure that the spell checker you select will be adequate.

Can I use the spell checker with the word processors I use? Sometimes a spell checker is specifically designed to work with certain word processors. Often minor alterations to a good spell-checking program will adapt it so that it can be used with a specific word processor. In any event, it is the responsibility of the vendor from whom you buy the product or the manufacturer of the product to help you make the connection. Don't purchase until you are sure that you can get good answers to this question. This is a good reason that your word processor be able to export ASCII.

Will the program indicate the number of words used in a document? Will it indicate the frequency of a specific word, if requested? These features are helpful when you are trying to break habitual modes of expression. When you discover that you are using the same tired word over and over again you can search and replace with words that add freshness to your document.

Will the program provide a list of synonyms for a given word in my document? If you discover that you have used a particular word excessively or if a word does not provide exactly the shade of meaning for which you are searching, then it's time to go synonym searching. Thus, it is extremely helpful for a spell checker to have a **thesaurus** feature that will display a list of synonyms for a word you indicate, as well as replace, at your request, the word in your document with one of the listed synonyms.

How easy is the program to use? Here's where you must really get down to the basics. There are a lot of programs on the market that sport catchy little utilities and exude praise for the tremendous size of their dictionaries, but when you attempt to run the programs they turn out to be either difficult or clumsy. The best programs start checking anywhere in a document that you indicate, check each word until they discover one that is not recognized, then stop, giving you a list of options from which to choose. These options should be very flexible, letting you handle text in a variety of ways. The options should be undergirded by important program utilities such as the following:

1. The program will list words from the dictionary that are spelled nearly like the one in the text that is not recognized by the dictionary. The user can elect to immediately replace the unrecognized word with any one of the listed words.
2. There are commands that cause the program to remember and ignore further occurrences of words in a document that are not recognized by the dictionary, without adding them to the dictionary.
3. There are commands that allow the user to stop or start spell checking at any point and return to or from the editing mode.

Of course, there are other features that a spell checker could have, but the ones we've listed are about the most important. After all, you don't want to get stuck with a spell checker that only lists the words it doesn't recognize, leaving it to you to find the appropriate spellings.

Grammar Checker

A spell checker can only find words that have been spelled incorrectly; it cannot tell you if the words are used correctly. Once you have written your document and checked the spelling, you might want to use a grammar checker for this and other functions. Grammar checkers are improving and will perform a number of important editing tasks in the future.

In a Nutshell

Certainly we have not listed all the characteristics a word processor, a spell checker, or a thesaurus can have. Far from it. In fact, by the time this book is published, there may be new features we have never dreamed of! This brings up an important issue. How can you avoid overkill? Some word processors include commands for attaining goals that are harder to use than attaining the goal in traditional ways. Another point: we are not suggesting that you obtain a word processor that has every feature we have discussed. Not at all! There are many tasks to be accomplished with a word processor: some easy, some hard, some long and complicated, and some short and sweet. Acquiring and learning to use a word processor requires an investment of money and time. You should analyze what you want to accomplish and buy a program that will do what you want, allowing room to grow. There is no reason, however, to spend time and money to acquire sophistication you'll never use.

With respect to spell checkers though, we suggest that you look for all the characteristics discussed and even more. As word processors become a more prominent educational tool, so will spell checkers. Thus, you should begin to look for features that are productive in the educational environment. These features may include keeping a list of the spelling errors with a list of corrected words for the user to have for reference. Moreover, the program could classify the types of errors that a user is making; for example, incorrect endings, not doubling letters appropriately, using *ie* and *ee* incorrectly. The spell checker may alert users to words used frequently so users may avoid redundancy. The spell checker could examine the text and tell the users how many common or unique words are used. This feature might help improve the users' vocabularies.

Well, that's enough for now. The main point is this: Examine your word processing needs and make purchases accordingly. To help you in this endeavor, we provide a detailed checklist at the end of this chapter. This checklist (Resource Sheet 10) will help you decide whether a word processing or spell-checking program is adequate for your needs.

Word Processing in the Classroom

We have made a lot of noise about features of word processors and what to look for when shopping. At least two more topics warrant discussion:

1. How does one learn to use a word processor?
2. How might word processors be used to enhance or manage traditional instruction?

In the remainder of this chapter we will explore answers to these questions.

Enhancing Instruction

There are countless ways teachers can use word processors to enhance instruction. Teachers can prepare hands-on activities that students complete using a word processor or they can prepare printed activities that students complete without any special equipment.

Hands-On Activities

When preparing hands-on activities, instructional objectives should be clear. The objectives may involve acquisition of word processing skills or acquisition of subject matter concepts. Of course, both types of objectives are important. Word processing will revolutionize written communication and replace pens, pencils, and typewriters for most tasks. To say that all students should learn word processing skills isn't an exaggeration. However, learning to use a word processor can't be an end in itself. Students must also learn new modes for processing information. Using pencil and paper, or even the typewriter, to write locks you into static modes. Once words are committed to paper, it's hard to change them. You erase, scratch out, cut, paste, staple, or redo and the results are not always attractive. Using a dictionary and thesaurus is time-consuming and tedious. Often you settle for less, choosing words that don't convey precisely what you want to say. With a word processor, the medium is *fluid*. You can capture spontaneous impressions and change the flow of ideas midstream. Words can be copied, deleted, rearranged, or modified with simple keystrokes. You learn to compose as you go, using trial and error to examine many possibilities quickly. What's more, you can do it privately. You don't have to share false starts or discarded efforts.

How does this relate to students? Whenever possible, educational opportunities should provide tools that extend problem-solving abilities. Schools should emphasize environments where students can try ideas, make mistakes, correct mistakes, and grow in the process. Students should have opportunities to privately view and modify ideas before submitting them for peer or teacher approval. They should develop skills for independently directing their learning. Of course, word processors can't do all this. But, with the direction of good teachers, the probability of achieving such goals is greatly increased.

The rest of this section will include sample hands-on activities that illustrate these ideas. Each activity involves two goals. One goal is to provide readers with experiences that develop word processing skills. The other goal is to illustrate activities for school students that develop traditional subject matter concepts and abilities. For each activity the following criteria are specified:

Title. Name of lesson.

Curriculum Area and Level. Precollege curriculum area and school level for which the activity is suitable.

Word Processing Objectives. List of word processing skills that the lesson emphasizes.

Subject Matter Objectives. List of academic skills and concepts the lesson emphasizes.

Directions to the Reader. Directions that tell the reader how to use the activity as a personal exercise for acquiring word processing concepts. If you have access to a computer and a word processor, you should complete each lesson. Prepare a special diskette for the exercises you complete. Use a word processor to log your experiences noting new word processing concepts you acquire. Save the lesson and the log on your word processing disk.

Lesson Preparation. Directions for preparing the lesson at the indicated school level. By preparing and saving these lessons, the reader acquires a set of sample activities for school students at different levels. Document names such as EX1, which indicates Student Exercise 1, are used. These documents should be saved using the suggested names so that they are easy to distinguish from other documents.

Directions for the Students. Directions for school students who complete the lesson to acquire subject matter objectives.

Sample. Many activities include a sample exercise, example, or puzzle.

Commentary. Suggestions for lesson delivery, appropriate prerequisites, and follow-up activites.

Study each activity. Note the word processing skills that are emphasized. Complete the lesson as directed in Directions to the Reader. Then consider the lesson from a teacher's point of view. Notice that many lessons could be presented in today's classrooms using traditional materials—pencil, paper, typewriters, and books. Try to decide why each activity might be more motivating or productive using a word processor. Think how students might respond differently to the activities depending on whether or not they are using a word processor. Contrast educational benefits of the sample activities with activities such as fill-in-the-blank, multiple choice, and exercises in which the student is to put an *x* next to the correct word that are widely used in today's schools.

ACTIVITY 10.1

Getting the Most out of Meaning

Curriculum Area and Level. Language Development. Suitable for fifth grade and above. With revision, the lesson might be used in lower grades or with low achievers.

Word Processing Objectives. To provide experiences using cursor keys, insert, and delete features. To provide experiences naming and saving a document file.

Subject Matter Objective. The student will use adjectives, adverbs, and other parts of speech to complete a simple paragraph.

Directions to the Reader. Use a word processor to enter the sample paragraph. Use the cursor keys to move the cursor to each * in the paragraph. Use insert mode to replace each * with an appropriate word. (See the directions for the students.) When you have finished, name your document file MOODY.DOC and SAVE it. Make a log to indicate the word processing skills you practiced in this lesson. Consider questions such as the following:

Does your word processor allow you to delete a word, sentence, or page in a single operation?

If you change your mind can you recover deleted text?

Lesson Preparation. Use a word processor to enter the sample paragraph and student directions. Save them as a file called EX1.DOC

Directions for Students. Read the following paragraph. Notice that it is not complete. In many places you will find either * or **. Replace * with one word. Replace ** with more than one word. When finished, name and save your paragraph.

Sample Paragraph.
When I leaned over the * rail of the * bridge and gazed into the * water below, I was **. It was * to see how the experiences of the last ** had * me. After what seemed to be ** I came back to **. I slowly looked around to see if **, then I moved * from the rail. I turned toward **. I had to go now and face **. As I * away, my * became *. My heart * a bit but my head said **. Well now, tomorrow is another day!

Commentary. Precede this activity with an activity in which students list adverbs and adjectives they know. Organize lists so that words having similar meaning are grouped together. Discuss words, allowing students to share ideas. As students complete the lesson, encourage them to experiment with different adjective and adverb replacements. The goal is to encourage the creative use of the students' vocabularies as well as to increase them.

ACTIVITY 10.2

Changing the Mood

Curriculum Area. Language Development. Suitable for fifth grade and above.

Word Processing Objectives. To provide experiences using cursor keys, insert, and delete features. To provide experience using block copy features. To provide experiences naming, saving, and loading a document file.

Subject Matter Objective. The student will practice using adjectives, adverbs, and other parts of speech to express different moods with the same basic paragraph.

Directions to the Reader. Use a word processor to enter the sample paragraph provided in Activity 10.1. Use its block copy command to make two more copies of the paragraph. Use the cursor keys and insert mode to replace the *s. Complete each paragraph differently to create contrasting moods. Name your document file MOODY2.DOC. Save and print it. Check to see if your word processor has other block commands such as block move and block delete. Determine how your printer works:

How do you align the paper at the top of the page?
How do you perform line feed and form feed operations?

Make a lesson log.

Lesson Preparation. Enter the paragraph and use the block copy command to make a document file containing two copies of the paragraph. Name the file EX2.DOC and save it.

Directions for Students. Load EX2.DOC. You will get a document with two paragraphs. In each paragraph you will find these symbols: * and **. Replace * with one word. Replace ** with more than one word. Finish each paragraph so their moods are different. Print your paragraphs.

Commentary. Students may require help loading and saving document files. Using the printer will pose problems for young or inexperienced students. They will need help aligning printer paper and form feeding. Precede this activity with discussion and examples of mood changes created by using different words in the same basic sentence.

ACTIVITY 10.3

Combining Sentences

Curriculum Area and Level. Writing. Fifth grade and above. Simpler paragraphs could be written for younger students.

Word Processing Objectives. Inserting and deleting. Setting margins and using tabs. Using text formatting commands such as the center, bold text, or underline command.

Subject Matter Objective. The student will combine short sentences to achieve precise, economic writing.

Directions to the Reader. Set the left margin to 10 and the right margin to 50. Enter and rewrite the sample paragraph, combining sentence pairs to produce a more fluid passage. Use the [Tab] key to indent the first sentence in the paragraph. Give the paragraph a title and use your word processor's center command to center the title two spaces above the paragraph. Save your document as BUS1.DOC, then print it. Determine special formatting commands of your word processor, such as bolding text, underlining, and so on. Bold or underline the title of the paragraph. Prepare a log that describes what you learned in this lesson.

Lesson Preparation. Use a word processor to enter the sample paragraph and student directions. Save them as a file called EX3.DOC

Directions to Students. Load the lesson file EX3.DOC. It is a paragraph composed of short, choppy sentences. Combine sentence pairs in the paragraph to make a more interesting and readable paragraph. *Example:* You might combine "It was a hot day." and "The sun was shining brightly." to produce the sentence "It was a hot, sunny day." When you are finished, save the new paragraph and print it.

Sample Paragraph.
It was a hot day. The sun was shining brightly. We were riding in an old bus. It was dusty. The smell of gas fumes floated in through the open windows. Yet riding in the bus was interesting. Old signs were on the wall. There was writing on the walls too. There was writing on the backs of the seats too. My friend, Alice, and I took turns reading the signs and handwritten messages. There were some that were really funny. One sign about banking said "The early bird gets the worm." Underneath this sign was a handwritten message that said "So who wants a pocket full of worms?"

ACTIVITY 10.4

Making Sense of It

Curriculum Area and Level. Logic, Math, and Language Arts. Fifth grade and above.

Word Processing Objectives. Using search and replace commands.

Subject Matter Objective. The student will detect and correct errors and solve problems.

Directions to the Reader. Enter the sample paragraph. There are consonants that must be replaced in the document so that it will make sense. Decide what those consonants are. Use the search and replace command of your word processor to replace inappropriate consonants. Use care and planning; the task is not as simple as it appears. You could accidentally make undesirable replacements. Save your new document as NUTS.DOC

Lesson Preparation. Use a word processor to enter the sample paragraph and student directions. Save them as a file called EX4.DOC

Directions to Students. Load the lesson file EX4.DOC. Your challenge is to read the paragraph and decide what two letters must be replaced in the paragraph so that it makes sense. Use the search and replace command of your word processor to replace inappropriate letters. Use care and planning; the task is not as simple as it appears. You could accidentally make undesirable replacements. When replacements are complete, solve the resulting problem.

Sample Paragraph.
Wagmar Wevlin packages Waphanie Woughnuss for Willi Welli. Waphanie Wevlin is Wagmar's mosher anw she person afser whom she woughnuss are namew. Waphanie is also she heaw chef for Willi Welli. Recensly she refinew she recipe for Waphanie Woughnuss, enlarging shem, awwing a special spice so she wough, leaving shem in she oven a minuse longer, anw wecorasing shem wish fluffy colorew creme. Wagmar Wevlin packs 15 of she bigger, welicious, wecorasew Waphanie woughnuss inso each Willi Welli #1 Box. Wagwoow Wevlin, Wagmar Wevlin's olwer brosher, places 8 Willi Welli #1 boxes of bigger, welicious, wecorasew woughness inso Willi Welli #2 boxes, so shas she woughnuss will nos ges crushew wuring shipmens. Waphanie's woughnuss are solw everywhere, from Wenver so Welaware. Waviw Wevlin, Wagmar Wevlins's cousin arranges 12 Willi Welli #2 boxes of bigger, welicious, wecorasew Waphanie woughnuss inso a Willi Welli Big Wozen. Warline Wevlin, Waviw Wevlin's mosher, manages she packing plans where she Big Wozen Packs of bigger, welicious, wecorasew Waphanie woughnuss are packew in shipping crases - forsy Big Wozen so a crase. Eighs crases of she Big Wozen Packs of bigger, welicious, wecorasew Waphanie woughnuss are ssorew in bins. Is sakes 75 bins so fill she Willi Welli Sranspors sruck shas sakes she bigger, welicious, wecorasew Waphanie woughnuss so she four corners of she nasion. How many bigger, welicious, wecorasew Waphanie woughnuss are in a sruckloaw? How mighs Waphanie anw Warline be relasew? Consiwer all possibilisies.

Commentary. Keep several backup copies of the original story handy. Some students will replace some consonants inappropriately. When this happens, document files become very confusing. Sometimes it is easier to start over than it is to try to correct replacements.

ACTIVITY 10.5

In Conclusion!

Curriculum Area and Level. Logic, English, and Math. Sixth grade and above.

Word Processing Objectives. General editing skills.

Subject Matter Objective. The student will use clues to arrive at logical conclusions.

Directions to the Reader. Read the clues given in the sample puzzle and solve it. Use your word processor to copy the clues in a column. Head the column with a centered, underlined title. Then write a paragraph using the clues that logically leads the reader through the clues to a logical conclusion. Give your paragraph a centered, underlined title. Use the Tab key to indent the first line in your paragraph and set the margins so that the paragraph is 40 columns wide. Save your document as LOGIC.DOC

Lesson Preparation. Use a word processor to enter the sample paragraph. Save it and the student directions as a file called EX5.DOC. Prepare printed copies to distribute.

Directions for Students. Read the clues given in the puzzle and solve it. Then use your word processor to write a paragraph using all the clues. The argument should smoothly lead the reader to the correct solution.

Make up a set of clues for your own puzzle. When you have finished, save your work on disk and print copies. Let your classmates try their skills at solving your puzzle.

Sample Exercise.

Problem: What day of the week is it?

Clues:

1. The only time I eat popcorn is on nights when we watch the late show.
2. If you are at Granny's, you can't watch TV, since she doesn't have one.
3. If tomorrow is a school day, then I must get to bed early.
4. I'm now eating popcorn.
5. If it is Friday, then we go to Granny's house and sit up late talking.
6. When I go to bed early, then I don't watch the late show.

Commentary. This should be preceded with a readiness activity in which students discuss how arguments are used in society for persuasion. Arguments are used to persuade people to buy goods, elect politicians, decide political issues, and so forth. Students should consider the importance of analyzing arguments to determine their validity.

ACTIVITY 10.6

Word Whirlwind

Curriculum Area and Level. Language Development and Spelling. Fourth grade and above.

Word Processing Objectives. General editing skills. Using a spell checker.

Subject Matter Objective. The student will develop spelling and word recognition skills.

Directions to the Reader. Enter the sample puzzle and solve it. Use a spell checker to check the words in your list. Prepare another puzzle and demonstrate a solution to your puzzle, spell checking the words in your solution. Save your work on disk and prepare printed copies.

Lesson Preparation. Prepare, save, and print a lesson that includes the sample puzzle and one you originate. Use the filename EX6.DOC. Your lesson should include directions to the student.

Directions for the Students. Here are some word puzzles for you to solve. Use a word processor and a spell checker. Start with the first word in each column and change one letter in each word to create a new word. See if you can make 10 new words without stopping. When your list is complete, spell check your words. Here is an example:

We start with	comb
we change the *b* to *e*	come
we change the *c* to *h*	home
we change the *m* to *l*	hole
we change the *l* to *p*	hope
and so on.	.
	.
	.

Sample Puzzle.

mark	pole	stem	. . .
____	____	____	
____	____	____	
____	____	____	
____	____	____	
____	____	____	
____	____	____	
____	____	____	
____	____	____	
____	____	____	

Commentary. Students should see demonstrations before working with puzzles independently. Group students in pairs so they can share ideas. Supply reference materials such as dictionaries, word lists the class generates, and word lists from spelling texts. Encourage students to try different words in the same spot to find choices that are most productive. Encourage them to put down words they think, but are not sure, are correct.

The next example is designed for history. Students are required to put statements describing historical events in chronological order. Similar activities could be designed for other subject areas. For example, for a civics class, activities could be designed that require students to order steps in some legal procedure such as steps necessary for becoming a citizen of the United States.

ACTIVITY 10.7

Good Timing

Curriculum Area and Level. History. Fourth grade and above, depending on the difficulty of expressions.

Word Processing Objectives. Using general editing commands and block commands.

Subject Matter Objective. The student will practice reference skills to list historical events in chronological order.

Directions to the Reader. Use your word processor to enter the sample exercise exactly as it is written. Use block commands to reorder events chronologically.

Lesson Preparation. Use a word processor to enter the sample exercises. Prepare directions for the lesson and give the lesson an appropriate heading. Save it as a file called EX7.DOC. Prepare printed copies of the lesson to distribute.

Directions for Students. Here is an exercise requiring you to put historical events in the order in which they occurred. As you order the events, insert a brief description naming important people and dates. Notice that the events are related to travel. Use the information to write a paragraph.

Sample Exercise.
Put these events in order, starting with the first event to occur. Tell the average speed in which each invention travels.
A. The invention of the first manned spacecraft.
B. The invention of the first hot air balloon.
C. The development of the first efficient automobile.
D. The invention of the first coal burning train.
E. The invention of the first jet plane.
F. The invention of the first propeller plane.
G. The invention of the first helicopter.

Commentary. Give students a printed copy of the exercise and provide resources for finding necessary information. When they have completed their research, the students should write their paragraphs using a word processor. Let students read their paragraphs aloud to one another.

The next activity is for vocabulary development and spelling. A word processor, a spell checker, and a synonym finder are used. Notice that students are encouraged to try to write words even if they are not sure of the spelling. This is a switch from what we generally do in the classroom.

ACTIVITY 10.8

Working with Words

Curriculum Area and Level. Language Arts. Fourth grade and above.

Word Processing Objectives. Using an electronic spell checker and thesaurus.

Subject Matter Objectives. Finding synonyms.

Directions to the Reader. Prepare the lesson as specified and follow the student directions. Then design files with other words for other student lessons.

Lesson Preparation. Use a word processor to enter this document: Six rows with the word *happy* written eight times. Prepare directions for the lesson and give the lesson an appropriate heading. Save it as a file called EX8.DOC.

Directions for Students. Load the lesson EX8.DOC. You will see a table with six rows. Each row has the word *happy* eight times. Starting with the second *happy* in the first row, type over each *happy* with another word that has a similar meaning. Don't worry if you are not sure of the exact spelling. Sound out the words as best you can. When you have thought of all the words you can, use the thesaurus to help you find other words. Spell check your work when finished. Next to each misspelled word, insert the correct spelling, and give a reason for each mistake.

For example, the first row could look like this:

happy cheerful content delighted elated glad joyful pleased

Commentary. Show students examples of why words are often misspelled. For example, words are often misspelled because certain letters are or are not doubled; for example, *writting* is often mistaken for *writing*. Have them formulate categories for mistakes and apply these categories to their mistakes. Perform the activity with the same sample word several times so that students can track their progress.

ACTIVITY 10.9

Better and Better!

Curriculum Area and Level. Writing. Second grade and above.

Word Processing Objectives. Using general editing commands. Using tab and indent keys or other keys that allow formatting text in columns. Saving and printing.

Subject Matter Objectives. The student will develop editing skills for creative writing.

Directions to the Reader. Use your word processor to enter the sample exercise exactly as it is written. Correct all grammar, punctuation, and capitalization errors. When you are finished, make a list of 10 suggested paragraph topics of interest to school students at different levels. Indicate suggested grade levels for each topic. Number the items in your list and arrange data in three columns: one for item number, topic, and level. Label your columns with boldface titles. Check your word processor's manual to see how columns are best formatted.

For example:

Number	**Topic**	**Level**
1.	Animals on the Farm	Grades 2 - 4

Make an entry for your log that describes new word processing techniques or commands you've discovered while doing this lesson.

Directions for the Students. Write your own story about the beach. Use only the word processor. Don't use any other materials. When you are finished, I will help you save your story. You can come back to this project every two weeks and improve your story based on what we've learned about reading, writing, and spelling.

Sample Exercise. Students may be directed to write a story about the beach. A story like this might be the result:

> last summer we went to the beech. It was very hot. i played all day in the water. My brother went to. His name is fred. we both got a bad sunburn. and we both tried to get up on a wind suffer. mr. randof told us you had to keep the wind to your back to get up. I got up. My brother fred had a hrder time then i did. we had a lot of fun i want to go back.

Commentary. Have students periodically edit their original story using new skills they have learned. Save each revision as a separate file so that progress can be charted. Encourage children to improve spelling, grammar, word usage, and style as they develop new skills, not all at once. Don't dwell on specific errors. Evaluate in terms of progress, not in terms of perfection. Tailor interim lessons to nuture needed skills.

In this section we have suggested several activites to be carried out by the student using a word processor. We called these activities hands-on activities because they are implemented under student control. These activities represent just a few of the possibilities that are open to educators.

Teacher-Made Materials

In the last section we explored learning activities in which students use word processors. What about learning materials such as tests, lessons, or activity sheets that teachers can prepare using word processors? The benefits are many. Lessons are easy to store, easy to change, and easy to retrieve. Furthermore, students complete lessons without the use of a computer. In this way a greater number of students are reached with the use of a smaller number of computers. Actually a school doesn't need a computer for every one or two students to affect curriculum in a positive manner.

To take full advantage of a word processor for designing instructional materials, teachers must know how to construct *electronic templates*. An electronic template is the skeleton of a document that is saved on disk. The template can be retrieved and used over and over again. By revising or completing the template, a useful instructional document is produced. The new document is saved under a new filename, leaving the original document intact so that it can be used frequently.

In the following pages we provide sample templates with explanations for constructing and using them. Sample Template 10.1 is a puzzle template; it is followed by Activity 10.10, a puzzle on U.S. presidents.

SAMPLE TEMPLATE 10.1

A Template for a Seek-and-Find Puzzle

Curriculum Area and Level. Can be adapted for most subjects. 3rd grade and above.

Directions to the Reader. This template is used to produce seek-and-find puzzles. The seek-and-find grid is constructed by typing in rows and columns of keyboard characters. A space is provided at the top of the document so that teachers can enter directions for completing a seek-and-find puzzle. The document is saved on disk using a name that identifies the template, such as SEEKFIND.DOC. When a seek-and-find puzzle is desired, the teacher retrieves the SEEKFIND.DOC document and replaces letters to construct a specific puzzle. Using the template saves a great deal of time. The puzzle's format is already constructed and it isn't necessary to enter new text characters into every cell of the puzzle. Once the template is designed and saved to disk, it can be retrieved and altered to meet new goals.

Directions for the Students. There are ## words in the puzzle that name *XXX*. They are displayed vertically, horizontally, or diagonally. See if you can find all of them. Don't be surprised if some of the words are written backwards.

E	F	G	H	F	V	B	U	J	K	V	N	M	L	D	E	G
W	M	L	P	D	R	B	Z	X	B	S	F	H	K	L	E	G
E	D	D	F	Y	U	R	W	M	X	C	F	T	J	L	A	D
K	H	B	M	N	R	I	O	X	W	Q	P	S	K	E	D	G
V	N	J	U	T	F	S	E	B	X	C	R	F	K	I	A	S
J	H	D	R	E	U	I	X	C	D	W	J	F	G	Y	J	B
E	G	M	F	S	J	L	F	R	J	U	M	L	S	A	U	I
E	D	D	Q	E	B	A	O	W	M	X	C	F	T	L	A	D
A	H	T	M	N	R	I	O	C	W	F	R	S	Y	E	D	G
V	N	J	U	T	F	S	E	B	X	C	R	F	K	I	A	S

ACTIVITY 10.10

The President Seek-and-Find Puzzle

Directions. There are 11 words in the puzzle that name U.S. presidents. They are displayed vertically, horizontally, or diagonally. See if you can find all of them. Don't be surprised if some of the words are written backwards.

W	F	G	H	F	V	B	L	J	K	V	P	M	R	D	J	G
M	A	D	I	S	O	N	I	X	O	N	F	H	E	L	E	G
E	D	S	F	Y	U	R	N	M	L	C	F	T	L	L	F	A
K	H	B	H	N	R	I	C	K	W	Q	P	S	Y	E	F	R
V	N	J	U	I	R	O	O	S	E	V	E	L	T	I	E	F
J	H	D	R	E	N	I	L	O	N	W	J	F	G	Y	R	I
E	G	M	F	S	J	G	N	R	J	U	M	L	S	A	S	E
E	D	D	Q	E	B	A	T	R	U	M	A	N	T	L	O	L
A	H	T	M	W	I	L	S	O	N	F	R	S	Y	E	N	D
V	N	J	U	T	E	I	S	E	N	H	O	W	E	R	A	S

ACTIVITY 10.11

A Reading Puzzle

Directions. Try to read each of the following passages, filling in the spaces as you go.

1. Th--- are se--- da-- in the we--. T-- of the da-- -t--t wi-- --e let--- T. I- is im---tant when writ--- the --mes of da-- to start the names wi-- capi--- ---ters.

2. -t -s -aid -hat "-arly -o -ed, -arly -o -ise, -akes a -an -ealthy, -ealthy, -nd -ise." -hat's -unny, -'m a -irl -nd I -et my -est -ork -one -ate -t -ight.

3. T-- t--ee p--mary c--ors a-- r--, b--e, a-- y--low. By m--ing t--se c--ors y-- c-- p--duce o--er c--ors. R-- a-- y--low m--e o--nge, y--low a-- b--e m--e g--en, a-- r-- a-- b--e m--e p--ple. B--ck a-- w--ite a-- n-- c--sidered c--ors. By a--ing b--ck and w-ite to c--ors y-- c-- p--duce d--ferent s--des.

A Template for a Math Activity

SAMPLE TEMPLATE 10.2

A Template for a Math Activity

Curriculum Area and Level. Can be adapted for most subjects. 2nd grade and above.

Directions to the Reader. This template consists of a lesson format and an unlimited number of mathematics expressions with blanks. Each expression is given a level of difficulty. To prepare a lesson using this template, use block moves to copy the lesson format and a selection of math expressions onto a new document. Complete all but one blank per line of the document to produce the desired lesson. Then save the lesson on disk until needed.

Directions for the Students. Fill in as many blanks as you can in the time you are given. Your score will be computed according to the level of difficulty. 1 point for *level one* blanks, 2 points for *level two* blanks, and so on.

Expression	*Level*
The product of —- and —- plus —- is —-.	2
—- times —-, divided by —- is —-.	2
The square of —- raised to the —- power is —-.	5
.	.
.	.
.	.

ACTIVITY 10.12

What's My Line?

Directions. Fill in as many blanks as you can in the time you are given. Your score will be computed according to the level of difficulty. 1 point for *level one* blanks, 2 points for *level two* blanks, and so on.

Expression	*Level*
The product of 5 and 7 plus 8 is —-.	2
12 times 7, divided by —- is 14.	2
The square of 4 raised to the 3rd power is —-.	5
.	.
.	.
.	.

Teachers are constantly looking for activities like those featured in the sample templates and Activities 10.10–10.12. These activities come in workbooks or textbooks, as ditto masters, or as black-line masters to be reproduced. Sometimes they are commercial products and sometimes they are made in the schools. Buying these activities is usually an all-or-nothing situation. You must buy a whole package. You can't scan lessons, selecting only those you want. After you get the package there's the problem of storage. You sometimes end up storing activities that are never used. When you've stored activities for a long time, it is hard to remember just where to find them. If you remember where, you locate them only to find that time has rendered them unusable.

Often teachers can't buy materials they want, either because they don't exist or there isn't money in the budget. So what do teachers do? They construct their own. Whatever the construction entails, you can be sure that using a word processor can make preparation and storage much easier than trying to design and keep up with activities using customary methods.

Managing Instruction

It is not unusual for a teacher to complain about the amount of required paperwork that doesn't directly relate to instruction. In recent years, with so many state departments of education gearing up to be "accountable," the complaint has become epidemic. Teachers everywhere are responsible for maintaining and reporting all kinds of student data to all kinds of audiences—to the public, to parents, to school administrators, and to state and federal officials. More and more you hear teachers claim that they are so bogged down with repetitive paperwork that they hardly have time to teach.

Computers and word processors cannot reduce the amount of paperwork demanded of teachers, but they certainly can lighten the loads. Templates for maintaining and updating class rolls and student profiles can easily be designed. Templates for managing textbook records and materials and equipment can be developed. Forms of all types can be stored on disks, retrieved, and used when necessary. Attendance information, form letters to parents, and reports to curriculum specialists are just a few of the documents that could be prepared using a word processor and a computer. In the Chapter Review, we will suggest templates for you to design. We will also ask you to dream up some original ways to use word processors for classroom management. Now, what about extracurricular activities? We haven't even touched on using word processors for these activities. Can you think of some ways?

Chapter Summary

In this chapter, we have described the features of word processors and have identified ways they may be used to both enhance and manage instruction. We hope that we have demonstrated that there is more to instructional computing than teaching programming or presenting trite tutorials. Despite all the glowing things we have said about word processors, they do have limitations. The search capabilities of word processors are limited and generally you can't sort items that are stored in documents. So, you may not want to construct many of the documents that we have suggested using a word processor. It's not that you will find it easier to design these items the traditional way, it's just that you may want to use some other generic computer tool, one that's more compatible with the goals that you are trying to achieve—like a data-base manager. So that's our next stop: Chapter 11, "Data-base Management."

Chapter Review

Knowledge Exercises

1. Define the term *word processor.*

   Answer: It is a computer utility for preparing and editing documents, with editing, file management, and printing components.

2. List and briefly describe the important features that a word processor editor should have.

   Answer:
   - Commands are available to allow the user to set margins and tabs.
   - Hyphenations are suggested to preserve margins, but the user has final say.
   - User may choose if text is to be right-justified or not.
   - When text is typed to the end of the line it automatically wraps to the next line.
   - Using special keys, the user may move anywhere on the screen, or move quickly through document.
   - User is allowed to insert or delete characters using special keys.
   - Passages can be isolated and identified as text with which to use special keyboard characters (underline, bold, italicize).
   - Blocks of text may be copied, moved, or deleted.
   - User may take materials from other files on the disk and read that material into the text that is being edited, or may block off parts of the text being edited and save the blocked text as a new file.
   - Page, line, and column references are readily available.
   - Commands are available for automatic pagination.
   - User may search for any set of characters in the text, and may replace them with another set of characters.
   - On-screen menus are provided that can be turned off and on as you are editing.
   - Help commands are available that can be used anytime in the program.
   - The program provides a utility that allows the user to see exactly what the text will look like when printed.

3. List and briefly describe the important features that a word processor file manager should have.

   Answer:
   - User must be able to easily save and retrieve files, and the save command should have a safety feature to prevent a previously saved file from being accidentally overwritten.

- User should be able to copy a file from the disk, then rename it and save the file on the same disk under the new name, as well as copy files from one disk to another disk without leaving the word processor.
- There is a built-in feature that automatically makes a backup copy of the file the user saves.
- User is able to specify paths to different subdirectories to implement a filing function.
- There is a command to allow the user to merge two or more files.
- The program allows the user to process and save non-document or ASCII files, eliminating codes that are defined uniquely by a particular word processing program.
- The program alerts the user when there is insufficient space on a data diskette to save a program that is being edited, and provides a way to retract a save command and prepare a new data diskette.

4. List and briefly describe the important features that the print manager of a word processor should have.

Answer:
- User should be able to easily configure the program to many different printers.
- User should be able to set the printing format easily and, ideally, choose to either place the format commands in the text or set them just before printing.

5. List and briefly describe five "extra" features of a word processor that are described in the chapter.

Answer:
1. An automatic outlining routine is provided that establishes numbering and lettering setups, and the user is able to insert new items and then give a renumber or reletter command that reorganizes the outline.
2. The user may stop while in the editor, turn on a screen calculator, and then return to the edit mode with calculations inserted where appropriate.
3. The screen is divided into different parts or windows, to enable the user to compare different sections of text while editing.
4. The program has an immediate mode so the user may enter a small amount of text and have it printed immediately.
5. The user may use a wildcard search to find a certain passage or name when the exact spelling is not known.

6. What important attributes should a spell checker have?

Answer: The dictionary should include the 10,000 most frequently used words and should allow users to add (and delete) words to fit their special needs. In addition, it would be useful to indicate the frequency of specific words in the document, provide a list of synonyms for a given word, be easy to use, supply a list of similar words from which the user may choose a word to replace the one in the text, and start or stop spell checking at any point and return to or from the editing mode.

Thought Exercises

1. Which of the editing features discussed in the chapter are essentially the same as those found on a typewriter? Which are quite different? Support your choices.
2. Which of the functions performed by the file manager of a word processor that are described in the chapter do you feel are essential for any word processor that you use? For any word processor that you use with elementary or secondary students? Are there any other functions that you would like to have? Explain.
3. Describe at least three types of documents that you would like to print using a word processing program for use with students you might teach. How would you construct the format for each one? Why?
4. Choose two of the "extra" word processing features described in the chapter and describe how you might use these features in a classroom to teach traditional skills or concepts.
5. Would you choose a literal or root-word dictionary for use with school students you teach or expect to teach? Support your choice.

Activities

1. Choose a word processor suitable for use with students at a level of your choice. Review the program and its documentation to see if it supports features on the word processor checklist included as Resource Sheet 10, following these exercises.
2. Repeat Activity 1 with a word processor suitable to the needs of the teacher. (What features are needed that students at the level you've chosen may not need?)
3. Select a word processing program that contains an indexing program or a mail merge. (If a word processor is not available, look through computing magazines to find an in-depth review or use available documentation or promotional material.) Describe how the indexing or mail merge programs work, and any shortcomings that you can observe. Would this feature help you as a teacher? How? Think about letters to parents.
4. Select a vocabulary list of 20 words. Use a word processor to write a short story suitable for use with students at a given level. As you write the

story, insert *** to indicate places where students are to insert words from the list of 20 words. Try the lesson with school students, if they are available.

5. Write a paragraph on the word processor using commonly misspelled words appropriate for students at a given level. Select two school students to go through the paragraph and correct misspelled words. Turn in a printout of the paragraph you develop and representative work from the students.
6. Write a paragraph on the word processor and underline words to be replaced with synonyms. Select two students to edit the paragraph. Turn in a printout of the paragraph you develop and representative work from the students.
7. Choose a list of at least 20 words suitable for use with students at a given level. They may be all nouns or all adjectives, or they may all relate to the outdoors, to the mountains, to the beach, or to the city. Write a brief paragraph using the words and a word processor.

Project

1. Have some students write a short story on some topic (What I Did on My Vacation, What I Want to Be When I Grow Up, My Favorite Animal, Space Travel, or any topic that would be of interest to them). Then go through the stories concentrating on one particular concept or error. Ask each student to correct his or her story. Then as you introduce another skill or concept, correct those same stories looking at one other area, and do this until they have gone through their stories several times, correcting errors each time.

   Then print out the students' stories. Let the students use illustrations, place their stories in folders and send them home, or make a class library using their own stories. (For this class, write a description of what you did, and bring in student work showing the progression on a particular story.)

Resource Sheet 10

Word Processing Checklist

Editor features	Yes/No	Comments
FULL SCREEN EDITING cursor moves easily and quickly		
INSERT/DELETE sentences, words, characters		
AUTOMATIC WORDWRAP		
CENTER TEXT		
JUSTIFY TEXT		
VERSATILE MARGIN SETTINGS		
AUTOMATIC HYPHENATION		
AUTOMATIC PAGINATION		
BLOCK MANIPULATION OF TEXT move, copy, delete		
READ AND WRITE COMMANDS insert/save excerpts from files		
FLEXIBLE HEADERS AND FOOTERS		
SEARCH/REPLACE		
File features		
SAVE/RETRIEVE		
COPY/RENAME		
AUTOMATIC BACKUP		
FILE MERGE		
PATH SPECIFICATION FOR FILES		
ASCII FILES		
AUTOMATIC DISK SPACE UPDATING		
Print features		
EASY CONFIGURATION		
EASY AND VERSATILE FORMATTING		
SPECIAL PRINT FEATURES		
Spell checker features		
APPROPRIATE DICTIONARY SIZE		
SCANS TEXT, STOPS ON ERROR		
PROVIDES REPLACEMENT LIST OF WORDS		
ALLOWS AUTOMATIC REPLACEMENT		
GIVES SYNONYMS		
HAS WORD COUNT AND OTHER FEATURES		

Bibliography

Aumack, J. "Computers for Nonwriters." *Principal* (November 1985): 46–48.

Becker, Henry Jay. "Computers in Schools Today: Some Basic Considerations." *American Journal of Education* (November 1984): 25. Teachers may use computers as administrative tools to manage individualized instructional programs, including analyzing student performance and routing students to different instructional or practice activities.

Costanzo, W. V. "Interactive Text Editors; A New Generation of Teaching Tools." *Educational Technology* (December 1985): 7–15.

Degnan, S. C., and J. W. Hummel. "Word Processing for Special Education Students: Worth the Effort." *T.H.E. Journal* (February 1985): 80–82. Discusses the benefits of word processing with special education students and how to integrate it into the curriculum.

Hammond, R. "Keywords." *Times Educational Supplement* (October 25, 1985): 48.

Hyer, D. "Word Processing Software." *Electronic Learning* (November–December 1985): 44–45. Reviews several word processing packages.

Lake, D. "Beyond Word Processing." *Classroom Computer Learning* (November–December 1985): 37+. Discusses how favorite writing activities take on new appeal when mixed with a modem and the class computer.

McCarley, B. "Why Teach Word Processing to Young Writers?" *Curriculum Review* (November–December 1985): 49–50.

Moen, N. B. "Word Processing Teaches the Basics—Plus!" *Business Education Forum* (February 1985): 10+.

Olds, H. F. "A New Generation of Word Processors." *Classroom Computer Learning* (March 1985): 22–25.

Seltzer, C. "The Word Processor—A Magical Tool for Kindergarten Writers." *Early Years* (January 1986): 51–52.

Wheeler, F. "Can Word Processing Help the Writing Process?" *Learning* (March 1985): 54–55. Four ways that word processing can teach writing, especially if you focus on writing as a process.

CHAPTER

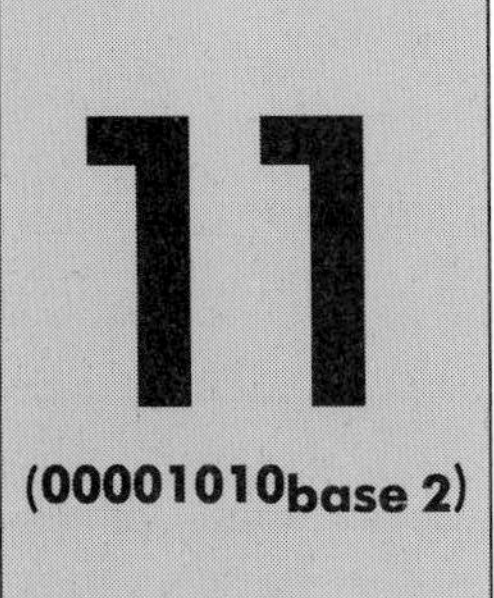

DATA-BASE MANAGEMENT
Filing without Frustration

Getting Started

In this chapter we will discuss a category of powerful software tools referred to as data-base management systems. While no other category promises to be more useful, no other category can be more intimidating if initial experiences are not appropriate. Obviously, one of the main purposes of this chapter is to remove any mystery that may surround the terms electronic data base *and* data-base management system. *To accomplish this we will make precise definitions, give concrete examples, and provide the reader with an example of a data-base program. (See the Program Disk.)*

The chapter is separated into three major sections. The first tackles the question, "What is a data base?" and discusses the advantages of understanding and using computer software to manage information. This section also lists some characteristics to look for when purchasing data-base management software. The second section of the chapter describes the small instructional data-base program that has been included with this book and provides examples of classroom lessons to be used with it. Our intent is to illustrate how a data base can be used to enhance a school curriculum subject area. In the third and final section, we provide suggestions for creating both instructional and classroom management data bases. We also list practical ways to use the suggested data bases.

Objectives for Teachers

To successfully complete this chapter, you should be able to

1. Define electronic data-base management.
2. Describe the attributes of a data-base management system.
3. List advantages that electronic data-base management has over traditional methods of organizing information.
4. List desired features of good data-base software.
5. Write specifications for creating an instructional data base.

6. Design lessons to be used with an instructional data base.
7. Describe an effective classroom management data base.
8. List practical ways to use data-base software in the classroom.

What Is a Data Base?

Today, teachers are being required to keep track of an ever-increasing amount of information, both student records and instructional data. The classroom teacher may be attempting to keep up with changes in curriculum objectives for mathematics, trying to stay abreast of updates in space travel for the science or social studies class, or just worried about maintaining accurate profiles for each student. Whatever the concern, you can be sure that when there is a large amount of information to be maintained, there is a need for a good computer software tool called a **data-base manager.**

Simply put, a data base is a collection of information organized and presented to serve a particular purpose. To get the feeling for what a data base is, think of a traditional dictionary. The dictionary represents a systematic way to store and retrieve words, their spellings, and their meanings. Even though it is not computerized, the dictionary provides a quick and easy way to retrieve information. The problem with the traditional dictionary is that the information in it cannot be manipulated. Words cannot be easily changed, added, or deleted. The same is not true of an electronic data base. How are words found quickly in a dictionary? They are listed alphabetically. When you find the word you are looking for, you also find its meaning and spelling. The word is the *key* to opening the lock of this simple data base. In any data base, information must be organized and presented in a way that makes it easy to find by the use of some key. Even information presented in tabular form can be considered a data base if such an organization lends itself to locating specific information quickly. In other words, there must be a key that facilitates the rapid location of information.

An electronic, or computerized data base is just a data base that is stored on a computer system, rather than paper. A data-base manager is a program used to access and maintain the information in an electronic data base. The term **data base** is frequently used to refer to both the information and the program that manages it. In this chapter, we will observe that convention. We will also refer to the term *paper data base,* or its equivalent, to refer to more traditional means of storing information.

How can the computer data base make work easier and more productive? The computer can really do nothing more than we can do with a paper data base, but it is able to do it at the speed of electricity. Just think of the savings in time that is. Consider another advantage of a data base. Imagine that you have recorded information about your students on 3″ × 5″ cards and stored the cards in a plastic box, arranged alphabetically by student name. One of your cards got in the way of your coffee mug; by now only the telephone number on the card is readable. What will you do with your paper data base? You will probably ask each student if the number is his or her number. What a chore that would be, especially if a few students are absent that day. With a computer data base, we could ask the computer to search for the person who belongs to the telephone number, and within seconds we would have the missing name. The computer can help you accomplish tasks that are not practical for you to do. It will do so quickly, easily, and without error.

To create a data base, you must have a data-base program. There are three types that are referred to as data bases: indexing systems, file managers, and relational data-base systems. There is a great range in the price that you might pay for a system, and the price depends on how much information you want to keep track of, how you want to store the information, and how quickly and in what form you want to find information once it has been stored. First, let's take a look at the general organization of a data-base management system and then take a brief look at the different kinds.

To understand the organization of a data base, you must be familiar with three terms: *file, record,* and *field.* A **file** is analogous to the plastic box containing the 3″ × 5″ cards in the previous example. In other words, the file is the entire collection of data. We may call our file STUNAMES, which is short for student names. PC DOS does not allow us to use more than 11 characters for filenames, so we must assign the file a name that is compact yet comprehensible. Our file has several **records,** one for each student. A record is analogous to one of the individual index cards stored in the plastic box. Each of the records is composed of the name, address, and telephone number of a student. A **field** refers to a particular part of a record. In the case of our example, there are three fields. You guessed it: there are fields for name, address, and telephone number. Be careful to make the distinction between a field itself and the name for that field. Student Name, Address, and Telephone Number are labels that indicate the nature of the contents of our fields, so we call them *field names.*

It takes time and personal commitment to learn to use a computer data base. Once you have learned to use one, it requires planning to decide how you will organize a useful file, and then time for entering data. However, the time saved and the release from dreary routine and seemingly endless filing jobs will be your reward. Once your file is intact, you can sort records in a variety of ways, alphabetically or by number, and you can easily search for specific records that you may require. Furthermore, most data bases have routines that allow the user to quickly add, delete, or change records. With just a little learning time, using a data base can become as easy as using your telephone directory. Remember, you are only learning a new set of functions for a machine that is designed to support your efforts in processing all kinds of information already familiar to you.

As we said earlier, there are three types of data bases that range in cost and sophistication. Deciding what data base to buy should depend upon the intended application. It is senseless to buy an unsophisticated system for a complicated task where many specific details need to be managed, even though the system may be inexpensive and easy to use. On the other hand, it is not prudent to buy a powerful, expensive data base when all you want to do is manage a greeting card list and organize recipes. Let's take a look at how each type of data base is constructed and what it will do.

Indexing Systems

An **indexing system** is one that allows the user to attach a list of key words to a paragraph or perhaps a page of text that is to be tracked. These programs usually provide flexibility in the amount and form of the text that is to be entered. They are usually easy to learn and to use. What is gained in the flexibility and ease of use is lost in speed of performance as well as power to search for specific bits of information. Also, these systems do not usually allow the user to tailor printed copies of information to specific needs; that is, the form in which the information was originally stored is the form in which the information is retrieved. Often, it is extremely helpful to bring information from a data-base file into another program. For example, you may want to incorporate student names you have organized in a data base into a document you are creating on your word processor. This operation is usually very difficult to do using an indexing system since the organization of information in such a system is not very flexibly structured.

File Management Systems

A **file management system** is usually **menu-driven.** This means that, at certain points in program execution, you are presented with a **menu** from which to choose options. Another feature that a file management system has is structured records. In fact, the first option that must be selected from the *main menu* of such a program is one allowing you to create the form of your record. You must specify the fields in your record and the number of characters you will allow to be entered as data in any one of the fields. For example, suppose you are trying to keep track of teaching resources for the courses to which you are usually assigned. You may want to create a file such as the following:

```
SUBJECT: ----
LEVEL: --
TYPE: ----------
TITLE: ----------------------------
AUTHOR: --------------
LEARNING OBJECTIVE: ----
PUBLISHER NAME: ----------------------------
PUBLISHER STREET ADDRESS: ----------------------------
PUBLISHER CITY & STATE: ----------------------------
PUBLISHER ZIP: ----
COMMENT 1: -------------------------------------------
COMMENT 2: -------------------------------------------
COMMENT 3: -------------------------------------------
```

Notice that by every field name there are spaces. These spaces indicate the maximum number of characters that can be entered in a specific field. For SUBJECT you must decide upon four-letter codes to represent each of the subjects you might want to enter, ENGL for English, MATH for Mathematics, and so on. The same thing must be done for all the other fields. That is, you should think long and hard about the data that you will want to enter, and determine codes that fit within the prescribed limits, yet provide the flexibility needed for comprehensiveness. In the field LEVEL, you may want to enter resources for kindergarten as well as 6th grade, so you must have codes that will handle both levels. You may want to collect information with regard to many types of resources: books, videotapes, software, journal articles, and so on. So, you must determine in advance which codes you will use for the field TYPE. Once you have settled on appropriate codes, the entry of data should be consistent. When it is time to search for data you need, it is important that you know how data have been entered. It would be difficult to search for all resources that are books if sometimes you use the code BK and other times you use BOOKS. Obviously, some data would get lost. Once you have decided on the form your records will take and what codes will be used, you can enter data. Here is what a completed record might look like:

```
SUBJECT: Read
LEVEL: 5-
TYPE: Book---
TITLE: Summer Fun
AUTHOR: Conrad, Richard
LEARNING OBJECTIVE: 5R-96
PUBLISHER NAME: Good Beginning Products------
PUBLISHER STREET ADDRESS: 3488 Melville
Street----------
PUBLISHER CITY & STATE: Tampa Florida----------------
PUBLISHER ZIP: 33612
COMMENT 1: GOOD book for teaching reading
comprehension,
COMMENT 2: Games and projects suggested for
leisure time
COMMENT 3: Students favor this book over
others.--------
```

Depending on the filing system being used, a number of things can be done with a file having records such as this. It is possible to *sort* records in a variety of ways. By sorting records, we mean that the data-base program could arrange the records in some meaningful way, alphabetically or numerically. For example, you could sort all the records in terms of grade LEVEL, in terms of TYPE, in terms of LEARNING OBJECTIVE, and so on. With many filing systems, you can sort with respect to more than one field, for example, sort in terms of LEVEL so that within a given LEVEL, items are grouped according to LEARNING OBJECTIVE.

All worthwhile filing systems allow the user to *search* for specific records. For instance, suppose you want to prepare a list of all software resources you have in the file for reading at LEVEL 5. Furthermore, you want the items arranged according to COST. First you must search the records with respect to three fields: SUBJECT, TYPE, and LEVEL. Then sort the records you find according to COST.

Another function to consider in a data base is flexibility of *reporting* data. If the searching and sorting routines supported by the filing system are efficient enough, then reporting routines are usually sufficiently flexible. In the example we have been discussing, the record is designed to make it possible to select particular fields for inclusion on printed reports. For example, we may want to retrieve publisher information for address labels. On the other hand, we may wish to retrieve TITLE, LEVEL, and COMMENTS so that particular teachers may plan their lessons. Still another use would be to retrieve TITLE, PUBLISHER, LEVEL, SUBJECT, and COST in order to inventory needs at different grade levels. Many filing systems come with capabilities for preparing different report formats and for calculating with numerical data given in particular fields, but many filing systems do not. If you are interested in these features, you must check software for them before you purchase.

As you can see, a filing system is more sophisticated than an indexing system. It allows you to do a greater number of things with the data you have stored. The price you pay for this greater flexibility is not all monetary. Learning to use a filing system is usually a little more difficult than learning to use an indexing system.

Relational Data-base Systems

The last type of data-base system we will explore is called a **relational data-base system.** We won't get bogged down in a technical definition because the theory that undergirds such a system is quite complicated. Suffice it to say that a relational data base is one in which each piece of data is ideally entered once and might appear in a number of records that may be retrieved in a number of different files. For example, in a large senior high school, it would be feasible to install a relational data base in which a variety of student information—attendance, grades, test scores, parental information, past school experience—could be entered once. Depending upon the need, different files could be built from the same pool of information and different records could be retrieved for the same student. Usually relational data bases allow the user to make changes in one file and have those changes reflected in related files. Relational systems are usually **command-driven.** This means that users must give commands to get results that are desired. The user cannot simply choose from a menu. In fact, most of the time these systems include a machine-code programming language for issuing multiple commands. Programs are written that provide the mechanism by which the data-base files are created and manipulated, as well as the means for allowing files to share data. This type of data base is by far the most powerful, the most expensive, and the hardest to learn and to use.

In a Nutshell

To sum it up, three kinds of data bases are available: indexing systems, filing systems, and relational data bases. These types vary greatly in power, ease of use, and cost. For the purposes of most teachers, a carefully chosen filing system will more than satisfy needs. Resource Sheet 11 contains a checklist that will help you evaluate data-base software. Many concepts indicated in the checklist have not been discussed thoroughly in this chapter since it has not been our purpose to present a detailed study of data bases. However, with a little research, you will find the checklist helpful when you get ready to evaluate or buy a data base.

Enhancing Instruction with a Data Base

There is no end to the applications that a teacher can implement with a data-base system. Most uses, however, fall into one of two categories. The categories are—you guessed it—computer enhanced instruction and computer managed instruction. Let us first turn our attention to enhancing instruction.

There are many ways that a data base can be used to enhance instruction; the difficulty is in choosing which ideas to illustrate. In using a data base, we want students to achieve two kinds of goals. The first kind has to do with developing the abilities to build and use a data base. The second kind has to do with developing traditional subject matter abilities as well as improving critical thinking abilities. Critical thinking involves using information in more than a cursory manner. In this section we outline lessons that will encourage the development of both kinds of abilities. Some lessons will lead to the production of a data base and others will demonstrate important ways to use the data base. Our intent is to provide a general set of strategies for organizing learning activities around a data base.

To begin, let's assume that we teach science and we want to develop a data base that will store information on different animals. We will call our data base ANIMALS and refer to our example lessons as ANIMAL ACTIVITIES.

The time required to complete each lesson will vary depending on the complexity of the tasks to be accomplished and the length of the class period. The level of the lesson can be adjusted to groups of students at various grade levels.

ACTIVITY 11.1

What Will We Search For?

Curriculum Area. Science or Biology.

Group Size. The entire class.

Objectives. In this activity, students will learn what a data base is and will learn to use appropriate terms such as field names and records to explain basic operations of a data base. They will also explore ways to obtain information about animals.

Materials. Resource materials for obtaining information about animals.

Directions. An essential part of this activity is student involvement. First you should conduct a class discussion on the concept of a data base. You should give examples with which students are familiar such as the telephone book, a dictionary, and a book's index. Appropriate vocabulary should be introduced and students should be given opportunities to relate terms to examples that are introduced. Students should be encouraged to think of examples.

When students have sufficient familiarity with data-base concepts, pose the problem of creating a data base about animals. Conduct brainstorming activity wherein students generate possible field names. Appropriateness of field names should not be discussed during the session; judgments and a final set of categories should be saved for a later lesson. During the discussion, you should build a table to keep track of every field name that is suggested. Only redundant names should be omitted. The table is referred to as an experience table and looks something like this:

EXPERIENCE TABLE FOR A DATA BASE ON ANIMALS:
Name of Data Base. ANIMALS
Question. What information do we want to collect about animals?
ANIMAL CLASS
DEVELOPMENT PERIOD BEFORE BIRTH
PERIOD BEFORE BECOMING FULL GROWN
AVERAGE WEIGHT WHEN GROWN
AVERAGE LENGTH WHEN GROWN
HIGHEST LAND SPEED
NUMBER OF LEGS
TYPE OF SKIN
AVERAGE LIFE SPAN
SIZE OF BRAIN
PARENTAL CARE
FOOD PREFERENCES
ENEMIES
CLIMATE THE ANIMAL LIVES IN

After the brainstorming session is complete, students should discuss resources they will need to find appropriate information.

ACTIVITY 11.2

Building a Record for the Animal Data Base

Curriculum Area. Science or Biology.

Group Size. This activity should involve the entire class, with students grouped in pairs.

Objective. The purpose for this activity is to have students evaluate field names that were generated in Activity 11.1.

Directions. Ideas gained through the brainstorming session in Activity 11.1 are applied here. Students should be given the experience table generated in Activity 11.1 and asked to rate each of the possible field names in order of importance. After rating activities are completed, the teacher and students in a large group activity should compile a composite rating. Questions should be raised that require students to explain why and how they made their choices. A final RECORD FORM for the data base ANIMALS should be the outcome of this lesson.

ACTIVITY 11.3

Collecting Information

Curriculum Area. Science or Biology.

Group Size. Pairs of students.

Objective. In this activity, students will practice using research skills. Techniques for following verbal and written instructions as well as organizing and recording data will be emphasized.

Directions. Before organizing students in pairs, the teacher should help students determine agencies where information on animals may be obtained; for example, the school library, the city or county library, wildlife associations, zoos, or perhaps a national telecommunications service with an on-line encyclopedia.

Each student pair should develop a plan for effectively enlisting help from suggested resources in gaining the needed information. After students have identified an organized plan, they should begin independent research activities. The importance of obtaining accurate records should be stressed. If possible, it is useful when information for each record is collected by at least two groups. This provides a method to check not only the accuracy of data collection, but also to compare information gained from more than one source. Each group should be given approximately one week to finish this lesson. In some cases, it will not be possible to collect all the necessary information in the given time frame. This may not be important. What is important is the final establishment of the data base, so that its functions can be used. Provisions for updating the data base on a consistent basis will be another lesson to learn.

During the week, each group's progress should be monitored. When difficulties occur, students may benefit from a brainstorming session by the class for possible solutions. At the week's end, data forms should be collected. A class discussion should follow, relating personal experiences and determining the next step in completing the project.

Before outlining the rest of the activities for this section, we would like to point out a few pedagogical considerations. So far, the activities have emphasized the following:

1. Learning what a data base is and learning related vocabulary.
2. Deciding upon a data base to build and brainstorming on possible field names.
3. Refining the field names and organizing them to produce a record.
4. Listing resources for obtaining information; devising a plan for using the resources.
5. Collecting accurate information. Building in methods to check accuracy.

The next set of activities involves the entering of data. This is an important step and is not as easy as it looks. The data should be prepared before they are entered and checked by different individuals. What is more, to prepare data for entry, codes for each field name should be established so that entry carried on by several people over a period of time will be consistent. The next obvious lesson concerns determining codes for entering information. You may be wondering why we didn't decide on codes before we collected information. We didn't because you can never be sure how the information you obtain will look. It is better to collect some of the information first to gain insight on how to define the codes.

ACTIVITY 11.4

Finding Codes for Field Names

Curriculum Area. Science or Biology.

Group Size. The entire class.

Objective. In this activity, students should decide on appropriate codes for each of the field names and the number of characters that will be allowed for each field.

Directions. An essential part of this activity is student involvement. First, you should conduct a class discussion on choosing the number of characters for each field and the codes. This decision is important and should involve three considerations.

1. How do I want the information to look when it is reported?
2. Do I want to conserve computer space?
3. Shouldn't the codes be easy to recognize?

Students should discuss the types of information they obtained for the different fields, then brainstorming activities should be conducted wherein students generate possible codes. During the discussion, a group leader should build a table to keep track of the codes that are generated and the field lengths. Students should be made aware of which fields are numeric and which fields are alphabetic.

ACTIVITY 11.5

Entering Data

Curriculum Area. Science or Biology.

Group Size. Pairs of students.

Objective. In this activity, students will practice entering data. Accuracy, editing, and checking will be stressed.

Directions. This activity requires the use of at least one computer and data-base software. It is important that the teacher or some leader has prepared the ANIMAL file ahead of time. Students should only be required to enter data, not design the form. Students should work together so they can check each other. A backup of the data base should be maintained in case errors occur that result in the loss of data. The teacher will have to plan a schedule for students to enter data according to the number of available computers. This schedule can easily revolve around other class work, so certainly a whole lab of computers is not necessary, though it may be ideal.

ACTIVITY 11.6

Using the Data Base

Curriculum Area. Science or Biology.

Group Size. The entire class.

Objective. In this activity, students will discuss ways to use the data base they have created and they will try some of the ideas that they suggest. The teacher should emphasize uses that not only involve data retrieval but also data comparisons and conclusions.

Directions. This activity assumes that the data have already been entered into our data base on animals. The following is a list of a few ideas for the creative use of this data base:

1. Search for all animals with large brains. Search for all animals who develop quickly before they are born. Compare the set of animals. Tell what you find out.
2. Sort animals on the basis of their fastest speeds on land. Put the animals into "speed" groups. Tell whether you notice any similarities in the animals in a group.
3. Search for all the animals that are mammals. On the basis of your search, speculate as to the characteristics mammals can and cannot have.
4. Search for the animals that are herbivorous. Search for the animals that are carnivorous. Compare the two sets of animals. Explain the similarities and differences that you notice. For example, which group of animals appears to be more aggressive?
5. Search for animals that sustain relationships with others of their own kind. What can you say about other characteristics they appear to have?
6. Make up a game of "Twenty Questions" (answered only by Yes or No) based upon search information that will allow you to find any animal in your data base.

Activity 11.6 is the last activity that we will discuss in any detail in this chapter. By now you have the picture. There are other important lessons that should occur often. For example, there should be lessons in which students maintain the data base. This, of course, requires correcting information, adding new information, and deleting information that is no longer desirable. There should also be lessons in which students evaluate the data base that has been constructed and revise it.

We will now complete the set of strategies that we emphasized after Activity 11.3. These are the important steps for using data bases in the classroom.

1. Learning what a data base is and learning related vocabulary.
2. Deciding upon a data base to build and brainstorming on possible field names.
3. Refining the field names and organizing them to produce a record.
4. Listing resources for obtaining information; devising a plan for using the resources.
5. Collecting accurate information. Building in methods to check accuracy.
6. Determining codes for fields and appropriate field lengths.
7. Entering accurate data, editing, and checking.
8. Using the data base to obtain and compare data to draw conclusions and make generalizations.
9. Maintaining the data base.
10. Evaluating the data base.
11. Revising the data base.

So that you can get the feel for how this set of activities proceeds, we have included an ANIMAL data base on the Program Disk. ANIMALS is the program and filename. An illustration of the record form for the file follows. Field names and lengths have been specified, but no data have been entered. Your task is to determine appropriate codes and enter data for 50 animals. Then you should plan and implement lessons for using the data base. (See Project 1 in Chapter Review.) Have fun!

```
              THE ANIMAL DATA BASE
ANIMAL CLASS: ----
DEVELOPMENT PERIOD BEFORE BIRTH: ----(specify in
days)
PERIOD BEFORE BECOMING FULL GROWN: ----(specify in
weeks)
AVERAGE WEIGHT WHEN GROWN: -----(specify in
kilograms)
AVERAGE HEIGHT WHEN GROWN: -----(specify in
centimeters)
AVERAGE LENGTH WHEN GROWN: -----(specify in
centimeters)
HIGHEST LAND SPEED: ----(specify in kilometers/hour)
NUMBER OF LEGS: -
TYPE OF SKIN: ---
```

```
AVERAGE LIFE SPAN: ----(specify in months)
SIZE OF BRAIN: -----(specify in kilograms)
PERIOD OF PARENTAL CARE: ----(specify in weeks)
FOOD PREFERENCES: --
ENEMY 1: -----
ENEMY 2: -----
ENEMY 3: -----
ENDURING RELATIONS WITH OTHER ANIMALS?: -(specify
Y or N)
SLEEPING HABITS: -----
MODES OF TRAVEL: ---(land, water, air)
CLIMATE WHERE ANIMAL LIVES: -------
CAN THE ANIMAL BE DOMESTICATED? -(specify Y or N)
IN WHAT COUNTRY DID THE ANIMAL ORIGINATE?: -----
MAIN WAY THE ANIMAL BENEFITS PEOPLE: -----
MAIN WAY THE ANIMAL PESTERS PEOPLE: -----
COMMENT: ----------------------------------------------------------
```

We have explored the possibilities of using only one data base. Are you getting ideas of your own related to your favorite subjects? There is almost no subject for which a data base would not be appropriate. You could prepare a data base on the history of flight, states of the Union, presidents, elections, nations, famous women, disease, important inventions, flowering plants, stars in the galaxy, or rare metals. We can go on and on. How about you?

Managing Instruction with a Data Base

Just as you have seen for enhancing instruction, there are endless ways to use a data base to improve the management of instruction. Many of these were demonstrated in Chapter 9. The programs BIBLIOGRAPHER and TEST ITEM BANK are both data-base management systems. We could demonstrate many more. However, once you recognize the advantages of using data bases to organize instruction and begin to get ideas of your own, then our task is complete. To wind up this chapter, we will simply list some areas of instructional management in which a data base may be useful.

1. Student profiles, grades, test scores, important personal information.
2. Learning objectives and related teaching resources.
3. Inventories of classroom equipment and furniture.
4. Grade reporting programs.
5. Attendance reporting.
6. Inventories of special aids, transparencies, manipulatives, and maps.
7. Test items, practice exercises, and contest items.
8. Data base on high-interest activities and games.
9. Data base on aids for children with special needs.

Chapter Summary

In this chapter we discussed data-base management systems and implications for education. First, we briefly described three different types of data-base programs, pointing out the good features as well as the limitations. Second, we demonstrated strategies for building an instructional data base in the classroom. Last, we generated ways in which data bases can be helpful for instructional management. The pre-1980 role of the teacher will be greatly transformed by the introduction of the microcomputer into education. Aren't you glad to be a part of the revolution?

Chapter Review

Knowledge Exercises

1. Define a data base.

   Answer: A collection of information organized and presented to serve a particular purpose.

2. Give an example of a non-computerized data base.

   Answer: A dictionary, card catalog, encyclopedia, or telephone directory.

3. List two advantages of an electronic data base.

   Answer: Saves time, makes searching easier and more efficient.

4. List three types of systems referred to as data bases (in order, with most powerful first and least powerful last).

   Answer: Relational data-base systems, file management systems, indexing systems.

5. Define the terms *file, record,* and *field.*

   Answer: File. The entire collection of data.
   Record. The collection of data on one person or object.
   Field. Each item (piece of information) in a record.

6. List two ways in which you can sort records in a computer data base.

   Answer: Alphabetically or by number.

7. Define an indexing system.

   Answer: Allows the user to attach a list of key words to a paragraph or a page of text.

8. List two pros and two cons of indexing systems.

   Answer: Pros. Provides flexibility, easy to learn and use.
   Cons. Slow, not easy to search for specific bits of information, don't usually allow user to tailor printed copies of information to specific needs.

9. What does it mean for a computer program to be menu-driven?

   Answer: At certain points in program execution you are presented a menu from which to choose options.

10. List four features of an effective file management program.

    Answer: Usually menu-driven, structured record, can sort for specific records, usually flexible reporting routines.

11. Define a relational data-base system.

    Answer: Each item of data may be entered once and may appear in a number of records that may be retrieved in a number of different files.

12. What does it mean for a computer program to be command-driven?

    Answer: Users cannot simply choose from a menu, but must give commands to get the desired results; often requires the use of a programming language.

13. Describe the two kinds of goals important for students to achieve when using a data base for instruction.

    Answer: 1. Developing abilities to build and use a data base.
    2. Developing traditional subject matter abilities as well as improving critical thinking abilities.

14. Which should be done first: collecting information to be input into a data base or determining codes for that information? Why?

    Answer: First collect at least some of the information, then define codes. You collect some information first to see how the data will look.

15. List the steps for using data bases in the classroom.

    Answer: See the list that follows Activity 11.6.

Thought Exercises

1. Describe an analogy for a data base other than a plastic box containing 3″ × 5″ cards. In particular, address the role of the terms *file, record,* and *field* for the analogy.

2. Describe at least two examples of how the ANIMALS data base might be searched to provide students with deeper insight into animal life. Give different examples than those used in the chapter.

3. List five subjects for an instructional data base other than those mentioned in the chapter.

4. Design a data base for managing information on students. Select field names, codes, and so on, and defend your choices.

Activities

1. Select a data-base management system. Analyze it using the checklist included at the end of these exercises as Resource Sheet 11. Write a short paragraph stating whether you would recommend its purchase by a school, citing specifics to justify your recommendation.
2. With a group of students, decide upon a subject for a data base and brainstorm possible field names. Have the class refine and organize those fields into a workable record. (Remember to consider the use of numeric data for ease of comparisons.)
3. Make up a game of "Twenty Questions" (each question must be answered Yes or No) to allow you to find a particular record in a data base. If possible, divide a group of students into teams and have them play the game to see which team will guess the correct record first.
4. Have students choose a data base and discuss and generate ideas for its creative use. List the ideas and indicate which ideas were actually used with the class and what conclusions were reached.
5. Input information for at least 10 students into the data base created in Thought Exercise 4. Document at least three ways you can search and sort to help with management tasks.

Projects

1. Using the program provided on the Program Disk, complete the ANIMALS data base with your students. Follow the procedures outlined in the chapter.
2. Build a data base with a group of students on a topic other than animals. Hold a brainstorming session to generate possible field names and construct an experience table. Then, compile a composite rating and a final record form. Have students compile information in pairs using data forms, and have more than one pair collect the same data, for a check.
3. After information is collected for a data base using data forms, have students determine codes and length of each field, and then proceed to input data. Have students discuss ways to use the data base. Emphasize comparisons and conclusions.
4. Enter data for a class into your data base from Thought Exercise 4. Keep updating the records for a month. At the end of that time, turn in your data diskette (with a printout, if possible) and a few paragraphs explaining problems and pitfalls and the best strategy for effective use.

Resource Sheet 11

Data-Base Checklist

Indexing systems features	Yes/No	Comments
WORD PROCESSOR OUTPUT CAN BE USED AS WELL AS KEYBOARD ENTRY		
SEARCH WORDS CAN BE ENTERED EASILY AND FLEXIBLY		
SEARCH FUNCTION IS FLEXIBLE you can use AND, OR, and NOT		
YOU CAN SORT RECORDS		
SEARCH WORDS THAT HAVE BEEN IDENTIFIED ARE LISTED		
SUFFICIENT SPACE IS PROVIDED FOR DATA IN RECORD		
PRINT OPTIONS PROVIDED		
File management system features		
SUFFICIENT RECORDS FOR YOUR NEEDS		
FAST ENOUGH		
MENUS ARE EASY TO FOLLOW		
YOU CAN DEFINE A SUFFICIENT NUMBER OF FIELDS FOR EACH RECORD		
YOU CAN CHOOSE THE NUMBER OF CHARACTERS TO USE FOR EACH FIELD THAT IS DEFINED		
AUTOMATICALLY COMPUTES USING DATA GIVEN IN A GIVEN FIELD FOR SEVERAL RECORDS		
DATA ARE EASY TO ENTER YOU CAN EDIT BEFORE YOU SAVE A RECORD		
SEARCHING IS FLEXIBLE you can use AND, OR, and NOT wildcard searches are available		
SORTING IS FLEXIBLE, you can sort with respect to several key words		
YOU CAN DESIGN DIFFERENT TYPES OF REPORTS TO PRINT		
CHANGING, ADDING, AND DELETING RECORDS IS MANAGED EFFICIENTLY		
MODIFYING THE RECORD FORM CAN BE MANAGED WITHOUT DESTROYING DATA		
FILES CAN BE TRANSFERRED TO OTHER PROGRAMS to word processors? to spreadsheets? to graphing programs?		
Relational data bases system features		
[FIRST, USE THE CHECKLIST SHOWN FOR THE FILE MANAGEMENT SYSTEM]		
IS THE COMMAND LANGUAGE REASONABLY EASY TO LEARN?		
HOW MANY FILES CAN BE OPENED AT THE SAME TIME?		

Bibliography

Freeman, D., and W. Tass. "Data Bases in the Classroom." *Journal of Computer Assisted Learning* (March–April 1985): 2–11. Summarizes Quest, a family of general-purpose data-handling computer programs which support existing curricula.

Garten, E. D. "Fifty 'Best' Data Bases and File Management Packages for Academic Libraries." *Library Software Review* (March–April 1985): 59–62. Discusses pros and cons of popular packages.

Greengrass, L. "Creating a Data Base with Children." *SLJ* (May 1985): 143–146. Discusses ways to use data bases in the classroom.

Honeyman, D. S. "Data Bases and Special Education IEP Reports." *Electronic Learning* (March 1985): 24, 26. Discusses the use of PFS File to store and sort IEP records and generate report information from these records.

Hsiao, F. S. T. "The Electronic Gradebook: An Application of dBASE II Program for Academia." *Collegiate Microcomputer* (February 1985): 59–67. Discusses methods of calculating students' average grades and assigning letter grades by using the dBASE II program on the IBM PC.

Hunter, B. "Problem Solving with Data Bases." *Computing Teacher* (May 1985): 20–27. Discusses typical uses of data bases and data management programs in the classroom; provides a learning plan to teach the usage of data bases.

Levinson, M. S., and J. A. Walcott. "On-line Data Bases—A School Project." *Media Methods* (September–October 1985): 13–15.

Mason, R. M. "Database Management Software." *Library Journal* (November 15, 1985): 4–5.

Olds, H. F., and A. Dickenson. "Move Over Word Processors—Here Come the Data Bases." *Classroom Computer Learning* (October 1985): 46–49. Gives suggestions on sorting through word processing features to better use them in the classroom.

Sopp, N. P. "Do You Really Need a Children's Data Base?" *Computing Teacher* (November 1985): 43–45. Opposing view to the teaching of a watered down version of integrated software to children. The author advocates teaching only the adult version and discusses how to accomplish it.

CHAPTER

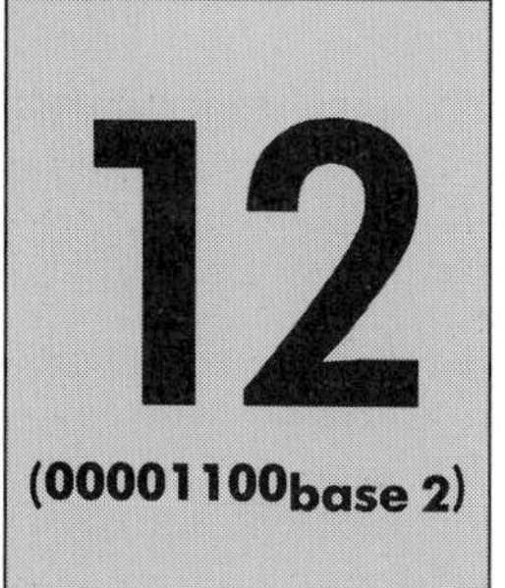

Electronic Spreadsheets
Calculating without Calluses

Getting Started

To a very large degree, electronic spreadsheet software is responsible for the continuing success of the microcomputer industry. Business users already had word processing technology, so they didn't need microcomputers for that. The financial modeling power of spreadsheets gave business users a reason to buy the first micros. Today, business users' demands form a large impetus for the ongoing improvement of hardware capabilities.

This chapter is designed to accomplish two things. First, it should give you an overview of what electronic spreadsheets are and what they can do. Once that's accomplished, we'll examine the potential instructional value of spreadsheets and introduce what we consider to be some meaningful models for using them.

Objectives for Teachers

After completing this chapter you should be able to

1. Describe what advantage(s) the first electronic spreadsheet had over the pencil-and-paper version.
2. Define the two different meanings of the term *spreadsheet* used in this chapter.
3. Explain the fundamental spreadsheet concept.
4. Explain what a cell is.
5. Describe two features common to all spreadsheets.
6. Describe what is meant by the relative method of addressing data cells in a spreadsheet.
7. Describe what is meant by the absolute method of addressing data cells in a spreadsheet.
8. Describe other features that a spreadsheet program might include.

9. Define integrated software.
10. Describe instructional management tasks that can be performed effectively using a spreadsheet or integrated software.
11. Describe instructional uses of spreadsheets or integrated software.
12. Develop an instructional plan using a spreadsheet or integrated software for management or for instruction.
13. Present a lesson to students using a spreadsheet or integrated software.

Spreadsheet Fundamentals

Once upon a time, people used to build mathematical models as a means of tracking and predicting the performance of a company. The tool for doing this was a large sheet of graph paper called a spreadsheet. Once a spreadsheet had been set up, a person could make changes in the model and see what overall effect those changes created. For example, an operations manager might ask, "If we halve the amount of stock in the warehouse by expediting deliveries from the manufacturer, will the savings in warehouse-related costs be enough to offset the costs incurred by expediting deliveries?" To find out, the manager could change the appropriate values in the spreadsheet model, recalculate all the values that depended upon the ones changed, and then get the bottom-line answer. The problem with spreadsheets was that all the calculations had to be done by hand or with a calculator.

All this changed with the creation of a program called VisiCalc. A student at Harvard Business School, Dan Bricklin, figured that computers might be able to help in the preparation of financial models. So he and a friend, programmer Robert Frankston, created VisiCalc. The advantage that VisiCalc had over paper spreadsheets was that when changes were made in a model, all recalculations were performed automatically by the computer. VisiCalc became a tremendous success, made lots of money for its creators, and in the opinion of many, had a lot to do with the success of the microcomputer by giving people a reason to buy one.

Spreadsheets have come a long way since VisiCalc. They have become more flexible and more powerful and have spawned a new genre: integrated software. Integrated software attempts to do many things at once by including a word processor, a data-base manager, a spreadsheet, graphics, and other features all in one big program package.

In this chapter, the term *spreadsheet* is used in two ways. First of all, it refers to the class of software products we have described. Second, it refers to the *models* that can be created with those products. Anywhere in this chapter that the difference matters, it should be clear from the context which way the word is being used.

Whatever frills, options, or features any particular spreadsheet product may have, there is one basic concept around which they all function. Let's call it the fundamental spreadsheet concept. That concept is that you, the user, may specify virtually any mathematical relationship you wish between data elements. Furthermore, once a relationship has been set up, if you change the value of an independent variable, all values that depend on it (that use it for computation) are automatically recalculated by the program. It's difficult to get a feel for what all this means from just a textual description, so let's look at some examples. Here is what a typical spreadsheet looks like when you first boot the program.

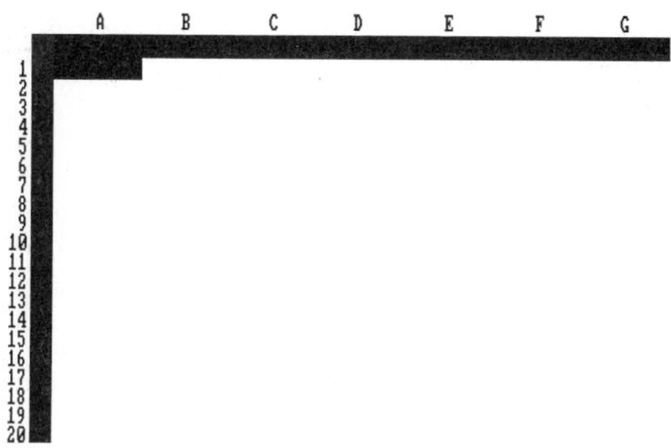

Not much to look at, is it? What you are seeing is like a piece of graph paper without the grid. Conceptually, that screen looks like the next illustration. Each of the little boxes formed by the grid is called a *cell.*

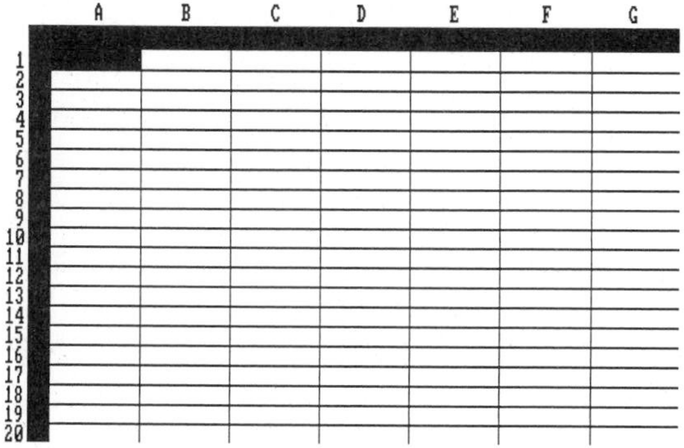

Notice the letters A, B, C, D, E, F, and G across the top of the screen. Down the left edge are the numbers 1 through 20. These borders form a coordinate system by which every cell in the spreadsheet can be uniquely addressed. For example, the cell in the upper-left corner is addressed as A1. The cell immediately to its right is B1. The cell below that one is B2, and so on. It is into these cells that you can enter numerical data, textual information, and formulas. Notice that cell A1 is painted solid. It represents the current location of the cursor. If you were to enter any information from the keyboard, it is into this cell that the information would go. Now, a spreadsheet wouldn't be very useful if all you had to work with was one screen full (140 in this example) of cells. In reality, the average spreadsheet is much larger, from tens to hundreds of thousands of cells. The computer's screen is your window into this large spreadsheet.

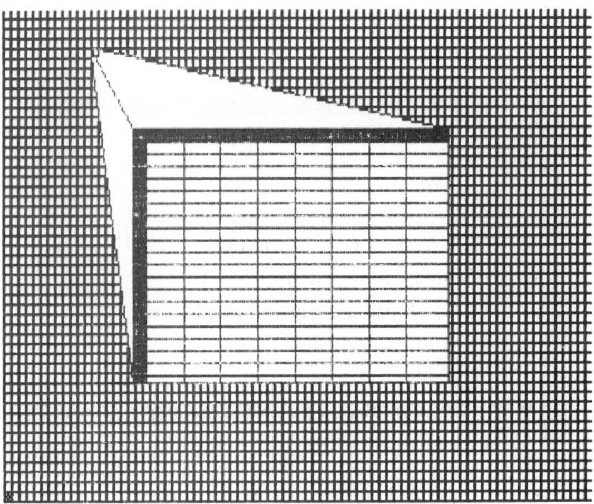

Most spreadsheets allow you to use cursor keys to navigate your cursor to any cell. As the cursor moves, the window follows it so that you see the cells around it. Also, you can usually split the screen into at least two vertical or horizontal windows so that you can see more than one area at the same time.

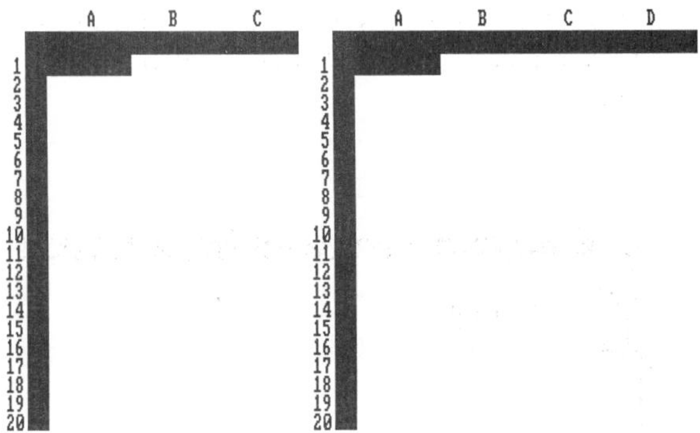

The following screens illustrate the fundamental concept of all spreadsheets. In the first illustration, the value of 5 has been entered into cell B2; 7, in B3; and we see the value 12 in B5.

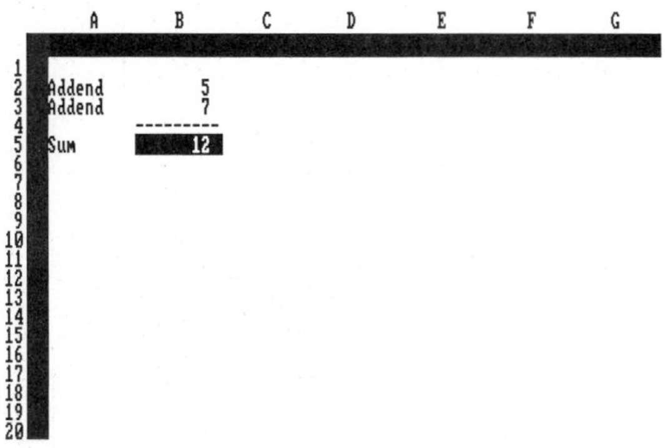

As illustrated in the next screen, the values in cells B2 and B3 are pure data. Cell B5 however, actually contains a formula that tells the program to add the contents of B2 to the contents of B3 and display the sum in B5.

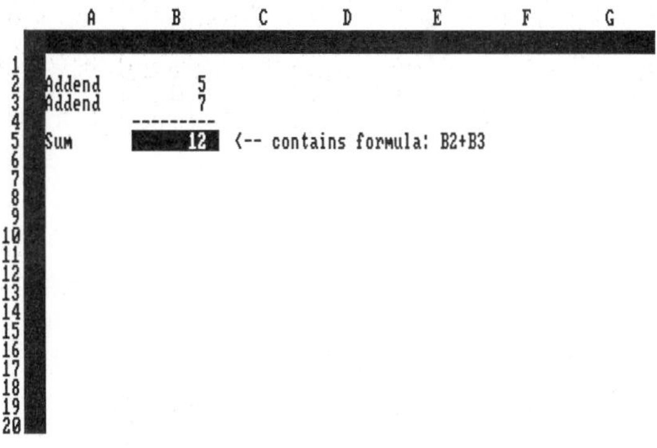

If you were to go back to B3 and change its contents to another number, 3 for example, the value displayed in B5 automatically changes to the new sum.

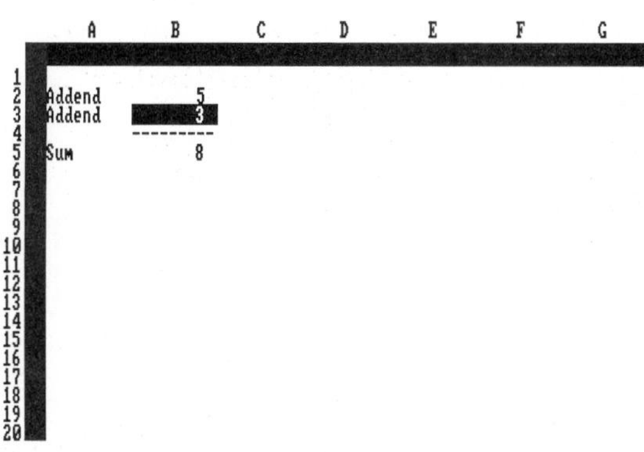

This is the magic of a spreadsheet. No matter what value is entered into either B2 or B3, the sum in B5 is always recalculated automatically. When you stop to consider that most spreadsheets allow you to use virtually any mathematical relationship in this manner, it becomes clear what a powerful tool this is.

Every spreadsheet on the market builds on the fundamental spreadsheet concept by offering you other features that make it easier to create your models. Notice, for example, the text labels in the last screen. In addition to formulas and numerical data, spreadsheets allow us to enter text information such as labels or even the line in cell B4 between the addends and the sum. Other features vary from one product to another, but two that are common to all products are the ability to copy and the ability to move the contents of any cell (or range of cells) to any other cell (or range of cells). This means that if you type a formula into a location on the sheet and later decide that you want to move it to some other location, you don't have to retype it—you can actually move it with a command. Additionally, if you need the same formula in a number of other locations (2, 10, 100, just about as many as you could want) you don't have to retype—you can copy the formula to all the cells you desire.

Oddly enough, the abilities to move and copy introduce a problem that tends to be one of the stickiest for spreadsheet novices. Let's refer back to the formula introduced before in which cells B2 and B3 contained data and cell B5 contained the formula B2 + B3. If we copy the contents of B5 to some other cell, what sum does that cell display? Is it the sum of B2 and B3 or some other pair of cells? The answer hinges on the concept of *relative* versus *absolute* referencing. To understand, let's introduce another example created on a specific spreadsheet product called Lotus 1-2-3.

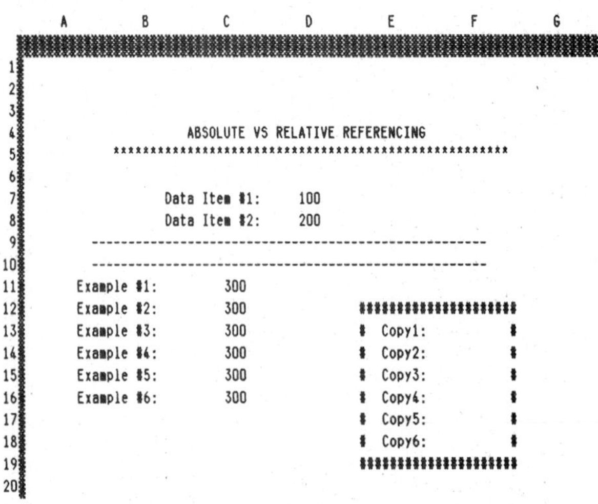

In this example, we see two cells, D7 and D8, which contain raw data, the values 100 and 200 respectively. Below these cells are six others, C11–C16, each of which contains a different formula for adding the contents of the data cells D7 and D8. We are going to take a look at those formulas, but first we are going to COPY the contents of all the formula cells to the area bounded by asterisks in the lower right-hand corner.

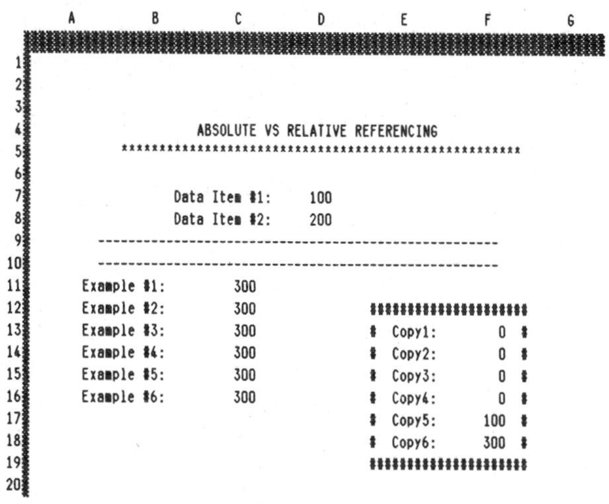

In this new screen, we see a startling revelation. After copying the formulas from cells C11–C16 to cells F13–F18, the sums are all different. The reason for this phenomenon is the manner in which each of the formulas addresses the data cells. To understand, we must examine those formulas in detail. The next screen shows the exact contents of each cell on the screen, including formulas.

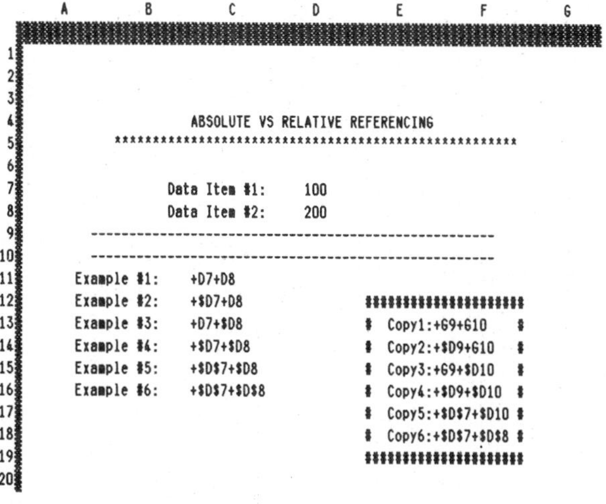

Look at the formula labeled Example #1. In the syntax of Lotus 1-2-3, this formula represents a completely relative method of addressing the data cells. Relative addressing means that whenever the formula is moved or copied, the addresses to which it makes reference are allowed to "float." In other words, they are adjusted by exactly the same number of rows and columns as the formula has been moved or copied. Look at the formula labeled Copy1. It displays the sum of cells G9 and G10. G9 and G10 don't contain anything. That is why the sum displayed in Copy1 is 0. How did D7 and D8 get to be G9 and G10? Counting up and to the right, how many cells distant is the Copy1 formula from G9? That's right, up 4 and over 1. Now, also count from Example #1 formula to D7. Isn't it also up 4 and over 1? The data cells referenced by the two formulas have the same location on the spreadsheet with relation to their respective formulas. This is what is meant by relative referencing.

Now compare the formula labeled Example #6 with its copy, labeled Copy6. When this formula was copied, there was no change. Both formulas refer to the same two cells. This is known as absolute referencing. In the syntax of Lotus 1-2-3, an absolute reference is represented by a dollar sign ($) in the formula. You can see that the formula in Example #6 uses only absolute referencing. All the other formulas, Examples #2 through #5, use mixed referencing. Study them and their respective copies. Make sure that you understand each one. While the syntax used in these examples is specific to Lotus 1-2-3, the concepts of relative and absolute referencing are common to all spreadsheets. A good understanding of them is a springboard to making intelligent use of spreadsheet software.

We have discussed a number of features that are common to all spreadsheets. Here is a list of other popular features that may or may not be included in any particular program. The following sections outline some things to look for when shopping for a spreadsheet.

Column Width

The ability to change the number of characters that can be displayed in any one column. Some programs only allow the user to change the entire spreadsheet (Global Column Width) while others allow more complete control under which any single column or range or columns can be adjusted.

Windowing

Most programs allow the user to view at least two different areas of the spreadsheet at the same time through different windows. Some allow as many as six. Additionally, some programs offer the choice of having windows scroll in synchronization or leaving them unsynchronized.

Titles

Titles are similar to windows in that they allow you to keep certain areas of the worksheet from scrolling off the screen. They are different from windows, however, in that they don't split the screen.

Color

A few programs (the number is growing) allow the user to customize the color pattern. In at least one product currently on the market, Microsoft Multiplan for the IBM PC, you can have six windows, each with different color combinations.

Protection

Some programs allow you to protect cells against accidental modification. Once protected, the only way to alter the contents of the cells is to intentionally unprotect them.

Cell Formatting

For text, some spreadsheets allow cells to be right-, left-, and center-justified. For numbers, cells can be formatted for scientific notation, fixed number of decimal places, currency, dates, and percentages.

Insertion/Deletion

In addition to moving and copying cells, some programs allow the user to insert blank rows and/or columns. Of course, entire rows and columns may be deleted as well.

Erasure

Most programs allow you to erase either the entire worksheet or any range of cells.

Recalculation

A handy feature to have is the ability to turn off automatic recalculation. It saves time to be able to edit all your changes and then have them all recalculated at once, rather than as you go.

Named Ranges

Another convenient feature is the ability to name ranges of cells. Then spreadsheet operations can be executed with labels rather than cell addresses. It's much easier to instruct the computer to reformat the DATA than it is to instruct it to reformat cells AA131 through BK200.

Printing

Some programs offer a wide variety of printing features to create hard copy of any area of the spreadsheet. With some programs it is possible to obtain printouts of cell formulas as well as data. Other features are headers, footers, and setup commands that allow you to invoke special features that your printer may have, such as compressed printing or italics.

File Handling

While any program will allow you to save and recall spreadsheets, some have additional features. Some programs will import data from other programs, such as word processors or data-base management systems. This feature allows you to have an integrated system where data can be freely exchanged between programs. Another feature offered by some products is the ability to "print" to disk files. This feature allows you to create forms to print out later, and it allows you to export data to other programs.

Macros

A very powerful feature offered by some products is the ability to program the spreadsheets to perform more than one function with just one command. These commands are called **macros.** For example, you might have a sequence of commands that you use frequently. Instead of typing all those commands every time you need them, you can link them together in such a way that they can all be automatically executed with one or two keystrokes.

Functions

Most spreadsheets offer a variety of mathematical operations and functions ranging from addition to arc cosine. Some programs offer other special features such as financial, date, statistical, and data-base functions. Available financial functions include rate of return, net present value, future value, present value, and payment. Date functions allow you to perform numerical operations on dates. For example, you can have a spreadsheet calculate how many days a payment is overdue by subtracting the dates. Statistical functions might include counting the number of items in a list, summation, calculating numerical means, finding minimum and maximum values, standard deviation, and variance. Data-base functions might allow you to have the computer locate a specific item in a list or table.

Integrated Software

Spreadsheets have led to the development of another class of microcomputer software products that integrate a number of functions into one program; for example, Lotus 1-2-3 and Symphony from the Lotus Corporation and Framework from Ashton-Tate. These programs differ from the spreadsheets mentioned before in that files don't have to be exchanged between different programs. Let's use Lotus 1-2-3 as an example. In Lotus 1-2-3, it is possible to model a spreadsheet and then use that same data to create line or bar graphs. You can also search that same data just like you might with data-base software. In addition, Lotus 1-2-3 has a very powerful macro command language. Some other integrated packages also offer the features of a word processor and a telecommunications program.

Instructional Uses

What can you do with spreadsheets in the classroom? Well, one obvious use is for management tasks. Spreadsheets can be very useful for keeping a computer gradebook. Once the formulas are set up, you can enter student scores and have the grades calculated automatically. Then you can produce a variety of reports with the program's printing capabilities. An extract from a gradebook created on Multiplan follows:

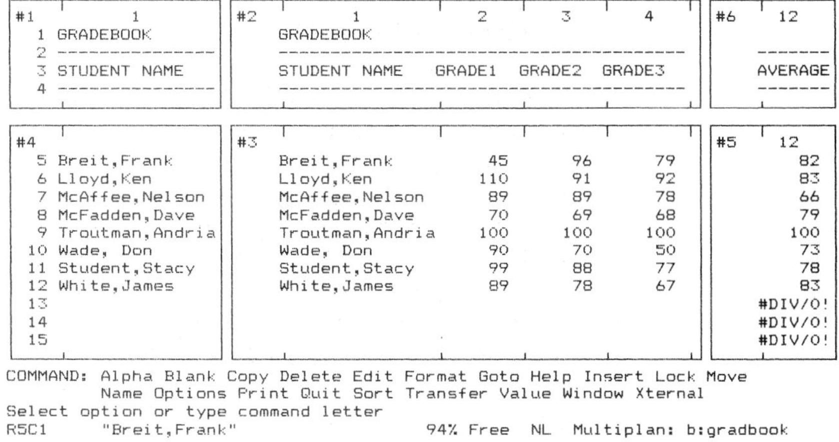

```
#1        1          #2       1           2         3         4       #6    12
 1 GRADEBOOK               GRADEBOOK
 2 ---------------         --------------------------------------           -------
 3 STUDENT NAME            STUDENT NAME    GRADE1    GRADE2    GRADE3        AVERAGE
 4 ---------------         --------------------------------------           -------

#4                   #3                                                   #5    12
 5 Breit,Frank             Breit,Frank         45        96        79           82
 6 Lloyd,Ken               Lloyd,Ken          110        91        92           83
 7 McAffee,Nelson          McAffee,Nelson      89        89        78           66
 8 McFadden,Dave           McFadden,Dave       70        69        68           79
 9 Troutman,Andria         Troutman,Andria    100       100       100          100
10 Wade, Don               Wade, Don           90        70        50           73
11 Student,Stacy           Student,Stacy       99        88        77           78
12 White,James             White,James         89        78        67           83
13                                                                         #DIV/0!
14                                                                         #DIV/0!
15                                                                         #DIV/0!
COMMAND: Alpha Blank Copy Delete Edit Format Goto Help Insert Lock Move
         Name Options Print Quit Sort Transfer Value Window Xternal
Select option or type command letter
R5C1     "Breit,Frank"                  94% Free   NL   Multiplan: b:gradbook
```

This particular spreadsheet is set up with six different windows (on screen, each window is in a different color) to keep the headings from scrolling off the screen as students are added to the list. Although this example calculates only individual averages, it is possible to generate virtually any kind of data, including class averages and class rankings.

Integrated packages are even more useful. With the addition of data-base capabilities, you can keep all kinds of records like textbook inventories or test item data banks. With word processing capabilities you can create documents such as personalized grade reports to parents that incorporate grade information calculated on the spreadsheet.

Economics and Consumer Education

The modeling power of spreadsheets can be used to great advantage in economics and consumer education. Students typically have difficulty understanding such topics as compound interest and amortization. It is difficult for a teacher to create good models because of the time and complexity involved in the calculations. With a spreadsheet, these kinds of things are a snap.

For example, an amortization model is shown in Activity 12.1. By changing the principal, interest, and term, students can gain an intuitive knowledge of how values are affected by observing the recalculation performed by the spreadsheet in mere seconds.

ACTIVITY 12.1

Understanding Amortization

Curriculum Area and Level. Economics and Consumer Education. Virtually any class in which the subject is taught, usually at the secondary level.

Objectives. To allow students to experiment with various principals, interest rates, and terms of payment to observe how monthly and total payments vary.

Directions. Prepare a work sheet ahead of time with sample data on it to be entered. Instruct students to use an amortization template to change the principal, interest, and term variables and observe how the monthly payment and total amount to be paid change. Instruct students to answer the following questions:

1. How does increasing the interest rate affect the monthly payment?
2. By what factor does doubling the term affect the total amount to be paid? Halving?
3. What is the disadvantage of getting small monthly payments by lengthening the term of the loan?
4. What is the advantage of taking the largest monthly payment you can handle for a given interest rate and principal?

Interest	14.0%		
Loan Amount	$10,000.00	** LOAN AMORTIZATION **	
Term (yrs)	30		
Mo. Payment	$118.49	Total cost:	$42,655.38

Month	Principal Pd.	Interest Pd.	Balance
1983			$10,000.00
1	$1.82	$116.67	$9,998.18
2	$1.84	$116.65	$9,996.34
3	$1.86	$116.62	$9,994.47
4	$1.88	$116.60	$9,992.59
5	$1.91	$116.58	$9,990.68
6	$1.93	$116.56	$9,988.75
7	$1.95	$116.54	$9,986.80
8	$1.97	$116.51	$9,984.83
9	$2.00	$116.49	$9,982.83
10	$2.02	$116.47	$9,980.81
11	$2.04	$116.44	$9,978.76
12	$2.07	$116.42	$9,976.70

Commentary. Students often fail to get an intuitive feel for the variables that affect a loan because the calculations are too tedious and amortization tables are too static. Yet, because common sense is what many people base judgment on, isn't the development of an intuitive sense of what is good and bad of utmost import to a student? Spreadsheets can be used as tools to remove the barrier of tedious calculation.

Ideas for Extension. Have your students shop around for loan advertisements in the newspaper. They can use an amortization spreadsheet to compare the varying terms of those loans to see which is the best deal.

Here are some other spreadsheet models for consumer education. What instructional objectives could you use these to meet?

```
#1   1      2               3                          4         5         6
  1 CHECKBOOK
  2 ***************************************************************************
  3 No.   Date      Description                      Debit     Credit    Balance
  4 ***************************************************************************

#2
  5         01/12/83 Initial Deposit                                       1000
  6   101   03/28/83 Mortgage                        254.9                745.1
  7         04/05/83 Income Tax Refund                         157.35    902.45
  8   102   04/13/83 Widgets                         99.95                802.5
  9   103   05/20/83 Magazine Subscription           19.95               782.55
 10   104   07/29/83 IBM PC                           4000             -3217.45
 11                                                                    -3217.45
 12                                                                    -3217.45
 13                                                                    -3217.45
 14                                                                    -3217.45
 15                                                                    -3217.45
COMMAND: Alpha Blank Copy Delete Edit Format Goto Help Insert Lock Move
         Name Options Print Quit Sort Transfer Value Window Xternal
Select option or type command letter
R10C5                              94% Free  NL  Multiplan: b:chekbook
```

```
***************************                MONTHLY BUDGET
Gross Income:              2200
```

CATEGORY	BUDGET	JAN ACTUAL	JAN DIFF.	FEB ACTUAL	FEB DIFF.
Telephone	30	23	7		30
Electricity	46	45	1		46
Gas	56	65	-9		56
Car Insurance	34.87	35.67	-0.8	34.87	0
Life Insurance	34.6	34.6	0	34.6	0
Car Payment	145.54	145.54	0	145.54	0
Mortgage	467	467	0	467	0
Food	450	400	50		450
Clothing	220	245	-25		220
Entertainment	110	65	45		110
Taxes at 0.25	550	550	0	550	0
TOTAL:	2144.01	2075.81	68.2	1232.01	30
DIFFERENCE:	55.99	124.19	68.2	967.99	

MONEY SUPPLY

	AMOUNT DEPOSITED	AMOUNT ON RESERVE	BORROWER	AMOUNT BORROWED	AMOUNT OF INTEREST
A. STUDENT	1000.00	100.00	TOM JONES	900.00	126.00
V. BLUE	900.00	90.00	MARY ROCK	810.00	113.40
H. O'DAY	810.00	81.00	M.T. CHASE	729.00	102.06
C. LEMON	729.00	72.90	I. BLANK	656.10	91.85
Y. RYAN	656.10	65.61	S. BROWN	590.49	82.67
TOTALS:	4095.10	409.51	TOTALS	3685.59	515.98

```
PREVAILING INTEREST                  TOTAL DEPOSITS   :        4095.10
     RATE:     14.00%                TOTAL RESERVE    :         409.51
                                     TOTAL LOANS      :        3685.59
                                     TOTAL INTEREST   :         515.98
             TOTAL AMOUNT OF MONEY CREATED
              BY DEPOSIT OF:        $1,000.00         :        8706.18
```

Mathematics and Science

One way in which spreadsheets can be helpful is in the creation of instructional support materials. Suppose you need a table of trigonometric functions for your next test, but the one in the textbook reproduces poorly and has values on it that you would like to exclude for some of the test items. Creating your own is very simple with a spreadsheet. For example,

X in RAD	SIN(X)	COS(X)	TAN(X)	CSC(X)	SEC(X)	COT(X)	X in RAD
0.000000	.0000	1.0000	.0000	undefined	1.0000	undefined	1.570796
0.030207	0.0302	0.9995	0.0302	33.1092	1.0005	33.0941	1.540588
0.060415	0.0604	0.9982	0.0605	16.5622	1.0018	16.5320	1.510381
0.090622	0.0905	0.9959	0.0909	11.0499	1.0041	11.0045	1.480173
0.120830	0.1205	0.9927	0.1214	8.2962	1.0073	8.2357	1.449965
0.151038	0.1505	0.9886	0.1522	6.6461	1.0115	6.5704	1.419758
0.181245	0.1803	0.9836	0.1833	5.5477	1.0167	5.4568	1.389550
0.211453	0.2099	0.9777	0.2147	4.7646	1.0228	4.6585	1.359343
0.241660	0.2393	0.9709	0.2465	4.1786	1.0299	4.0572	1.329135
0.271868	0.2685	0.9633	0.2788	3.7240	1.0381	3.5872	1.298927
0.302076	0.2975	0.9547	0.3116	3.3613	1.0474	3.2091	1.268720
0.332283	0.3262	0.9453	0.3451	3.0656	1.0579	2.8979	1.238512
0.362491	0.3546	0.9350	0.3792	2.8200	1.0695	2.6368	1.208305
X in RAD	COS(X)	SIN(X)	COT(X)	SEC(X)	CSC(X)	TAN(X)	X in RAD

Virtually any kind of table of numerical relations is easy to reproduce.

LENGTH CONVERT Input	Inches	Feet	Yards	Miles	Mm	Cm	Meters	Km
1 In.	1	0.083333	0.027777	0.000015	25.4	2.54	0.0254	0.000025
3 Ft.	36	3	1	0.000568	914.4	91.44	0.9144	0.000914
5 Yd.	180	15	5	0.002840	4572	457.2	4.572	0.004572
7 Mi.	443520	36960	12320	7	11265408	1126540.	11265.40	11.26540
2 Mm	0.078740	0.006561	0.002187	0.000001	2	0.2	0.002	0.000002
8 Cm	3.149608	0.262467	0.087489	0.000049	80	8	0.08	0.00008
9 Mm	354.3309	29.52756	9.842517	0.005592	9000	900	9	0.009
4 Km	157480.4	13123.36	4374.452	2.485484	4000000	400000	4000	4

These models are examples of some rather simple ideas, however. Surely something more significant can be accomplished with spreadsheet software.

The modeling power of spreadsheets is valuable for studying the nature of functions. Once modeled, a function's domain can easily be varied with resulting changes in the range instantly observable. Integrated packages with graphics are even more powerful. Once a function has been modeled, changes can be made in its constants and a new graph quickly plotted.

With electronic spreadsheets and integrated software, students can be given the tools to explore mathematical and scientific relationships in much the same way as Logo is used (see Chapter 5), except with speed and accuracy never before possible. When teaching mathematical relationships, teachers typically demonstrate a few examples, explain the concepts involved, and then expect the students to gain deeper cognitive level understanding by performing exercises. There are a number of problems with this approach. For one thing, teachers aren't perfect. Even we make mistakes. When class time permits only a few examples to be shown, a mistake or hesitation in even one example is enough to confuse students and destroy the effect of the lesson. Teachers rationalize and say to their students, "Well, you get the idea from the other examples." Often they don't. What about textbook exercises? Students are even less accurate than teachers. Exercises that are completed improperly frequently lead to little learning.

In our discussion of Logo, we talked about discovery learning as a more effective means of teaching. A major concept embodied in Logo is to place the student in an environment conducive to learning. Teachers with spreadsheet software can create powerful environments for learning mathematical relationships. Let's look at a few examples.

One place to start is with a subject-specific textbook. Many of the problem-solving activities posed in textbooks are perfectly appropriate for spreadsheet solution. The following example is a teacher-prepared template that removes the stumbling block of computation and allows the student to concentrate on problem-solving strategies.

THE CANDY STORE

There are many different ways to spend $5.00 at the candy store. One is show here. How many can you find? Buy no more than five of each item and come as close to $5.00 as you can without going over.

ITEM	AMOUNT	PRICE	TOTAL
Candy Cane	1	0.49	$0.49
Chocolate Bar	1	0.99	0.99
Licorice	1	0.89	0.89
Mints	0	1.98	0
Gum Drops	1	0.25	0.25
Lollipop	1	0.79	0.79
Jelly Beans	1	1.19	1.19
Bubble Gum	1	0.39	0.39
			$4.99

The first example required little student knowledge of how to operate a spreadsheet, but the next one requires partial construction of the template.

PETE'S PAYCHECK

Pete is trying to figure out how much money he has earned this week. See if you can help him out by completing this template. He makes $3.75 per hour.

PETE	S	M	T	W	R	F	S	TOTAL
HOURS	7	5	2	8	8	6	8	
TIPS	5.75	3.50	2.20	10.00	9.75	3.25	5.50	
TOTAL								

Discovery learning is much more widely used in science classes than in mathematics classes. Spreadsheets can be used either to create discovery environments or as recording tools in the traditional discovery environment, the laboratory. It is not at all uncommon for chemistry students, for example, to record and plot data collected from an experiment. Many spreadsheets allow limited bar graphs, so data collected during experiments and recorded on the spreadsheet can easily be accurately represented graphically. Purists might question this use of the software saying, "The student isn't doing the work." We would ask, "What is the objective of such an activity: to develop students' skills in graph plotting, or to give them an understanding of the scientific method?" Using a spreadsheet to create the graph removes a stumbling block that stands in the way of understanding.

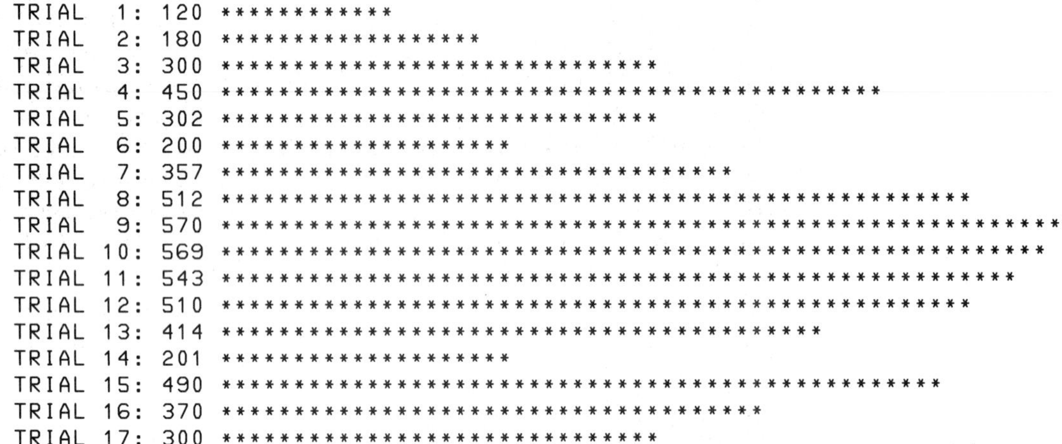

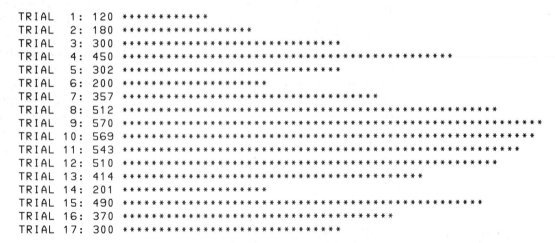

```
TRIAL  1: 120 ************
TRIAL  2: 180 ******************
TRIAL  3: 300 ******************************
TRIAL  4: 450 *********************************************
TRIAL  5: 302 ******************************
TRIAL  6: 200 ********************
TRIAL  7: 357 ***********************************
TRIAL  8: 512 ***************************************************
TRIAL  9: 570 *********************************************************
TRIAL 10: 569 ********************************************************
TRIAL 11: 543 ******************************************************
TRIAL 12: 510 ***************************************************
TRIAL 13: 414 *****************************************
TRIAL 14: 201 ********************
TRIAL 15: 490 *************************************************
TRIAL 16: 370 *************************************
TRIAL 17: 300 ******************************
```

Here is an example of a spreadsheet that presents a discovery environment for physics or chemistry. In either of those courses, students often study Boyle's Law, Charles's Law, and the Combined Gas Law Equation, all of which have to do with the relationships between temperature, pressure, and volume for gases. The following spreadsheet goes a long way toward making these laws come alive for students. By manipulating values and observing the results, students can achieve very concrete understandings. Here we have the spreadsheet as it is loaded into the computer.

	TEMPERATURE	VOLUME	PRESSURE
VOLUME (m^3):	22.40	22.40	22.40
PRESSURE (cm Hg):	76.00	76.00	76.00
TEMPERATURE (C):	273.00	273.00	273.00

Here is the same spreadsheet after some values have been changed.

```
One kmole of a gas occupies 22.4 cubic meters
volume at standard temperature and pressure. In
the column labeled TEMPERATURE, change the volume
and the pressure and observe how the temperature
is affected. In the column labeled VOLUME, change
the pressure and temperature to observe how the
volume is affected. In the last column, labeled
PRESSURE, change volume and temperature to see
how pressure is affected.

                          TEMPERATURE   VOLUME   PRESSURE
VOLUME (m^3):                 22.40      44.80      22.40
PRESSURE (cm Hg):             76.00      38.00     152.00
TEMPERATURE (C):             273.00     273.00     546.00
```

Just as the techniques of graphing or manipulating formulas can be obstacles to learning for science students, so too can tedious calculation stand in the way of the mathematics student. The authors have very vivid memories of trying to teach students how to find square roots by the divide-and-average technique. This technique is very simple in concept; there are only two steps. The technique is difficult for students to execute because it requires comparatively tedious calculation. Students get so caught up in juggling the numbers, which they already know how to do, that they can't keep track of the two simple steps in the technique. Now, whether or not you believe in teaching students how to compute square roots, the point here is that calculation, which is not part of the learning objective, can interfere with students' achieving the objective. Spreadsheet software can be used to remove the interference at least until the objective has been accomplished. Students can either perform the calculations themselves, or use a spreadsheet—such as the one that follows—that demonstrates the process.

```
            ------------ SQUARE ROOT ALGORITHM ------------
        ************
        *    2.000 *          <<<  NUMBER TO FIND THE SQUARE ROOT OF
        ************

             2.000                     1.414                     1.414
        -----------               -----------               -----------
1.000 :      2.000      1.414 :        2.000      1.414 :        2.000
             1.333                     1.414                     1.414
        -----------               -----------               -----------
1.500 :      2.000      1.414 :        2.000      1.414 :        2.000
             1.412                     1.414                     1.414
        -----------               -----------               -----------
1.417 :      2.000      1.414 :        2.000      1.414 :        2.000
             1.414                     1.414                     1.414
        -----------               -----------               -----------
1.414 :      2.000      1.414 :        2.000      1.414 :        2.000
```

An area of mathematics on which spreadsheets and integrated software can have tremendous impact is the teaching of how functions are related to their graphs. Using trigonometry as an example, once students have learned how to plot functions point by point, they are usually introduced to more powerful graphing techniques. These techniques depend upon the relationships between the graph and the constants in equations of the form

$$f(x) = C + A\sin B(x + D)$$

These constants all affect the graph independently of one another. Many instructors teach this topic by demonstration because it's the easiest way out. We have already mentioned some of the problems associated with the I-Demonstrate, You-Go-Home-and-Work-the-Problems-in-the-Book mode of instruction. The problems are even more acute when graphing is involved. There are precious few teachers who can consistently produce accurate graphs, and probably even fewer who have time to prepare visual aids ahead of time. Spreadsheet software can do a little to alleviate the problems. Even many of the older programs can produce graphs like this one.

```
       X    SIN(X)
       0         0 .
0.157079 0.156433 ++++
0.314158 0.309015 +++++++++
0.471237 0.453988 +++++++++++++
0.628316 0.587783 +++++++++++++++++
0.785395 0.707104 +++++++++++++++++++++
0.942474 0.809014 ++++++++++++++++++++++++
1.099553 0.891004 ++++++++++++++++++++++++++
1.256632 0.951054 ++++++++++++++++++++++++++++
1.413711 0.987687 +++++++++++++++++++++++++++++
 1.57079         1 +++++++++++++++++++++++++++++
1.727869 0.987689 +++++++++++++++++++++++++++++
1.884948 0.951058 ++++++++++++++++++++++++++++
2.042027 0.891010 ++++++++++++++++++++++++++
2.199106 0.809022 ++++++++++++++++++++++++
2.356185 0.707113 +++++++++++++++++++++
2.513264 0.587793 +++++++++++++++++
2.670343 0.454000 +++++++++++++
2.827422 0.309027 +++++++++
2.984501 0.156446 ++++
 3.14158 0.000012 .
```

Integrated software can have a dramatic effect. The following spreadsheet is one of a series created with Lotus 1-2-3 for graphing functions. This one just graphs sine functions. The following depicts the computer display as it first appears to the student. By changing the values of A, B, C, and D, the student can almost instantly view the resulting graph.

```
GRAPHS OF TRIGONOMETRIC FUNCTIONS - THE SINE
FUNCTION
 ---------------------------------------------
          Observe how the values of the parameters
          A, B, C, and D in the equation
          f(x)=C+ASINB(x+d) affect the shape of
```

```
the graph by changing them and
regraphing. First, view the standard SIN
graph by pressing F10 and then any key
to return.

          C-Vert Disp    D-Horiz Disp
          -----------    ------------
               0              0

          A-Amplitude    B-#Cyc. in 360
          -----------    --------------
                1              1

          *** press ALT-G to graph ***
```

The following graph corresponds to the values shown. Although it can't be seen in this reproduction, there are actually two curves present; one superimposed over the other. One graph is a standard—f(x) = sin(x)—the other is the graph corresponding to the values entered by the student.

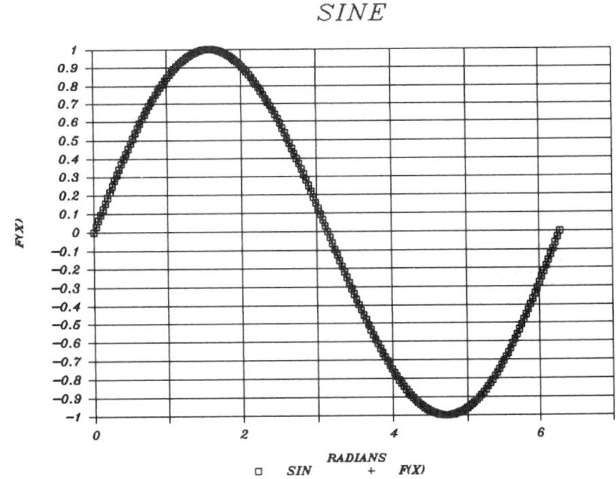

If we return to the display of constants, we can alter the values to these; for example,

```
GRAPHS OF TRIGONOMETRIC FUNCTIONS - THE SINE
FUNCTION
-----------------------------------------------
          Observe how the values of the parameters
          A, B, C, and D in the equation
          f(x)=C+ASINB(x+d) affect the shape of
          the graph by changing them and
          regraphing. First, view the standard SIN
```

```
graph by pressing F10 and then any key
to return.

          C-Vert Disp    D-Horiz Disp
          -----------    ------------
                    0               0

          A-Amplitude    B-#Cyc. in 360
          -----------    --------------
                    2                 3

          *** press ALT-G to graph ***
```

By pressing the proper keys, we can cause the spreadsheet to recalculate 200 different ordered pairs and then, in seconds, present us with this graph.

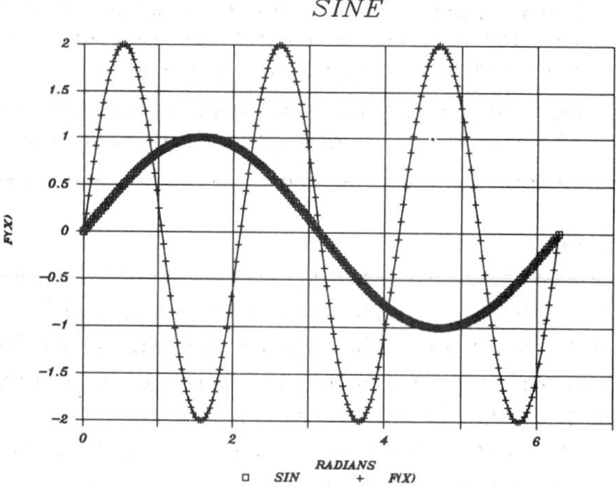

We think this represents a pretty powerful environment for learning about functions and graphs. Activity 12.2 should convince you, too.

ACTIVITY 12.2

Graphing SINE Functions

Curriculum Area and Level. Secondary Mathematics. Eleventh and Twelfth Grades.

Objective. The student will be able to use the B coefficient in equations of form

$$f(x) = C + A\sin B(x - D)$$

to predict the period of the function and how the graph is affected.

Directions. Have students work in pairs and use the spreadsheet to aid them in completing the sample work sheet (included at the end of the chapter as Resource Sheet 12) by "discovering" the answers to the questions listed.

Commentary. The students should already know how to plot functions, know the terms *period* and *cycle,* and know radian notation. Some previous experience with the spreadsheet is also helpful.

Ideas for Extension. After students have completed the work sheet and "discovered" the relationships, review to reinforce those concepts.

Chapter Summary

In this chapter, we have examined what spreadsheets are all about and have seen that all spreadsheets, no matter what other features they may encompass, are tools for dynamically modeling quantitative relationships between data or sets of data. We have also looked at a number of models for using spreadsheets in different curriculum areas. There is a common theme among all the models. That theme is to use the software to create learning environments that remove obstacles encountered with "normal" instruction. The spreadsheet is a powerful tool for handling calculations and its dynamic nature can be used to make difficult concepts much more attainable to students.

Chapter Review

Knowledge Exercises

1. What was the first computer spreadsheet program to be developed, and what was its advantage over pencil-and-paper spreadsheets?

   Answer: VisiCalc was so successful because all recalculations were done automatically by the program; whereas before, all recalculations had to be done by hand or by calculator.

2. What are the two ways the term *spreadsheet* is commonly used?

Answer: 1. A spreadsheet is a computer program for dynamically modeling quantitative relationships.
2. Spreadsheet also refers to the models that can be created with such a program.

3. What is the fundamental spreadsheet concept?

Answer: The concept is that the user may specify almost any mathematical relationship desired between data elements, and that if a value of an independent variable is changed, all values that depend on it are recalculated by the program.

4. What is a cell in a spreadsheet program? How should you address the cell in column H and in row 14?

Answer: A cell is the "receptacle" for an element of data or a formula. The grid of a spreadsheet program gives each cell a unique address. The cell in column H, row 14 should be addressed as H14.

5. Name two features common to almost all commercial spreadsheets.

Answer: Two features that are common to almost all products are the ability to copy and the ability to move the contents of any cell (or range of cells) to any other cell (or range of cells).

6. Define the relative method of addressing data cells in a spreadsheet.

Answer: Relative addressing means that whenever the formula is moved or copied, the addresses to which it makes reference "float" or change. They are adjusted by exactly the same number of columns and rows as the formula has been moved or copied.

7. Define the absolute method of referencing or addressing data cells.

Answer: Absolute referencing means that when a formula is copied, there are no changes in the address(es) of the cell(s) referenced. The formula still refers to the same cell(s).

8. List and briefly describe at least 10 additional features that are available with some spreadsheet programs.

Answer:
- Column Width. The ability to change the number of characters that can be displayed in any one column.
- Windowing. The user can view at least two different areas of the spreadsheet at the same time through different windows.
- Titles. These allow the user to keep certain areas of the work sheet from scrolling off the screen, but don't split the screen.
- Color. The user can customize the color pattern.
- Protection. The user may protect cells from accidental modification.
- Cell Formatting. Text in the cells may be justified (left-, right-, or center-) and numbers can be formatted for scientific notation, percentages, and so on.

- Insertion/Deletion. The user may insert or delete entire rows and/or columns.
- Erasure. The entire work sheet or any range of cells may be erased.
- Recalculation. The user may turn off automatic recalculation until all data have been entered.
- Named Ranges. The user may name ranges of cells.
- Printing. A wide variety of printing features are available to create hard copy of any area of the spreadsheet.
- File Handling. The program allows the user to import or export data from other programs such as word processors or data-base management systems.
- Macros. The user may program the spreadsheet to perform more than one function with just one command.
- Functions. Some programs offer special functions (in addition to mathematical) such as financial, date, statistical, and data-base functions.

9. What is integrated software?

   Answer: These are programs that integrate several functions into one program; for example a spreadsheet, data base, graphing capabilities, word processor, telecommunications, and a macro command language might all be included in one program.

10. What are some uses of spreadsheets and integrated software in education?

    Answer: Spreadsheets and integrated software can be used to make computerized gradebooks, textbook inventories, and test item banks; to teach economics and consumer education (for example, compound interest and amortization); to study the nature of mathematical functions by developing function tables and graphing functions; to explore the laws of physics; to find square roots by the divide-and-average technique to name a few.

Thought Exercises

1. Write an appropriate lesson plan for the checkbook template illustrated in this chapter (following Activity 12.1).

2. Write an appropriate lesson plan for the budget template illustrated in this chapter (following Activity 12.1).

3. Write an appropriate lesson plan for the money supply template illustrated in this chapter (following Activity 12.1).

4. List some ways that spreadsheets could be used to create instructional support materials, other than those suggested in the chapter. Be as specific as you can.

Activities

1. If you have access to spreadsheet software, learn to use it. Many programs provide tutorials to help you master them.
2. Whatever program you end up learning, use it to replicate some of the spreadsheets shown in this chapter, especially the ones for checkbook, budget, and money supply.
3. If possible, use your spreadsheets and lesson plans developed in the Thought Exercises to present a lesson to students. Write a brief description of student reactions and motivation, along with successes and problems you encounter.
4. If possible, use either Activity 12.1 or Activity 12.2 for a presentation to students. Write a brief report of student reactions to the lesson, and detail successes, problems, and suggested modifications for a particular student group.

Projects

1. Develop an instructional unit of at least one week's duration using a spreadsheet for instruction. You have at least two major problems before you.
   - How do you get students up to speed with the software?
   - How will your activity best be presented?

   Write a rationale for how you will incorporate the spreadsheet into your plan, along with detailed lesson plans. Keep a log describing successes, problems, student reactions, modifications, and suggestions for improvement for each lesson.
2. Use a spreadsheet for instructional management tasks. If you have students, let them help you develop your materials. Keep a log describing successes, problems, modifications, and suggestions for improvement. Was this use of a spreadsheet more efficient? Would you use it again?

Resource Sheet 12

Sinusoids: Period of Sin
Student Work Sheet

Name: **Period:**

Instructions. Use the spreadsheet provided to answer the following questions. Use the table at the bottom of this page to gather and organize information by graphing the indicated functions.

1. From your observations, list the values of B that squeeze, or compress, the graph (more cycles over the same distance on the X axis).
2. What general observation(s) can be made about values of B that squeeze the graph?
3. From your observations, list the values of B that stretch, or expand, the graph (fewer cycles over the same distance on the X axis).
4. What general observation(s) can be made about values of B that stretch the graph?
5. How does the value of B relate to the number of cycles? What would be a good name for B?
6. What effect(s) do negative values of B have on the graph?
7. What is the relationship between B and the period of the function? (For example: 2 times B = period, or 1/B = period.)

Function	B	#Cycles in 2PI	Period	Other observations
Y=SIN X				
Y=SIN 2X				
Y=SIN 3X				
Y=SIN 4X				
Y=SIN 10X				
Y=SIN .5X				
Y=SIN. 33X				
Y=SIN .25X				
Y=SIN .1X				
Y=SIN −X				
Y=SIN −2X				

Bibliography

Allen, V. "Spreadsheets." *Electronic Learning* (April 1985): 52–53. Reviews of several spreadsheet packages.

Bowman, C. "Integrated Software Solves Scheduling Problems." *Electronic Learning* (April 1985): 22–24. How one school used a spreadsheet and data base to reroute buses.

Dribin, C. I. "Spreadsheets and Performance: A Guide for Student-Graded Presentations." *Computing Teacher* (June 1985): 22–25. Describes a student-centered grading system in which students evaluated and graded peer performance; management is facilitated through an electronic spreadsheet.

Lynn, L. E. "Integrated Software: A Versatile Management Tool." *Principal* (January 1985): 44–46. Integrated software is available to help with many of the small-to-medium-sized schools' management tasks requiring data analysis.

Pogrow, S. "Microcomputerizing Your Paperwork: Easy, Economical, and Effective." *Independent School* (December 1982): 45–46 and 49–52. Advocates using microcomputers to reduce school administration paperwork through three categories of general applications programs: word processors, spreadsheets, and data-base management systems.

Stang, D. J., and M. Levinson. "Spreadsheets Come to School." *Media and Methods* (September 1984): 28–29. Describes ways of using spreadsheets to maintain gradebooks; includes reviews of current programs.

Tinker, R. "Idea Exchange: Spreadsheet Math . . . An Example of Educational Applications of General Software Tools." *Hands On* (Spring 1984): 19–21. Discusses the nature of electronic spreadsheets and their educational applications.

CHAPTER

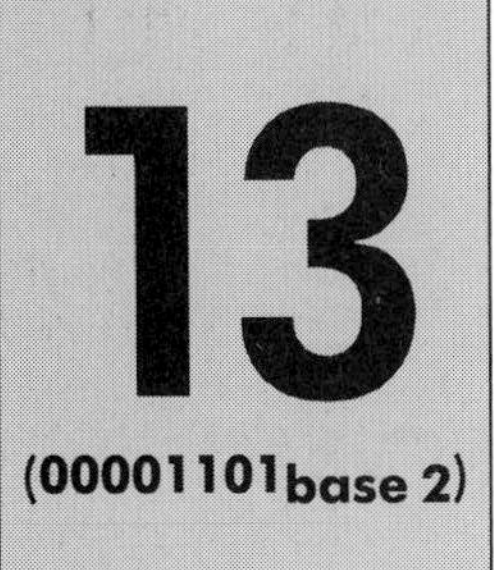

13 (00001101base 2) SILIcon SUPERSTITION
What Are We Doing Here?

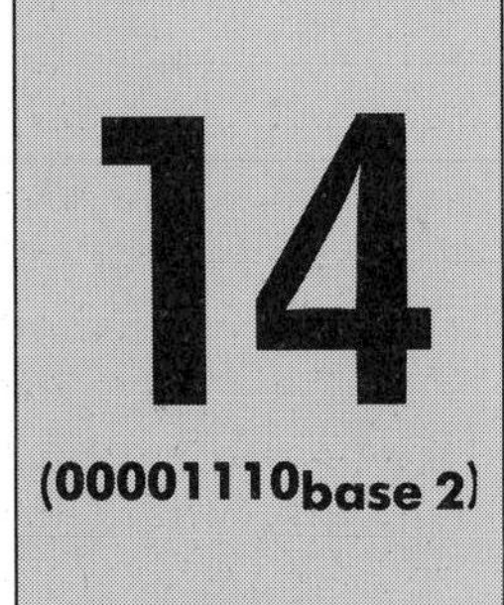

TELECOMMUNICATIONS

Terminating Telephone Tag

Getting Started

There are two purposes for this chapter. The first purpose is to familiarize you with telecommunication concepts and terms necessary for general literacy. With such a foundation you will be comfortable when reading related publications or attending professional meetings. What's better than talking about telecommunications? Right: telecommunicating! So, the second goal is to provide you with concepts and skills necessary for setting up to telecommunicate. Our third and most important goal is to explore implications for education. So, with no further ado, let's get started.

Objectives for Teachers

To successfully complete this chapter, you should be able to

1. Define the term *telecommunications.*
2. Differentiate between a smart and a dumb terminal.
3. Describe the difference(s) between serial and parallel interfaces.
4. Describe the difference(s) between acoustic and direct-connect modems.
5. Define baud rate and state the advantages and disadvantages of using 300 baud versus 1,200 or higher transmission speed.
6. Describe what is meant by the statement that two computers must be set to compatible parameters.
7. Define the following parameters: full duplex and half duplex, originate/answer mode, data bits, start/stop bits, and even/odd parity.
8. Evaluate a telecommunications software package.
9. Define the term *information utility* and describe three services such utilities provide.
10. Identify telecommunications resources available to education.
11. Describe 10 ways in which telecommunications can be used with students.

What Is Telecommunications?

The first thing we should be concerned with is the term **telecommunication.** The meaning of this term, very simply put is this: telecommunication is the telephone communication of data from one computing device to another. This is not a new idea. Whenever any two computers or peripherals are connected and operating, there is communication between them. Whether the communication is from a computer to a printer or between two computers, the end result is the same: data are electronically communicated from one device to another. Telecommunication expands on this concept by incorporating telephone technology.

Terminals

Now, if you are going to take part in telecommunicating, you need some equipment. For starters, you need a **terminal.** There are two kinds of terminals; you can have your choice of either a *dumb* terminal or a *smart* terminal. Both dumb and smart terminals consist of a keyboard, a **monitor,** and a modem. **Modems** handle the translation of data into and out of a mode suitable for telephone transmission. A dumb terminal is an inexpensive device that will send and receive information, but that's about it. It won't store telephone numbers, it won't dial automatically and repeatedly should a line be busy, and it won't go through complex automatic log-on procedures that are required when you use remote information utilities. (More about this later.) In fact, a dumb terminal does not have a central processing unit—that is, it isn't a computer.

Another limitation of dumb terminals is that incoming information appears a line at a time on the monitor until the screen is full, then the screen scrolls up so that as each new line of text is added at the bottom of the screen, a line from the top of the screen vanishes into that great digital graveyard in the sky, never to return. In short, there's no way to store information, and if you can't remember it, you've lost it. To eliminate this problem, you need a terminal with a printer.

Smart terminals are more expensive than dumb terminals because they contain more sophisticated parts. In particular, smart terminals contain a microprocessor and memory so they can automatically dial telephone numbers, automatically log onto various telecommunication systems, and capture and store incoming data. In short, they are *programmable.* Considering all the limitations of dumb terminals, it may be wasteful to commit yourself to one if you can afford a microcomputer. With the appropriate hardware, you can set up most micros to operate like smart terminals. Why? Because they have microprocessors and memory-storage capabilities. To make an IBM PC into a smart terminal, you need a communications adapter, a cable, a modem, and communications software. The sophistication of the software will determine the intelligence of the microcomputer as a terminal. The other enhancements carry out transmission tasks. Oh yes, you also need a telephone line.

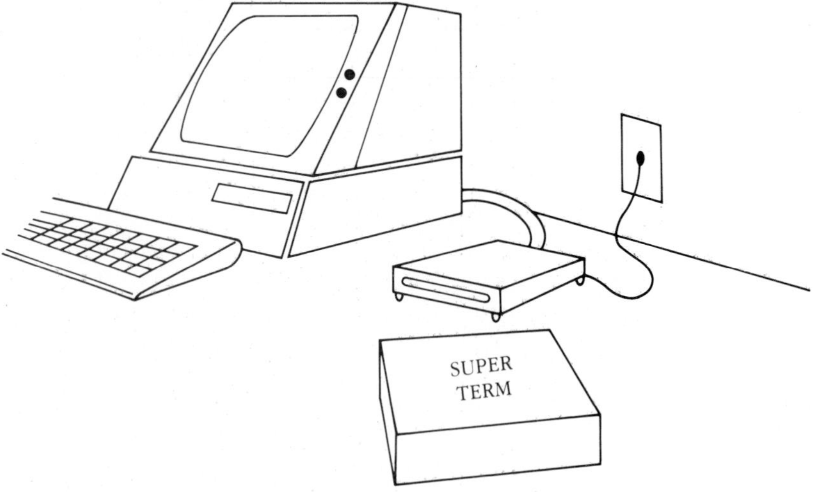

Communications Interfaces

Communications interface is one of the many terms used to name a circuit board that allows a microcomputer to perform external communications. Other names that are often used are serial port, async adapter, and **serial interface.** If you remember, back in Chapter 1 we discussed the fact that a computer manipulates data stored as 0 and 1 digits in what are referred to as bytes, where each byte stores eight digits, or bits. When an adapter transporting a byte of data from one location to another is made up of eight parallel wires that can send all eight bits of the byte at the same time, then it is called a *parallel* adapter; its operations are called **parallel communications.**

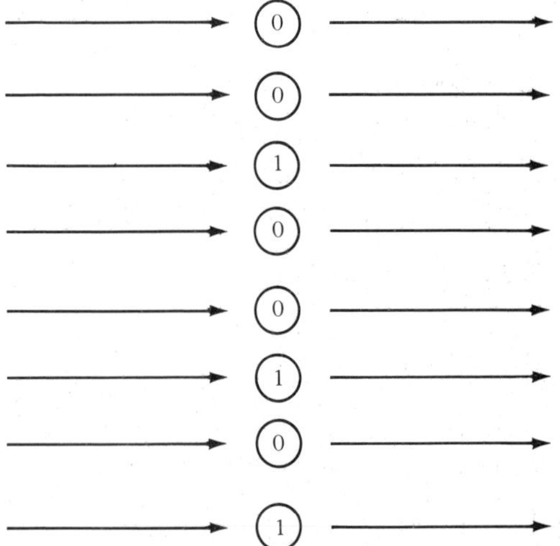

Parallel Communications

If the adapter sends only one bit at a time, then it is called a *serial* connection; its operations are called **serial communications.**

Serial Communications

The communications interface that allows the IBM PC to communicate externally sends out and takes in data one bit at a time. It is, therefore, a serial device. IBM calls it the *asynchronous communications adapter.* Asynchronous means that the time between the sending of any two complete characters may vary. After all, isn't that the way people type at a keyboard? (Some kinds of telecommunications require synchronous, or timed, transmission, but they are not important to us.)

Now, you might be asking yourself, "Wouldn't it be more efficient to send out data eight bits or one byte at a time?" The answer is that the efficiency gained would not be worth the increase in cost. Back to Chapter 1 again. Even though the IBM PC communicates internally eight bits or one byte at a time, it would be very expensive to establish parallel connections over long distances. Remember that ordinary telephone equipment is already in place, ready to accept a flow of sequential serial bits. So, there you have it. For the PC to communicate externally and take advantage of ordinary telephone equipment, there must be a device that makes, among other things, parallel-serial conversions. That's just what the asynchronous communications adapter does.

Modems

It would be nice if all the converting to be done could be accomplished by the communications adapter, but that is not the case. You also need a modem. A modem is a device that prepares outgoing signals to be sent out over the telephone lines or incoming signals to be received in from the telephone lines to a terminal. The word *modem* comes from MOdulate/DEModulate. A modem takes signals generated in a sending terminal and *modulates* them into electrical impulses that can be sent over telephone lines. When receiving information, it *demodulates* signals, changing them from electrical impulses to data codes that the terminal can recognize. Different modems may have different attributes, but three major attributes to consider are how the phone connection is made, the speed of transmission, and command protocols.

Making the Connection

There are two ways a modem can be connected to a phone line: acoustic and direct. An *acoustic* modem has a pair of rubber cups that are placed over the ear and mouthpiece of a telephone handset. It sends and receives tones in the same way that your voice is transmitted during a telephone conversation. A *direct-connect* modem differs from an acoustic modem in that a direct connection is made with the telephone line. The connection is usually achieved by plugging the modem into a modular wall jack or by plugging the modem into a jack that is located on the telephone itself. In the latter case, of course, the telephone must be connected, too.

A direct-connect modem is usually more reliable than an acoustic modem and has more features, but an acoustic modem has some definite advantages. It can be used with any telephone at almost any time, whether or not a modular wall jack is available. You can use an acoustic modem in your motel room when you are away from home or even in a telephone booth. Of course, the major advantage of a direct-connect modem is freedom from outside noise. A direct-connect modem transmits electrical impulses, whereas an acoustic modem transmits sounds, which can include interfering background noises. Other advantages that some direct-connect modems have over acoustic modems are the abilities to automatically dial phone numbers and to automatically answer the phone. With acoustic modems, these tasks must be performed manually.

Speed of Transmission

Modem transmission speed is measured in **baud rate,** which indicates the amount of time required to transmit one bit of data. The formula looks like this:

baud rate = l/bit signal duration

Whenever the bit signal duration is short, the baud rate is high. On the other hand, when bit signal duration is long, the baud rate is low. Theoretically, messages could be sent at any rate of speed, but since both the sending and receiving machines must interact effectively, only a limited number of speeds, or baud rates, are standard. The most common rates are 300 and 1,200, which translate very roughly into 30 and 120 characters per second. Older and less expensive modems transmit at only one baud rate or the other. Some newer ones support both 300 and 1,200 and offer 2,400 as well. Naturally, the faster transmission system requires more expensive components, so 1,200-baud modems are more expensive than 300; modems that allow a choice of either 1,200 or 300 baud are more expensive still; and 2,400-baud modems are even more expensive. As for the advantages of one baud rate over the other, information services and other computer hosts with which you might communicate have charges that differ with baud rate. Many do not even offer 2,400 baud, and 1,200 baud is considerably more expensive than 300. The additional cost is money well spent, however, if your work is not interactive—that is, if you are sending and receiving files that have been prepared on disks before you get on-line. Overall, you will spend less. If, on the other hand, you are entering information on the keyboard, waiting for responses, and reading and reacting to responses, you will pay a lot more for little advantage over the 300-baud rate.

Here are two important things to remember about baud rates.

1. Both the sender and the receiver must have the same baud rate.
2. The faster baud rate is worth the additional cost when you are doing straight transmitting, but not when you're composing or exploring menus or exchanging ideas spontaneously with someone at the other end of the line.

Command Protocols

Every modem observes a predetermined set of commands for operation. These commands cover how to dial automatically, how to answer automatically, and similar operations. Although the protocols used by one major manufacturer, Hayes Microcomputer Products, have emerged as the dominating standard, there are many modems available that observe other protocols. What is important is that the software you purchase be able to talk to the modem you buy. There is more on this subject in Chapter 15.

Cables, Anyone?

So far we have not discussed how the modem and the communications adapter inside the computer are connected. You're right, you need a cable. It is commonly referred to as a serial cable, or **RS-232-C** cable, and has connectors that plug into the asynchronous communications adapter in the computer on one end and the modem on the other. The cable, the connectors on each end, and the receptacles in the computer and the modem all conform to a standard defined and published by the Electronic Industry Association in 1969: the RS-232-C. There is nothing mysterious about this designation. The RS stands for Recommended Standard, 232 is the identification number for the standard, and C refers to the latest revision of the standard. The reference RS-232-C indicates the use of a DB-25 connector that is manufactured to meet the standard. (Don't panic. DB-25 is just another part number.) This connector has 25 pins ordered in two rows, one row with 12 and one row with 13. Each pin has a specific job to do and, in the case of telecommunications, not all the pins are used.

Telecommunications Parameters

Once your PC is outfitted with a communications adapter, serial cable, and modem, all you need is some good software, a telephone line, and a friend at a distance who wants to communicate. Before talking about telecommunications software, let's talk about some of the things that software must manage, the most difficult concepts involved in telecommunications. It's not all that hard if you don't let the terminology frighten you.

First of all, one must control the parameters of computer communications. The term *parameter* means a variable, or more simply, a setting that can vary. In telecommunications, parameters must be set in specific ways. The basic principle to remember is that the two computers involved in the communication must be set to compatible parameters. While many of the parameters involved in telecommunications have standard settings that are consistently used, there are a few parameters that either you or the software you are using must control. It's great to leave it to the software and just relax and enjoy, but the more parameters you know how to control, the more flexible your communications can be. Unfortunately, more parameters mean more conscious choices, more time spent, and more opportunities for confusion if you don't select compatible settings with the computer operator with whom you hope to talk. The parameters you must adjust most frequently are

Baud rate. Speed of transmission, usually 300 to 1,200.
Duplex. Type of transmission, full or half.
Mode. Which computer calls and which computer answers?
Data bits. How many bits are used to represent each character, 7 or 8?
Start and stop bits. How many bits will be transmitted to indicate where a cluster of bits representing a character to be transmitted starts and stops?
Parity bits. Bits that check for proper transmission, even or odd.

We have already discussed baud rate at some length, so let's start with duplex.

Full or Half Duplex?

Another parameter choice is whether to select full duplex or half duplex for the transmission of your data. Again, this concept is easy once you understand the terminology. Remember the World War II films in which the radio operator had to say, "Over" at the end of each transmission? This was so the listener could switch to the sending mode at the same time the sender switched to the listening mode. That system used half duplex, meaning that only one side can transmit at a time.

With modern computer communications, we do not have to constantly switch back and forth between sender and receiver. We just set the parameter at half duplex; the software and the computers do the rest. The important thing to remember is that when the parameter is set to half duplex, both communicating computers cannot send or receive at the same time. They must take turns. Furthermore, one computer cannot be set to full duplex and the other to half duplex.

Full duplex, on the other hand, is comparable to our modern telephone, with both sides able to send information simultaneously. Again, as in half-duplex telecommunicating, both computers must have the same duplex setting.

Originate or Answer Mode?

Much as modern telephone switching systems use different sound tones to activate switches, modems use sets of tones to activate the switches that shift them from sending to receiving mode. Many modems have a switch giving you a choice of originate or answer. If you want to call a bulletin board or information utility to use their resources, then you will set this parameter to the originate mode and leave it there. After all, you will be the one who is doing the calling. If you want to interact with another person using telecommunications, then one of your computers will have to do the calling (originate mode) and the other will have to answer (answer mode). When you encounter problems telecommunicating, the problem may stem from something as simple as forgetting to set this parameter correctly. It's certain you won't get anywhere if both computers are sitting there waiting to be called.

Number of Data Bits

Another parameter you may be required to set is the number of bits your computer will use to transmit each character. The typical choice is 7 or 8 per character. You may be wondering why there is a choice at all. After all, each character corresponds to one byte and, as we saw in Chapter 1, each byte has 8 bits. (You may want to review binary notation at this point.) When would 7 bits ever be appropriate? The answer has to do with the ASCII set. Remember: the ASCII set is the universally adopted character code. Also remember that while 8 bits give us a potential for 256 different codes, only the characters with codes less than 128 are standard. It only takes 7 bits to represent numbers from 0 to 127, and that takes care of just about any text you might wish to telecommunicate.

Now that the 7-bit option is clear, you're probably wondering when using 8 bits is ever appropriate. Text is not the only information that is telecommunicated. It is also possible to transmit and receive programs. Programs for any given computer typically include bytes with values of 128 and greater. In order for them to be transmitted, an 8th bit is required. Another use of the 8th bit is to define special characters not represented in ASCII, for example, graphics characters and reverse video. It doesn't hurt to transmit text using 8 data bits. If the setting is 8, we still use ASCII codes and an extra digit of zero is annexed to the seven-digit code. After all, this extra zero doesn't change the value of the byte. The important thing to remember is that if you set your communication at 8 bits per character, then your computer will be expecting to send and receive just that for each character. It's a bad time in telecommunicationsland when two communicating computers have different settings.

Start and Stop Bits

In order for one computer to understand another, it has to know which group of bits represents one keyboard character and which group represent another. But, characters are entered with different lengths of time between entry, so how does the computer on the receiving end know where one character stops and another starts? The solution is simple. The sending computer adds *start and stop bits* to each character. Most systems running at 300 baud use a start bit preceding the data bits for each character and a stop bit behind. Slower systems sometimes use one start bit and two stop bits. If 7 data bits are used per character, and start and stop bits were set at 1 and 2 respectively, then your computer would expect to send and receive 10 bits per keyboard character. The first bit announces the character's arrival, the next 7 represent the character, and the last let the computer know that the character is complete.

Even or Odd Parity?

A final parameter you may be required to choose is the *parity bit,* or *check bit.* Parity is a means of giving you some assurance that the characters you transmit really arrive as you send them. This is the way it works. In setting parity, you specify either even parity, odd parity, or you turn it completely off (no parity). By specifying even parity, you instruct the computer to send and receive 8-digit character codes made up of an even number of 1 bits. Consequently, if you send a character such as the lowercase letter *a,* that has only three 1 bits (binary for a is 01100001), an 8th bit of 1 is annexed. This makes the number of 1 bits in the code even. If, on the other hand, you send a character like the capital letter *A,* that already has two 1 bits (binary for A is 01000001), an 8th bit of 0 is annexed. Odd parity instructs the computer to send and receive an odd number of 1 bits for each character. By the way, the parity bit is in addition to the 7 bits for character definition and any start and stop bits.

During transmission, if the receiving machine is expecting to receive codes with even parity and it doesn't, it knows that either this parameter is not set correctly or something else is wrong with transmission. In most cases, you won't have to worry about setting the parity parameter; your software will probably make the choice for you. But just as with most other parameters, both the sending and the receiving machine must be set in same way.

A Point to Remember

The range of parameters of your telecommunications system is limited by the hardware you purchase, and the control of these parameters is often limited by the software you purchase to run your telecommunication activities. If you buy a 300-baud modem, for example, you can never transmit at the more rapid rate of 1,200 baud. On the other hand, you can have the most sophisticated hardware in the world, but if you purchased limited software, your telecommunications system will be limited. The ideal, of course, is to have both sophisticated hardware and sophisticated software, and to let the software control your parameter selection whenever the selection doesn't matter much. But, because parameter selection will sometimes matter to you, you want to have the option of seizing control and making your own choices.

Okay, so we hope we have made an important point. In telecommunicating, there are parameters that must be coordinated between the sending and receiving computers, as follows:

The baud rate must be the same.
The duplex selection must be the same.
The calling machine must be in originate mode and the other in answer mode.
The number of bits per character must be the same.
The stop bits and start bits for each machine must have the same setting.
The parity bits for each machine must have the same setting.

But here's the good news: If you have a smart modem and good software, you won't have to worry about coordinating these elements all by yourself. The software and the smart modem will give you plenty of help.

Telecommunications Software

With your computer and modem matched and linked, you only need software to start operations. Remember that your software determines whether or not you have a smart terminal, even if you've made all the hardware purchases to get the best. In selecting your software, go all the way for a smart terminal. In the following sections, we outline some specific questions you will want to ask.

How Easy Is Installation?

There are many easy to install and operate telecommunications packages that are written for micros in the IBM PC family. In some cases, all you need to do is put the software in the drive and turn on the PC. Other telecommunications software packages may need to be installed on the PC. *Installing* a program is usually as easy as making a set of selections from a menu and proceeding to telecommunicate. This cannot be said of all programs. Some may require the writing and assembling of a set of computer instructions that modify the program. Such a set of statements is called a program *patch*. Always review the **installation** procedures on the software packages you are considering for purchase.

Are System Commands Easy to Access?

Here's another important question to ask when you are ready to buy software: How easy is it to use *system commands* when you are on-line? Can you check your disk directory, delete files, change disks, or perform other housekeeping tasks without disrupting your session? With some software, you can take care of these operations right in the middle of communication transmission. With other programs, you must leave the program, while still maintaining telephone connection, in order to get to system commands. With still others, you must leave the program, break your telephone connection, and eventually start telecommunications over—all just to use the system commands for some simple little housekeeping task. Obviously, this latter procedure is irritating, time-consuming, and costly.

Is the Package Menu-Driven or Command-Driven?

Here's another choice you can make as you select your software. Do you want to communicate your commands to the computer directly (command-driven), or do you want the computer to present a list of choices and let you take your pick (menu-driven)? The command format is usually faster, more direct, more powerful, and less consuming of memory. It is a little like recall questions on a test: you have to know your material and originate the action. The menu-driven format is like a simpler recognition question on an objective test: the menu presents the choices, and you only have to recognize which one is appropriate. You may need menus as you begin to use a program, but they will get in the way when you master the program and know how to originate the commands on your own. The best software lets you easily turn off menus when you no longer need them, allowing you to go directly into the command mode.

Does the Program Support Macros?

Any time you call an information system or a bulletin board, there is a logging-on dialogue that rarely changes. It typically includes such information as what kind of computer you are using, your account or member number, and your password. As you may remember from Chapter 12, a macro is a "script" that can direct your computer to do everything from dialing the phone to answering all the log-on queries and providing all the necessary information, all with the touch of a single key. Not only do macros make the telecommunications process easier, they also save you money because they are faster than you. If you are still not sure about whether or not you need macros, take our word for it, they are invaluable.

Does the Package Have Help Screens?

We all need help when we're learning to use a new program, and we all get lost occasionally, having momentary lapses of memory even when using a familiar program. Many programs provide *help* systems that we can enlist to get us back on track when we need it. Often, programs have simple instruction pages that can be called up from almost any point in program execution. By pushing a button or two, you can locate momentarily forgotten instructions on how to turn the printer on or off, how to print to disk, or how to hang up the telephone electronically. Some programs provide a toggle control for obtaining help. Such a control allows you to turn the help screen on and off, keeping the main screen uncluttered when you don't need help.

Does the Package Have an Information Capture Feature?

The memory that is left over after a program is loaded into the computer can be set aside as a **buffer** for storing incoming or outgoing information. Many programs ignore this space, which can be extremely important if efficient communication is desired.

When you load a communications program into your computer there is almost always additional unoccupied space left in memory. That constitutes an area of memory that can be set aside as a working space or buffer area in which you can store incoming information to be printed or saved on a disk, or in which you can load material waiting to be transferred. Be sure you choose hardware and software tools that allow you to use this space.

Does the Program Support XMODEM or other Binary Protocols?

As we've mentioned, it is also possible to transmit binary information such as programs. There are many bulletin boards around the country that maintain on-line libraries of programs that you can **download,** or into which you may **upload** a program of your own to share with others. Although many programs can be handled in text format, binary is faster. Some programs cannot be sent in text format at all.

Some of the telecommunications packages on the market do not support binary transmission. Among the ones that do, a protocol known as XMODEM is popular. If you expect to be able to transmit programs, be sure the package you buy is capable of doing so. As you'll learn in Chapter 15, this can be a great source of free software.

How Should You Shop?

When buying telecommunications software, be sure to choose wisely. Remember not to be too conservative if you don't want to be chained to a rigid system having limited capabilities. Consider how much you know about computers and the degree of complexity you are willing to tackle. The more complexities you can handle, the less you will need to depend on attributes of software and hardware but the more trouble and frustrations you may encounter. Try to make selections that will allow you the flexibility to choose when and what variables you will control. Consider the capabilities you need now and those you will need in the future. Last, and probably most important—if you are a novice, go with a standard that has weathered the test of time, a system for which information and service are readily available. Let those experienced at telecommunications try the off brands.

Be sure to select a variety of sources. One source you will surely want to check is the user-support network. Currently there is a user-supported program called PC-Talk III that can be freely copied. (See Chapter 15 for more about user-supported software and how to get it.) This communications package is excellent and very widely used.

How Can You Use Telecommunications?

There are a number of ways you can use telecommunication systems. You can gain access to an information utility, you can call an electronic bulletin board, or you can telecommunicate with a friend who has the proper equipment.

What Is an Information Utility?

An **information utility** is a computer facility that hosts a network of computers. It stores and retrieves information for the network as well as managing communications among the computers in the network. For a small fee, you can join such a network, gaining access to an *information data base.* This can be compared to using a library, but with important differences. You don't need to physically go to the library, you will never misplace a book, you can choose to read the same material many other people are reading simultaneously, and the information you obtain can be up-to-the-minute with barely any turn-around time from collection to publication. Some information utilities focus on specific areas or subjects, while others are encyclopedic.

An information utility may also provide *transaction services* so that you can complete bank transactions, pay bills, or order services without leaving home. Such services may allow you to shop at stores around the world, or make plane, hotel, and restaurant reservations at many locations. In fact, they may make it possible for you to buy, sell, and barter almost anything with on-line classified ads.

The *communication services* provided by most information utilities allow you to plan and hold conferences on-line without travel problems or expenses. These services allow you to post notices on electronic bulletin boards for all to read and respond to, as well as to send electronic mail to specific individuals. Such mail moves instantaneously and waits patiently until recipients are ready to read and respond. Just think, no more telephone tag as caller and receiver continually miss each other.

But how do you save money if you're paying a fee to the utility as well as paying long-distance bills for direct telephone access? In some cases, it is worth the cost of direct access; but often the company managing the information utility will eliminate long-distance costs by providing a local telephone number, probably provided by contract with a *communications switching network* such as Tymnet, Telenet, or Uninet.

What Is a Bulletin Board?

An **electronic bulletin board** really is an information utility, but in many cases, bulletin boards are less formally organized, primarily designed to let users exchange messages. A bulletin board operates something like this. A host computer is established at some location and remains in answer mode during certain periods of time. Users can call the bulletin board during the specified time periods to read messages or leave messages. Users can download public domain software, exchange program patches, tips, and product information. By frequently using the bulletin board, you can find other individuals who have interests similar to yours and who would like to exchange messages with you. Subsequently, you can communicate directly from your computer to theirs.

What Can Educators Do Using Telecommunications?

There are obvious uses for telecommunications in the area of instructional management; for example, the electronic transfer of student records. Such activities are already being conducted and usually require initiative at the state or district level. But what about in the classroom? What are some things that the classroom teacher can do with students?

Imagine sitting in the classroom, keying in your access code, and instantly tying your terminal to one of thousands of information sources. Imagine exchanging ideas with creative teachers nationwide and encouraging your students to communicate with long-distance peers. Imagine swapping public domain software, using special data bases, and locating software reviews on computer utilities thousands of miles away. All this—and more—can happen with telecommunications. Telecommunications has the potential to revolutionize communications and radically change the method and content of education. With a terminal, a modem, some communications software, and a telephone, the small world of the classroom can open up quickly and conveniently to encompass the entire globe. Applications of telecommunications in education exist today, but the surface has barely been scratched. In the following sections, we'll describe some ways in which educators can use telecommunications to enhance learning. We suggest possibilities related to both student and teacher activities. No doubt you will be able to add to the list.

Activities for Students

Simply learning to use telecommunications is valuable in its own right as a student activity, considering that this method of communication will grow tremendously in the coming years. Students who learn telecommunication skills today in our schools will no doubt be better prepared to meet future demands than students who do not. At the present time, using telecommunications to tap resources of information utilities may not be as cost effective as using printed materials, but learning to locate, capture, and store information is a set of skills with great future value. Moreover, it's a highly motivating activity. Since many information utilities provide special rates to schools, it may soon be well worth the expenditure. In any event, there are many activities that schools can plan that involve neither information utilities nor long-distance telephone calls. Neighboring schools can plan telecommunications activities in which students learn to set communication parameters, send, receive, and capture information.

Using an Electronic Encyclopedia

If possible, schools should consider subscribing to an information utility that has educational resources. One such utility is Compuserve. Compuserve maintains a huge electronic encyclopedia for its subscribers. After logging onto Compuserve, the user only needs to type *GO AAE* at any prompt. At this point, beginning students could elect to read a guide that will familiarize them with methods for using the encyclopedia, while the experienced students could search for information on an assigned topic. The latest information on many likely school topics is waiting at the fingertips of students who know how to use key words for searches. If instructed, Compuserve's encyclopedic data base will immediately retrieve articles on these topics, sending them over the telephone lines to the computer screen in the classroom. This will take place in a matter of seconds. Students can then read the articles, save them to disk, or print them. Of course, reading and taking notes on articles you've retrieved takes more time than printing the articles, and printing them takes more time than saving them to disk. To get the most from the school's investment, it is usually most productive for students to save information on a disk, delaying careful review of the information to a time when telephone telecommunication is terminated.

Researching Current Events

The Source, another information utility, maintains the service of United Press International (UPI) on-line. If students want the very latest information available on a given subject, perhaps recent developments in cancer treatment, they enter *UPI* when The Source prompt appears. The UPI line presents a series of menus from which the student can select National News, then General Interest. After these choices have been made, students will be prompted to give key search words and will be asked to designate a time period not to exceed the last seven days (since The Source retains news stories for only seven days). If students request a search on the keyword *cancer* and designate the last three days, the computer will retrieve all news bulletins that have accrued on that subject in the last three days. Finding this kind of recent information sure beats looking for the same information in school reference materials that may be 10 years old. Also you can be sure that students will get whatever news has been reported, without any filtering by the local news media.

Actually, activities that can take place between schools and a national information utility such as The Source can take place on a smaller scale between schools and a central library. In a collective effort, schools could prepare data bases on any number of subjects. These data bases could be stored on a host computer at a central location, just waiting to be accessed by local schools. Of course, the sophistication would not be the same, but the educational results could be powerful in more ways than one.

Even More Possibilities

The foregoing are just three of the most obvious activities for students. There are many more exciting possibilities just waiting to be dreamed up by creative educators. Here are some possibilities.

Organize students to develop and manage local bulletin boards.

Organize on-line interviews of students with important people—politicians, authors, artists, law enforcement officials, and so on—both locally and nationally.

Arrange software exchanges between students in other parts of the school district or the nation.

Develop telecommunications pen-pal activities among students in the school districts.

Arrange creative writing activities that students from different schools can share using telecommunications.

Simulate news reporting. Let students prepare news reports of school activities and share them using telecommunications.

Provide learning experiences for children who are in hospitals or homebound.

These are just a few instructional ideas that presently are economically feasible. We are sure that you can add to the list, especially if you have already had telecommunications experiences.

School Resources

In the following sections, we'll highlight some of the special resources available to schools through telecommunications.

Latest Education News

Both The Source and Compuserve carry Ed-line, a news and information network of the National School Public Relations Association. Daily news affecting the world of education appears on-line. The full texts of many major educational reports are available as soon as they are released. What a great resource to have available if teachers and administrators want to seriously consider the issues having impact on education—from legislation to innovations in technology.

Connecting for Special Interests

The ability to telecommunicate affords great potential for people with special interests to "talk" even though there may be many miles that separate them. This potential is not restricted to adults. Just think of the possibilities for children. At present, we know of a couple of these **special interest groups,** or **SIGs,** already in operation. The coming years should see these groups emerge in great numbers. Check the back of magazines for a listing of special interest communications groups designed with children in mind. Typically they are free, except for the cost of the phone call.

Special Education Information

SpecialNet, operated by the National Association of State Directors of Special Education, provides daily updates on legislative developments and issues in special education. It also offers bulletin board services and electronic mail. Any school system that seriously wants to better education for special students would do well to access this telecommunications network.

Software Reviews

Almost any educator would agree that keeping up with educational software releases is tough. Assessing whether new products are appropriate for educational needs is even tougher. There's hope though, since there are many credible agencies now providing software reviews through telecommunications. (See Chapter 16 for more discussion about reviewing software.) You can find these agencies through your library or listed in some of the popular computer magazines. Two such agencies are listed here.

The Educational Products Information Exchange provides reviews for educators. Certain commands on Compuserve will retrieve information on evaluations of software and allow users to exchange news and ideas about educational products, courseware, and services. If you are a teacher interested in buying new software, you might be interested in getting this service.

The Florida Information Resource Network (FIRN) has a data base of software reviews available at the cost of a phone call. This data base was created and is maintained by the Florida Center For Instructional Computing, University of South Florida, in Tampa. To get reviews on-line, set your terminal for full duplex, 300 or 1200 baud, null or even parity, 7 data bits, 1 stop bit, and call (813) 974-3890. Then, follow these steps:

1. When asked PLEASE TYPE YOUR TERMINAL IDENTIFIER, press the [A] key.
2. At the PLEASE LOGIN prompt, respond *SERENET.*
3. When asked to enter the USERNAME, respond with *DOE.*
4. At the LOCAL prompt, respond *C SERVAX.*
5. Once again, respond to the USERNAME prompt with *DOE.*
6. When asked for the password, respond *BULLETIN.*

After a few seconds, you will be logged in and at command level. Next, type in *@MICRO* and then *HELP* to get instructions. After a few seconds of study, you will be able to tap the software review resources. The return on the money that you spend for the telephone call can be substantial.

Communicating with Other Educators

The Department of Education of the State of Florida provides an electronic mail service, along with other information services, to Florida educators. School people can communicate quickly and economically with other school people throughout the state. There are also forums and bulletin boards for special interest groups. Many other states have similar systems, or are investigating the possibilities.

Joining an Information Utility

Here are the addresses of the information utilities we consider currently of greatest interest to educators. Write to them for more detailed information about their services, costs, and about how to get on-line.

Compuserve
5000 Arlington Centre Blvd.
Columbus, OH 43220

The Source
1616 Anderson Road
McLean, VA 22102

SpecialNet
1201 16th St. NW Suite 404E
Washington, DC 20036

Florida Information Resource Network
Knott Building, Room 1702 C
Department of Education
Tallahassee, FL 32301

Chapter Summary

In this chapter we have discussed telecommunications concepts that will help you get up and running. We have described some ways in which telecommunications is being used to serve education. We have also dreamed a little. Hardware and software capabilities are present realities. Cost is, to be honest, still a little high if you want to access some of the expensive information utilities. Yet these costs are getting lower as time passes, just as the cost of telecommunications equipment and software is coming down. In fact, the biggest problem many teachers have encountered is persuading a reluctant principal to provide them a direct phone line under their supervision. For obvious reasons, most phone lines in school are routed through central switchboards. Unfortunately, having to call through a switchboard can remove many of the advantages provided by modems that can automatically dial and answer. A direct phone line is really what you need.

We predict that by the time you read this book, it will be economically feasible for almost any school in the U.S. to provide activities for its student to engage in some type of telecommunications activities. So what are we waiting for? With the mobilization of human talent and effort, we can push back the walls of the classroom to take in the world!

Chapter Review

Knowledge Exercises

1. Give a definition for the term *telecommunication.*

   Answer: The telephone communication of data from one computing device to another.

2. What is the difference between a dumb terminal and a smart terminal?

   Answer: Dumb terminal. An inexpensive device to send and receive information. It won't store telephone numbers, dial automatically and repeatedly if line is busy, or go through complex automatic log-on procedures. It doesn't store information.
   Smart terminal. Has microprocessor and memory so it can automatically dial telephone numbers, automatically log onto various telecommunication systems, and capture and store incoming data.

3. Can a microcomputer serve as a terminal? Explain.

   Answer: Yes. Microcomputers have microprocessors and memory storage capabilities. You need a communications interface, cable, modem, and communications software.

4. What is the difference between a parallel interface and a serial interface?

   Answer: Parallel interface. Made up of eight parallel wires that can send all 8 bits of a byte at the same time.
   Serial interface. Sends data 1 bit at a time.

5. Define the term *modem.* Where does the word come from?

   Answer: A device that prepares incoming signals to be received from the telephone lines to a terminal or outgoing signals to be sent over the telephone lines. Modem is short for modulate/demodulate.

6. What are three important attributes to consider when selecting a modem?

   Answer: You should consider how the phone connection is made, the speed of transmission, and command protocols observed.

7. What are the differences between acoustic and direct-connect modems?

   Answer: Acoustic. Has a pair of rubber cups that are placed over the ear and mouthpiece of a telephone handset; sends and receives tones same way voice is transmitted during telephone conversation.

Direct-connect. Direct connection is made with the telephone line; can be plugged into a modular wall jack or into a jack located on the telephone itself.

8. What does baud rate mean?

   Answer: Baud rate indicates the amount of time required to transmit one bit of data.

9. Are data transmitted faster at 300 baud or at 1,200 baud? Explain.

   Answer: 1,200 baud is faster. The higher the baud rate, the faster the transmission.

10. What is an RS-232-C cable and what is it used for? What is the significance of RS-232-C?

    Answer: An RS-232-C cable connects the modem and the communications interface inside the computer. RS-232-C refers to a recommended standard for data communications.

11. What does the term *parameter* mean?

    Answer: A variable or a setting that can vary.

12. What is the difference between half and full duplex?

    Answer: Half duplex. Only one side can transmit at a time; computers must take turns.

    Full duplex. Both communicating computers can send or receive simultaneously.

13. What is the difference between the originate and answer mode? Give an example of when you would use each mode.

    Answer: Originate. Your computer is doing the calling; use when calling a bulletin board or information utility.

    Answer. Your computer is doing the answering; someone is calling you.

    When interacting with another person using telecommunications, one computer must be in originate mode and one in answer mode.

14. How many bits per character are usually chosen as a parameter? Why?

    Answer: Either 7 or 8 are usually chosen; ASCII text requires seven digits to represent each of the standard keyboard characters, so 7 bits are commonly used. If using 8 bits, the 8th bit can be used to define special characters not represented in the ASCII code set, or to transmit binary data.

15. What do start bits and stop bits mean in telecommunications?

    Answer: They tell the modem which group of bits represents one keyboard character and which group represents another.

16. What is parity?

    Answer: Parity is a check system that gives you some assurance that the characters you transmit really arrive as you send them.

17. What are six things to look for when selecting communications software?

    Answer:
    1. Ease of installation.
    2. Access to system commands.
    3. Menu or command driven, macro support.
    4. Help features.
    5. Information capture features.
    6. XMODEM or other binary protocols.

18. What is an information utility? Name and discuss three services offered by many of these utilities.

    Answer: An information utility is a computer facility that hosts a network of computers. Three services offered are electronic mail, special interest groups, and on-line data bases. (See the text for a discussion of these services.)

19. What is an electronic bulletin board? Describe some of its uses.

    Answer: Like an information utility, but smaller and less formal. May be run by one person with one computer. Forum for exchange of ideas, software tips, special interests, uploading and downloading software.

Thought Exercises

1. What type of modem would you recommend that a school purchase? Describe the use(s) to be made of it. Defend your choice.
2. Elaborate on the statement, "two computers involved in telecommunications must be set to compatible parameters."
3. A new computer has just been introduced into the American market, which is far superior for the price to anything else available. It has its own code, and it does not use the ASCII character set. Would you advise your school to purchase these computers? Why or why not? What problems, if any might arise?
4. You are trying to communicate with another computer using telecommunications, but something is obviously not working. What are some of the things you should check?
5. Try out a communications software package, evaluating it on the five points listed in the chapter. Write a review, including a final recommendation for use in your school.

Activities

1. Use telecommunications to access a bulletin board, search for information on a data base, or communicate with another computer. Write a short report on any problems or successes encountered.
2. Name and briefly describe 10 ways in which telecommunications activities can be used with students.
3. Write to an information utility and request information regarding what services are available. Submit this information in a short report, emphasizing the features you think would be beneficial to education.
4. You want to organize an electronic bulletin board for your school, but the principal is reluctant to give you the phone line you need. Write a paper outlining the benefits to be accrued by your proposed activity in such a way that you are sure to convince the principal.

Projects

1. Choose a telecommunication activity to perform with a class of students. Keep a log, recording successes and problems.
2. There are probably students in your school who have a lot of experience with telecommunications. Seek them out. Enlist their aid by asking them to demonstrate for your class. Possibly they can help you download programs for your computer(s).

Bibliography

Here are a number of references on telecommunications. The ones that are marked with an asterisk (*) are good first references containing substantial information, written so that a beginner in telecommunications can understand them. Other references listed provide the more advanced reader with something to think about.

*Adler, Carolyn, Andria P. Troutman, and William West. *Telecommunication and Teachers.* Tampa, Fla.: Florida Center for Instructional Computing, University of South Florida, 1984. Introduction to telecommunications, instructional uses.

Glossbrenner, Alfred. *The Complete Handbook of Personal Computer Communications.* New York: St. Martin's Press, 1983.

Jordan, Larry D., and Bruce Churchhill. *Communications and Networking for the IBM PC.* Bowie, Md.: Robert J. Brady, 1983.

Schawaderer, David W. *Digital Communications Programming on the IBM PC.* New York: Wiley, 1984.

*Stone, David D. *Getting On-Line.* Engelwood Cliffs, N.J.: Prentice-Hall, 1984.

PART

5 OFF AND RUNNING

The last two chapters of this book are designed to pull together a lot of things we haven't covered elsewhere. First, we'll look at what you can do to really make your PC shine. Not only will we name some particularly attractive software products, we'll also tell you about hardware additions to your system that will really enhance its capabilities.

In the last chapter we're going to cover some real nuts-and-bolts issues about using computers in schools. Where do you get software? What is copy protection and how do you deal with it? Where should you put the computers in a school? How do you set up a computer lab?

After reading this section, you should really be off and running!

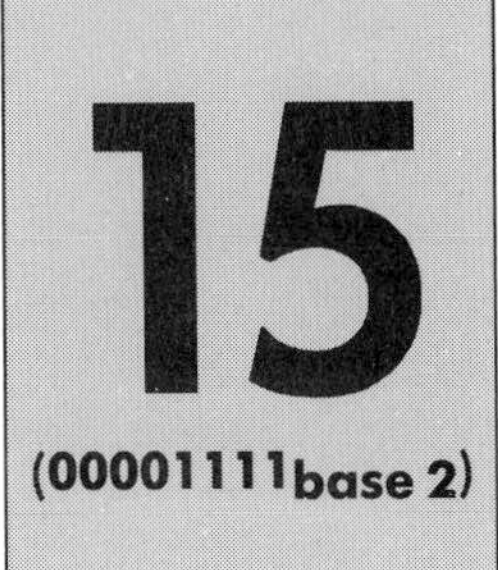

PC PYGMALION

Really Turning the Computer On!

Getting Started

This chapter is about the many products, both software and hardware, that you can purchase for your IBM PC to bring out the best in it. The software products are a collection of our favorites: sophisticated but easy-to-use programs that allow students to draw pictures, compose music, and a variety of other activities. The hardware products are, again, some of the things we have discovered that we think have a place in education, additions that extend your computer's capabilities or make it easier to use. Although this chapter, like the rest of the book, will refer specifically to the IBM family of microcomputers, most of the devices and software mentioned are available for many other types of microcomputers as well.

This chapter is intended to be an overview of some of the more useful and interesting enhancements you can make to your PC. It is not a detailed tutorial on installing hardware. You can get that information from your local retailer, users' groups, or one of the many magazines that caters to the PC market.

Objectives for Teachers

After completing this chapter, you should be able to

1. Identify some special programs for the IBM PC in the areas of microcomputer applications, authoring, graphics, logic, music, programming, word processing, and utility software.
2. Explain what an interface is and name two common types.
3. Define, name four typical features, and describe the advantages and disadvantages of a multifunction card.
4. Give four examples of microcomputer peripheral input devices that have educational applications, explain how they differ, and give the advantages/disadvantages of one compared to another.
5. Identify and describe two common types of microcomputer printers.

6. Explain what a modem is and what it is used for.
7. Compare and contrast floppy diskettes, fixed disks, and laser disks.

Special Software

In this section, we want to talk about some of the kinds of software that we think are very useful, but haven't sufficiently discussed elsewhere in the book. In addition, most of these programs are especially good bargains. Of course, the information provided here will be dated by the time you read it, so don't rely on specific details. But, not only will the same or similar products always be available, they'll undoubtedly get even better.

Public Domain and User-Supported Software

Not all good software is for sale and not all great programmers work for big companies. There is a lot of software available for free. The authors of public domain programs take pleasure in creating them and making them available for all to use. Some of these programs answer users' needs that are not addressed by available commercial products. Many of them are games or utilities that make life a lot easier.

User-supported programs are not entered into the public domain. But, their owners still give them away with the hope that you will send them some money if you like the program. There is more detail on public domain/user-supported software and where to get it in Chapter 16. The important point to remember is that it is free. Of the hundreds of programs available, here is a selection of some of our favorites:

ANIMAL. A BASIC version of the classic Logo program. The computer guesses what animal you are thinking of.

ELIZA. A BASIC version of an early Artificial Intelligence program. Eliza is a kind of computer psychiatrist.

HANOI. A BASIC version of the classic Towers of Hanoi game.

LADYBUG. A version of Logo.

NUKE-NY. A BASIC program that graphically illustrates the potential for destruction if nuclear weapons were used on New York City.

PC-FILE. An excellent program for data-base management.

PC-MUSICIAN. A program enabling you to make music on your PC.

PCPG. The name stands for PC Picture Graphics; it is a drawing program.

PC-TALK III. A highly acclaimed telecommunications program. As good as almost anything on the market.

PC-WRITE. A highly regarded word processor. Better than many high-priced commercial programs.

RBBS. This program helps you set up your own computer bulletin board.

SDIR. This program gives you a sorted directory (DOS DIR command doesn't do this).

VIEW. A fancy version of the DOS TYPE command. It pauses when the screen is full.

Graphics Programs

Your computer can be a powerful tool for drawing, drafting, and creating art. PC Design is the drawing program that comes with the PC version of an inexpensive graphics tablet called the Koala Pad. This combination of software and hardware gives you some very powerful drawing tools at a very low price. PC Paint, PC Paintbrush, and other programs like them are newer, more powerful programs that give you even more features. Often, they can be purchased at reasonable cost packaged with a mouse (which we'll discuss later in this chapter in the section on alternative input devices).

Spelling Checker and Thesaurus

Many of the better word processors on the market now come with an integrated spelling checker and on-line thesaurus. But, if yours doesn't, then IBM's Wordproof is one to consider. This is not a new program, but it is still one of the best and can be purchased at very low cost. It works with most word processors that can store files in ASCII format.

Authoring Systems

Authoring systems are programs that allow you to create computer-based tutorials, lessons, and tests on just about any subject you desire. Their advantage is that you don't have to know how to program to use them. The disadvantage is that they have limitations. Some don't allow graphics, some have very limited formats, and some surprisingly expensive ones don't keep very good records of student progress. A very inexpensive program to get started with authoring systems is, again, from IBM. Among other features, Private Tutor can integrate with graphics and supports the use of videodiscs. It compares very favorably with many much more expensive programs.

Utilities

There will come a day when, with the stroke of a finger, you will destroy untold hours of work. It doesn't matter how experienced you get. It is going to happen. When it does, you'll wish you had a copy of the Norton Utilities. This program has many features, but what sells it is its ability to restore deleted files. It isn't cheap, but it can be worth its weight in RAM chips. You can probably find a free program that does the same thing, but it won't be as easy to use or have as many features. Even if you never use it, think of the Norton Utilities as an insurance policy.

Internal Hardware Additions

We've talked about some software that can make your computer special. Now let's consider some hardware. In theory, any microcomputer is capable of having virtually any kind of additional equipment connected to it. In practice, that theoretical capability is limited by the manufacturer's choice of design and marketing practices. Some computers are easier to enhance than others.

One of the factors in the rise to prominence of the IBM PC has been its open design. The company encouraged other manufacturers to create products that worked with its computers. The IBM PC has **expansion slots** in it that allow you to plug in additional circuit boards, called *cards,* that perform special functions. All you have to do is remove the lid and plug in the card.

The cover of the system unit is very easy to remove. There are either two or six screws on the back to take out, depending upon the vintage of your computer, and the cover slides off. Removing the cover reveals that the PC has five expansion slots. The PC/XT has seven slots. If you were to open your PC, you would probably find that at least two of these slots are already occupied. The slot closest to the middle of the computer probably has a *disk drive adapter* card in it. This device allows your PC to communicate with the floppy disk drives that are installed in it. One of the four remaining slots probably has a *display adapter* card plugged in. IBM makes four different display cards for the PC, each having different capabilities. These cards are required to allow your computer to communicate with its monitor. If you have a PC/XT, you'll find that a third slot is occupied by a *fixed disk adapter* that allows your computer to communicate with its fixed disk drive.

What can you plug into the open slots on your computer? There are many products on the market, each of which is designed to perform a specific task or tasks. You can even replace some of the cards we have already mentioned. Many PC users found fault with the two original display cards IBM sold for the PC: the Color Graphics Display Adapter and the Monochrome Display Adapter. The monochrome card was criticized because it didn't allow graphics. The color graphics card was criticized because it allowed users to draw graphics in only four different colors at one time and displayed text that was harder to read than the monochrome display. Many manufacturers other than IBM, frequently called **third party manufacturers,** answered this need by producing display cards for the PC that allow graphics on the monochrome monitor, provide more than four colors on the color display, or have other capabilities.

Let's turn our attention to some other products that you can plug into your open slots. Before we do, however, there is one caveat that should be discussed. Whenever you add to or replace something in your PC with a product that is made by another manufacturer, you are taking the risk of introducing incompatibilities. Computer manufacturers—including IBM—don't guarantee that, down the line, they won't make changes in their products that might render some other manufacturer's product completely or partially inoperable. How big a risk you are taking depends upon the product. Investigate your options thoroughly before buying.

Interface Cards

If you would like to use a printer with your computer, you'll have to install an interface card that allows your printer and computer to communicate with one another. Since there are two different possible types of interfaces, you'll need to determine which your printer requires. If you have a dot matrix printer, you will probably require a *parallel printer adapter* (or *parallel port*). However, some printers use an *asynchronous communications adapter* (sometimes called an *async card* or *serial port*). What is the difference between the two? Recall that to represent any single character of text, your computer requires eight pieces of information called bits. Together, these eight bits form a byte. When the computer sends a character to the printer over a parallel adapter, it sends all eight bits at the same time, in parallel. On an asynchronous adapter, the eight bits are sent one at a time. In the microcomputer community, asynchronous communications interfaces are often called serial interfaces. Parallel interfaces are most commonly used for printers. Serial interfaces are used not only for printers, but for a variety of other peripheral devices as well. A PC can have up to three different parallel cards and two different async cards installed. There is a third, less common, standard interface for the PC; the *game port adapter.* It is used for such devices as joysticks and graphics tablets.

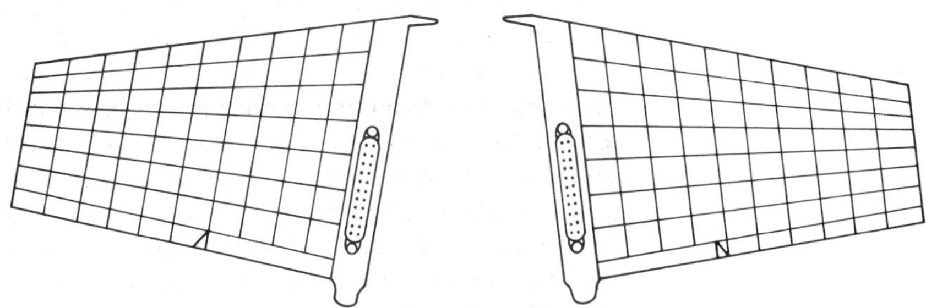

Additional Memory

As more and more software is written that requires copious amounts of memory, you may need to install a **memory expansion card.** An unenhanced PC can have up to 256KB of memory installed on its system board, but the computer is capable of addressing up to 640KB. All the memory above 256KB must be installed on a separate card that is plugged into one of the expansion slots. Since the introduction of the PC, memory prices have fallen dramatically. In early 1984, retail prices for 64KB (nine chips) ran as high as $185. In early 1986, you could buy exactly the same chips for $10. This makes it almost inexcusable for your PC not to have 640KB.

Multifunction Cards

You may be wondering what happens when all the slots are full and you want to add something else. One solution is to conserve slots by purchasing a **multifunction card.** This is a device that typically handles all of the tasks just mentioned. It usually has a parallel port, a serial port, a game port, and sockets for memory expansion all on one card that occupies only one slot. In addition, multifunction cards also usually have battery-powered clocks on them and software for automatically entering the time and date when you boot your computer. Along with all its benefits, the multifunction card does bring one disadvantage: if something on it needs repair, you must remove the entire card for servicing. Taking out all your interfaces and extra memory will probably render your computer just about unusable until the card is fixed.

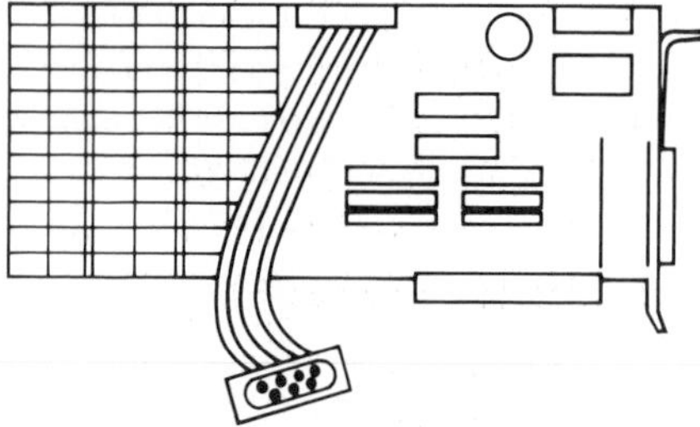

Fixed Disk Drives

As fixed disk drive prices have fallen, it has become increasingly popular to add them to PCs. Internally mounted drives can be purchased with storage capacities of 10 megabytes, 20 megabytes, or even more. All that is usually required is to insert an interface card, possibly remove a floppy diskette drive, install the fixed drive, and perhaps set some switches. Many magazines have published articles on how to do this. There is one warning, however. The power supply in the PC was not designed to handle a fixed disk. One of the differences between a PC and a PC/XT is a bigger power supply. If you install a fixed disk in a PC, you may also have to purchase a bigger power supply.

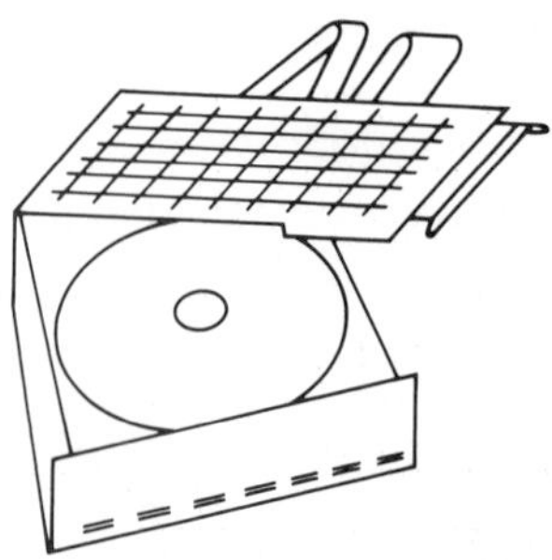

The 8087 Coprocessor

As explained in Chapter 1, the microprocessor in the IBM PC is capable of performing only simple mathematics. Any program that does a lot of math has to contain a lot of code to do so. This extra code makes the program bigger and slower. If the PC could do more powerful mathematics, computation-intensive programs would be smaller, run faster, and be easier to write. Well, there is a way to make your PC a better mathematician.

If you remove the cover from a PC and locate the 8088 microprocessor, you'll probably see an empty socket next to it. This socket is designed to receive a companion to the 8088, the 8087 math **coprocessor.** The 8087 can dramatically increase the speed of some programs. Unfortunately, existing programs must undergo significant modification to use it. In 1984, the price of the 8087 fell to under $100. As more programs are written to use it, and more people buy it, the price will fall even more. The 8087 can be installed in every member of the PC family except the PCjr and the PC/AT. The PCjr has no socket in which to install the chip. The PC/AT, which has a different microprocessor, the 80286, has its own math coprocessor, the 80287.

External Hardware Additions

There are many devices that you can connect to the IBM PC. All of them require interfaces that are usually installed internally like the ones we've already mentioned. Most use either parallel, async, or game ports; some, however, require their own, special interfaces.

Alternative Input Devices

There are many ways to input information to the computer other than the keyboard. In fact, for some applications (graphics, for example), the keyboard is an inefficient device. One device that is becoming more and more popular is the **mouse.** A mouse is usually used to move a pointer on the display. Moving the mouse moves the pointer. That pointer is used to control software by selecting options from menus. A mouse with software that is designed for it can make a computer much easier to use, especially for beginners.

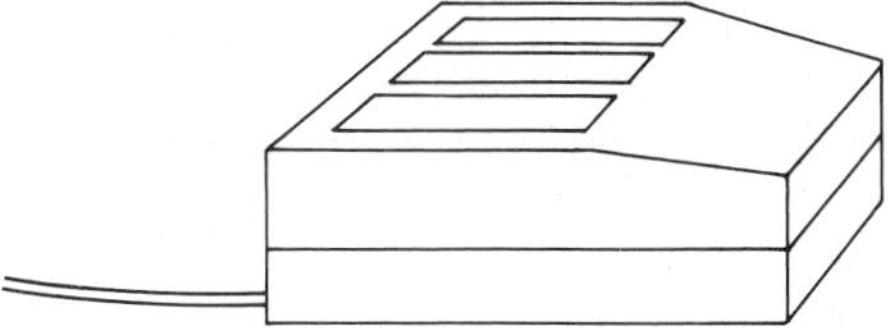

There are two general types of mouse devices. One has a rolling ball underneath it that will function on most flat surfaces. The other type has no moving parts, but uses infrared light to sense its position on a special pad that it must use. Both types are accurate and function well. The ball type has the advantage of not needing a special pad. The infrared type has the advantage of no moving parts, so it probably lasts longer. Many mouse devices interface through an asynchronous adapter. Some come with their own special interfaces that must occupy an entire slot in your PC.

Joysticks are among the more popular alternatives to keyboards. They are popular for use with games and have many of the same advantages as mice. They tend to be less expensive and, as you might expect, are less accurate, providing much cruder control. Joysticks usually interface through a game control adapter.

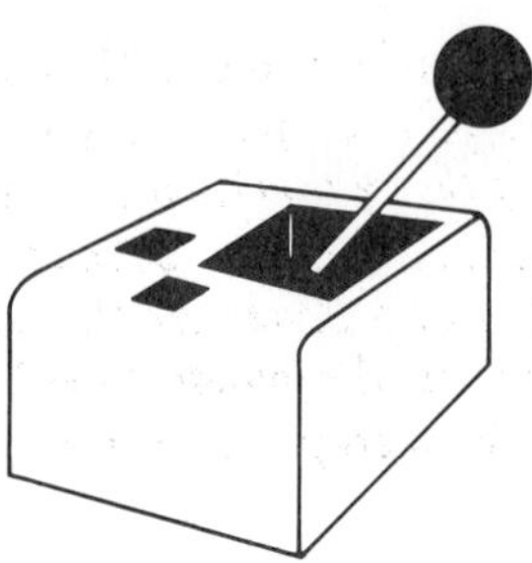

A close relative to the joystick is the **track ball,** which is rolled to control the computer. The track ball has the potential to be as accurate as a mouse. There are keyboards available that have joysticks or track balls built right in. These can be used to replace the keyboard that comes with the computer.

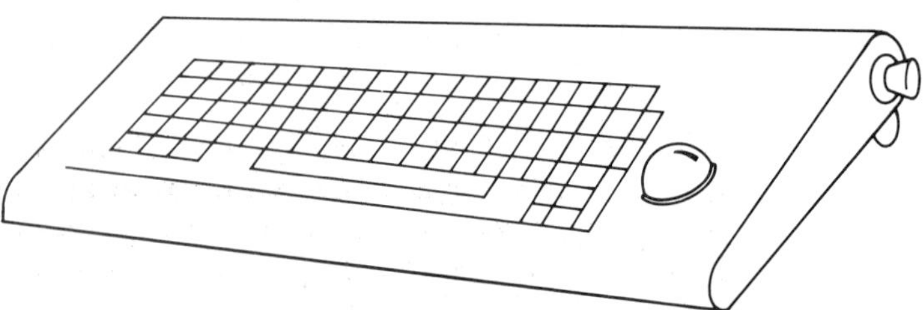

A popular device for creating art or drafting is the **graphics tablet.** Information is input through a graphics tablet by moving a stylus over its surface. One advantage that this method has over other input devices is that it can be used to trace existing drawings. It also has the potential for great accuracy. Graphics tablets range in features and price from very expensive, highly accurate models designed for **Computer Aided Design (CAD)** to less accurate, inexpensive, handheld models. Many graphics tablets interface with the computer through the game port. Some use asynchronous adapters or special interfaces.

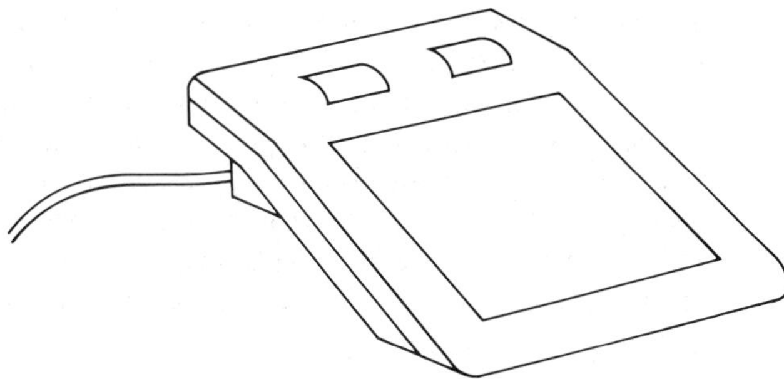

The **light pen** is an alternative to the keyboard that has been around quite a while, but that you don't see used very much. This type of device allows you to input information by touching it to the display. As you might imagine, there is great potential here for educational software. Even very young children can respond to a computer by touching the screen. This device could also be a boon to the handicapped. Light pens are usually connected to the computer through game ports or special interfaces.

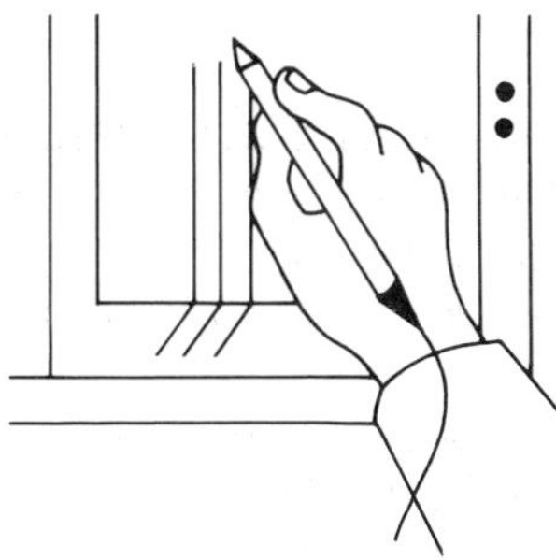

The final alternative input device we'll look at is one that you may have already used: an **Optical Character Reader (OCR).** Even if you haven't used one, you probably know that many schools currently employ such devices to grade standardized tests or read other information from cards marked with a number 2 pencil. What you may not know is that these devices can be interfaced with the PC through an asynchronous adapter.

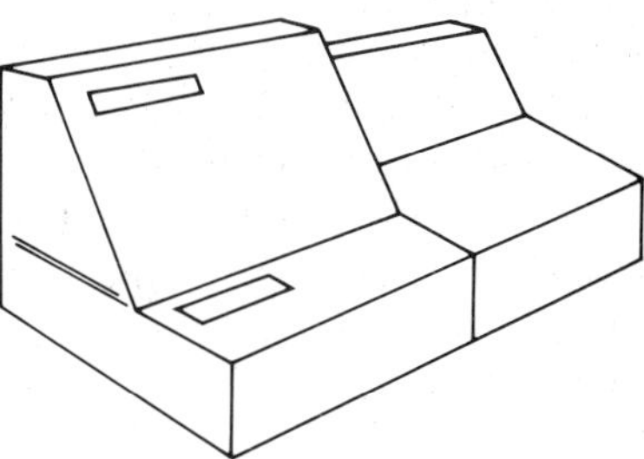

Systems like this are already beginning to appear in classrooms, especially places like remedial learning labs where student progress is measured quite frequently. The teacher or aide need only pass the student's answer sheet through the reader to have the computer grade it, record the result, update the student's record, and print out a suggested follow-up activity based on the results of the test. This scenario is becoming even more realistic as lower-priced OCRs are beginning to appear on the market.

Printers

Probably the single most useful addition to a computer system is a printer. The two most widely used types of microcomputer printers are dot matrix and daisywheel. A **daisywheel printer** works much like a typewriter. It has a print wheel that rotates to the appropriate character and strikes a ribbon. A dot matrix printer has a print head that consists of a matrix of pins that can be shot out in any combination to form characters. For example, when the letter A is printed, the pins are shot out in just the right arrangement to form an A.

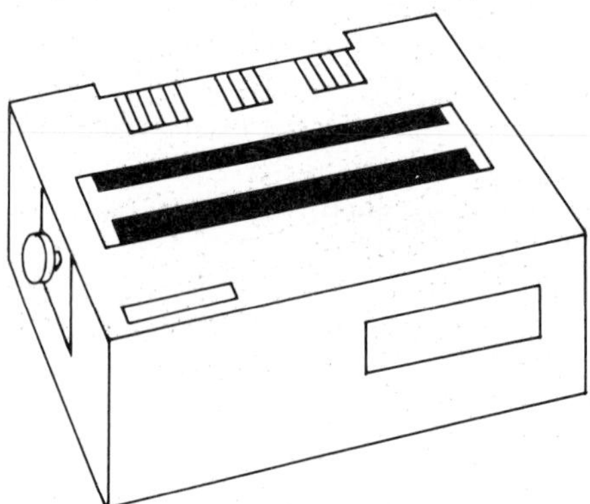

What are the respective strengths and weaknesses of these devices? Dot matrix printers tend to be faster and more versatile than daisywheels. They can be programmed to print virtually any kind of character, font, or picture.

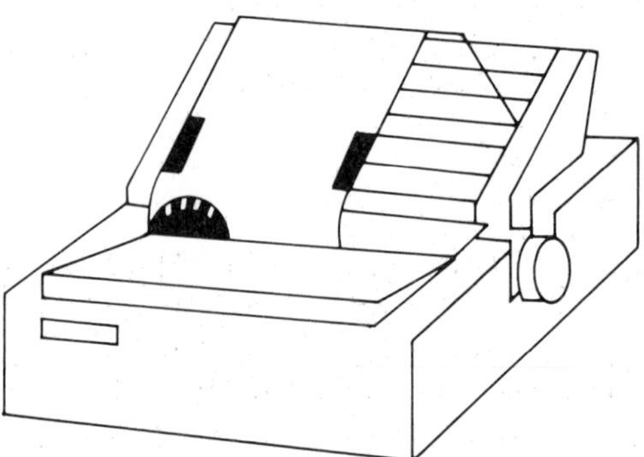

Their print speeds typically range from 40 to 200 characters per second. Daisywheel printers produce better quality text than dot matrix, but are slower, more expensive, and cannot produce graphics. In fact, as the text quality of dot matrix printers improves, and as new print technologies have emerged, fewer and fewer daisywheel printers are being sold.

The major new print technology that is displacing daisywheel printers is the **laser printer.** Laser printers bring the technology of the copier industry to the microcomputer arena. They have all the advantages of both daisywheel and dot matrix printers. They are fast, reliable, have excellent print quality, can be programmed to print in virtually any font, can produce very high quality graphics, and their prices start at that of a good daisywheel.

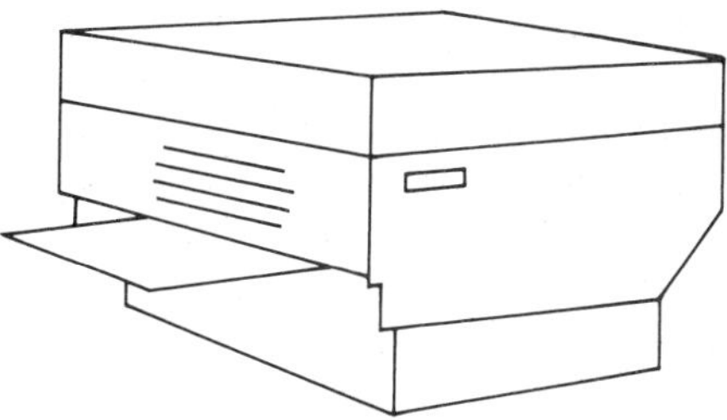

Most dot matrix printers for the PC interface through a parallel port. Some daisywheels use parallel ports, some asynchronous adapters. Laser printers interface through the asynchronous adapter. If you are in the market for a printer and have a small budget, look at dot matrix printers. If you want the best in print quality and have a little more money to spend, get a laser printer.

One last consideration about printers is color. Color print technology does exist, but it is not sufficiently developed. The most reasonable alternatives for schools today are the inexpensive color **ink-jet printers** produced by some manufacturers. These devices work by spraying dots of colored ink to form images on paper. Unfortunately, the image quality is only high when a special type of paper is used. In our opinion, color print technology will really arrive when color laser printers become available at reasonable cost. Right now, a color printer shouldn't be high on your list of priorities unless you have a special need for one (if, for instance, you happen to be an art teacher).

Modems

As telecommunications becomes more and more common, every computer is going to need a modem. This is the device that allows your computer to talk over the telephone. A major feature to look at in modems is speed. On the telephone, time is money. So, for many applications, the faster your modem, the lower your cost. Of course, the faster the modem, the higher its cost. Early modems for the PC were 300 baud (see Chapter 14). Then 1,200 baud became prevalent, followed by even faster speeds.

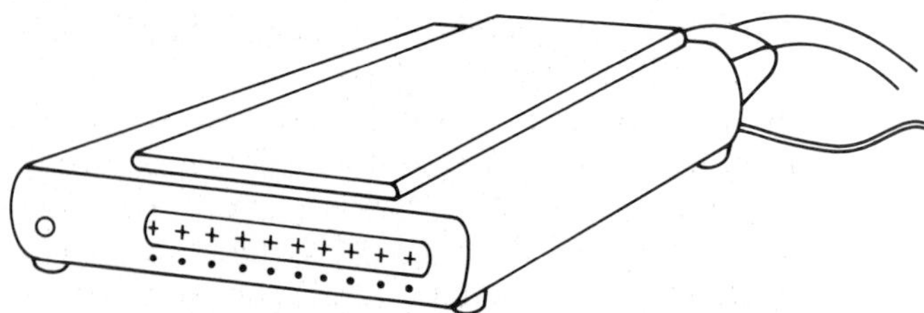

Another important factor to look at in a modem is how the software "talks" to it. This is a totally arbitrary standard, and it is possible that every modem could be different. However, for the PC, the standard set by one manufacturer has emerged as dominant. It is referred to as the Hayes standard. There tends to be much more software available for it than other standards, and many other manufacturers have adopted the Hayes standard as well. If you buy a modem that observes a different standard, make sure that you also know where to get software that works with it.

Modems come in two flavors for the PC; *external* and *internal.* External modems connect with your computer through an asynchronous adapter and have their own power supplies. Internal modems look like interface cards and plug right into a slot in your computer. They require no additional asynchronous port. External modems have the advantages of being portable, you can easily move them to another computer, and they place no demands on your computer's power supply. Also, down the road when you get rid of your old computer and buy a new one, you'll probably be able to use your old modem with it. Internal modems are less expensive and don't take up any precious shelf space.

Speech Synthesizers

Speech will probably become an important feature for microcomputers, especially those used in education. *Speech synthesizers* are devices that can allow your computers to talk to you. The ones available for the PC family are either internal cards or, in the case of the PCjr, an attachment that plugs into one end of the computer.

Computer speech is usually generated one of two ways. Often, the synthesizer will have a fixed set of words encoded and stored in its own ROM. Also, many synthesizers have **phonemes** stored in ROM that you can use to assemble words phonetically. The main advantage of the first method is that it sounds very human and is easy to understand. The disadvantage is that your computer has a fixed vocabulary. The advantage of phoneme-based speech is that it is versatile. You can make your computer say almost anything. The disadvantage is that you may not know what it is saying. This kind of speech synthesis sounds very robotic and is difficult to understand. Another, newer method of making computers talk allows you to "record" your own words and store them on disk for playback. This method has both the advantages of versatility and understandability, and it has the added feature of allowing you to store words in any voice you want. This could be important in education because it means you can provide any child with an appropriate verbal role model. The disadvantage of recorded speech is that it takes up more RAM than the other two types. As computer memories get larger, however, that is becoming less of a problem. The IBM PCjr Speech Attachment is able to generate all three of the types of speech mentioned here.

CD ROMs

This budding technology is a variation on the laser disk theme: information can be digitally encoded *optically* rather than *magnetically*. With this technology, information is encoded in the form of depressions made in the surface of the disk. These depressions can then be decoded by scanning them with a laser. The advantages of optical storage systems are manyfold. They are very durable and require no special handling, the integrity of data stored on them should degrade much more slowly than with conventional magnetic storage, and they can be used to store incredibly large amounts of data, such as high-resolution images, for use with your computer. Most of them interface with the PC through an asynchronous port. Already, some software products (for example, authoring systems) are able to make use of them. These technologies promise to revolutionize high-speed data storage; however, they have not quite arrived. A major problem is that they are, as yet, mostly read only technology. That means that you, the user, cannot record information on them. You can only read information from them. This state of affairs will change. It's only a matter of time.

Chapter Summary

In this chapter, we have looked at some special products, both hardware and software, that put your PC to good use or extend its capabilities. We feel that it is important to acquaint you with some of the products available on the market, but remember, much of this information is subject to change. Things move very quickly in the world of microcomputers. New technologies are announced almost every day, so just use this chapter as a starting point from which to explore on your own.

Chapter Review

Knowledge Exercises

1. What kinds of free software are available for the IBM PC?

   Answer: There are programs available of almost any kind; from public domain utilities such as SDIR and VIEW to user-supported communications programs such as PC-TALK III. Much of this software is as good as or better than comparable commercial programs.

2. Why are interfaces needed? Differentiate between the three types of standard interfaces described in this chapter. Can you install them yourself?

   Answer: Interfaces allow peripheral devices to "talk" to the computer. Parallel interfaces send data in parallel, eight bits at a time, and are commonly used for printers. Serial interfaces, or asynchronous communication adapters, send data one bit at a time and are commonly used with mouse devices, modems, and some printers. Game ports are used to interface with joysticks and some graphics tablets and light pens. All of these devices are easy to install. They just plug into PC expansion slots.

3. What are multifunction cards? What are their features? What disadvantage(s) do they have? Why would you want one?

   Answer: Multifunction cards contain all the circuitry for a number of functions. They typically contain such features as parallel ports, serial ports, game ports, memory expansion sockets, and battery-powered clocks. They are less expensive than buying all the components separately and occupy only one expansion slot in the computer. The major disadvantage comes when something needs repair and the whole device must be removed for servicing.

4. What do light pens, graphics tablets, mouse devices, joysticks, and track balls all have in common? How do they all differ?

   Answer: They are microcomputer input devices, alternatives to the keyboard. Each is manipulated differently to generate input to the computer. A mouse is a handheld object that is moved across a surface. A joystick has a lever that is manipulated. With a graphics tablet, one moves a stylus across a surface. Light pens are a kind of stylus that is used to point directly at the computer display. A track ball is like an upside-down mouse and may be part of the keyboard. The user manipulates the ball directly.

5. Why should you not purchase a daisywheel printer? How do they compare to dot matrix or laser printers?

   Answer: Daisywheel printers are a dying technology. Compared to dot matrix, they are expensive, slow, less reliable, and cannot print graphics.

Laser printers equal or exceed the print quality of a daisywheel, but can also print graphics and different text fonts as a dot matrix can.

6. What device do you need to perform telecommunications with your computer? What are some things to look for?

   Answer: A modem. Modems come with different speed capabilities; generally, the faster the modem, the greater the cost. The safest purchase is probably Hayes-compatible, since that has emerged as something of a standard for PCs.

7. What advantages does a fixed disk have over a floppy diskette? Can you add one to a PC? What about CD ROMs?

   Answer: The major advantages of fixed disks are storage capacity and speed. They can be added to PCs, but may require a new power supply. CD ROMs offer even greater storage than fixed disks, but are not yet very common.

Thought Exercises

1. If you are going to purchase microcomputer peripheral devices or hardware enhancements, do you buy local retail, local discount, or mail order? What do you imagine might be the advantages and disadvantages of each method?

2. Of all the peripheral devices, hardware, and software mentioned in this chapter, which do you think are most important to acquire for your classroom?

3. Can you think of any software or hardware that is not mentioned in this chapter that would be of use in schools? If so, describe what features it should have in as much detail as you can.

Activities

1. Try to talk your instructor or some other trusting person into letting you "tour" the insides of his or her PC. Locate as many of the devices and components mentioned in this chapter as you can.

2. Visit a computer laboratory in a school. See how many programs and devices they have that are mentioned in this chapter. Ask the teacher in charge why the school has what it does, what factors influenced the purchases, and what will be acquired next.

3. Try to view or get your hands on as many of the programs and devices mentioned in this chapter as possible. Visit or join a computer users' group and obtain some of the public domain or user-supported software. Ask your instructor to try to set up some demonstrations of hardware and software. Try some local businesses to see if they'll let you view or borrow some items.

Projects

1. Pretend you are writing a grant proposal for funding an instructional computing project. Identify a specific student population, specific instructional goals, and make some justifiable decisions as to what software and hardware resources you require to help students achieve those goals. Write a report specifying all the details. Cite your references.

2. If you think that you've done a good job on Project 1, submit your proposal to the education divisions of some major microcomputer manufacturers. You might be surprised at the results. Be prepared to add to your proposal how you plan to evaluate student progress and whether or not the computers had any impact on it.

Bibliography

Arabia, T. "Choosing a Printer." *Classroom Computer Learning* (October 1985): 20–22. Discusses what the hardware has to offer.

Chertok, Barbara Lee, Dov Roseneld, and James H. Stone. *IBM PC and XT Owner's Manual.* Bowie, Md.: Robert J. Brady, 1984.

Cortesi, David E. *Your IBM Personal Computer: Use, Application, and BASIC.* New York: Holt, Rinehart, & Winston, 1982.

Dyrli, O. E. "Input Devices—Joysticks, Mice, and Lightpens." *Classroom Computer Learning* (November–December 1985): 10–11. Discusses these devices and their impact on educational opportunities that were never before possible.

Dyrli, O. E. "Input Devices—Graphics Tablets and Alternate Keyboards." *Classroom Computer Learning* (January 1986): 14–15. Discusses the devices that bridge the gap between the keyboard and handheld control devices.

Gader, Bertam, and Manuel V. Nodar. *Free Software for the IBM PC.* New York: Warner Books, 1984.

Ginther, D. W. "Microcomputers Are Talking Back in the Classroom: The Promise of Speech Technology in Education." *Technological Horizons in Education* (October 1983): 105–107. Explores past and future uses of speech synthesizers, describing new features that allow considerable control of speech output.

Goldstein, Larry Joel, and Martin Goldstein. *IBM PC: An Introduction to the Operating System, BASIC Programming, and Applications.* Bowie, Md.: Robert J. Brady, 1984.

Green, John O. "New Ways for Special Education Kids to Communicate." *Classroom Computer Learning* (October 1984): 24–29. The challenge is to enhance hardware and software to open new avenues for children with special needs.

Hagen, D. "Jason Says 'Yes'." *Pointer* (Winter 1984): 40–43. A seven-year-old non-vocal blind child with cerebral palsy and probable mental retardation learned basic cause and effect tasks via a speech synthesizer and microcomputer.

Johnson, C. W., and D. A. Orban. "Light Pens as a Magic Wand: Computerize Classroom Visual Aids Using an Extended BASIC." *Educational Technology* (March 1985): 20–24. Provides examples of the custom instructional applications that can be created using extended BASIC and a light pen.

McConnell, B. "The Handicapple: A Low Cost Braille Printer." *Creative Computing* (October 1982): 186–188. Describes the technique of combining the Apple computer and Braille-writer to produce hard copies in Braille.

Rogers, S. "The Talking Apple." *T.H.E. Journal* (March 1985): 102–103. Discusses the adaptive equipment that this blind author uses for word processing.

Sachs, Jonathan. *Your IBM PC Made Easy*. Berkeley, Calif.: Osborne/McGraw-Hill, 1984.

St. Lawrence, Jim. "The Interactive Videodisc—Here at Last." *Fast Forward* (April 1984): 49–57. Sound and graphics become alive with this new interactive medium.

Spence, D., and M. Williams. "Getting Started with Braille-Edit." *Education of the Visually Handicapped* (Spring 1985): 31–38.

Vincent, A. T. "Computer Assisted Support for Blind Students: The Use of the Microcomputer-Linked Voice Synthesizer." CAL Research Group Technical Report No. 10, January 1981, 21 p. Paper presented at CAL Symposium on Computer Assisted Learning, Leeds, England, April 8–10, 1981.

White, D. W. "Creating Microcomputer Graphics with the Koala Pad." *Art Education* (March 1985): 10–14.

Williams, J. M. "When the Classroom Computer Talks, Handicapped Children Listen." *American School Board Journal* (March 1985): 43–44.

Wilton, J., and R. McLean. "Evaluation of a Mouse as an Educational Device." *Computers and Education* 8, no. 4: 455–461. Describes the mouse and other pointing devices used to facilitate easier user-microcomputer interaction.

CHAPTER

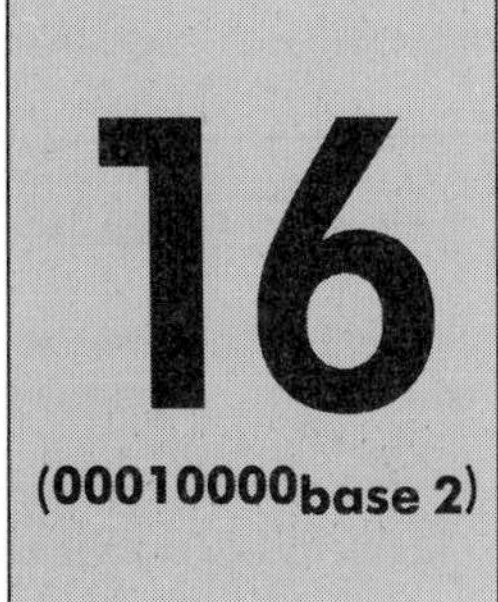

FINAL FORGET-ME-NOTS

Organizing the Elements of Instruction

Getting Started

This chapter is all about what you need to do to prepare to teach with computers. Developing your personal skills and learning to use computers is just the beginning. There are a myriad of factors to be dealt with also; the nuts and bolts, you might say. Where do you put the computers? Is it better to put them all in one dedicated classroom under the control of one teacher, or to put one in every classroom? What about putting them in a resource center that is available to all teachers? Speaking of making computers available to all teachers, do they have a place in teacher work areas? How does one prepare a space to house the computers? Are any special wiring requirements necessary? Do you need to beef up your source of power? What steps need to be taken to ensure proper security.

Once the computers are in the environment, what makes them go? Of course, the answer to that is software. With the limited availability of educational dollars, software must be carefully screened before purchase. How do you obtain reliable software reviews? Can you look at a program before you buy it? If so, how do you get a copy of it? If you decide to use it, how many copies will you need? Can you make copies yourself? Is that legal? In this chapter, we'll take a look at all of these questions.

Objectives for Teachers

After completing this chapter you should be able to

1. State relative strengths and weaknesses of different computer classroom models: the one-computer classroom, the dedicated classroom, the computer resource laboratory, and the teacher workroom.
2. Identify which, if any, of the models stated in our first objective is most appropriate for a given instructional task or situation.
3. Describe important issues to consider when preparing a computer laboratory.

4. Describe important considerations related to evaluating software.
5. Understand software company policies for previewing software and making multiple copies available for classroom use.
6. Specify a new computer laboratory for a given application within your school, justifying each recommendation.
7. Create an overall computer plan for your school.
8. Write a report concerning copyright laws as they pertain to computer software.

Where Do the Computers Go?

In the early eighties, as microcomputers were first placed in schools, two arrangements began to evolve. At first, since numbers were usually small, computers were frequently allocated one to a classroom. Then, as larger numbers of computers were purchased, some schools placed them all in one classroom, under the control of one teacher. This often occurred because the programming and computer literacy teachers were those who had the ear of their principals. Other teachers, unsure of how to use computers, made no demands and expressed no interest. The programming and computer literacy teachers had clear and definable needs for the computers.

Now that computer use is becoming more widespread, across all subject areas, these early models for installation are proving inefficient. All the computers in a school are tied up all day long by a handful of teachers. One answer to this problem is to buy more computers. Obviously, that solution introduces more problems. The biggest one is cost. Just how many computers can a school afford to purchase and maintain? Another problem is one of space. Many schools are already overcrowded. Even if large numbers of computers are purchased, how many schools can afford to build or allocate the space to house them?

The best number of computers to have is probably one per student. Clearly, that ratio represents the ideal, but how realistic is it? Will it ever be the obligation of the school to provide a computer for every student? As computer prices and sizes continue to decrease, no one can predict what the future may hold. In his book *Mindstorms,* Seymour Papert maintains that the goal of a computer for every child is attainable; that the costs would "represent only about 5 percent of the total public expenditure on education." That scenario has not yet been played and there are no signs that it will be in the near future.

Fortunately, there are other, more efficient models for placing computers in schools. These models allow more teachers to use a limited number of computers without trading off too much in exchange. Let's examine a number of different models in detail, including the two already mentioned.

Which models are appropriate for a given instructional activity? Which are the most efficient? Then, at the end of this section, we'll propose an overall model for placing computers in schools.

The One-Computer Classroom

Let's begin by expanding this category to include larger numbers of computers. Any classroom in which there are not enough computers to serve the entire class simultaneously is, strategically, the same as a one-computer classroom. This model places the greatest demand on the management skills of a teacher. It requires simultaneous attention to students working with the computer and students working without the computer. Teachers who have endured this experience can testify to the difficulty of attempting to work with a group of children while cries of "This disk won't boot." or "Billy kicked out the plug!" arise from the computer corner. Even when the teacher is technically competent and the students are well enough trained to use the computer without assistance, the software is rarely up to the task. Few programs are capable of providing feedback to the teacher about a student's performance. How valuable is time spent on the computer when the teacher has no way to evaluate what learning took place? Because few teachers possess the skills to manage one computer in a classroom, that computer frequently ends up being the reward for good behavior or for completing assignments on time. While that can be a valuable tool, it is certainly an inefficient use for a powerful device.

This is not to say that there are no ways to use one or a small number of computers. Computer projects, classroom demonstrations, and selected group activities are all valuable learning experiences that can be executed with one computer. However, machines employed this way probably don't get used 100 percent of the time. Other teachers could use the machine during the slack time, but not if it's in another teacher's classroom.

The Dedicated Classroom

The dedicated classroom refers to the second arrangement mentioned earlier. This is where a *classroom set* of computers is placed in one room for use by one teacher all day long. This teacher is usually a programming or computer literacy instructor. Even in school districts in which these topics are given high priority, do these teachers really need those computers 100 percent of the time? Although they may rarely admit it, the answer is, in our opinion, an emphatic no. The dedicated classroom may be the most inefficient arrangement of all.

The teaching of programming might seem like it requires constant computer use. The truth is that programming teachers only use the computers part of the time. In fact, allowing novice programmers too much computer time at too early a stage can lead to the development of poor programming habits. Student programmers need to be taught to thoroughly analyze problems or tasks before writing code. Having computers constantly present encourages students to attempt to write code before the task to be accomplished is fully understood.

Having computers constantly present may also interfere with the execution of other types of instruction. There is always a place in the classroom for activities that don't require hands-on. Few teachers are so entertaining that they can successfully compete with a microcomputer. The teaching of computer literacy is even less computer-intensive than programming. The literacy topic that requires the most computer use is the teaching of programming. All the factors mentioned before apply here as well.

The dedicated classroom has one major advantage over other arrangements. It lends itself best to tight security. With only one or two teachers and their classes using the computers, it is much easier to maintain control of the computers and software. But, is that advantage worth trading off efficiency?

The Computer Resource Laboratory

One answer to the major flaw of the first two arrangements, that of inefficient use, is the resource laboratory. This is an arrangement where a classroom set of computers is placed in a room to which all teachers have access, much like a media center. To use the lab, a teacher must reserve it ahead of time. In this fashion, all interests may be served. Programming teachers may reserve space on a regular basis and teachers whose needs are less frequent may still be given access. In addition, software may also be housed in the lab. The resource lab is the most efficient use of computer hardware and software resources. With careful scheduling, 100 percent usage is possible. There are, however, two major problems with a lab arrangement. First of all, it does require careful scheduling and the facility requires management, again, much like a media center. If the lab is the responsibility of no specific teacher, then who will make up the schedule and who will manage the resources? The second problem associated with the resource lab is that of security. With many different teachers and students using the computers, there is great potential for loss of equipment and software. Unauthorized copying of software is also more likely to take place.

Some schools have had success in answering these problems by designating a teacher or an aide as a lab manager. This person spends some part of the day managing the lab and providing support to teachers who are using the lab. In cases where no such appointment is made, the responsibility for the lab is usually undertaken by one or more teachers.

The Teacher Workroom

One place where computers can be used to great effect is in teacher work areas. Schools all too often make the mistake of expecting teachers to teach with computers without providing those teachers with training. This same mistake is propagated when teachers cannot have uninterrupted, student-free access to computers in order to prepare for instruction. By placing computers in teacher work areas, this need is answered.

The Teacher's House

We are constantly amazed at the number of schools that don't allow teachers to take computers home on weekends or over the summer. A school district has much more to gain from allowing the practice than it does to lose. The biggest expense related to putting computers into schools is teacher training. Time and time again we have seen teachers make tremendous gains in knowledge at no expense to the school when they are allowed to take computers home. What if a school does lose one computer in 100? Isn't it worth it?

The Overall Model

All of these arrangements have advantages, so it makes sense that an ideal arrangement is a combination of all of them. Start with a resource laboratory. Despite the problems it presents, it still results in the most efficient and versatile use of limited hardware resources. Then, place at least one computer in a teacher work area, off limits from students. This way, teachers can learn without interruption from students and they can prepare instructional activities. Allocate a few computers as floaters that can be checked out like movie projectors are. These computers will answer instructional needs that are not appropriate to the laboratory setting. Finally, establish a fair procedure for allowing teachers to take computers home on weekends and over the summer. Whether administrator or teacher, we don't think you'll regret it.

Preparing a Computer Lab

There is more to establishing a computer lab than just setting up some computers in a spare room. There are many variables to be dealt with, some of which we discuss in the following sections.

The Power Supply

If you are designing a computer laboratory, it is best to plan from the beginning for your lab to have its own private power supply. Electrical current is full of irregularities that don't affect most appliances. Microcomputers, however, are very sensitive to these irregularities. We're not talking about things like lightning strikes or large power surges. It doesn't take that much to cause trouble. Even minor fluctuations in voltage level or the slightest interruption in a computer's power source can result in the loss of data. Ideally, every computer should be on a circuit that is specially treated to remove irregularities.

The best system is called UPS (for Uninterruptable Power Supply). In addition to filtering the power supply against irregularities, UPS provides an emergency power supply in case of blackout or brownout. The disadvantage with UPS is that it can be very expensive. When deciding whether or not to install UPS, you have to consider what your potential losses can be without it. Businesses frequently require UPS because the loss of even the slightest amount of productivity can affect profits. There are not many situations in education where data is generated that is so valuable as to require UPS.

What can be done short of UPS? There are less expensive modules with fewer capabilities for protecting computers. They vary greatly in price, but for the most part, you'll get what you pay for. Another thing to consider is having a master power control switch installed in your lab. It saves wear and tear on the computers' off/on switches and when you shut down the lab at the end of the day, you *know* that everything is, indeed, off.

In whatever room is chosen for your computer lab, you'll probably have to install additional electrical outlets. It isn't safe to rely on extension cords, and don't let the electrician install outlets that project from the floor. Both are potential hazards. Have power strips installed at table height on the walls of the room, and arrange the computers accordingly, or have the power dropped from the ceiling with special posts made just for that purpose. If you have to install outlets in the floor, make sure that they are flush with the surface.

The Environment

If possible, place your computers in a cool, clean, and vibration-free environment. Dust, dirt, and smoke are the biggest enemies of computers and magnetic media.

Both computer units and monitors have to be ventilated. Always position a computer so that air can be circulated through it. Never cover the ventilation slots on the top of a monitor.

There is some question about the proper level of humidity for computers. While the hardware lasts longer in a dry environment, that same dry environment is ideal for the development of static electricity. Static discharges can zap diskettes, cause strange problems called **glitches,** and destroy integrated circuits. Geography seems to be an important factor. The western coast of Florida has a naturally humid environment, so we keep our computers (and people) in air conditioning almost all the time. In all our experience with micros, we have never had a serious problem that we thought was caused by static electricity. It is our understanding that in other parts of the country, where the climate is dry, static can be a very big problem.

Although there is some question about the proper humidity for computers to live in, there is none whatsoever with respect to extremely humid conditions such as rain, leaky roofs, and floodwaters. For this reason, computers should be kept indoors and, if possible, not on either the first or

top floor of a building. In a two-story building, the floor computers are placed on is usually best determined by local conditions. If the roof is about to fall, it doesn't make sense to place them on the top floor to avoid a potential flood. Never place computers in the basement or in a room with exposed pipes overhead.

Furniture

There has been a great deal of press about buying special *ergonomically* designed computer furniture. While you should certainly get the best furniture your budget will afford, remember that very few students will have the luxury of sitting in front of a computer all day long. You definitely need furniture and furniture funds should always be included in a computer purchase. But expensive, specialized computer furniture should not be a high priority. Good, sturdy tables and chairs will suffice for most applications. One exception to this rule might be vocational training in word processing or the like, where it is important to develop good work habits.

If you plan to keep software in your lab, you will need sufficient shelving. For maximum security, lockable cabinets are best. This is more than just an issue of theft prevention. Software can be stolen without being removed from the lab by simply copying it. The best way to keep your school out of trouble with copyright infringement is to maintain close control over all software. Keep it under lock and key when it's not being used.

How one arranges the computers and furniture in a lab depends upon instructional needs and physical limitations. Contrary to a "normal" classroom, the best place for the teacher's desk-cum-master computer is—as many teachers have found—on a platform at the back of the lab. That way you can see what's on everybody's monitor. Here are some typical arrangements.

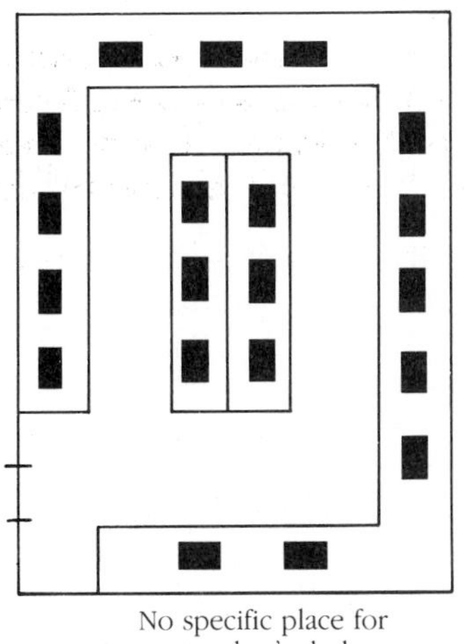

No specific place for a teacher's desk.

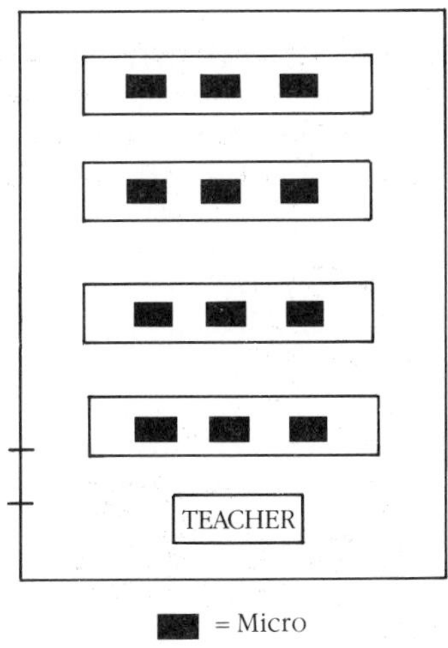

■ = Micro

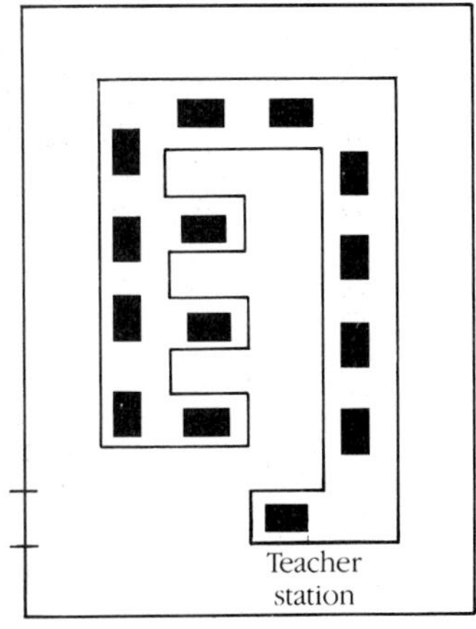

Odds and Ends

Every computer lab should have at least one fire extinguisher. The halon kind is best since it will probably do less damage to the computers than other types of extinguishers.

If you're planning on telecommunications activities in your lab, you'll need at least one dedicated telephone line, tone-dial if possible. Start campaigning for one as soon as possible. You'll be amazed at how difficult it can be to get the principal to give you a phone line, even one in a room that is kept under lock and key. The phone company does market special high-quality data-transmission lines, but a normal private phone line will suffice for most educational purposes. It's a real pain to have to call through a switchboard with a computer, so try to get a line with its own number so you can dial out directly.

Software Review

Once computers are established in the environment, the next consideration is purchasing quality instructional software. In the typical educational environment, money for the purchase of software is at a premium, so it is important to have reliable information about a piece of software before you buy it. What is this information composed of and how do you obtain it?

The most obvious way to obtain software reviews is to perform them yourself. This task is too difficult for even a large school district, let alone a single school faculty. Reviewing software is time-consuming, it requires machines that could otherwise be used for instruction, and it is very difficult to obtain the necessary quantities of software. Thus, the best way to obtain reliable information about software is to obtain it from an agency organized to perform software reviews. In reality, the most important task for a school faculty is to know where to get reliable reviews and how to interpret them.

Technical Characteristics

What information should a good review contain? The first and most important question: Is it technically sound? This question relates to both the program and its documentation. A program that is not technically sound, no matter what other advantages it may have, could well be worthless. The vast majority of technically unsound programs should be rejected with no further consideration. The following list sets forth concerns that relate to technical characteristics:

Ease of use. How easy is it to use without documentation? Are the directions easy to follow? Is on-line help available? Are the keystrokes necessary for entering commands both concise and consistent? Is the printed documentation consistent with the way the program actually behaves?

Reliability. Is the program free from programming and operational errors?

Information displays. Are text screens well formatted and grammatically accurate? Is the print suitable for the target audience? Is the variety of screen displays appropriate for the target audience? Are graphics displayed promptly and accurately?

Documentation. Is necessary information for program use included? Are tutorials available? Are instructions clear and easy to use? Are accurate pictures and diagrams provided that help the reader? Are comprehensive indexes included? Is resource information easy to find?

Instructional Characteristics

If the technical characteristics fly, then it's worth the time it takes to look at the instructional characteristics. An informative review is based upon the objective collection of program characteristics. Such a review includes a minimum of subjective statements such as, "This program is boring." or "This program is wonderful!" What is boring to an advanced student may be perfectly appropriate for a student who has special learning difficulties. What is wonderful for an advanced student might be frustrating to a learning-disabled student. What an informative review does is concisely list the instructional characteristics of a program so that educators can match them with given learning objectives for specific student groups. Some important characteristics that should be addressed follow:

Instructional purpose. For what purpose is the program most appropriate—Computer Directed Instruction, Computer Enhanced Instruction, or Computer Managed Instruction? Are elements of more than one of these categories present? (In Chapters 7–9 we addressed the elements that define each of these categories.)

Program objectives. Is the program designed specifically for instruction? If so, are student learning objectives clearly delineated in terms of expected outcomes? Is the level of instruction indicated? Are intended target audiences indicated?

Program content. Is the program up-to-date, accurate, and free from stereotypes? Does the program make optimal use of hardware capabilities?

Program design. If the program is designed specifically for instruction, will it respond to individual students by branching on the basis of their responses? Is the student able to direct the program flow, or must the student simply respond to the program's demands? Can students and/or teachers modify the content of the program? Are printed reports available? If so, do they give both quantitative and qualitative information? How are text and graphics used? Do they display instructional models, are they used only to motivate responses, or both? Does the program use sound to build concepts, provide feedback, or to motivate?

Another 10,000 words could be spent on the topic of software review. In a sense, a major portion of this book has been devoted to this topic. The preceding provides a brief summary of important considerations. For more detailed treatments, consult some of the sources cited in this chapter's bibliography.

Other Software Issues

As one prepares to execute instruction using computers, all kinds of unforeseen problems with software may arise. Unavailability, high cost, restrictive licensing agreements, inflexibility, and copy protection are all potential sources of difficulty. The following sections provide a typical example of what you can end up going through.

Ella's Story

This is the story of Ella Mentry, a typical computer-using teacher. While Ella may be fictional, her experiences as detailed here are a composite of things that have actually happened to people.

Getting Software for Preview

My name is Ella Mentry and I teach sixth grade at Hardly Fundamental School in Techno City, Florida. Last year, I took a computer literacy course at State of the Art University, so this year I thought I would use the computers at Hardly to design some instructional activities for my students. Have I got a story to tell you!

The first thing I did was to contact our district's computer resource person, Golda Mein, to seek her advice. Golda put me on to some catalogs of computer software and I spent quite a bit of time going through them in search of something I wanted to use. Finally, after lots of research, I settled on two programs: Master Math Skillblaster from The Tenderware Company and The Spiffy Spelling Program by OverByte Products. From the descriptions in the catalog and some very favorable reviews I saw in *The Computer Teacher's Friend,* it seemed like these two programs were exactly what I was looking for. They were pretty expensive, though, so I called the companies to see if they could send me preview copies. Boy, was I ever naive!

At first, The Tenderware Company treated me pretty nicely.

"Oh sure," the nice man said, "we'll be happy to send you a copy. What company did you say you were with?"

I told him I was in education.

"Oh," the nice man said, "what university?"

I told him I was with the public school system.

"Well, what do you do? Are you the district-level computer specialist?"

I told him I was a classroom teacher.

"You're just a teacher?" he said, incredulously. I heard laughter in the background. "I'm sorry," he said, "I can't help you. If we loaned software to every classroom teacher who wanted it we'd go broke!"

OverByte was even worse.

"Good morning, this is OverByte Products. My name is Susan. How may I help you?"

I thought I'd try the bold, forthright approach.

"Hello, Susan. My name is Ella Mentry and I teach sixth grade at Hardly Elementary School in Techno City, Florida. I am interested in your Spiffy Spelling program. I am calling to order a preview copy."

"Let me put you on hold," she said, "while I connect you with the appropriate person."

Susan put me on infinite hold. After 10 minutes I hung up and called back. All the lines were busy.

In desperation, I called Golda to tell her what happened and to see if she could get copies for me.

"I'm sorry," she said, "but I can't do it. I happen to know that those companies send out demo copies of their programs that have been 'crippled' so that you can't really use them. Not only would you be unable to get a true evaluation of them, the district has established a policy that prohibits ordering that kind of preview copy. That's the only way we can discourage the practice. But, don't give up hope yet. Let me call the Computer Resource Center at State of the Art U. Maybe they have the programs you need."

Golda called back later and told me that the University did, indeed, have the programs that I wanted, but that I would have to go over there (a 30-mile drive) to preview them. The next day, I previewed the programs and they turned out to be just what I needed. So when I got back to school I ordered them.

Copy Protection

A month later, my programs arrived and I began to make final preparations. I put the polishing touches on the support materials I developed and had copies run off.

Hardly Elementary has a lab of 15 computers that teachers can reserve for their classes. My activities were designed in such a way that I planned to take my students to the lab and have them use the computers to complete the activities I prepared. I planned to put two students on each computer, so I figured that I needed 14 more copies of each of the programs, one for each computer. I bought a couple of boxes of blank diskettes and went down to the lab one day after school to make the copies. I booted a computer with the DOS diskette and executed the disk copy routine. After a few seconds, the computer started to beep and messages like "Read error on track 9 sector 7" began to scroll up the screen. When the copy process finally stopped, I used a compare utility to check the copy. The program indicated that there were a number of comparison errors on the target diskette, but I decided to try it anyway. It wouldn't run. I looked more closely at the diskette and saw at the bottom of the label the legend, "COPY PROTECTED." Much to my dismay, it seemed that the manufacturer used some arcane procedure to render the diskette uncopyable! In desperation, I opened the other program and looked at the diskette. It, too, said "COPY PROTECTED." I could see my carefully laid plans going up in smoke. My budget just would not bear the purchase of additional copies, even with the manufacturer's educational discount. What was I to do?

When my despair subsided, I sat down with the programs and ran one of them again to see if I could think of some way out of my situation. I noticed that once I had booted the program the disk drive never again came on throughout the entire program execution. Excitedly, I removed the diskette from the drive and tried to boot another computer with it. It worked! Pretty soon, I had the program running on every computer in the lab. How could I have been so stupid? Of course, I remembered, a computer program loads into memory and executes from there. Once it has been loaded, there is no need for the diskette to remain in the drive. It seemed that I had found my way out. Just to be sure, I took the other program from its package and booted it, too. This time, however, I noticed that the disk drive came on quite a few times during the run of the program. I tried to boot some other computers with the same program, but no matter how I tried, the program always crashed unless the diskette was in the drive. Apparently, this program needed to read some kind of data from the diskette during the operation of the program. Well, I had figured out how to use one program; maybe someone else would know what to do with this one. It was time to call Golda again.

Legalities

"You what?" Golda exclaimed.

"I said that I tried to make copies of the programs I bought, but they don't work. The diskettes say that they are copy protected. What should I do?"

"Ella, I've got a program that might copy them, but don't you know that's illegal?"

"Illegal? Then why does the DOS have a copy command?"

"That's so you can copy DOS files and files that you create. Commercial programs that you purchase are protected under the law. When you buy a program, technically, you purchase the blank diskette that it comes on and the manufacturer is licensing you to use the program. The actual program code belongs to the manufacturer, who retains all rights to it."

"Wait a minute, Golda. Didn't you just say that you had a program that might copy them? Is that something you wrote yourself?"

"No, I bought it from Sneaky Pete Software. It's called The Replicator."

"I don't understand. If it's illegal to copy software, how can a company get away with making and selling a program that copies copy-protected software?"

"Well, it's really more complicated than what I told you. Software is extremely volatile and a user can be put to a great deal of expense and inconvenience if the only copy of a program happens to crash. Therefore, the law allows a user to make one archival copy of program, solely for the purpose of using in the event that the original fails to work. The makers of programs that circumvent copy protection schemes advertise that their products are only for this purpose. It's still illegal to use their program to make copies for use by other people on other computers."

"Golda, I can see how it would be illegal if I made copies and then sold them or gave them away to other people. But, how can it be illegal for me to copy them for use with my classes?"

"Making copies of those diskettes for use with your class amounts to the same thing as buying just one textbook and having it duplicated for use with your class. The development of a sophisticated software product can require a tremendous investment and sometimes takes over a year to bring to market. When you copy it, you are depriving the manufacturer of the profit that would have been made had you purchased it instead."

"Hold on a minute. I took a computer literacy class over at the University and the professor let us copy some programs for use during the course. He had us all sign a paper stating that we would return the copies for destruction at the end of the semester. Can't I do something like that?"

"Ella, your professor almost certainly knew that what he did was in violation of the licensing agreement that the manufacturer issued with the programs. But, he probably doubted the illegality of his actions. You see, a lot of these things have yet to be tested in court. You know how much of the law is based on interpretation. My best guess is that what he did was illegal and that he was taking a chance. He probably figured that there was very little probability of what he was doing coming to the attention of the manufacturer. He also probably figured that, even if it did, nothing would happen. What company wants to generate the kind of negative publicity that might come with suing an educational institution?"

"Well, if that's the case, who's to know if I just borrow your copy of The Replicator and make myself 14 archival copies for use with my class?"

"I'll know, you'll know, and most important of all, your students will know. Are you willing to set that kind of example for them? Also, we educators have a bad enough image with the public already. Do you want us to make things worse by being thieves and hypocrites?"

"No, I guess not. Well, I'll just give up on the one program. At least I've got the other."

"What do you mean? I thought you only had one copy of each."

"Oh, I forgot to tell you. One of the programs can only be used on one computer at a time because it constantly reads from the diskette. The other program resides entirely in memory, so, even though it's more work, I can boot the entire lab with one diskette."

"I hate to tell you this, Ella, but if you read your licensing agreement more carefully, you'll probably find that your plans are also in violation. Legally speaking loading a program into a computer's memory constitutes making a copy. Most manufacturers license you only to copy the program into the memory of one computer, and that means *one computer,* period. You're not supposed to use the program on different computers even if it's not at the same time. That means if you bought the program for use on a particular computer in the lab, you can't use it on any other computer."

"Oh, no! Let me look. . . . You're right. It says 'For Use On One Machine Only.' What am I going to do? What do other people do?"

"It's a sorry state of affairs, but many people, educators among them, routinely violate licensing agreements. Some even knowingly violate the law. In practical terms, the laws associated with computer software are unenforceable. People just know that they are not going to get caught. Either that, or they figure that the particular clause of the licensing agreement they are violating would never stand up in court. I, too, think that some of them probably wouldn't, but that's beside the point. What it boils down to is that individually, we have to decide for ourselves what is acceptable. I can tell you one thing, though. You're on your own if you decide to take any steps of questionable legality. The district will support only strict compliance with licensing agreements. If a product has an agreement that you just can't live with, then my advice is don't buy it."

"Well, I guess I'll just give up the entire idea of using computers and send these programs back for a refund."

"I'd hate to see you give up, Ella. Besides, you might have some difficulty getting refunds. If you'll recall, the programs were probably packaged so that you could read the licensing agreement without opening the package. Furthermore, the manufacturer probably takes the position that your opening of the package constitutes acceptance of the agreement. It's your responsibility to see that the product meets your needs."

"Boy, what a racket! First I can't use them, now I can't even send them back. I can't see how computers are ever going to become a force in education."

"I can understand how you feel, but there is some hope on the horizon. There are some things we can do. First of all, we educators have finally begun to learn that we need to budget funds for software acquisition instead of channeling every free dollar toward the purchase of hardware. Second, one major reason for all these problems to have developed in the first place was that the manufacturers were not prepared to deal with education. In the past, they haven't understood what our needs are. Now they are beginning to catch on. A number of companies are developing innovative licensing policies that make it realistic for schools to be able to purchase multiple copies. Some companies are just flat reducing their prices for us. They figure it's an investment in the future. Some farsighted companies are even giving away substantial numbers of products to schools. Some have joined forces with book publishing companies and are collaborating to produce integrated materials and software packages that are realistically priced. Believe me, both software and hardware manufacturers desperately want to be a part of education. But in order to do so, the bottom line is that they still have to be able to turn a profit."

Public Domain and User-Supported Software

Although informative, Golda's lecture about the software facts-of-life did nothing to help my problem. I asked her if there wasn't something else I could do.

"You know, there are other sources of software you can try," she said.

"Other sources? What are they?"

"There's an entire class of software that has been entered into the public domain. Anyone is free to copy, modify, and use them in any way whatsoever."

"Oh, I saw some of that stuff at the University. Most of it is just utility programs and games. I didn't see much that would be of use in the classroom."

"That's true, but there is a new kind of software that is beginning to appear that solves that problem. It is called user-supported software. The difference between this kind of software and public domain software is that it is not placed in the public domain. The authors have chosen to retain all rights, but they encourage copying and distributing their programs. Some of these guys are former professional programmers for software manufacturers, so the stuff they're turning out is often as good or better than anything else on the market at any price. They use a kind of honor system to generate funds. Most of the programs contain some kind of statement requesting that you send in a small registration fee to support their efforts if you plan to use their program. They figure that if only a small percentage of all copies are registered, they'll make more money than if their product has been distributed through normal channels. There's some very good software available under this format: word processors, spreadsheets, database managers, graphics programs, and more."

"What about educational software?"

"I'm afraid that's a weak link in the chain. There are a few educational user-supported programs floating around, but not many. I don't see why not, though. It seems to me that there must be thousand of teachers who have written good programs for their own use. The user-supported format would be an ideal way for them to get distribution."

"Wouldn't that be a lot of work, having to duplicate and distribute diskettes?"

"Yes, but you don't even have to do that if you don't want to. There are mail-order clearinghouses for user-supported and public domain software. Many of them advertise in nationally distributed magazines. There's even one that caters to educators. All you have to do is send your program to one of these places and they'll advertise and distribute it for you. Another option would be to place your program on a computer bulletin board, where interested users can download it."

"Why do people register when they can use the programs for free?"

"Usually, registration brings some other benefits with it. For example, some authors promise to send you the next program revision. Some grant you a fixed number of telephone calls for support or information. Others send you a typeset copy of the program manual. Registration details vary greatly among the different programs. They are controlled by the author's wishes."

"Where can I get some of these programs?"

"I'll send you the addresses of some mail-order clearinghouses. Also, I have a small library myself. I'll send you some copies."

Epilogue

Well, that's almost the end of my story. I'm making do this year with some public domain programs I obtained. When I looked at the diskettes that Golda sent me, I discovered that some of the educational programs had been written by a teacher in our district. I contacted her and she was willing to send me some other programs that have been very useful. She even modified some of them for me. This situation might seem unusual, but I'm beginning to see what Golda meant when she said that there must be many educators who have written good, useful programs that nobody knows about. Even Golda didn't know about this person in our own district!

Individual educators writing their own software seems like a stopgap measure to me. For computer use to reach its full potential in education, I think more commercial software manufacturers are going to have to come up with innovative distribution and pricing procedures. This game of copy-protection has to come to an end. We educators, too, must make a contribution. We must all become informed about copyright law and stop depriving programmers and manufacturers of their hard-earned profits.

Chapter Summary

There are many small, difficult details to be handled in the integration of computers into instruction. This is unfortunate, because they get in the way of the more important theme of using computers to enhance students' learning experiences. We hope that the material presented in this chapter has helped you to understand those details. We have covered the where, how, and why of placing computers in schools. We have talked about the most efficient arrangements of computers for given instructional tasks. We have examined the importance of reviewing software on the basis of technical and instructional characteristics. Finally, we have discussed many of the problems concerning the acquisition, maintenance, and use of microcomputers and microcomputer software.

Chapter Review

Knowledge Exercises

1. State strengths and weaknesses of the one-computer classroom.

   Answer: It makes the computer theoretically available to every student in the classroom, but it taxes the management skills of the teacher to the utmost. Many teachers are intimidated by the machine, and even those technically competent have difficulty using the machine effectively since most software doesn't give the teacher a report of how the student performed. However, computer projects, classroom demonstrations, and selected group activities are possible.

2. State the strengths and weaknesses of the dedicated classroom.

   Answer: It lends itself best to tight security, but may well be the most inefficient arrangement of all. Neither a single teacher nor that teacher's students need computers 100 percent of the time.

3. State the strengths and weaknesses of the computer resource laboratory.

   Answer: Since all teachers have access to this classroom set of computers, the resource lab is the most efficient use of hardware and software. The two major problems are that careful scheduling and management are required and there can be a problem with security. Some schools have answered these problems by designating a teacher or an aide as a lab manager.

4. State the strengths and weaknesses of the teacher workroom.

   Answer: With limited resources, this arrangement is often seen as just one more machine that is not available to students; however, many times teachers are expected to teach with computers without being given sufficient time to develop personal skills. A computer in a teacher work area also gives the teacher time to prepare for instruction without student interruption. Indeed, if a school has only one computer designated for instruction, the teacher work area is where it belongs.

5. What are some issues to consider concerning the power supply when preparing a computer lab?

   Answer: Plan from the beginning for the lab to have its own power supply. Ideally, every computer should be on a circuit that is specially treated to provide flawless service. A master power control will save wear and tear on the computer's off/on switches and it is easy to shut everything down at the end of the day. Don't rely on extension cords; have additional outlets installed either at table height on the wall of the room or have the power dropped from the ceiling with special posts for protection.

6. What are some issues to consider concerning the environment when preparing a computer lab?

   Answer: Keep the computers in a cool, clean, vibration-free environment, away from dust, dirt, and smoke. Be sure to position system units and monitors so they are well ventilated. Protect both hardware and software from static electricity. Be sure the computers are away from possible flooding or leaking, ideally not on the first or top floor of a building and never where there are exposed pipes overhead.

7. What are some issues to consider concerning furniture when preparing a computer lab?

   Answer: When funding is limited (When isn't it?), specialized computer furniture should not be a high priority. Good, sturdy tables and chairs are fine for most applications. An exception might be vocational training. Lockable cabinets are best for storing software, thus discouraging illegal copying of software as well as outright theft.

8. What are some miscellaneous issues related to preparing a computer lab?

   Answer: Every lab should have at least one fire extinguisher, preferably halon. If you're planning on telecommunications activities in your lab, a direct dedicated phone line will be necessary, tone-dial if possible.

9. Name three important technical characteristics to consider when reviewing software.

   Answer: Answers will vary, but might include ease of use, reliability, information displays, and documentation.

10. Name three important instructional characteristics to consider when reviewing software.

    Answer: Answers will vary, but might include instructional purpose, program objectives, content, and design.

Thought Exercises

1. Which arrangement of computers makes the most sense for a given specific group of students? Support your answer.
2. You have just been asked to design a new computer laboratory at your school. Write a plan and justify each recommendation that you make, since the principal will have final say on how much money can be spent on the project. Also, submit a sketch of the room showing placement of student computers, location of the teacher's desk and computer, outlets, windows, and door, and any other pertinent items.
3. Describe a particular instructional task or situation that is best suited for each of the types of computer arrangements discussed in this chapter. Support your choices.
4. Use the information provided in Chapters 7–9 and the information provided in this chapter to design a model for reviewing software designed expressly for education.

Activities

1. Select at least two pieces of software (at least one of them should be an educational program) and investigate the company's licensing agreement

and preview policy for educators. What steps can a school district or teacher take to obtain access to more software?

2. Visit a computer laboratory in a school, comparing the setup with the recommendations in this chapter. Write a brief description, justifying any differences that you feel are necessary because of conditions in the school.
3. Visit or join a computer users' group and obtain some public domain or user-supported software. Evaluate it for its applicability to education and make judgments about how well it compares to similar commercial products.
4. Use the form that you developed in Thought Exercise 4 to review three software packages of your choice. Assess the usefulness of your model and describe possible refinements.

Projects

1. Write a report covering copyright laws as they pertain to computer software. Cite your references.
2. Interview a school district computer resource person to discuss how he or she is preparing the district to meet the demands of the future. Ask about such points as previewing software, obtaining multiple copies of software at reasonable prices, teacher training, and hardware purchase policies. Write a report of your findings and share it with other teachers in your class.
3. Obtain and compare some software review forms or models used by various agencies that publish software reviews.

Bibliography

Adams, D. "Choosing Software? Let Your Students Help." *Electronic Education* (November–December 1985): 12–13. Provides a form to be used with your students for reviewing software.

Bothwell, Mary. "Jefferson High School's Computer Program: A Curriculum Development Model for the Future." *The Computing Teacher* (October 1982): 20–25. A model program in a high school setting is outlined with emphasis on the integration of computers into the total program.

Bramble, William J., and Emanuel Mason. *Computers in Schools.* New York: McGraw-Hill, 1985. A comprehensive treatment of the field with specific guidelines for setting up a computer classroom.

Cauchon, Paul A. "Computers at Canterbury School." *The Computing Teacher* (May 1983): 71–74. The article discusses hardware configuration and presents a course outline for literacy.

Coburn, Peter, and Peter Kelman. *Practical Guide to Computers in Education.* Reading, Mass.: Addison-Wesley, 1985. Good discussion of the issues involved in setting up a computer lab.

Dauite, Collette. *Writing and Computers.* Reading, Mass.: Addison-Wesley, 1985. Chapter 13 provides a useful discussion of designing computer writing environments.

Dearborn, D. E. "How States Evaluate Software." *Electronic Learning* (October 1985): 27. State departments of education have several ways of helping districts evaluate software. Discussed are seven different ways, and the states that employ them.

East, Phillip. "Ethical and Social Concerns." Topic presented before the Association of Computer Machinery, January, 1981. Presents the necessity of teacher stimulated discussions on privacy, human rights, and moral and legal issues surrounding the use of computers.

Finkel, LeRoy. "Buying a Micro: What Every Educator Should Know." *Electronic Learning* (1983): 26–28. Selecting a dealer, demonstration materials, and the creation of a districtwide computer selection committee are topics covered.

Finkel, Leroy. "When Is a Pirate a Thief?" *Electronic Learning* (1985): 26, 28. Suggestions on district software copyright policy are presented.

"Guidelines to Get Your Computer Center Organized." *Teaching and Computers* (1985): 10–12. Fifteen guidelines are given for setting up a computer center. Maintenance and security tips are set forth.

Hannah, Larry, and Charles Matus. "Teaching Ethics in the Computer Classroom." *Classroom Computer Learning* (April–May 1984): 33–36. By discussing real-life computer related issues, students can examine their values and develop reasoning and decision-making skills.

Harris, Thorne D. "You Should Know What the Copyright Law Says." *Classroom Computer Learning.* (October 1984): 16–20. An attorney addresses the legal issues a teacher faces every time software is booted up.

Heller, Norma. "Computers in an Urban Library Media Center." *The Computing Teacher* (February 1983): 51–55. A discussion of one example of hardware placement.

Hively, W. "TESS Points the Way to Quality Software." *Electronic Education* (October 1985): 10. Discusses the usefulness of The Educational Software Selector (TESS).

Kreidler, William J. "Teaching Computer Ethics." *Electronic Learning* (January 1984): 54–57. Thirteen classroom activities to teach various ethical aspects are given.

Lent, John. "A Computer Center from Scratch." *Instructor* (March 1983): 67–70. Examples of how teachers in four different schools set up computer learning environments.

Papert, Seymour. *Mindstorms: Children, Computers, and Powerful Ideas.* New York: Basic Books, 1980. The classic book by the author of Logo contains his discovery philosophy and practical examples.

Phillips, Wayne. "How to Manage Effectively with Twenty-five Students and One Computer." *The Computing Teacher* (March 1983): 32. Various strategies are presented for managing hardware under poor situations.

"Planting a Software Evaluation Exchange Development (SEED) in the South." *Electronic Learning* (November–December 1985): 8–9. Discusses a program that seven Southern states have developed to pool their knowledge about reviewing software.

Post, P. E., and M. I. Sarapin. "Writing and Evaluating Educational Software: Some Key Elements." Paper presented at the Annual Conference of the American Vocational Association, Anaheim, Calif., December 3, 1983.

Radin, Stephen, and Fayvian Lee. *Computers in the Classroom: A Survival Guide for Teachers.* Chicago: Science Research Associates, 1984. In addition to explaining BASIC programming, this text provides guidelines for funding and equipping a computer facility.

Reynolds, K. E. "How to Use the Software Evaluation Form." *Science and Children* (September 1985): 18–20. Describes what to look for in evaluating software.

Sirotnik, K. A. "Evaluating Computer Courseware." *Educational Leadership* (April 1985): 39–42. Discusses subjecting computers and software to the same evaluation criteria used for other aspects of the curricula.

"Study Examines How Teachers Organize Computer Use." *Electronic Learning* (February 1985): 16–21. News article referring to Henry Becker's work at John Hopkins. With various classroom settings, different organizational strategies are necessary.

Sullivan, David R., and T. G. Lewis. *Computing Today* Boston: Houghton Mifflin, 1985. Chapter 17 of this comprehensive text provides a good discussion of software piracy and computer trespass.

Whiteside, C. "Software Checklist: An Evaluator's Best Tool." *Electronic Education* (March–April 1985): 20–21. Provides a reproducible checklist for evaluating software.

APPENDIX
BASIC Minibook

This appendix is for those individuals who wish to explore BASIC further than what was presented in the main text. It is organized in exactly the same fashion as the chapter on BASIC (Chapter 5).

Appendix Lesson 1

Preliminaries

In the text, we said that a good programming language must have statements that can be used to create programs that can repeat a task. BASIC meets that criterion with the FOR . . . NEXT statement. These statements are used in conjunction with sets of numbers that indicate how many times the task is to be repeated. For example, if we said, "Write your name one time for each of the numbers in the set 1 through 10," you would, if you felt agreeable, write your name 10 times. If, in a program, we say:

```
FOR I=1 TO 20
(do something)
NEXT I
```

then the program will start with I = 1 and proceed to do the *something* once. When the statement NEXT I is encountered, the program will increase the number for I by 1 and do the *something* again. This procedure will continue until the task has been completed 20 times. Notice that the task you want repeated must be indicated between the FOR and the NEXT statements. The set of statements formed by a FOR . . . NEXT, and the statements in between is called a FOR . . . NEXT *loop*. Why is this name intuitively pleasing? The I represents each of the values 1–20, one-at-a-time, as the task is being completed. I is called a *variable*. We will discuss variables in more depth in Appendix Lesson 2.

Discovery 1: Color Me BASIC

Objectives. In this lesson, you will learn to use FOR . . . NEXT statements to repeat tasks. You will also learn to use the COLOR, SOUND, SCREEN, and BEEP statements to add a little zest to your programs.

Materials. Your formatted data diskette, and a little imagination.

1. Read Program 8 on the Program Disk carefully. Analyze the purpose of each line and the purpose of each character in the line. Predict what you think the program will do when executed. Then, run the program to find out whether or not you are correct. Notice how the statement on line 130 has been indented two spaces. This is a common programming practice to enhance program readability. The purpose of the indention is to emphasize which line is being repeated.

```
90 REM PROGRAM 8 - WOLF
100 PRINT "The boy cried,"
110 PRINT
120 FOR I=1 TO 20
130  PRINT "WOLF,",
140 NEXT I
150 PRINT
160 PRINT "But nobody came!"
170 END
```

2. Now enter Program 9 and run the program. Compare the effort that is involved in entering the program to the amount of work done by the program.

```
90 REM PROGRAM 9 - DR. M'KROBYRTS
100 FOR I=1 TO 500
110  PRINT "I promise never to be late to Dr. M'Krobyrts' class again."
120 NEXT I
130 END
```

3. Now, load Program 10. You will revise the program so that the cars change colors. You will use a FOR . . . NEXT loop to repeatedly print cars on the display. (*Hint:* Insert lines and RENUM.)

```
90 PROGRAM 10 - CARS IN COLOR
100 CLS
110 FOR N=1 TO 15
120    COLOR N,3
130    CLS
140    PRINT "          ____     "
150    PRINT "     --__/_¦_o\__  "
160    PRINT "   -- /__________]"
170    PRINT "    --   O      O  "
180    FOR I=1 TO 500
190    NEXT I
200 NEXT I
210 END
```

4. Did you notice a vacant spot on the screen? How can you account for this spot?

5. What is the purpose of the FOR . . . NEXT loop in lines 180–190?

6. Now let's get a little more complicated. You will build a skyscraper using the FOR . . . NEXT statement. Enter the program and analyze what each statement accomplishes. Draw a sketch to show what you think the skyscraper will look like when the program is executed. Decide why the NEXT statement is in line 170 rather than line 200. Run Program 11 to see if your conclusions are correct.

```
90 REM PGM 11 - SKYSCRAPER
100 CLS
110 COLOR 4,1
120 PRINT "            ____________________"
130 PRINT "            {                   }"
140 FOR I = 1 TO 8
150   PRINT "            { [] [] [] [] [] [] }"
160   PRINT "            {                   }"
170 NEXT I
180 PRINT "            {        [~~~~]     }"
190 PRINT "            {_______[____]______}"
200 PRINT
210 COLOR 14,1
220 PRINT " New York, New York! What a wonderful town!"
230 END
```

7. Now you will use FOR . . . NEXT statements to print your name several times on the display. To accomplish this, you will also use the LOCATE statement. Instead of using specific values in the LOCATE statement, you will use a variable: I. The value of this variable is incremented by one each time the program goes through the loop, so naturally this changes the position of the printed message on the display. Before you run the program, predict its output. Sketch what you think will happen. Run Program 12 to see if your conclusions are correct.

```
90 REM PROGRAM 12 - YOUR NAME
100 CLS
110 FOR I=1 TO 15
120   COLOR I
130   LOCATE I,I
140   PRINT "(your name)"
150 NEXT I
160 END
```

8. You can design FOR . . . NEXT loops so that the increment is some number other than 1. Try this: Modify lines 110 and 140 to read as follows:

```
110 FOR I=1 TO 15 STEP 2
140   PRINT I;"(your name)"
```

Run the program to see what happens. Experiment with this program line, changing the value of the STEP several times.

9. Now try this: Modify line 110 to read as follows:

```
110 FOR I=15 TO 1 STEP -3
```

Run the revised program and observe the results.

10. As we saw in Program 12, FOR... NEXT statements can be used to build loops within loops. Using this technique, all kinds of complicated tasks can be repeated. Enter Program 13 to see the power of this idea. Notice that the first FOR... NEXT statement directs the computer to repeat a task 24 times. The variable used in this loop is I. So that you can tell when this statement is being executed, we have inserted a statement that will print an asterisk every time the task is initiated. The primary task to be performed also involves a FOR... NEXT loop directing the computer to print the letter *C* 60 times. The variable for this loop is J. Every time an asterisk is printed on the same line, J is incremented. The program outputs a heap of Cs even though only one has been entered. A warning: This program is bound to make you C-sick!

```
90 REM PROGRAM 13 - C-sick
100 CLS
110 FOR I=1 TO 24
120  FOR J=1 TO 60
130   PRINT "C";
140  NEXT J
150  PRINT "*"
160 NEXT I
```

11. Enter Program 14, one more program that has loops within loops. Call it Loopa De Lou.

```
90 REM PROGRAM 14 - LOOPA DE LOU
100 CLS
110 FOR I=1 TO 10
120  PRINT "Once more, with feeling!"
130  FOR J=1 TO 3
140   SOUND I*J*100,1
150  NEXT J
160 NEXT I
170 PRINT "The party's over for awhile."
180 END
```

12. Enter Program 15. In this program, a FOR... NEXT loop is used to show off the colors of the IBM display.

```
90 REM PROGRAM 15 - COLORS
100 CLS
110 FOR BACKGROUND=0 TO 15
120  FOR BORDER=0 TO 7
130   FOR FOREGROUND=0 TO 31
140    COLOR FOREGROUND,BACKGROUND,BORDER
150    PRINT "COLOR ME HAPPY!";
160   NEXT FOREGROUND
170  NEXT BORDER
180 NEXT BACKGROUND
190 END
```

13. Sometimes the most elegant and useful is the most simple. We will end this session with such a program. You saw it in Program 10. What is a FOR . . . NEXT loop with nothing inside? It is called a *time loop* or *delay loop*. Experiment with the values given in line 130 of Program 16.

```
90 REM PROGRAM 16 - TIME LOOP
100 COLOR 7,2
110 CLS
120 COLOR 7,0
125 LOCATE 10,1
130 FOR DELAY=400 TO 1 STEP -5
140  PRINT " ";
150  SOUND 50000!/DELAY,1
160  FOR TIME=1 TO DELAY
170  NEXT TIME
180 NEXT DELAY
190 END
```

Programming Particulars

In this lesson, we have tried to demonstrate how a microcomputer can be programmed to repeat a task. The programming tool we used was the FOR . . . NEXT statement. Normally, the variable in a FOR . . . NEXT loop is incremented by 1 each time the loop is executed. Some of the examples in this lesson demonstrated how the STEP option makes the variable increment or even decrement by values other than 1. For example, the statement

```
FOR N=20 TO 1 STEP -3
```

causes N to *count down* from 20 to 1 by threes.

While exploring the FOR . . . NEXT statement, we have introduced a number of important ideas. If programmed to do so, most IBM microcomputers can produce and change colors, they can make sounds, and they can process numerical information stored as variables. In Appendix Lessons 2 and 5, we will discuss variables and sound. Here, however, we will try to get some closure on color. If you have a color monitor, then there are many options open to you. First of all, you can be working on one of three screens: SCREEN 0, SCREEN 1, or SCREEN 2. Normally, SCREEN 0 is the default. That is, when you enter BASIC, you are in SCREEN 0. This screen is devoted to text and is called the *text screen*. You cannot perform true graphics on this screen, such as drawing circles or intricate patterns. Those types of images, often called *bit-mapped* graphics, are possible in SCREEN 1 and SCREEN 2, which we will explore in Appendix Lesson 5.

On SCREEN 0, You can only use keyboard characters to create graphic images that you want to deliver. Even so, there are many colors at your disposal. The COLOR statement allows you to make three choices: you can choose foreground color, background color, and border color. Color numbers 0–7 are available for the foreground, background, and border. Colors 8–15 are lighter shades of the colors assigned to the numbers 0–7. These colors are only available as foreground and border colors. The table that follows gives number-hue assignments. Adding 16 to a foreground color makes the characters flash. The syntax of the COLOR statement is

```
COLOR foreground,background,border
```

Color number	Color	Color number	Color
0	Black	8	Dark Grey
1	Blue	9	Light Blue
2	Green	10	Light Green
3	Cyan	11	Light Cyan
4	Red	12	Light Red
5	Magenta	13	Light Magenta
6	Gold-Brown	14	Yellow
7	White-Grey	15	Bright White

Program line 200 will create a display with a bright white foreground, a blue background, and a magenta border.

```
200 COLOR 15,1,5
```

You don't have to specify all three of these options, but when there are omissions, the statement must include commas so that it is clear what the desired options are. For example, in

```
200 COLOR 20,1
```

the foreground is changed to flashing red, the background is changed to blue, and the border is not changed. In

```
200 COLOR ,,2
```

the foreground and background are not changed. The border is changed to green. In

```
200 COLOR ,3,12
```

the foreground color is not changed, the background is changed to cyan, and the border is changed to light red.

The SOUND statement has the following syntax:

```
SOUND f,d
```

The *f* stands for frequency expressed in hertz (cycles/second) and the *d* is for duration in seconds. The BEEP statement produces one general purpose tone.

Appendix Lesson 2

Preliminaries

So far we have been concerned with controlling the way text appears on the screen. The biggest idea we have worked with is the idea of building programs that repeat tasks. We have not yet explored programs that process information nor have we discussed programs that interact with the user. In this lesson you are going to learn some BASIC statements that allow the creation of powerful programs. The LET statement allows us to define *variables*. For example, the following statement assigns the value 25 to the variable X:

```
200 LET X=25
```

The concept of variables is sometimes confusing, but this confusion can be eliminated if you carefully distinguish between the variable's name and the data that are assigned to it. In the example just given, X is the *name* for the variable and 25 is the assigned *value*, or *data*. To get a better feeling for this distinction, think of a safe-deposit box in a bank. The safe-deposit box may have a name like X. This name allows you to identify the location of the box. What's in the box is another matter. There may be 25 dollars in the box. When you use the LET statement, the computer identifies a location in memory, gives it a variable name, and stores in that location the data you have assigned to the variable. Often, you will want to change the contents of a variable just as you may want to change the contents of your safe-deposit box. You can do so by using the LET statement again. In this lesson you will discover how this works. It is important to note that the variable in a LET statement always goes on the left of the equal sign. In other words, the statement

```
LET 25=X
```

is incorrect.

There are two kinds of variables: numeric and alphanumeric, or *string*. *Numeric variables* are ones that have number assignments. String variables are ones that have data assignments that are not numbers. *String variable* is a good name since a string variable can represent any string of characters. To let the computer know that a given variable is a string variable, the variable name is always terminated with a dollar sign ($) and the assigned data are enclosed in double quotation marks. Let's look at some examples.

```
10 LET X=32              (Numeric variable named X, value assigned is 32)
10 LET X$="Bonnie"       (String variable named X$, data assigned is Bonnie.)
```

There is much more that you need to know about strings, but we will save that information for Appendix Lesson 4. In this lesson we will concentrate more on numeric variables. We will also introduce you to the INPUT statement. This statement allows values to be assigned to variables interactively, while a program is executing. With this powerful tool we can build programs that can collect information from the outside environment to be processed. It's time for us to stop talking and you to start doing.

Discovery 2: INPUT and VARIABLES

Objective. In this lesson, you will learn to use the INPUT and LET statements. You will also learn about numerical and string variables and variable arrays.

Materials. Your formatted diskette.

1. Enter Program 17. Make sure that you copy each character in every line.

```
90 REM PROGRAM 17 - VARIABLES
100 LET X=3
110 LET Y=10
120 LET Z=X+Y
130 PRINT Z
140 END
```

2. Now enter Program 18. This program is like Program 17 but it is more flexible. When you run this program, it will sit and wait for the user to input values for X and Y. The INPUT statement displays a question mark on the screen, and awaits your input for X. After you type in a value for X and press [Enter], then the process repeats for Y. Run the program to see how the INPUT statement works.

```
90 REM PROGRAM 18 - INPUT VARIABLES
100 INPUT X
110 INPUT Y
120 LET Z=X+Y
130 PRINT Z
140 END
```

3. Go back to Program 18. Eliminate line 100 and change line 110 to read

```
110 INPUT X,Y
```

Run the revised program and tell what effect these changes have.

4. In Program 19 you will INPUT strings. You should notice this form of INPUT allows you to display a prompt before the question mark. You should also notice that variable names are used that relate to the data that are requested. Naming variables this way makes them easier to remember, which is convenient when you are writing a complex program. This technique can also be used for numeric variables. Enter the program and run it to see how the INPUT statements work.

```
90 REM PROGRAM 19 - DESSERT
100 CLS
110 INPUT"What is your first name";NAYME$
120 INPUT "What is your favorite dessert";DESSERT$
130 CLS
140 LOCATE 12,1
150 PRINT NAYME$;" likes to chow down on";DESSERT$;"."
160 END
```

5. Program 20 involves INPUT statements requiring the user to input numbers and strings. The program also involves variables. Enter and run the program.

```
10 REM PROGRAM 20 - HEARTBEAT
100 CLS
110 WIDTH 80
120 INPUT "What is your first name";NAYME$
130 INPUT "How old are you";AGE
140 CLS
150 LET HEARTBT=60*24*365*AGE
160 LOCATE 10,1
170 PRINT NAYME$;", Your heart has beat about";HEARTBT;"times."
180 LET HEARTLF=60*24*365*72
190 LOCATE 12,1
200 PRINT "It will probably beat";HEARTLF-HEARTBT";more times."
210 END
```

What's this? If you are 32, this program states that your heart has beat 1.68192E + 07 times! That funny-looking number is how the computer writes *exponential notation.* It means 1.68192 times 10 to the seventh power. That equals 1.68192 times 10,000,000, or 16,819,200. The IBM PC, like many microcomputers, automatically displays numbers larger than a certain fixed value in exponential notation. Experiment with your computer to find that value. Note the use of the asterisk to signify multiplication. If you are accustomed to normal algebraic notation, you're going to find yourself leaving out multiplication signs. The computer treats AB as a variable distinct from A and B, not the product of A times B. Addition and subtraction are indicated in the customary fashion. The symbol for division is the slash (/).

6. Program 21 uses an INPUT statement within a FOR . . . NEXT loop. This is a handy tool. The program accepts the input of five scores. The total number of points, of course, starts off at 0. Each time a score is given, the total number of points is updated to reflect the new score. Notice the peculiar LET statement in line 150. This form is called an *accumulator* because the expression

```
TOTAL=TOTAL+SCORE
```

takes the last value of the variable TOTAL and adds to it the new score that is entered. Then the new number is assigned to the variable TOTAL. This continues until all the scores are entered. Then the average is found in line 170. Enter the program and run it a few times. Be sure you understand how it works. For example, why does line 170 divide by I-1 instead of just I? The techniques applied in this program can be used in many situations.

```
90 REM PROGRAM 21 - SCORES
100 CLS
110 LET TOTAL=0
120 FOR I=1 TO 5
130   PRINT "Score ";I;"=";
140   INPUT SCORE
```

```
150  LET TOTAL=TOTAL+SCORE
160 NEXT I
170 LET AVERAGE=TOTAL/(I-1)
180 PRINT "Your average is ";AVERAGE
190 END
```

7. As we have said many times, the computer can solve problems that are very tedious and time-consuming for human beings. The next program will illustrate this point. For this problem, assume that you run a sandwich shop. You want to be able to tell the computer how many and what kinds of sandwiches you are prepared to make on a given day. You want to furnish the same information for drinks. You want the computer to list all the drink and sandwich combinations that are possible. After you study the list, you will decide on a daily special.

Using INPUT, LET and FOR... NEXT statements, we can build a very economical program that will do a lot of work and will save human time. We are also going to cheat a bit by using a concept that we have not introduced yet. This is the idea of *arrays.* In line 170 of Program 22, we request input, using a variable, SAND$(I), that is obviously related to the variable I. We do likewise with the variable, DRINK$(J). This variable is related to the variable J. Lines 120, 140, 220, and 280 will also look a little strange. Try not to be too concerned with these lines right now. The important thing is to enter this program accurately and recognize its power. For very large values of both the variables, SAND and DRINK, the program will crank out lists of sandwiches and drinks that would take you precious hours to compile.

```
90 REM PROGRAM 22 - SANDWICHES
100 CLS
110 INPUT "How many sandwiches can you make today";SAND
120 DIM SAND$(SAND)
130 INPUT "How many drinks can you make today";DRINK
140 DIM DRINK$(DRINK)
150 FOR I=1 TO SAND
160  PRINT "What kind of sandwich is #";I;
170  INPUT SAND$(I)
180 NEXT I
190 CLS
200 FOR J=1 TO DRINK
210  PRINT "What kind of drink is #";J;
220  INPUT DRINK$(J)
230 NEXT J
240 CLS
250 PRINT "Get ready for the list!"
260 FOR I=1 TO SAND
270  FOR J=1 TO DRINK
280   PRINT SAND$(I),DRINK$(J)
290  NEXT J
300 NEXT I
310 PRINT "That's all y'all."
320 END
```

8. Okay, now let's talk about arrays. The previous program would be pretty clumsy if we had to use a different variable name for each kind of sandwich and each kind of drink. We would also have to define ahead of time the maximum number of each we wish to have possible, and put enough variables in the program to accommodate that maximum number, whether or not that many are used each time. For example, to accommodate up to 10 different drinks, we might use variables like:

DRINKONE$, DRINKTWO$, DRINKTHREE$, . . . , DRINKTEN$

If you have difficulty seeing how this would be a problem, try rewriting Program 22 in this fashion, without the arrays. You will find that the problem very quickly becomes unmanageable. Variable arrays allow us to group large numbers of variables under a common variable name and then refer to them as elements of the array. In Program 22, an array named SAND$(*n*) was used to store all the different kinds of sandwiches. Sandwich #1 was stored as the first element of the array, SAND$(1). Sandwich #2 as SAND$(2), and so on. Once all the different kinds of sandwiches are entered, they can all be referred to with the same variable name, SAND$(*n*), and differentiated between by their respective element numbers. While this might seem difficult, and Program 22 may look complicated, it does make the task a manageable one. The DIM statements in lines 120 and 140 are used to tell the computer the *dimensions* of an array. These statements are optional for arrays with fewer than 11 elements (0–10), but must be used for arrays larger than that.

9. Here's another program that uses an array for you to study. It is a modification of Program 21. Program 21 loses all the individual scores as you enter them. What if you want to keep them? An array is handy for that. Also, notice that the average is now computed by reading the scores out of the array, not as the scores are entered. Load Program 21 and edit it to get this.

```
90 REM PROGRAM 21R - SCORES REVISED
100 CLS
110 DIM SCORES(5)
120 LET TOTAL=0
130 FOR I=1 TO 5
140  PRINT "Score";I;"=";
150  INPUT SCORES(I)
160 NEXT I
170 CLS
180 FOR I=1 TO 5
190  PRINT "SCORE";I;"=";SCORES(I)
200  LET TOTAL=TOTAL+SCORES(I)
210 NEXT I
220 LET AVERAGE=TOTAL/(I-1)
230 PRINT "YOUR AVERAGE IS";AVERAGE
240 END
```

Programming Particulars

Let's talk a little more formally about variable names, because there are some restrictions on them. You may have wondered why the variable NAYME$ was used in Programs 19 and 20 instead of just NAME$. This is because NAME is a *reserved word*. There are many words that are reserved for the exclusive use of the BASIC interpreter. Most of them are the names of the various commands and statements. You may not use these words as variable names. A complete listing of them can be found in the BASIC manual. Just look in the index under *reserved words.*

IBM BASIC can discriminate between variable names of up to 40 characters in length. This means that you can create very descriptive variable names if you wish to do so. For example, you might wish to use names like PROFITSAFTERTAXES or CHIEF.OPERATING.OFFICER$. By recognizing up to 40 characters, the computer knows the difference even between these variables:

```
PRODUCT.IDENTIFICATION.NUMBER.0000000001
PRODUCT.IDENTIFICATION.NUMBER.0000000002
```

Attempting to use variable names of greater than 40 characters will result in a syntax error.

Appendix Lesson 3

Preliminaries

The IBM PC is excellent at arithmetic. It can add, subtract, multiply, and divide very efficiently. In the last lesson you saw how to use special symbols for conveying these operations to the computer. Besides the basic operations, the computer can find roots and powers of numbers. Certainly, you are familiar with the four fundamental operations, but you may not be as familiar with finding roots and powers. A *root* of a number is a special factor of that number. For example, the square root of 16 is one of two equal factors of 16. That is,

4 * 4 = 16

so 4 is a square root of 16. The cube root of 27 is 3, since 3 is one of three equal factors of 27, that is,

3 * 3 * 3 = 27

The fourth root of 16 is 2 since

2 * 2 * 2 * 2 = 16

A *power* of a number is found by using the number itself as a factor. In the number sentence

3 * 3 = 9

the 3 is used as a factor twice, so 9 is the second power of 3. We express it this way: "3 raised to the 2nd power is 9." To get the computer to evaluate roots or powers, you define a variable and use the PRINT statement. In any case, you must know how to write numerical expressions that represent powers and roots. Expressions for both roots and powers are written in terms of powers.

An expression for the 4th power of 3 is 3^4. If you want to store this power as a variable, you do something like this.

```
LET X=3^4
```

The 3 is referred to as the *base* and the 4 is called the *exponent*. An expression for the 4th root of 256 is 256^(1/4). To indicate that a root is desired, we write a fraction using 4 as a denominator and 1 as a numerator. This is because taking the 4th root of a number is the same as raising the number to the 1/4th power. If you want to store the root as a computer variable you do something like this.

```
LET X=256^(1/4)
```

The computer is very systematic and routinely does tasks in a certain order. When computing, as long as there are no parentheses, brackets, or braces, the computer will evaluate expressions in a specific order. First, the computer looks for and evaluates powers and roots from left to right, then it computes products and quotients, and finally sums and differences. For example, the expression

6 * 4 + 3 ^ 5 − 7

will be computed as follows:

6 * 4 + 3 ^ 5 −7

6 * 4 + 243 −7 *(The 5th power of 3 is computed.)*

24 + 243 −7 *(Then 6 times 4 is computed.)*

267 −7 *(Next the sum is computed.)*

260 *(Finally, subtraction is computed.)*

When parentheses and other symbols of inclusion are involved in a numerical expression, the computer starts with the innermost set and computes from the inside out. Here is an example to give you the idea.

((4 * 5) ^ 2 − 20)/(3 + 7)

(20 ^ 2 − 20)/ 10 *(Compute 4*5 and 3+7.)*

(400 − 20)/ 10 *(Raise 20 to the 2nd power.)*

380/10 *(Subtract 20 from 400.)*

38 *(Divide 380 by 10.)*

These concepts will become clearer as you work through this lesson. As you enter and run the programs, you will profit most by making careful and detailed observations.

Discovery 3: Number Fun

Objective. In this lesson, you will learn to write numerical expressions for the computer to evaluate. In some expressions, you will use symbols of inclusion. You will also learn to define a variable using a numerical expression.

Materials. Your formatted diskette.

1. Enter and run each of the programs. Make sure you know the answer to each of the questions that is asked before moving on to another program.
2. Program 23 is a reminder. Its purpose is to remind you that whenever the PRINT statement is used and quotation marks are not used, then the intention is to print data assigned to a variable or to print a number. What symbols are used in programs to indicate multiplication and division?

```
90 REM PROGRAM 23 - FUN
100 CLS
110 PRINT 8*4
120 PRINT 8+4
130 LET A=8-4
140 PRINT A
150 LET A$="Computing is fun."
160 PRINT A$
170 LET B$="8/4"
180 PRINT B$
190 PRINT 8/4
200 END
```

3. Read Program 24. Predict the results of each print statement. Enter and run to check your predictions.

```
90 REM PROGRAM 24 - ENOUGH
100 CLS
110 LET A=3*9-6
120 PRINT A
130 LET B=3*(9-6)
140 PRINT B
150 PRINT "B=";B
160 PRINT A+B
170 PRINT A;"+";B
180 PRINT "That's enough printing for one program!"
190 END
```

4. Enter Program 25 exactly as you see it. Try to RUN it. See what happens and tell what's wrong.

```
90 REM PROGRAM 25 - FIXIT
100 CLS
110 PRINT Do not worry, I can be fixed!
120 END
```

5. Predict the results of each print statement in Program 26. Enter the program and run it to check your predictions.

```
90 REM PROGRAM 26 - THANK GOODNESS
100 CLS
110 PRINT 3+4^2
120 PRINT (3+4)^2
130 PRINT 6+18/3
140 PRINT (6+18)/3
150 PRINT 2^5-4
160 PRINT 2^(5-4)
170 PRINT 3^5-4^(1/2)
180 PRINT 3^(5-4)^(1/2)
190 PRINT 3^5-(4^1/2)
200 PRINT 3+4-6/2
210 PRINT (3+4-6)/2
220 PRINT "The end is here, thank goodness."
230 END
```

6. Parentheses can be placed in each of the numerical expressions given in Program 27 so that the resulting numerical expression will equal 17. Place the parentheses so that when the program is executed, each print statement yields 17. If a statement does not need parentheses, explain why.

```
90 REM PROGRAM 27 - PARENTHESES
100 CLS
110 PRINT 3*2+4-1
120 PRINT 3*2+2*2+7
130 PRINT 3^3-2+8
140 PRINT 1/2*40-3
150 PRINT 24/3+16^1/2+5
160 PRINT 3*5+4^1/2
170 END
```

7. Program 28 is a simple program, yet it shows off the capability of the computer. Enter and run the program. Analyze it carefully so that you understand what it does.

```
90 REM PROGRAM 28 - ROOTS
100 CLS
110 FOR I=1 TO 25
120  PRINT I;"squared is";I^2
130  PRINT "The square root of";I,"is";I^(1/2)
140 NEXT I
150 END
```

Programming Particulars

Most of the work a computer does is with numerical expressions, so it is important that you can write such expressions accurately. Two important things to remember follow:

1. You can assign the value of a numerical expression to a variable.
2. When the PRINT statement is used with a numerical expression not enclosed in quotation marks, the print statement will evaluate the expression.

Appendix Lesson 4

Preliminaries

Arithmetic is not all that is mathematical about the IBM PC family. IBM BASIC permits the use of functions. Some functions are built into the system and some can be defined by the user. A *function* is a routine that, once defined, can be used over and over again. Say that I'm going to double any number you tell me. We could call this the Double It function. You say 3, I say 6. You say 2, I say 4. In this case, we would say that Double It is the function and the number that you supply is the *operand*. So:

DOUBLEIT (4) = 8
DOUBLEIT (.3) = .6

Not all functions operate on numbers and return numbers. Some operate on strings and return strings. To illustrate, we will define a function called BACKWARDS this way: reverse the letters of the operand. Thus,

BACKWARDS (CAT) = TAC
BACKWARDS (EVIL) = LIVE

BASIC has many functions built into it and most of them are rules that return numbers. Four interesting functions that operate on numbers are CINT, INT, RND, and STR$. Some functions that operate on strings that you will find useful are CHR$, LEFT$, LEN, MID$, RIGHT$, STRING$, and VAL.

There are others that you should become acquainted with, but we're talking too much! It's time for you to get those fingers moving and find out what these functions do.

Discovery 4: Functions

Objectives. In this lesson, you will learn to use some of the IBM BASIC predefined functions. You will also learn to define functions of your own. To get the most from this lesson you must make careful observations.

Materials. Your formatted diskette.

1. Enter Program 29 and then run it using the numbers 2.88, 2.501, 2.99, and 2.78912. What does it do?

```
90 REM PROGRAM 29 - THE CINT FUNCTION
100 CLS
110 FOR I=1 TO 4
120  LOCATE 2,1
130  PRINT "Enter a decimal fraction that is between"
140  PRINT "2 and 3 but closer to 3."
150  LOCATE 5,8
160  INPUT X
170  LOCATE 5+I,8
180  PRINT X;"is closer to";CINT(X)
190  LOCATE 5,8
200  PRINT "            "
210 NEXT I
220 END
```

2. After you have run this program once and made observations, edit line 140. Instead of having the program request a number closer to 3, have it request a number closer to 2. Run the program again using the numbers 2.34, 2.1117, 2.49999, and 2.009.
3. Write a definition of the CINT function. Later you will want to check your definition with that given in the "Programming Particulars" section.
4. Modify the program again by editing line 180. Change the function CINT to INT. Repeat Steps 1–3. Be sure that you can explain the difference between the functions.
5. A handy application of CINT is a program that rounds numbers to specified powers of 10. Enter Program 30, input the numbers 3.5678, 9.9999, and 2.00007, and observe the results.

```
90 REM PROGRAM 30 - ROUNDING
100 CLS
110 INPUT A
120 ROUND A=CINT(A*100)/100
130 PRINT A;" rounded to the nearest hundredths is ";ROUNDA
140 END
```

6. The next function you will investigate is the RND function. It will be useful in a number of ways. When the computer processes the RND function,

it returns a number between 0 and 1. You will note that it is not necessary to specify an operand. Enter Program 31 to see how the RND function works.

```
90 REM PROGRAM 31 - LOOKING AT RND
100 CLS
110 FOR I=1 TO 10
120  LET X=RND
130  PRINT X
140 NEXT I
150 END
```

7. When you ran Program 31, what was the largest number generated? What was the smallest? How many decimal places were in each numeral? Edit line 120 to read

```
120 LET X=RND*50
```

Run the modified program a number of times. Notice that each number in the new set is between 0 and 50; that is, no number is negative and all numbers are smaller than 50. Experiment by replacing 50 with other numbers. Observe the results.

8. Modify Program 31 again by changing line 120 to read

```
120 Let X=INT(RND*50)
```

Try to predict the results of the program before running it.

9. Modify Program 31 again. This time, line 120 should read

```
120 LET X=INT(RND*50+1)
```

What kind of numbers will this statement generate? What effect did adding 1 have?

10. Have you noticed that if you run the same program more than once, the same "random" numbers appear each time? RND can't, of course, generate *true* random numbers. It uses an algorithm that does a pretty good job, but it must have a number to start with. This number is called the *seed*. If it starts with the same seed each time, as we have been doing up to now, it generates the same random sequence. To reset the seed, use the RANDOMIZE statement, which will prompt you to enter a new seed. Place it early in your program, before the first RND statement. Add the following line to Program 31 and try it out:

```
105 RANDOMIZE
```

11. Now, let's look at some string functions. Enter and run Program 32. It will reveal a lot of information in a hurry. Run it several times to determine the meanings of all the functions used in the program. You will find these functions very helpful when you want to manipulate strings.

```
90 REM PROGRAM 32 - STRING FUNCTIONS
100 CLS
110 INPUT "Enter a word with at least six letters.";A$
120 FOR I=1 TO 3
```

```
130  PRINT LEFT$(A$,I),RIGHT$(A$,I),MID$(A$2,I)
140 NEXT I
150 PRINT "The number of characters in ";A$" is ";LEN(A$)
160 PRINT TAB(45);A$
170 END
```

12. Here's a program that will come in handy. It prints the symbols that are associated with the IBM character codes. If you remember, each character that can be displayed has a code assigned to it. When the computer processes the statement

```
PRINT CHR$(code number)
```

it prints the associated symbol. Enter and run the program; then you will feel comfortable with how CHR$ works.

```
90 REM PROGRAM 33 - AN INTRODUCTION TO CHR$
100 CLS
110 SCREEN 0
120 LOCATE 1,27
130 PRINT "CHARACTERS AND CODES"
140 LOCATE 3,1
150 FOR I=32 TO 255
160  PRINT I;" ";CHR$(I),
170 NEXT I
180 END
```

13. Enter and run Program 34. Decide what the function STRING$ does.

```
90 REM PROGRAM 34 - WHAT DOES STRING$ DO?
100 CLS
110 INPUT "Enter a number from 33 to 254";A
120 FOR I=1 TO 10
130  PRINT STRING$(I,A)
140 NEXT I
150 END
```

14. It is often necessary to be able to change a number to a string and vice versa. Luckily, BASIC gives us the tools for that. Try Program 35 to determine what STR$ and VAL do.

```
90 REM PROGRAM 35 - STR$ AND VAL
100 CLS
110 LET NUMBER=1234
120 LET WORD$="5678A"
130 PRINT NUMBER, WORD$
140 PRINT
150 LET NUMBER=VAL(LEFT$(WORD$,2))
160 LET WORD$=STR$(NUMBER/2)+"A"
170 PRINT NUMBER,WORD$
180 PRINT
190 END
```

15. This section would not be complete if we did not introduce you to "Do it yourself" functions. IBM BASIC refers to these functions as *user-defined* functions.

Suppose you worked in a clothing store where customers paid 5 percent tax on all purchases. It would be convenient to have a register that would calculate the tax and add the tax to the purchase price. The register would print a bill indicating the purchase price, the tax, and the total price. Program 36 simulates these conditions with a function that is defined by the programmer.

```
90 REM PROGRAM 36 - REGISTER
100 CLS
110 DEF FNTX(P)=CINT(.05*P*100)/100
120 DEF FNTOT(P)=P+FNTX(P)
125 INPUT "How much is the item";P
130 PRINT "PRICE";
140 PRINT "TAX",FNTX(P)
150 PRINT "TOTAL",FNTOT(P)
160 END
```

16. User-defined functions work for strings as well. Study, enter, and run Program 37.

```
90 REM PROGRAM 37 - PIG LATIN
100 DEF FNPIG$(WORD$)=RIGHT$(WORD$,N-1)+LEFT$(WORD$,1)+"AY"
110 INPUT "WORD";WORD$
120 LET N=LEN(WORD$)
130 PRINT FNPIG$(WORD$)
140 END
```

Programming Particulars

The INT function and the CINT function differ in the following ways. For positive numbers, INT truncates. In other words, it strips off all the decimal places. For example,

$$INT(2.85) = 2$$

For negative numbers, INT rounds to the next smallest integer. For example,

$$INT(-2.35) = -3$$

(Remember, -3 is smaller than -2.)

CINT genuinely rounds numbers according to the rules of mathematics. For example,

$$CINT(2.35) = 2$$

and

CINT(2.85) = 3

Similarly,

CINT(− 2.35) = − 2

and

CINT(− 2.85) = − 3

There is an aspect of the VAL function of which you should be aware. When VAL is used on a string containing letters, it only returns the value up to the first letter. If the first character of the string is a letter, then the value returned is always 0. For example,

VAL("123ABC") = 123

and

VAL("ABC123") = 0

Two other handy functions are TIMER and TIME$. TIMER is available only in Disk Operating Systems more recent than version 2.00. It returns the number of seconds elapsed since the last system reset or midnight, whichever came last. You can use it to automatically seed the random number generator with the statement

```
RANDOMIZE TIMER
```

Try it.

TIME$ returns the current date as a string in the form "hh:mm:ss." The statement

```
LET HOUR$=LEFT$(TIME$,2)
```

returns the hour of the day in the variable HOUR$.

Appendix Lesson 5

Preliminaries

In this lesson, we'll take a break and explore some BASIC statements that illustrate the PC's graphics and music capabilities. However, the graphics statements will work only if your computer is equipped with a *color graphics adapter*. That is the interface in the computer that allows it to work with an **RGB** color display, or a composite display. Many PCs are equipped with a *monochrome display adapter* that will display only text characters on a special high-resolution monochrome display. We hope yours isn't one of them. The graphics statements you'll see in this lesson are COLOR, CIRCLE,

DRAW, LINE, PAINT, PSET, and PRESET. The statements for producing sound and music are BEEP and PLAY.

Before we start, we'll need to discuss the environment in which the graphics statements function. In Appendix Lesson 1, you saw how to create drawings with special line drawing characters. At that time, we also referred to another kind of graphics called bit-mapped. The statements demonstrated in this lesson create bit-mapped images. That means they create images from tiny little dots. These tiny little dots are called *pixels* (short for picture elements). To use them, we must put the PC in SCREEN 1. This screen is composed of 64,000 pixels arranged in an array of 320 × 200. Each pixel has unique coordinates. For example, the top, leftmost pixel is addressed as (0,0). The bottom, rightmost pixel is addressed as (319,199).

SCREEN 1 allows us to display graphics in four colors. The background can be one of eight different colors, as in SCREEN 0. Figures drawn on the screen can be one of four different colors, the background color and three others chosen from one of two different *palettes.*

Discovery 5: Some FUN Things

Objectives. In this lesson, you will become acquainted with some BASIC statements for graphics and sound. As always, make careful observations as you proceed and try to maximize your understanding.

Materials. Your formatted diskette.

1. Enter and run Program 38. See if you can determine how the COLOR and PSET statements function. Experiment with different values for background and palette.

```
80 REM PROGRAM 38 - OH, STARRY NIGHT
90 REM REQUIRES COLOR GRAPHICS ADAPTER
100 SCREEN 1
110 KEY OFF
120 CLS
130 INPUT "Background (0-7)";BACKGROUND
140 INPUT "Palette (0-1)";PALETTE
150 COLOR BACKGROUND,PALETTE
160 CLS
170 FOR I=1 TO 50
180  FOR KOLOR=1 TO 3
190   LET X=RND*320:LET Y=RND*200
200   PSET(X,Y),KOLOR
210  NEXT KOLOR
220 NEXT I
230 END
```

2. There are two easy ways to undo a pixel set with PSET. One is to set it again, but with the same color as the background. This has the effect of making it invisible. The other way is to use the PRESET statement. (Read that *p-reset,* not *pre-set.*) Enter, run, and study Program 39. Try changing some of the values for color and the X and Y loops.

```
90 REM PROGRAM 39 - FOLLOW THE DOT
100 REM REQUIRES COLOR GRAPHICS ADAPTER
110 SCREEN 1
120 KEY OFF
130 COLOR 0,1
140 CLS
150  FOR Y=0 TO 199
160   FOR X=1 TO 319-Y
170   PRESET (X-1,Y)
180   PSET (X,Y),3
190  NEXT X
200 NEXT Y
210 END
```

3. PSET and PRESET are very tedious for drawing figures. Fortunately, IBM BASIC provides us with some other, more powerful ways to make graphics. Enter and run Program 40. See if you can figure out how CIRCLE and the different variations of the LINE statement work.

```
80 REM PROGRAM 40 - CIRCLES, LINES, AND BOXES
90 REM REQUIRES COLOR GRAPHICS ADAPTER
100 SCREEN 1
110 KEY OFF
120 COLOR 1,0
130 CLS
140 CIRCLE (100,100),40,1
150 CIRCLE (100,100),50,1
160 LINE (10,180)-(280,10),2
170 LINE (10,10)-(280,180),2
180 LINE (250,10)-(250,180),2
190 LINE (60,60)-(140,140),3,B
200 LINE (75,75)-(125,125),3,B
210 END
```

4. The PAINT statement allows us to fill in figures like those drawn in the preceding programs. To PAINT, you must address a point inside the object to be painted, tell what color to paint with, and tell the color of the boundary. Insert the following lines into the previous program, run it, and observe the results.

```
155 PAINT (100,85),2,1
185 PAINT (200,100),1,2
205 PAINT (65,65),3,3
```

These statements also allow us to use variable arguments. That makes them much more useful. Run and study Program 41.

```
80 REM PROGRAM 41 - VARIABLE CIRCLES
90 REM REQUIRES COLOR GRAPHICS ADAPTER
100 SCREEN 1
110 KEY OFF
120 COLOR 0,1
130 CLS
140 INPUT "CENTER (X,Y)";XCNTR,YCNTR
```

```
150 INPUT "RADIUS";RADIUS
160 INPUT "COLOR (0-3)";KOLOR
170 CIRCLE (XCNTR,YCNTR);RADIUS,KOLOR
180 END
```

5. The last graphics statement that we will study is DRAW. DRAW has a sublanguage of its own that gives us very flexible ways to create images. The syntax of the statement is

DRAW *"directions"*

Some of the directions are highlighted in the following table:

Code	Explanation
U *n*	Draw up *n* units (in pixels).
D *n*	Draw down *n* units.
L *n*	Draw left *n* units.
R *n*	Draw right *n* units.
B	Placed before any direction, moves without drawing.
TA *n*	Turn *n* degrees, from −360 to +360. In DOS version 2.00 and later, + turns counterclockwise and − turns clockwise.

If you are interested in DRAW, there are more directions that you can look up in the BASIC manual. Use Program 42 to explore with DRAW.

```
80 REM PROGRAM 42 - WHAT A CHARACTER!
90 REM REQUIRES COLOR GRAPHICS ADAPTER
100 SCREEN 1
110 KEY OFF
120 COLOR 1,0
130 CLS
140 LET H$="U90 R30 D30 R40 U30 R30 D90 L30 U30 L40 D30 L30"
150 LET I$="U90 R30 D90 L30"
160 DRAW "BL80 BD30"
170 DRAW H$
180 DRAW "BR130"
190 DRAW I$
200 END
```

6. Appropriately, DRAW can also take variable input. Can you figure out how Program 43 works? Be sure to try some big numbers.

```
80 REM PROGRAM 43 - RECTANGLES
90 REM REQUIRES COLOR GRAPHICS ADAPTER
100 KEY OFF:CLS
110 SCREEN 1
120 CLS
130 COLOR 1,0
140 INPUT "HOW BIG";S
150 INPUT "HOW MANY";H
160 LET T=360/H
170 BOX$="U=S;R=S;D=S;L=S;"
```

```
180 FOR TURN=T to 360 STEP T
190   DRAW BOX$
200   DRAW "TA=TURN;"          'DOS2.00 and later
210 NEXT TURN
```

7. Now let's take a look at how to make noise with BASIC. We have already seen the SOUND statement, which allows us to generate a tone, given the frequency and duration. For cases where you just want to get someone's attention and you don't care what the tone is, try the BEEP statement. BEEP and SOUND are not very good for making music. For that, we have the PLAY statement. PLAY allows us to specify notes in the standard form *ABCDEFG*. The syntax is

```
PLAY "notes"
```

Other options allow you to specify octave, tempo, length of note, and so on. Run and study Program 44.

```
90 REM PROGRAM 44 - DO, RE, MI
100 LET SCALEUP$="CDEFGABO5C"
110 LET SCALEDOWN$="CO4BAGFEDC"
120 PLAY SCALEUP$
130 PLAY SCALEDOWN$
140 END
```

Another way to specify notes is by number, from 0 to 84, corresponding to the keys on a piano.

```
90 REM PROGRAM 45 - PLAYING BY THE NUMBERS
100 FOR NOTE = 0 TO 84
110   LET NOTE$="N"+STR$(NOTE)
120   PLAY NOTE$
130 NEXT NOTE
140 END
```

As with other statements we have introduced, you can find more about PLAY in the BASIC manual.

Programming Particulars

Varying with what version of DOS you have, there are many more statements for producing graphics on the PC. We have just scratched the surface. If you like this kind of programming, we encourage you to probe further. In particular, there are techniques and statements for producing animation, which we only touched upon in Program 39.

The PC also has a higher-resolution mode, SCREEN 2, that can be used to produce finer graphics, but without color. The PCjr is even more powerful, providing other screen modes that allow a wide array of resolutions and colors to be used.

Appendix Lesson 6

Preliminaries

Brace yourself. We've saved some pretty heavy-duty stuff for this lesson. Up to now, just about every program demonstrated has executed in linear fashion. In other words, they have executed line by line, in numerical order. The only exceptions have been the programs that used FOR . . . NEXT loops, which caused a block of statements to be executed multiple times. It's just about impossible to write a significant program that doesn't use instructions that *branch,* or alter the flow of execution. We'll introduce the major ones in this lesson.

Another important structure that we have ignored is *decision making.* Any program worth a hoot has to be able to make decisions and branch on the basis of those decisions. We'll look at two important decision-making statements in this lesson. Finally, we will introduce another way for a program to get input from the keyboard and another way for a program to assign values to variables.

Discovery 6: Some Biggies

Objectives. This lesson, you will become familiar with the format and function of IF. . . THEN, WHILE . . . WEND, GOTO, GOSUB . . . RETURN, INKEY$, and READ . . . DATA statements.

Materials. Your formatted diskette.

1. Let's start with decision making. A frequently used tool for this in BASIC is the IF. . . THEN construct. The format is as follows:

IF *condition* THEN *do this*

We are also going to use GOTO in this program. GOTO is a branching statement. Whenever it is encountered, the flow of execution is altered. Enter and run Program 46. Study how IF. . . THEN and GOTO are used.

```
90 REM PROGRAM 46 - WHO AM I?
100 CLS:KEY OFF
110 INPUT "What kind of computer am I";ANSWER$
120 IF ANSWER$="IBM" THEN PRINT "THAT'S RIGHT!":END
130 PRINT "No, try again"
140 GOTO 110
150 END
```

An option for the IF. . . THEN statement is to include an ELSE condition. In Program 46, when ANSWER$ did not equal "IBM," the program flow "fell through" line 120 to line 130. The action in lines 130 and 140 was our ELSE condition.

2. Program 47 demonstrates another way to specify the ELSE statement.

```
90 REM PROGRAM 47 - WHO AM I? (REVISED)
100 CLS:KEY OFF
110 INPUT "What kind of computer am I";ANSWER$
120 IF ANSWER$="IBM" THEN PRINT "That's Right!"
           ELSE PRINT "No, try again."
130 END
```

3. You have to be very careful about using GOTO. Using it too much and unwisely can result in a program that is difficult to understand, modify, and debug. In fact, many authorities suggest that it should not be taught at all. Program 48 is an extreme example of how GOTO can render a program difficult to understand. Try to figure out what it does before you run it. Although this program is silly, it does illustrate what *can* happen in a program that is not *supposed* to be silly.

```
90 REM PROGRAM 48 - WHO'S THERE?
100 CLS:KEY OFF
110 PRINT "Knock! Knock!"
120 INPUT "(respond)";RESPONSE$
130 IF RESPONSE$="Who's there?" THEN GOTO 180
140 GOTO 250
150 GOTO 300
160 PRINT "Not me!"
170 GOTO 330
180 FOR N=1 TO 8
190  PRINT "dither.. ";
200  FOR I=1 TO 500
210  NEXT I
220 NEXT N
230 PRINT
240 GOTO 160
250 PRINT "try again, ";
260 GOTO 150
270 PRINT"Me and my PC."
280 END
290 GOTO 180
300 PRINT "Sam"
310 GOTO 110
320 END
330 GOTO 270
```

4. GOSUB is often used in place of GOTO because it is more difficult to use unwisely and encourages you to write programs that are *modularly structured.* A modular program is one that is built from smaller subprograms called subroutines. GOSUB means go to a subroutine. The difference between GOSUB and GOTO is that GOSUB RETURNS to where it came from. Study Program 49. Isn't it easier to understand the flow of execution here than in Program 48? (We'll explain the INKEY$ statement used in line 120 when we get to the next program.)

```
90 REM PROGRAM 49 - SKETCHPAD
100 SCREEN 1:KEY OFF:CLS
110 WHILE I$<>"Q"
120  LET I$=INKEY$
130  IF I$="8" THEN GOSUB 1000
140  IF I$="2" THEN GOSUB 2000
150  IF I$="6" THEN GOSUB 3000
160  IF I$="4" THEN GOSUB 4000
170  GOSUB 5000
190  IF I$="C" THEN CLS
220  LOCATE 25,1:PRINT "NUMLOCK ON 8=UP 2=DN 6=RT 4=LT";
230 WEND
240 END
998 '
999 REM move up 10 units
1000 LET MOVE$="U10"
1010 RETURN
1998 '
1999 REM move down 10 units
2000 LET MOVE$="D10"
2010 RETURN
2998 '
2999 REM move right 10 units
3000 LET MOVE$="R10"
3010 RETURN
3998 '
3999 REM move left 10 units
4000 LET MOVE$="L10"
4010 RETURN
4998 '
4999 REM draw move
5000 DRAW MOVE$
5010 LET MOVE$=""
5020 RETURN
```

5. The INKEY$ statement is another way to get input from the keyboard. One problem with INPUT is that your program stops execution until the Enter key is pressed. That is not appropriate in cases where you want the program to continue execution while waiting for input, like in an arcade-type game, for example. INKEY$ solves this problem by scanning the keyboard whenever the statement is encountered and then continuing execution. INKEY$ has the additional advantage of not requiring the Enter key to be pressed. Study this demonstration of INKEY$.

```
90 REM PROGRAM 50 - PRESS-A-KEY
100 PRINT ".";
110 LET I$=INKEY$
120 IF I$<>"" THEN PRINT I$;
130 GOTO 100
```

6. Here's an example of a more useful application—a typing drill. We want the program to give the user a finite amount of time in which to respond, so it must count while it checks the keyboard.

```
90 REM PROGRAM 51 - TYPING DRILL
100 KEY OFF:CLS
110 RANDOMIZE TIMER
120 FOR HOWMANY=1 TO 10
130  X=INT(RND*26)
140  X$=CHR$(X+65)
150  LOCATE 10,10
160  PRINT "TYPE ";X$
170  FOR I=1 TO 250
180   LET I$=INKEY$
190   IF I$=X$ THEN BEEP:R=1
200  NEXT I
210 IF R=0 THEN SOUND 50,10
220 LET R=0
230 NEXT HOWMANY
240 END
```

7. Earlier we introduced the FOR . . . NEXT structure as a way of making a program repeat or loop a block of statements. One of FOR . . . NEXT's limitations is that it is intended for loops in which the number of repetitions is known. What if you wish to design a loop that terminates when a condition is met? For that, you need WHILE . . . WEND, which is like a FOR . . . NEXT loop with a built-in IF. . . THEN. Program 52 is a simple example of a loop that waits until a specific key is pressed.

```
90 REM PROGRAM 52 - WAIT ON Q
100 KEY OFF:CLS
110 PRINT "PRESS Q TO QUIT"
120 WHILE INKEY$<>"Q"
130  PRINT ".";
140 WEND
150 PRINT "ALL DONE!"
160 END
```

8. The last new concept we'll introduce is the READ . . . DATA construct. Take a moment to turn back to the SANDWICHES program (Program 22) in Appendix Lesson 2. One problem with this program is that you must type in all the sandwiches and drinks every time you run it. Wouldn't it be nice if you could keep their names in the program and edit them every time there was a change? READ . . . DATA lets us do that.

```
90 REM PROGRAM 53 - SANDWICHES (REVISED)
100 SCREEN 0:WIDTH 80:KEY OFF:CLS
110 PRINT "Get ready for the list!"
120 READ SAND
130 DIM SAND$(SAND)
140 READ DRINK
150 DIM DRINK$(DRINK)
160 FOR I=1 TO SAND
170  READ SAND$(I)
180 NEXT I
190 FOR J=1 TO DRINK
200  READ DRINK$(J)
```

```
210 NEXT J
220 FOR I=1 TO SAND
230  FOR J=1 TO DRINK
240   PRINT SAND$(I),DRINK$(J)
250  NEXT J
260 NEXT I
270 PRINT "That's all, y'all!"
280 END
1000 REM NUMBER OF SANDWICHES
1010 DATA 8
1020 REM NUMBER OF DRINKS
1030 DATA 5
1040 REM SANDWICHES
1050 DATA HAM,BEEF,BOLOGNA,TURKEY,CHICKEN
1060 DATA PEANUT BUTTER & JELLY,CHEESE,LIVERWURST
1070 REM DRINKS
1080 DATA COFFEE,TEA,MILK,SODA,LEMONADE
```

9. It's difficult to give good examples of the powerful statements covered in this lesson without using many of them in the same program. Programs 54 and 55 make use of much of what we have covered in this lesson and the previous one. Study them carefully and observe how they are used.

```
80 REM PROGRAM 54 - RANDOM RECTANGLES
90 REM REQUIRES COLOR GRAPHICS ADAPTER
100 SCREEN 1
110 KEY OFF
120 CLS
130 RANDOMIZE TIMER       'only DOS 2.00 and later
140 WHILE INKEY$<>"q"
150  LOCATE 25,1
160  PRINT "PRESS `q' TO QUIT, `p' TO PAINT";
170  LET X1=RND*319
180  LET X2=RND*319
190  LET Y1=RND*219
200  LET Y2=RND*219
210  LET KOLOR=RND*4
220  IF INKEY$="p" THEN GOSUB 1010
230  IF INKEY$<>"p" THEN GOSUB 2010
240 WEND
250 END
990 '
1000 ' FILLED BOX
1010 BEEP
1020 LINE(X1,Y1)-(X2,Y2),KOLOR,BF
1030 RETURN
1990 '
2000 ' BOX
2010 LINE(X1,Y1)-(X2,Y2),KOLOR,B
2020 RETURN
```

```
90 REM PROGRAM 55 - SING-A-LONG
100 KEY OFF:WIDTH 80:CLS
110 WHILE MUSIC$<>"END"
```

```
120   PRINT WORD$;
130   PLAY MUSIC$
140   READ MUSIC$,WORD$
150 WEND
160 PRINT:PRINT TAB(30)WORD$
990 '
1000 ' PUT YOUR SONG HERE
1010 DATA "G","Ma","Fa","ry","E-","had ","F",a "
1020 DATA "G","lit","G","tle ","G","lamb, "
1030 DATA "P16","","P16","","P16","","P16,""
1040 DATA "F","lit","F","tle ","F","lamb, "
1050 DATA "P16","","P16","","P16","",P16",""
1060 DATA "G","lit","B-","tle ","B-","lamb. "
1070 DATA "P16","","P16","","P16","","P16",""
1080 DATA "G","Ma","F","ry ","E-","had ","F","a "
1090 DATA "G","lit","G","tle ","G","lamb, "
1100 DATA "G","whose ","F","fleece "
1110 DATA "F","was ","G","white ","F","as "
1120 DATA "E-","snow !!"
1130 DATA "END","The End"
```

Programming Particulars

You may be wondering how BASIC knows where to return after a GOSUB. The computer makes a little note to itself whenever a GOSUB is executed, and that note tells it where to return. You can put GOSUBs inside of other GOSUBs, and the computer won't get mixed up. It always returns to the last note made for where to return.

You may have made the observation that Program 49 is easier to understand than Program 48 because it is organized more clearly. That is exactly the point. GOTO is much more generous about allowing you to write a confusing program (programmers call this *spaghetti code*) than GOSUB. Because GOSUB always RETURNs, you almost have to write a better organized program. Oh, you can still mess it up, but you have to work harder at it.

You may also have noticed that the READ statement knows what data have already been read. BASIC maintains a pointer that tells it which data to read next. If you wish to reuse the data in a program, the RESTORE statement resets the pointer back to the beginning of the data.

In our final lesson, we'll stand back and look at the overall process of assembling a program.

Appendix Lesson 7

Preliminaries

It's now time to tie all the pieces together. Despite all the programs that we've looked at, we have really yet to write a program. By that, we mean that all the programs we have seen so far are all pieces, or subroutines, for larger, more useful programs. In this section we'll study the programming process in detail. We will take a look at how to conceive, plan, and write a complete program.

Discovery 7: Greater Than the Sum of the Parts

Objectives. In this lesson, you will become familiar with the concepts of *top-down* and *bottom-up* thought processes, *modular programming, subroutines,* and how to clearly define a programming task and then break it into smaller tasks.

Materials. Your formatted diskette.

Where Do You Start?

The first step is to think the problem through. What are the things we wish to accomplish? How should we go about them? What kinds of problems might arise? Good programmers often say that most of the programming they do is on paper or in their heads, not on the computer. Only when the problem is thoroughly understood is one ready to write code.

The next step is to plan the actual writing of program code. This is where you translate your ideas into a structure suitable for the programming language you plan to use. (Often, programmers must also decide what language is best suited to the task. Since we're learning BASIC, we don't have to make that decision.) Flowcharting can be an invaluable tool for planning a program. It forces you to think about how your program should be structured. You should make your important decisions at this stage. If you wait until you begin to write code, you may find that you have to make many revisions and do a lot of debugging.

There are two ways to plan a program: top-down and bottom-up. When you use the top-down method, you start with the big ideas and work your way down to the little ones. For example, you start with the main concept of the program:

THIS PROGRAM IS GOING TO DO *(task)*

Then you think about all the things you have to do to accomplish your task.

TO GET *(task)*, WE HAVE TO DO *(subtask$_1$), (subtask$_2$), (subtask$_3$)*, . . .

Now analyze each of the subtasks and break them up into their logical components. Repeat the process until you get to a level where the subtasks are coherent, achievable jobs. By planning and programming top-down, you stand a better chance of writing a successful, error-free program.

Bottom-up programming takes place when you start with the small ideas and work your way up to the big ones. It's probably contradictory to say that bottom-up programs are planned. They usually occur when you just sit down at the computer and start entering code. This might be known as the It-Grows-As-I-Write-It school of programming. Don't misunderstand. We're not saying that you have to plan every little thing you do ahead of time or that, unless you have planned for something, you can't put it in your program. What we're saying is if you make it a way of life, you're looking for trouble. Bottom-up programming usually results in programs that are harder to understand, modify, and debug. The programming that we are going to demonstrate is top-down.

Once the planning is complete, we're finally ready to write the program code. Instead of writing one long step-at-a-time program to do a complex task, good programmers will write many small programs that work together to complete the task. Each little program, called a *subroutine,* is usually designed to do a specialized task. This technique is useful for two important reasons. Many carefully labeled small programs, each with a single objective, are easier to keep track of than a long step-by-step program. Complicated programs made up of small programs are usually more efficient than big programs that are not made of small logical parts. Whenever certain tasks need to be done, program control is turned over to the small special program that does that job. As the large program is executed, small programs are called in at different stages. In this way, small programs are used efficiently, each usually more than one time.

Think of it this way: Suppose you are a maintenance dispatcher in a large apartment complex. When carpets need to be cleaned in apartment 408 you send out a carpet cleaning crew. When pest control is needed in apartment 203 you send in the pest control agents. To make this work there must be a central body—you, as the dispatcher. This central body must stay informed of the maintenance needs and must turn control over to the specialized crew when a specialized task needs to be done.

A good program has a central component or main module that controls and monitors the rest of the program. The central component regulates the flow of the program among all of the little programs. The following diagram illustrates this idea:

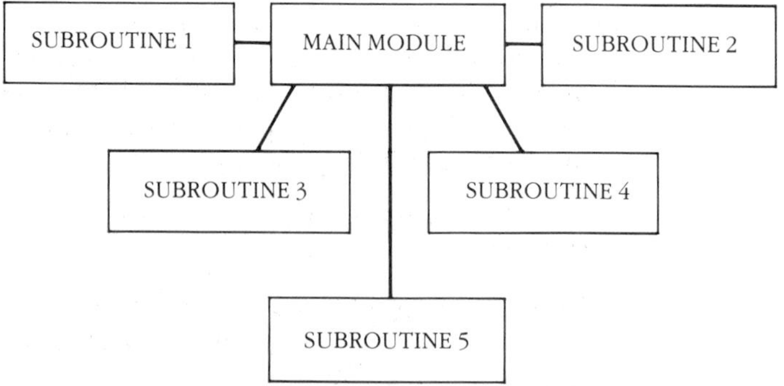

Now, let's build some subroutines and put them together so that you can better understand this idea. We will henceforth refer to this idea as modular programming. Each subroutine will address a small part of the overall program and will be called a program *module.*

The Estimate Program

We are going to build a drill and practice program. This program will provide the user with practice estimating the product of two numbers between 10 and 1,000. To start, we must decide exactly what we want to do. The big jobs are to provide exercises, check the learner's responses for accuracy, and give feedback to the learner.

These big jobs, however, need to be broken into smaller jobs. First, let's look at providing exercises. To provide exercises we must set up the screen so that the display is pleasing and easy to follow. We should indicate some name for the program and give some directions. If we want to personalize the program and any reports that are generated, then we must get the user's name. To display exercises, we must have numbers. If we define the numbers ourselves, then the program will be very limited. If we generate random numbers, there will be more variety. Once we obtain numbers, we can display exercises. Here is a summary of the smaller tasks into which we have broken up the big job of providing exercises.

SET UP SCREEN
GET NAME
RANDOMIZE
GET RANDOM NUMBERS
DISPLAY EXERCISE

Once we have an exercise, we must give the learner an opportunity to respond. Once a response is entered, the program must compare the response to the actual answer. Feedback must be given to advise the learner of the accuracy of his or her response. Let's summarize these steps.

GET LEARNER'S RESPONSE
CHECK RESPONSE
GIVE FEEDBACK

Now, when that's all done, we have two more things left to do. At this point the learner must be given the option to continue practicing or quit. If the learner wants to continue, we must repeat certain steps. If the learner wants to quit, we should give some report of his or her progress. This report should be available on the display or as a printed copy. When this last job is completed, we end the program.

FIND OUT IF LEARNER WISHES TO CONTINUE
PRINT REPORT OF RESULTS

Okay, we've thought our program through pretty thoroughly. We're finally ready to write the code. Our main module might look like this.

```
10 REM This program provides practice estimating
20 REM  products of numbers less than 999.
30 '
97 '-----------------------------------
98 ' MAIN PROGRAM MODULE
99 '-----------------------------------
```

```
100 GOSUB 1000              ' set up screen
110 GOSUB 2000              ' randomize
120 GOSUB 3000              ' get student name
130 LET ATTEMPTS=0                ' initialize ATTEMPTS
140 LET AGAIN$="Y"          ' initialize AGAIN$
150 WHILE AGAIN$="Y" OR AGAIN$="y"     ' another exercise?
160  LET ATTEMPTS=ATTEMPTS+1        ' increment ATTEMPTS
170  GOSUB 4000             ' get numbers
180  GOSUB 5000             ' display exercise
190  GOSUB 6000             ' get and check response
200 WEND
210 GOSUB 7000              ' progress report
220 CLS
230 END
```

So far, so good. This makes sense. We know where we are headed and we can begin to build other small programs or modules to do all the tasks we want done. First, we will build a module that will arrange the display as we want it. In this program module we set the width of the screen to 40 columns, we choose colors that are visually effective, and print the title of our program. When this module's work is done, program control is turned back over to the main module. This is accomplished using the RETURN statement in line 1070.

```
997 '---------------------------------------
998 ' SET UP SCREEN
999 '---------------------------------------
1000 KEY OFF
1010 COLOR 15,1,4
1020 WIDTH 40
1030 CLS
1040 LOCATE 2,10
1050 COLOR 10
1060 PRINT"ESTIMATING PRODUCTS"
1070 RETURN
```

Next, we will seed the random number generator. Why? Because we want the program to generate different numbers every time we run it. We randomize using four functions: TIME$, MID$, RIGHT$, and VAL$. In lines 2000 and 2010 we define SECONDS and MINUTES both in terms of the string returned by TIME$. The reason for using this method instead of the TIMER function demonstrated in Appendix Lesson 4 is that TIMER is not present in IBM BASIC before DOS 2.00. This routine will work with any version of IBM BASIC (and many other BASICs, as well).

```
1997 '---------------------------------------
1998 ' RANDOMIZE
1999 '---------------------------------------
2000 LET SECONDS=VAL(RIGHT$(TIME$,2)) ' get seconds
2010 LET MINUTES=VAL(MID$(TIME$,4,2)) ' get minutes
2020 RANDOMIZE SECONDS+MINUTES      ' seed random generator
2030 RETURN
```

Now we will write a program module to get the user's name. Again, we locate the cursor and choose a color. In line 3020 we use the INPUT statement to get the string variable, NME$. This input statement prompts the user with

```
"ENTER YOUR NAME"
```

The program will sit patiently until the learner inputs his or her name. When the work is done, program control will be turned over to the main module.

```
2997 '---------------------------------------
2998 ' ENTER NAME
2999 '---------------------------------------
3000 LOCATE 10,1
3010 COLOR 15
3020 INPUT "ENTER YOUR NAME";NAYME$
3030 RETURN
```

Now we will get the numbers we need to exhibit an appropriate exercise. Line 4000 defines the variable FACTOR1 as some integer less than 1,000. Line 4010 defines FACTOR2 as an integer less than 100. Again, program control is then turned over to the main module. Since this is an estimation program, we'll also define variables for plus and minus 20 percent of the exact answer. Those are the limits within which we will consider the learner's response to be "correct."

```
3997 '---------------------------------------
3998 ' GET NUMBERS
3999 '---------------------------------------
4000 LET FACTOR1=INT(RND*1000)     ' assign 1st factor
4010 LET FACTOR2=INT(RND*100)      ' assign 2nd factor
4020 LET ANSWER=FACTOR1*FACTOR2      ' calculate exact answer
4030 LET LESS20=ANSWER-.2*ANSWER    ' calculate lower limit
4040 LET PLUS20=ANSWER+.2*ANSWER    ' calculate upper limit
4050 RETURN
```

This next routine will display the exercise and problem number. The PRINT USING statements are a handy way to format the way the factors are displayed and also print other characters, in this case, the times sign.

```
4997 '---------------------------------------
4998 ' DISPLAY EXERCISE
4999 '---------------------------------------
5000 CLS
5010 LOCATE 2,12
5020 PRINT "PROBLEM NUMBER";ATTEMPTS
5030 LOCATE 12,8
5040 COLOR 10
5050 PRINT USING "### X";FACTOR1;      ' format display
5060 PRINT USING " ### ";FACTOR2;      '  of factors
5070 PRINT "IS ABOUT";
5080 RETURN
```

This routine gets the learner's response and checks to see if it is within our 20 percent range (line 6050.) If not, the exact answer is immediately displayed. If it is within the range, it is then checked to see if it is equal to the exact answer. If so, the learner is given appropriate feedback and the exact answer is displayed. If not, the learner is told that he or she is within 20 percent and the exact answer is displayed. Finally, the routine finds out if the user wants to continue. Let's take a look.

```
5997 '---------------------------------------
5998 ' CHECK RESPONSE
5999 '---------------------------------------
6000 COLOR 14
6010 INPUT RESPONSE$            ' get response
6020 COLOR 15
6030 LOCATE 15,1
6040 LET RESPONSE=VAL(RESPONSE$)    ' convert to number
6050 IF RESPONSE<LESS20 OR RESPONSE>PLUS 20 THEN GOTO 6090
6060 COUNT=COUNT+1 '<-increment # correct  ^-is it wrong?
6070 IF RESPONSE=ANSWER THEN COLOR 28:PRINT TAB(15)
     "PERFECT!!!" :COLOR 15
6080 IF RESPONSE<>ANSWER THEN PRINT" YOU ARE WITHIN 20% OF THE EXACT ANSWER"
6090 PRINT
6100 PRINT"   THE EXACT ANSWER IS";
6110 COLOR 10
6120 PRINT ANSWER
6130 COLOR 15
6140 LOCATE 21,5
6150 PRINT"Do you want to try another? (Y/N)"
6160 LET AGAIN$=INPUT$(1)
6170 RETURN
```

When the learner no longer wishes to continue, we'll display the results of the session on the display and ask if a printout is desired.

```
6997 '---------------------------------------
6998 ' PROGRESS REPORT
6999 '---------------------------------------
7000 CLS
7010 COLOR 10
7020 LOCATE 2,10
7030 PRINT"ESTIMATING PRACTICE"
7040 LOCATE 5,5
7050 COLOR 14
7060 PRINT"NAME: ";
7070 COLOR 15
7080 PRINT NAYME$
7090 COLOR 14
7100 LOCATE 7,5
7110 PRINT"NUMBER OF PROBLEMS ATTEMPTED: ";
7120 COLOR 15
7130 PRINT ATTEMPTS
7140 COLOR 14
7150 LOCATE 8,5
7160 PRINT"NUMBER CORRECT: ";
```

```
7170 COLOR 15
7180 PRINT COUNT
7190 LOCATE 11,5
7200 COLOR 14
7210 PERCENT=COUNT/ATTEMPTS*100
7220 PRINT"PERCENT CORRECT: ";
7230 COLOR 15
7240 PRINT USING "###.##";PERCENT    'print percent to 100ths
7250 LOCATE 23,2
7260 PRINT"DO YOU WANT A PRINTED REPORT? (Y/N)"
7270 LET A$=INPUT$(1)
7280 IF A$="N" OR A$="n" THEN RETURN
7997 '
7998 ' PRINTED REPORT
7999 '
8000 LPRINT"  ESTIMATING PRACTICE"
8010 LPRINT
8020 LPRINT
8030 LPRINT" NAME: ";
8040 LPRINT NAYME$;TAB(30)"DATE: ";DATE$
8050 LPRINT
8060 LPRINT" NUMBER OF PROBLEMS ATTEMPTED: ";
8070 LPRINT ATTEMPTS
8080 LPRINT
8090 LPRINT" NUMBER CORRECT: ";
8100 LPRINT COUNT
8110 LPRINT
8120 LPRINT" PERCENT CORRECT: ";
8130 LPRINT USING "###.##";PERCENT    'print percent to 100ths
8140 RETURN
```

Programming Particulars

In this lesson we have constructed a program from several small programs. The name for this program is Estimating Products. In this program, no instruction on how to estimate products is given. The program simply provides practice exercises and a progress report. For these reasons, the program is an example of drill and practice.

We have discussed good programming practices and modeled what we consider to be a good example. This concludes our minibook on BASIC and programming concepts. Remember, though, this has just been a sampler and we've only scratched the surface. But if you have mastered everything in this section, you've got a good start toward becoming a programmer.

GLOSSARY

This glossary is a general-purpose resource for microcomputer terminology. As such, it contains many terms that are not discussed in detail in the text and terms that don't appear in the text at all. In fact, that has been our emphasis: to provide an additional resource for material that is not specifically addressed in the book. If you can't find what you want here, look in the Index. There's a good chance that the information you need is covered in one chapter or another.

access ID or code A combination of letters and numbers assigned to a user which allows access to information utilities or other services provided by telecommunications systems.

acoustic coupler A modem designed to transmit and receive data through a telephone handset. The modem contains rubber cups that are placed over the ear and mouthpiece of a telephone handset. This type of modem is useful when a direct connection between the telephone line and a modem is not possible; for example, in an office, telephone booth, or motel room.

adapter *See* **interface.**

AI *See* **Artificial Intelligence.**

algorithm A finite set of steps that, when executed, will consistently achieve specific goals.

alphanumeric Data consisting of alphabetic characters and/or digits.

ANSI American National Standards Institute, an organization of computer professionals responsible for setting standards for everything from floppy disk quality to computer languages.

archival copy A legal copy made of a commercial software program, solely for use in the event that the original fails to work.

arguments The value(s) upon which a function acts.

Artificial Intelligence (AI) The development of computer systems which allow a computer to behave in ways that humans would recognize as intelligent, such as thinking and reasoning.

ASCII (pronounced "as'key") Acronym for American Standard Code for Information Interchange. The standard code for the representation of characters through binary numbers in microcomputers. These codes are used in communications between personal computers. The standard ASCII code set consists of 128 numbers ranging from 0 to 127, each of which represents a letter, number, or other computer character or keystroke. This code is used in communications between personal computers.

ASCII code *See* **ASCII.**

asynchronous communication Data communication of the start-stop variety. Each character is transmitted as a discrete unit with its own start bit and one or more stop bits. This is what most personal computers use whether "talking" on the telephone or "talking" to another computer. Synchronous communication is also possible, but it most often used when a personal computer is talking to a corporate mainframe or a local network of computers linked together within a group of offices.

authoring language/system Programs that allow the user to create computer-based tutorials, lessons, and tests on any subject area.

BASIC Acronym for Beginner's All-purpose Symbolic Instruction Code. A high-level programming language commonly used on microcomputers. In many cases, a BASIC interpreter is built into the hardware of a microcomputer.

baud A unit for measuring the speed at which data are transmitted from a computer to some other device. It is approximately equivalent to one bit of data per second. The baud rate is commonly used as a measure of the speed of data transmission through a modem. The most common baud rates are 300 and 1,200, but newer modems offer 2,400 as well.

BBS *See* **Bulletin Board.**

benchmark A test or the testing process used to determine the capabilities of a computer or a program. The tests are often ones of speed. (How long does it take to sort a certain amount of data? How much time is required to perform a given set of calculations?) Magazines will frequently benchmark several machines or programs by feeding them identical sets of data and reporting the results. Hardware manufacturers will also report benchmark results of their equipment. But here you have to be careful, because companies tend to choose tests that show their products in the best possible light. Without a detailed knowledge of the conditions of the test, it is difficult to form a judgment on the basis of advertised benchmarks.

binary The base-2 numbering system used in computers, which uses only two digits, 1 and 0.

bit Abbreviation for Binary digIT. The smallest unit of information used within a computer. In the computer, these digits are signified by either a higher voltage (1) or a lower voltage (0). Eight bits together are called a byte, and four bits are called a nibble.

block commands Commands used in a word processing program that allow the user to identify a block of text to be copied, moved, or deleted, or have some other operation performed upon it.

boot The process of placing parts of the Disk Operating System into internal memory such that information can be moved between the CPU and internal memory and an external storage unit. A cold boot is the process carried out when the computer system is initially turned off. A warm boot is the process carried out when the computer system is already turned on.

branching A type of programming language instruction which allows the program to diverge from one sequence to another.

buffer Any portion of a computer's internal RAM that is set aside by a program as a temporary "holding tank." In a word processing program, the software may create a *type-ahead* or *keyboard buffer* to allow you to type faster than the computer can display characters on the screen. It may also create a buffer to hold the blocks of text you want to move from one page to another. A communications program may set aside a *capture buffer* into which you can pour incoming data instead of waiting for the printer to print it. The technique of *print spooling* sets up a buffer to temporarily hold text before it is sent to the printer.

bug Broadly speaking, any kind of malfunction, whether of hardware or software. One explanation for the origin of this term involves the doorbell-like relay circuits that were used in the first computers. This type of switch works by causing a bar of metal to move physically toward an electromagnet. It is thought that a moth or some other insect at one time managed to get in the way of the contact and caused the computer to malfunction. Whether true or not, the logbook for one of the early computers built under the aegis of the Department of the Navy has a desiccated moth pasted into it with a notation in the computer operator's handwriting that he had found a bug in the system.

Bulletin Board An information utility accessed through the use of a modem which allows the user to exchange electronic messages or use other services such as downloading public domain software.

byte The number of bits used to represent a single letter or other character in a computer. In microcomputers, a byte is usually eight bits. The unit used to describe the amount of storage space in internal memory or various forms of external storage.

C A very popular, powerful high-level programming language used to write the Unix operating system and many powerful commercial software packages.

CAD *See* **Computer Aided Design.**

CAI A widely recognized acronym for *Computer Assisted Instruction.* CAI has evolved into a blanket term that embodies almost all applications of computers to instruction. It is most often broken up into four categories: drill and practice, tutorial, simulation, and problem solving.

CAL Acronym for *Computer Assisted Learning;* it is gaining acceptance as a replacement for CAI. The term has been employed to mean a number of different things.

cassette recorder A peripheral device that allows information to be transferred back and forth between a computer and an audio cassette.

catalog To display the contents of a disk.

CDI *See* **Computer Directed Instruction.**

CD ROM Acronym for Compact Disk Read Only Memory. A new technology which stores digital information optically rather than magnetically on the surface of a plastic disk. The information on the disk is read by a laser beam. The advantages of the technology are the durability of the medium and the incredible amount of information that can be stored in a small space. *See also* **laser disk.**

CEI *See* **Computer Enhanced Instruction.**

central processing unit (CPU) The part of the computer that acts as the computer's brain. It carries out arithmetic and logical operations and controls instructional processing. In addition, it provides timing signals and performs other housekeeping operations.

Centronics Interface *See* **parallel interface.**

chat mode A method of telecommunication in which two or more users can talk to each other in real time.

checksum One of several techniques computers and programs may use to verify accuracy whenever data are transmitted from one place to another. When two personal computers are linked by telephone, for example, one may send a file and then say to the other, "I sent you 1,000 characters. How many did you receive?" The other machine will have been counting the characters as they came in and if it says, "Yup, I got 1,000 characters," it is an indication that the file was received accurately. If the other machine says, "Oh-oh, I only got 981 characters," the sending machine will say, "Hmm. Must be a problem. Hang on, I'll send the same file again." Checksum is used to count characters (or bytes). Parity checking counts the number of bits in each character.

circuit board A plastic rectangular board which contains integrated circuit chips and other electronic components.

clock speed All microprocessors in personal computers have a built-in clock that ticks with a frequency of anywhere from one million times a second to ten million times or more. The speed is measured in *megahertz* (MHz). The significance of the clock speed is that nothing can happen inside a computer until the clock "ticks" or pulses. No data can be transferred. No instructions can be executed. The faster the clock, the faster the computer can work. The standard Intel 8080 chip found in many eight-bit computers has a clock speed of 2 MHz; other versions are faster. The Zilog Z80 chip runs at 3 MHz. The Z80A used in the TRS 80 Model III computers runs at 4 MHz. The Intel 8088 that is the heart of the IBM PC runs at 4.77 MHz. All of which is interesting but largely irrelevant. Some people get caught up in clock speed, but it is not a good way to pick a computer. Concentrate on the software that is available for the computer instead, and have faith that no major company is going to offer a machine with a clock speed so slow that you would notice it in most applications.

clone A computer built to function exactly like another computer already on the market, usually from another manufacturer. *See also* **compatibility/incompatibility.**

CMI *See* **Computer Managed Instruction.**

COBOL Acronym for COmmon Business-Oriented Language. One of the oldest high-level languages, COBOL is widely used in business and many programs are written in it.

cold boot *See* **boot.**

command-driven When a program is command-driven, you as the user must remember what commands to type to get the software to perform a particular task. (Your computer's DOS is a good example.) Though more difficult to master than menu-driven programs, by eliminating the need to wait for and interact with on-screen menus, command-driven software offers the advantage of speed to experienced users. *See also* **menu-driven.**

compatibility/incompatibility Two different types of computers that are able to use all the same software and accept all the same hardware additions would be 100 percent compatible. Most computers from different manufacturers have some degree of incompatibility with one another.

compiler A program that converts high-level programming languages to machine code. A text source code file is read by the compiler, translated to machine code, and a second, executable program file is created. Most languages are implemented this way.

computer An electronic device that accepts input, stores information, processes information, and produces output.

Computer Aided Design (CAD) The use of special computer graphics programs to help in the design of three-dimensional objects.

computer chip A small piece of silicon on which literally thousands of electronic circuit elements are imprinted. These chips are the heart of all integrated circuits used in computer technology.

Computer Directed Instruction (CDI) A computer software program in which the computer directs instruction on one of many instructional tasks. The program installed in memory, the computer, and the learner are sufficient conditions for completing a lesson.

Computer Enhanced Instruction (CEI) A computer software program that allows the user to create teaching aids and instructional support materials, and to enhance student self-directed learning with appropriate software tools.

computer literacy Term coined by Arthur Luehrmann to describe the basic understanding and skills associated with using a computer. It has been interpreted to mean many different things, including a general knowledge of computers and how they are used in the modern world.

Computer Managed Instruction (CMI) A computer software program that performs a variety of managerial tasks for the teacher. Two major categories of managerial tasks are (1) tasks that involve students indirectly (for example, grade reporting, attendance reporting, test item banks); and (2) tasks that involve students directly (for example, using student records of acquired objectives accomplished to track progress, using computer graded tests to identify learning difficulties).

computer program A finite set of precise, logically organized statements which will achieve goals when executed by the computer.

concept development The process leading to the understanding of a new idea. Concept development activities are those that a teacher would use to teach a new idea.

concept reinforcement The process (following concept development) of ensuring long-term retention via the repetition of a newly learned concept.

configure To set up or customize a hardware or software installation. For example, many software packages have to be "told" what computer to operate on, what printer to use, which parallel port to send data to, what color to display on the screen, and so on.

control codes The first 31 values in the ASCII set, which are used to request such operations as line feeds, carriage returns, tabs, and so on.

control key A key, designated in this text as Ctrl, which is used in conjunction with other keys to produce specific results.

coprocessor A microprocessor CPU chip that is plugged into the computer's circuit board to assist the main CPU. The IBM PC is designed to accept an Intel 8087 chip to complement its main 8088, which then serves as a coprocessor to handle the keyboard, disk drives, and other chores. The 8087 is meant to help out the 8088 by handling heavy-duty math applications faster than the 8088 alone could manage.

copy protection Techniques used by the software manufacturer to make a program on a diskette difficult if not impossible to copy. If a diskette is copy-protected, making a copy of it through any means is illegal.

courseware A program or collection of programs designed around a specific curriculum.

CP/M Acronym for Control Program for Microcomputers. A disk operating system for microcomputers, CP/M was the closest thing to a standard operating system for microcomputers prior to the release of the IBM PC. Since the inception of MS/PC DOS, use of CP/M has dwindled to a very small fraction of the market.

CPU *See* **central processing unit.**

crash A drastic halt or break in the execution of a program. Typically, control is either passed back to the operating system or lost altogether.

cursor keys The arrow keys on a computer keyboard, usually used to move the cursor around the screen, in the direction the arrow points.

daisywheel printer A type of printer used with microcomputers that works much like a typewriter. It has a print wheel that rotates to the appropriate character and strikes a ribbon. Produces letter-quality type, but compared to dot-matrix printers, daisywheels are expensive, slow, less reliable, and cannot do graphics.

data Any kind of facts (numbers, letters, codes) that can be input and processed by a computer.

data base Any collection of information. If the information is stored on a computer system, it is more properly called an electronic data base. A data base can be your address list, your personnel files, your inventory, or anything else. The term is also used to refer to electronic data bases: the collections of information available over the telephone and to the organizations that provide it (The Source, Dow Jones News/Retrieval, CompuServe, NewsNet, and so on).

data-base manager A program written for the specific purpose of setting up, searching, and maintaining electronic data bases.

data diskette A formatted diskette which will be used for the storage of information.

decimal The base-10 numbering system we use in everyday life.

dedicated classroom An arrangement in which a classroom set of computers is placed in one room for use by one teacher all day long. This teacher is usually a programming or computer literacy instructor.

dedicated word processor A computer that is specialized to perform only the task of word processing.

default A concept used in software design in which a specific value is assigned to a variable unless the user makes a choice. One common example is the assignment of a specific disk drive to be the object of a command unless otherwise specified in the command line.

DIF Acronym for Data Interchange Format. A technique for storing information designed by Software Arts, Inc. (creators of VisiCalc). The goal is to make it possible for different programs from different software houses to share the same data files.

digitize To store information as a series of discrete binary values. Information stored in this format can be more easily used by a computer.

Direct Distance Dialing (DDD) The technique most personal computer owners use to access data bases, computer bulletin boards, and other on-line services. The term is most significant in the data communications industry where DDD is but one form of computer access.

directory To catalog or display the contents of a disk.

disk drive A peripheral device that allows information to be transferred back and forth between a computer and a diskette.

disk(ette) A thin, circular piece of plastic coated with a metallic material and placed inside some type of protective covering. Used as an external storage medium for microcomputers.

Disk Operating System *See* **DOS.**

documentation Information about a specific item of computer hardware or software that describes the item's characteristics and instructions on how to use it. The information may be in the form of a manual or user's guide. Internal documentation refers to a programmer's comments in the program code.

DOS Acronym for Disk Operating System. The collection of utility programs designed to integrate one or more disk drives with the rest of the computer system.

dot matrix printer A type of printer used with computers in which the print head consists of a matrix of pins that can be shot out and impacted with the ribbon in any combination to form characters. Dot matrix printers do not create true letter-quality print, but are inexpensive and can print graphics.

download To capture the information sent to your computer by another computer, as opposed to letting it disappear as it scrolls off the screen.

editor A software program which allows information that has been input into a computer to be modified. Editors are usually part of larger programs, such as programming languages or applications programs.

Electronic Bulletin Board Service *See* **Bulletin Board.**

electronic data base *See* **data base.**

electronic mail Messages sent from one computer to another by telecommunications. Usually a service available through an information utility.

E-mail *See* **electronic mail.**

embedded codes Special control characters placed into a document to control how the document is formatted when printed.

ENIAC Acronym for Electronic Numerical Integrator And Calculator. Built in 1946, this was one of the first true digital computers. It used vacuum tubes as memory devices.

enter key The key, designated in this text as [enter], is used to signify the completion of a command and to submit the command to the computer. In word processors, it also serves as a return key.

EPROM Acronym for Erasable Programmable ROM. This is a PROM chip that can be erased and reprogrammed an indefinite number of times. The chip has a little window in its casing and when high-intensity ultraviolet light is shined through it for 15 to 20 minutes, all of the bit patterns are erased. The chip can then be reprogrammed with a special machine. EPROMS are useful to software houses or other firms wishing to develop programming that will eventually be hardwired into a ROM chip. *See also* **ROM** and **PROM.**

ergonomics The study of workplace design efficiency. For example, ergonomically designed computer furniture is theoretically less fatiguing to use, resulting in greater user productivity.

expansion slots Slots inside the computer which allow additional circuit boards, called cards, to be added to the computer. The cards that are added can perform a number of special functions from additional internal memory to the ability to use a modem.

expert system A program that contains both factual (data) and procedural (rules for making decisions) information to model the performance of human experts in a given field. For example, expert systems have been developed that diagnose illnesses more accurately than any human doctor.

extended character set A set of special characters that is appended to the normal ASCII set, that correspond to the numbers 129 through 255. These characters can be produced on the screen by holding down the [Alt] key and typing the three-digit code on the numeric keypad.

external command A DOS command in the form of a program file which resides on the DOS diskette. The disk must be in the drive for the command to be used.

external memory Secondary memory. *See* **memory.**

field The computer equivalent of the blanks you fill in with your name, address, and other information when completing a sweepstakes entry, driver's license, or other form.

file The computer equivalent of all of your cancelled checks for the month, the year, or some other period. Each check is a record. Each blank on the check is a field. The whole collection is a file.

file management system A type of data-base program which allows for the entry and updating of records in a file and the sorting and selecting of a subset of records for a printed report. Its main limitation is the ability to work with only one file at a time.

fixed disk *See* **hard disk.**

flag Variable or constant used to indicate the states of a variable condition.

floppy disk(ette) *See* **disk(ette).**

flowchart Both the act and the product of graphically depicting the structure of a computer program. Usually done as a means of figuring out or documenting program logic.

font The physical appearance of printed information. Many printers and software packages allow the user to determine the type of font in which a passage of text will be printed.

footprint The area on your desk or table occupied by any piece of computer equipment.

format To organize a diskette by using DOS to make it ready for the storing of information in files.

forum A telecommunicated, topic-specific running conversation between computer users, usually hosted on a bulletin board or information service. For example, The Source has an education forum.

function keypad A set of keys which can be preset to different functions by a program.

game port A point of connection which allows the computer to connect up with a joystick or paddle for playing computer games. Some computers have a game port built in. Other computers allow a game port to be added through an expansion card.

generic software tools The all-purpose tools of the microcomputer: spreadsheets, word processors, data-base managers, telecommunications programs, and graphics programs.

glitch A sporadic hardware bug, usually untraceable. Often caused by power supply irregularities or static charges.

global character *See* **wildcard.**

grammar checker Also called syntax checkers. A program that analyzes writing style. Such programs usually provide reading level, a list of unusual vocabulary, and point out possible run-on sentences, complex verb forms, or other unnecessarily complicated forms of usage.

graphics Visual material created with the help of computer software programs.

graphics tablet A peripheral device that allows for the creation and storage of graphics by the movement of a stylus over a flat surface.

halon fire extinguisher The best kind of extinguisher for computers. Halon is an inert gas that will not damage electronics as will carbon dioxide or other extinguisher types.

handshaking The little ritual of signals exchanged between two computers before communications can begin. Signals are sent back and forth so that each machine is prepared for the other's input or output.

hard disk Also, fixed disk. Hard disks are a very high density storage medium. Unlike a floppy diskette, the disk in a hard drive is metallic and permanently sealed in the drive. This allows data to be placed on a hard disk about 100 times more densely than on a floppy. Where 5 1/4″ floppy disk capacity is measured in hundreds of kilobytes, hard disk capacity is measured in tens of megabytes.

hardware All the physical components of a computer that enable operation.

hexadecimal The base-16 numbering system. In the decimal system there are 10 digits (0 through 9) to use in expressing numbers. In "hex" there are those 10 digits plus six letters (A, B, C, D, E, and F). The main advantage of the hexadecimal system is that it is easier to read and deal with than the 1s and 0s of the binary system. It also lets you express the same number in less space. For example, the decimal number 14 can be expressed in binary as 1110 or in hex as D. Similarly, the decimal number that would require 16 digits in binary (1000100110101101) can be written in hex as 89AD.

high-level languages Programming languages that are far removed from the actual machine code which must be produced for them to be executed. Such languages must be either compiled or interpreted to machine code. Examples are BASIC, Pascal, Logo, FORTRAN, and COBOL. There are hundreds of others. *See also* **compiler** and **interpreter.**

hi-res or **hi-res′** Short for high resolution. The abbreviation is pronounced "hi-rez," even if it isn't always spelled that way. See **resolution.**

host computer The controlling computer in a link between two machines. A computer which serves as the control center of a set of computers arranged in a network.

IC *See* **integrated circuit.**

indexing system A very simple type of data base program, allowing the user to tag information items for later retrieval with a limited number of key words.

indexing utility A feature offered by some top-of-the-line word processors. The user may instruct the computer to assemble an index for a given body of text.

information capture The preservation in a disk file of all text appearing on the screen in a telecommunications session. When checking one's electronic mail, it is not uncommon to capture the text of incoming messages. This way, the text can be used to assist in composing a reply off-line, to be sent at a later time.

information utility A general-purpose computer subscription service that allows a computer user with a modem to access many different data bases, programming languages, electronic mail, or other services via telecommunications. Examples are The Source and Compuserve.

ink-jet printer A type of printer used with computers which forms characters by spraying liquid or powdered ink on the surface of the paper.

input Data entered into a computer by the user.

input device A device through which data are entered into the computer's memory, such as a keyboard, diskette drive, light pen, cassette recorder, joystick, or graphics tablet.

installation *See* **configure.**

instructional framework In the case of microcomputer applications to education, a means of classifying computer programs in terms of student behaviors that are stressed.

instruction set The set of basic operations that the computer's microprocessor can perform, such as comparing two numbers or moving a byte from one memory location to another, which are hardwired into the microprocessor.

integrated circuit (IC) Miniaturized versions of electronic circuits formed on the surface of small silicon chips.

interactive mode A reciprocal dialogue between the user and the system; interactivity.

interactive video The integration of a computer, program, and computer-controlled video source such as a videotape or videodisc player to produce information displays or lessons containing photographic images.

interface The boundary between two parts of a computer system. Usually used in discussing the connection of a computer to a peripheral.

internal command A DOS command which resides in the command processor. When the command processor is loaded, the DOS diskette need not be present in the drive for the command to be executed.

internal memory Primary memory. *See* **memory.**

interpreter A program for converting a high-level language to machine code. Differs from a compiler in that the translation is done on-the-fly every time the program is executed. Very few languages are commonly implemented this way, primarily BASIC and Logo.

I/O Acronym for Input/Output. *See also* **input** and **output.**

joystick A peripheral device that allows the input of information into a computer through the movement of a vertical rod connected to a base. Used most often with computer games.

justification A term adopted into word processing to describe the way the text is aligned on the page with regard to the margins. Most word processors automatically align words on the left margin and offer right margin alignment as an option.

keyboard The most common device for entering information into a microcomputer. Usually contains keys for all the characters along with cursor keys and special control keys.

keyboarding The use, or instruction in the use of, a keyboard to input information involving either a typewriter or a microcomputer.

key word A word used as a search criterion when querying a data base.

kilobyte A unit of 1,000 bytes, or more precisely, a unit of 1,024 bytes (but no one worries about the 24 bytes). One kilobyte or K of memory can hold 1,000 characters, or about half a double-spaced, typewritten page.

LAN *See* **local area network.**

laser disk A kind of videodisc, usually random access. Used with microcomputers to produce interactive video displays or lessons.

laser printer A type of printer used with microcomputers. It uses the technology of copiers to produce excellent print quality, can be programmed to print in virtually any font, and can produce very high-quality graphics.

learning aids In the case of microcomputer applications to education, learning aids are microcomputer-generated instructional materials such as manipulatives, work sheets, and so on.

letter-quality Typewriter-like printing, in contrast to printing with a dot matrix printer. A letter-quality printer uses a printing element containing fully formed letters, whereas a dot matrix printer creates each letter as necessary by pushing forward the correct number of wires in its printing element. *See also* **daisywheel printer** and **dot matrix printer.**

licensing agreement The rules governing the usage of a given software product. Programs are rarely purchased by the user. They are licensed by the manufacturer for use by the consumer. The specific licensing agreement included with the package details how it may be employed.

light pen A pen-like device that, with appropriate software, may be used to indicate locations on a computer display as a way of inputting information.

LISP Acronym for LISt Processor. Most widely used language for artificial intelligence research and applications.

listing A printout of a computer program.

local area network (LAN) Hardware and software for linking a number of microcomputers into a system for sharing common information and hardware resources.

Logo A programming language designed for discovery learning of mathematics and science. Created by Seymour Papert at MIT. Widely used in education.

log-on To sign on to a bulletin board or mainframe computer system. Usually involves typing in name or account number and password.

lo-res or **low-res'** Short for low resolution. The lowest display quality on a given system. *See* **resolution.**

machine code/ language The binary representation of computer instructions. The only form of programming with which the computer actually operates. All other languages must be assembled, interpreted, or compiled.

macro Short for macro-expansion or macro-instruction. A sequence of instructions that can be programmed to be initiated with a single keystroke and to carry out a task without further intervention by the user. For example, you might load today's date into a key and then, later, press that key to insert the date at the beginning of a letter.

magnetic media The predominant form of computer storage. Information is represented by using magnetic fields to first rearrange (write) and then later interpret (read) the arrangements of minute iron particles suspended in an inert medium. Disks and tapes are magnetic media.

mainframe Large computer system appropriate to handle the computing needs for an entire company or community. CPU and storage devices are usually installed in a room or building all to themselves with many (hundreds of) terminals distributed around a large building or area.

megabyte or **meg** Nominally, one million bytes. Actually 2^{20} or 1,048,576 bytes. Abbreviated M or MB.

memory The device(s) used by a computer to store information. Primary memory usually refers to integrated circuit chips housed within the CPU and consists of RAM and ROM. Secondary memory usually refers to storage devices such as disk drives. Memory is usually measured in bytes, kilobytes, and megabytes. *See also* **RAM** and **ROM.**

memory expansion card A circuit board used to add primary memory to a computer system.

memory-resident software Program that loads into memory and hides there, invisible to other applications, waiting to be called to life with a special key combination. Usually utility programs like calculators or calendars.

menu A list of options from which to choose.

menu-driven Refers to a program style in which the user chooses options from a menu rather than having to remember and enter commands to gain results. Often considered a key element in the user-friendliness of a program. *See also* **command-driven.**

microcomputer A complete computer system suitable for use by one individual or in the home. Uses a microprocessor for its CPU. Usually the CPU, console, and storage devices are in close proximity.

microprocessor A computer on a chip. An integrated circuit chip which contains all the circuitry to be a CPU.

minicomputer A complete computer system suitable for use by a number of individuals or a small business. A step between a microcomputer and a mainframe. Usually installed with the CPU and storage devices in one central location with consoles distributed throughout the workplace.

MIS Acronym for Management Information System. Usually, a corporate division responsible for supplying all levels of management with the information they need to make decisions. The information typically comes from the firm's computers and data bases.

modem Acronym for MOdulate/DEModulate. A device that translates information from a computer into a form that can be transmitted over standard telephone lines. A modem also translates incoming signals into a form that a computer can understand. Two modems, one for each computer, are needed for any data communications over telephone lines. Most modems are direct connect (the phone line plugs right in). Others, mainly for portable computers, are acoustic; that is, they have rubber cups that fit over the ends of a standard telephone receiver.

monitor A device, like television, for displaying video output.

mouse A handheld peripheral input device. Movement of the mouse over a surface controls the display cursor. From one to three buttons are used to select menu choices highlighted by the cursor.

multifunction card A circuit board that adds a number of different enhancements to a microcomputer system. These enhancements are commonly memory; a battery-powered clock; serial, parallel, and game ports.

network *See* **local area network.**

NTSC Acronym for the National Television Standards Committee. This committee has set the American television standard at 525 lines.

null modem (cable) A plug or cable designed to connect two computers via their serial ports when the computers are physically close to one another and telecommunication is therefore unnecessary. The null modem substitutes for a modem by crossing over the appropriate communication lines.

numeric keypad A 3×3 array of number keys, usually on the right of the keyboard, designed for the rapid entry of number data.

OCR *See* **Optical Character Reader.**

OEM Acronym for Original Equipment Manufacturer. An OEM usually manufactures computer components and then sells them to other companies that assemble complete computer systems.

on-line In computer communications, on-line means "connected to a remote data base." With regard to on-line help, the term also means "when you are in the middle of using a program."

open architecture Method of designing a computer system and publishing specifications so that other manufacturers can easily design, manufacture, and market products designed to work with it. The Apple II and the IBM PC are examples of open architecture.

Optical Character Reader (OCR) Device for optically scanning and inputting to the computer text or other character data. For example, some OCRs are used to enter documents into a word processor.

optical disk A digital disk that uses a light beam to read information from the surface of the disk. Used with microcomputers as a form of external memory. *See also* **laser disk.**

output Data produced by a computer for use by the user.

output device A device to which information is directed by the computer, either for storage, presentation, or transfer. Storage devices include magnetic disks and tapes. Presentation devices include video displays, printers, and other devices driven by the computer, such as speakers. Modems are transfer devices.

overlay A segment of an applications program that is loaded into the computer from disk on an "as needed" basis.

parallel communications Sending information from one computer to another, or from a computer to a peripheral device, one byte (eight bits) at a time (as opposed to serial, which sends one bit at a time). *See also* **serial communications.**

parallel interface A circuit board that employs the parallel communications protocol to link a computer to a peripheral device, usually a printer. Also known as a Centronics interface.

parameter Similar to an argument, a stipulation to a command which specifies an explicit option or mode of operation as opposed to the default mode.

Pascal A high-level programming language specifically designed to teach programming concepts. Created in 1971 by Nicklaus Wirth of Zurich, Switzerland. Very widely used in education, it was named in honor of the mathematician Blaise Pascal, who devised an early calculator.

patch A small modification to a program, usually no more than a few bytes. Usually made directly to the machine code, often with the use of a debugger.

pel *See* **pixel.**

peripheral(s) Auxiliary devices exterior to the computer. For example, printers, modems, and mouse devices are all peripherals.

phoneme A sound, a unit of speech. A component of a word. One method of synthesizing speech on computers is to provide a library of phonemes that can be assembled into words. The resulting speech tends to sound robotic.

Pilot An authoring language widely employed in education. *See* **authoring language.**

pixel Short for picture element. The smallest addressable dot of light on the screen that your computer is capable of displaying. Also called a pel.

playing turtle A Logo-related activity in which students physically perform the steps of an algorithm.

populate To fill in completely, as with a memory expansion board. When all the sockets for memory chips are filled in, the board is said to be fully populated.

power down To turn off your computer system and peripherals.

power supply In general, the source of power for a computer system. Also, a specific component in the computer that converts line voltage to the appropriate levels for use within the system.

power surge Sudden, abnormally high level of power, such as caused by lightning. Can cause extensive damage to a computer, often even with a surge protector installed. *See also* **voltage fluctuation.**

power up To turn on your computer system and peripherals.

primary memory *See* **memory.**

problem-solving software Educational programs designed to cause the student to integrate skills to perform tasks to find solutions to puzzles.

programming The process of creating a combination of instructions to the computer which causes it to perform a desired task.

PROLOG Acronym for PROgramming in LOGic. A programming language widely used in Artificial Intelligence applications. Second in use only to LISP.

PROM Acronym for Programmable ROM. Programming can be placed in a PROM chip one time after its manufacture. By way of contrast, ROM chips can only be programmed at the time of manufacture. *See also* **ROM** and **EPROM.**

protocol An established or standard procedure for accomplishing a task. In particular, getting two programs or two computers to communicate with one another.

public domain software Software to which the rights have been placed in the public domain. Distributed primarily by bulletin boards, users' groups, and mail-order clearinghouses. Many public domain programs are of very high quality and fill needs not answered by commercial products.

query To search a data base using specific criteria.

RAM Acronym for Random Access Memory (also called user memory). Primary memory for the temporary storage of information in a microcomputer. The contents of RAM can be both read and written to by the computer. Power must constantly be applied to RAM in order for it to retain its contents. When the computer is turned off, RAM reverts to a blank slate. *See also* **memory.**

Random Access Memory *See* **RAM.**

Read Only Memory *See* **ROM.**

record An integral collection of data items. Analogous to a page in a file folder or to a section of an electronic data base containing all the information related to an individual person. Also, part of a disk format.

recursion When an algorithm refers to or calls itself. An elegant, but often inefficient programming technique permitted by Logo and Pascal, it is a powerful problem-solving tool.

RGB Acronym for RED/GREEN/BLUE, this term is used to refer to a type of color monitor in which the signals for the three primary colors are carried on separate lines. This results in a very high quality picture. By contrast, **composite** color monitors blend all three signals on one line.

relational data-base system Data-base system in which one common base of information may be accessed and manipulated by a number of different applications. When one application updates the data, it is automatically updated for all the others.

resolution The fineness or smoothness of a computer's display. Typically, the more pixels (picture elements) or pels, the higher the resolution. *See also* **pixel.**

return key Now, another name for the enter key. Key used to signal the computer that information is ready to be processed.

ROM Acronym for Read Only Memory. Primary memory for permanent storage of information in a microcomputer. It does not require power to retain its contents. ROM can be read by the computer, but it cannot be written to. It typically contains the programming necessary to boot the computer before control is passed to the operating system. Also usually contains most or all of the BASIC interpreter. *See also* **memory.**

RS-232-C A standard developed by the Electronics Industry Association (EIA) specifying the transmission of data from a computer to a modem. Also commonly used to refer to the 25-pin plug used to make the connection.

screen dump A technique for easily replicating the contents of the computer's display on a printer. For example, on the IBM PC, the key combination [Crtl]-[PrtSc] will dump the screen to the printer.

search/replace Common feature of a word processor, the user may specify text to be searched for in a document and, optionally, additional text with which the program will replace it.

secondary memory *See* **memory.**

serial communications Sending information from one computer to another, or from a computer to a peripheral device, one bit of information at a time (as opposed to parallel, which sends eight bits at a time). *See also* **asynchronous communications, parallel communications,** and **RS-232-C.**

serial interface A circuit board that employs the serial communications protocol to link a computer to a peripheral device, such as a printer, modem, or a mouse.

set up *See* **configure.**

SIG *See* **special interest group.**

simulation In software, using the computer to feign an experience difficult or impractical to actually provide. Examples include operating a nuclear power plant and taking a wagon train West from Ohio to California.

skill development The acquisition of a new ability, usually implying memorization of a set of behaviors.

skill reinforcement Practice and application of a skill already learned.

soft-sectored The non-permanent sectoring of floppy diskettes by the operating system, as opposed to hard-sectored diskettes, which are presectored at the time of manufacture and cannot be changed.

software Computer programs.

software evaluation The product or process of closely examining software against a set of predefined standards as a means of identifying its quality and/or usefulness.

special interest group (SIG) Group of computer users organized around a topic of interest. Often convened on a computer bulletin board system, with members residing in all parts of the country.

spell checker A feature of many word processors, identifies the user's spelling errors, usually suggesting alternate spellings.

split-screen *See* **window.**

spooler/spooling A mechanism/technique for printing out information while simultaneously using the computer for other processes.

statements The vocabulary of a high-level programming language. Special reserved words which translate into machine-code instructions.

storage device Hardware for recording information. Internal computer memory is primary storage. Diskette drives and other media are secondary storage. *See also* **memory.**

string A word or sentence or any other continuous string of characters. Always treated as text, even if composed entirely of numerals.

style checker Auxiliary program for a word processor, performs stylistic writing analysis, typically providing such information as reading level, average sentence length, and a list of unusual vocabulary.

subdirectory Catalog or directory for a portion of a mass storage device like a hard disk. Used to make a voluminous storage medium more manageable.

syntax The grammar and punctuation conventions of an operating system, language, or program.

synthesize To create by artificial means, as in speech synthesis.

sysop Short for system operator, pronounced "sigh'-sop." The individual who owns, operates, and maintains a computer bulletin board system.

system reset Restarting a microcomputer system from scratch without turning it off and on again. Usually implies rebooting with the Disk Operating System. On the IBM PC, it is accomplished by pressing the [Del] key while holding down the [Ctrl] and [Alt] keys.

telecommunications The process of using computers and telephone lines to communicate between users. Includes micro-to-mainframe links, calling a bulletin board, and direct micro-to-micro communications.

template A partially completed application for a generic software package, to be completed by the user. For example, in a spreadsheet application for amortizing a loan, the user need only enter the principal, term, and interest rate.

terminal Device for communicating with a mainframe computer. Usually not much more than a screen and a keyboard. The typical terminal cannot be used independent of the mainframe system.

terminal mode When communicating with a mainframe computer, a microcomputer must be programmed to emulate, or act like, a terminal. Many telecommunications programs provide this capability.

thesaurus A feature of many word processors, an electronic version of Roget's creation. Provides the user with synonyms and antonyms for a given word.

third party manufacturer/vendor The computer manufacturer and the owner/user are the first two parties. Third parties are other companies or individuals that manufacture or market hardware designed to work with a given system.

toggle/toggle key A key action that reverses the status of some variable condition. Frequently used to change the meanings of other keys. Examples: [Num Lock], [Scroll Lock], [Caps Lock], and [Ins] (or overtype) keys.

touch screen An input device. Senses where the user points on the display to indicate an instruction.

track ball An input device, like an upside-down mouse. Consists of a ball mounted in a surface, manipulated by hand to control the cursor; used in many arcade games.

transistor The successor to the vacuum tube as the logic device in computers. An active semiconductor device, usually made of silicon or germanium.

Turtle Graphics A system of creating graphics implemented in Pascal, Logo, and Pilot. Allows the user to draw lines by specifying distance and direction (vectors) instead of coordinates.

tutorial Software that attempts to teach a new concept, as opposed to drill and practice of a concept already taught.

typematic key A key that will repeatedly print when it is held down.

typewriter mode A feature of some word processors, this mode feeds keyboard input straight through to the printer. Handy for addressing envelopes and such.

UART Acronym for Universal Asynchronous Receiver/Transmitter. Pronounced "you'-art," an IC used for converting parallel signals into serial signals and vice versa; the heart of a serial interface card.

UCSD p-System Operating system developed by the University of California at San Diego. One implementation of Pascal for the IBM PC and compatibles runs under this system. Once very popular, p-System use is on the decline.

UNIVAC Acronym for UNIVersal Automatic Computer. Commonly considered to be the first commercial computer of the transistor generation.

Unix An operating system (like MS DOS) with multiuser and multitasking capabilities. Unix use is becoming more widespread.

upload To send information over the telephone lines to another computer directly from your floppy disk, cassette tape, or buffer, as opposed to typing at your keyboard.

user friendly Indicates that a program is easy to use, jargon held to a minimum, and not intimidating to novices. Has evolved into a superlative (like "new and improved") that software and hardware producers routinely stamp on their product labels, ads, and brochures.

users' group Organization of computer users who own or are interested in the same brand of computer. Such groups commonly sponsor regular meetings, newsletters, public domain, software libraries, and bulletin boards.

user-supported software Variation on public domain software. Creator keeps copyright but permits free duplication and use of software. If user finds program of value, voluntary registration fee is requested and brings various additional benefits such as a newsletter and upgrades.

utility software Programs for pragmatic, practical purposes; for example, diskette organizers, file compressors, print spoolers, and files to unerase deletions.

vacuum tube Predecessor to the transistor. Once used as the logic device in computers.

variable A quantity or quality that is not fixed in value; for example, programming language variables and information in a data-base field.

voltage fluctuation Irregularity in power supply. May cause glitches in computer systems or even damage hardware. *See also* **glitch** and **power surge.**

warm boot *See* **system reset.** *See also* **boot.**

wildcard Also called global character. Characters used to match any character in a command or search criterion. For example, the characters ? and *, when used in a DOS command to represent any single character or series of characters, respectively, in a filename.

Winchester *See* **hard disk.**

window Area of the display which, under software control, displays a different kind of output, or output from a different program, than the rest of the display.

word processor Generic applications software for entering, editing, formatting, and printing text on a microcomputer.

wordwrap A feature of almost all word processors. When typist reaches margin, program automatically wraps word being typed to the next line.

WORM Acronym for "write once, read many." A digital (laser) disk that can be written to one time.

write-enable notch Notch on the right edge of the diskette, which allows the diskette to be written to. If this notch is covered with a write-protect tab, or not present at all, the diskette cannot be written to.

write protect *See* **write-enable notch.**

INDEX